Dictionary
of Anagrams

Dictionary of Anagrams

Samuel C. Hunter

Routledge & Kegan Paul

London, Boston and Henley

First published in 1982
by Routledge & Kegan Paul Ltd
39 Store Street, London WC1E 7DD,
Broadway House, Newtown Road,
Henley-on-Thames, Oxon RG9 1EN and
9 Park Street, Boston, Mass. 02108, USA
Printed in Great Britain by
Redwood Burn Ltd, Trowbridge, Wiltshire
© Samuel C. Hunter 1982

Library of Congress Cataloging in Publication Data

Hunter, Samuel C., 1919–

Dictionary of anagrams.

1. Anagrams—Glossaries, vocabularies, etc.
I. Title.
GV1507.A5H86   793.73   81–23445

ISBN 0–7100 9006 4   AACR2

Contents

Introduction

An anagram is a word, phrase or sentence formed by transposing the letters of a different word, phrase or sentence. Anagrams, principally in respect of phrases and sentences, have a long history: they were known to the Greeks and Romans and were popular throughout Europe during the Middle Ages. Some scientists of the seventeenth century embodied their discoveries in anagrams, and pseudonyms are often anagrams of the original name.

Today, anagrams are frequently used by compilers of crosswords, especially cryptic crosswords, in both clues and solutions although, in the absence until now of any comprehensive anagram dictionary, single-word solutions have often been hidden in the letters of two or more words appearing in the clue construction.

The author of this dictionary, himself a crossword compiler, has, over the last twenty-odd years, collected together the material now incorporated in this work. The collection is confined to single-word anagrams, arranged in strictly alphabetical order, tabulated according to the number of letters (five to thirteen). Words are only given in the plural when, by the addition of the letter 's', further words are possible, for example:

> NECTARINES – TRANSIENCE
> BALANCE-SHEETS – TEACHABLENESS
> CREDENTIALS – CENTRALISED
> MODERATORS – ASTRODOME

Acceptable hyphenated words have been included, but the author has resisted the temptation of including such interesting items as SALVAGES and TEA-GARDEN since their anagrams LAS VEGAS and GREAT DANE involve the use of two separate (un-hyphenated) words, and such a practice would depart from the self-imposed rule outlined above. A number of proper names have been incorporated into this dictionary and these are indicated by an asterisk against the word where it appears in the first column on the pages, e.g.

> *HILDEBRAND – BRIDLE-HAND
> *PTERELAUS – PULSE-RATE
> *CORNELIUS – INCLOSURE
> *MINNESOTA – NOMINATES
> *LANCASTER – ANCESTRAL

Each of the above pairs, and of course all the other groups included, also appear in their alternative settings. Thus HILDEBRAND, above, will also be found under its anagram BRIDLE-HAND. This cross-referencing equally applies to cases where more than one anagram is applicable. For instance ELIMINATORS, MISRELATION, ORIENTALISM and RELATIONISM appear separately in the eleven-letter section, each giving the three alternative anagrammatic words. Thus whatever the known word, its anagram will immediately be available when reference is made to that section of the Dictionary dealing with the appropriate number of letters.

This anagram dictionary is the only one of its kind ever published and will be invaluable not just to crossword compilers and to many of those millions who regularly attempt to solve crossword puzzles the world over, but also to an ever-increasing number of people for whom anagrams have a special appeal and fascination. This is evident from the popularity of numerous radio and television panel programmes that serve anagrams in their fare – fair enough?

HAPPY ANAGRAMMING!

Five letters

ABEAM Ameba
ABELE Albee
ABETS Baste, Bates, Beast, Beats, Esbat, Sebat, Tabes
ABLER Baler, Blare, Blear
ABLET Blate, Bleat, Table
ABODE Adobe
ABORD Board, Broad, Dobra, Dorab
ABORT Boart, Rabot, Tabor
ABOUT U-boat
ABRIN Bairn, Brain, Brian
ABRUS Bursa
ABSEY Abyes
ABSIT Baits
ABUTS Tabus, Tsuba, Tubas
ABYES Absey
ABYSS Bassy
ACERA Areca
ACERB Brace, Caber, Cabre
ACERS Acres, Cares, Carse, Races, Sacre, Scare, Scrae, Serac
ACHES Chase
ACHOR Orach, Roach
ACLIS Laics, Salic, Scail
ACRED Arced, Cadre, Cared, Cedar, Dacre, Raced
ACRES Acers, Cares, Carse, Races, Sacre, Scare, Scrae, Serac
ACRID Caird, Daric
ACTED Cadet, Ectad

ACTIN Antic
ACTON Canto
ACTOR Croat, Rocta, Taroc
ADDER Aredd, Dared, Dread, Dreda, Readd
ADDLE Daled, Dedal, Laded
ADEPS Sepad, Spade
ADEPT Pated, Taped
ADITS Staid
ADMAN Daman
ADMEN Amend, Mande, Maned, Menad, Named
ADOBE Abode
ADORE Oared, Oread
ADORN Andro, Radon
ADSUM Dumas, Mauds
ADULT Tauld
ADUST Dauts
AEGER Agree, Eager, Eagre, Ragee
AESIR Aries, Arise, Raise, Resai, Serai
AFIRE Feria
AFRIT Frati
AGAIT Taiga
AGIST Gaits, Staig
AGLEE Eagle
AGNEL Angel, Angle, Glean
AGREE Aeger, Eager, Eagre, Ragee
AGRIN Grain
AHEMS Hames, Heams, Shame
AIDER Aired, Irade, Redia
AIDES Aside, Ideas, Sadie

1

AILED	Eliad, Ideal	ALTER	Alert, Artel, Later,
AIMED	Amide, Media		Ratel, Telar
AIMER	Marie, Ramie, Rimae	*ALTON	Notal, Talon, Tolan,
AIRED	Aider, Irade, Redia		Tonal
AIRTS	Astir, Sitar, Stair,	ALTOS	Sloat, Stola, Tolas
	Stria, Tarsi, Trias	ALURE	Ureal
AISLE	Slaie	*ALVES	Elvas, Laves, Salve,
AITCH	Atchi		Slave, Vales, Valse,
ALARM	Malar, Ramal		Veals
*ALBAN	Banal, Laban	AMAIN	Amnia, Anima, Mania
ALBEE	Abele	AMASS	Assam, Massa
ALBIN	Blain	AMBER	Brame, Bream, Embar
ALCES	Claes, Laces, Scale	AMBLE	Blame, Embla, Mabel
ALDER	Daler	AMBOS	Bomas, Moabs, Sambo
ALERT	Alter, Artel, Later,	AMBRY	Barmy
	Ratel, Telar	AMEBA	Abeam
ALGAE	Galea	AMEER	Ramee
*ALGER	Elgar, Glare, Lager,	AMEND	Admen, Mande, Maned,
	Large, Regal		Menad, Named
ALGIN	Align, Liang, Ligan,	AMENE	Enema, Meane
	Linga	AMENS	Manes, Manse, Means,
ALGOR	Argol		Mensa, Names, Samen
ALGUM	Almug, Glaum, Mulga	AMENT	Manet, Meant
*ALICE	Ileac	AMIDE	Aimed, Media
ALIEN	Aline, Anile, Elain,	AMIGO	Imago
	Laine, Liane	AMINE	Anime
ALIGN	Algin, Liang, Ligan,	AMITY	Atimy
	Linga	AMNIA	Amain, Anima, Mania
ALINE	Alien, Anile, Elain,	AMONG	Mango
	Laine, Liane	AMORT	Morat
ALISH	Hails	AMPLE	Maple, Pelma
ALIVE	Avile, Velia	AMPLY	Palmy
ALL-BE	Be-all, Bella, Label	AMSEL	Almes, Lames, Leams,
ALLOT	All-to, Atoll		Males, Meals, Melas
ALLOY	Loyal	ANCLE	Clean, Lance, Lenca
ALL-TO	Allot, Atoll	ANCON	Canon
ALMAH	Halma, Hamal	*ANDES	Danes, Deans, Sedan,
*ALMAS	Lamas		Snead
ALMES	Amsel, Lames, Leams,	ANDRO	Adorn, Radon
	Males, Meals, Melas,	ANEAR	Arena
	Mesal, Salem, Samel	ANGEL	Agnel, Angle, Glean
ALMRY	Marly	ANGER	Areng, Range, Renga
ALMUG	Algum, Glaum, Mulga	ANGLE	Agnel, Angel, Glean
ALOFT	Float, Flota	ANGOR	Argon, Groan, Nagor
ALONG	Logan		Orang, Organ
ALOOF	Loofa	ANGRY	Rangy
ALPEN	Panel, Pelan, Penal,	ANGST	Gants, Gnats, Stang,
	Plane		Tangs
ALTAR	Artal, Ratal	ANILE	Alien, Aline, Elain,
			Laine, Liane

ANILS	Nails, Salin, Slain, Snail			AREDE	Areed, Eared, Reeda	
ANIMA	Amain, Amnia, Mania			AREED	Arede, Eared, Reeda	
ANIME	Amine			ARENA	Anear	
ANKER	Naker			ARENG	Anger, Range, Renga	
ANNAT	Tanna			ARETE	Eater, Reate	
*ANNES	Senna			ARETS	Aster, Earst, Rates, Reast, Resat, Stare, Strae, Tares, Tarse, Tears, Teras	
*ANNIE	Inane					
ANTIC	Actin					
ANTIS	Saint, Satin, Stain, Tains, Tanis			ARETT	Tater, Tetra, Treat	
ANTRE	Retan			ARGIL	Glair, Grail	
ANVIL	Vinal			ARGOL	Algor	
APART	Trapa			ARGON	Angor, Groan, Nagor, Orang, Organ	
APERS	Asper, Pares, Parse, Pears, Prase, Presa, Rapes, Reaps, Spaer, Spare, Spear			ARGOT	Groat	
				ARGUE	Auger	
				ARGUS	Sugar	
APERT	Pater, Peart, Petar, Petra, Prate, Taper, Trape			*ARIES	Aesir, Arise, Raise, Resai, Serai	
				ARIOT	Ratio	
APERY	Payer, Repay			ARISE	Aesir, Aries, Raise, Resai, Serai	
APEST	Paste, Pates, Peats, Septa, Spate, Speat, Tapes			ARISH	Hairs	
				ARLES	Earls, Lares, Laser, Lears, Rales, Reals, Seral	
APHIS	Apish, Spahi					
APISH	Aphis, Spahi			ARMED	Derma, Dream, Madre, Ramed	
APNEA	Paean					
APORT	Porta			ARMER	Rearm	
APPAL	Papal			ARMET	Mater, Metra, Tamer, Terma, Trema	
APPEL	Apple					
APPLE	Appel			ARMOR	Morra	
APRIL	Pilar			ARNEE	Ranee	
APRON	No-par			ARNOT	Orant, Toran, Trona	
APSOS	Psoas, Soaps			AROID	Radio	
APTLY	Patly, Typal			ARRET	Rater, Retar, Tarre, Terra	
*ARCAS	Sacra					
ARCED	Acred, Cadre, Cared, Cedar, Dacre, Raced			ARSES	Asser, Rases, Rasse, Sarse, Sears	
				ARSIS	Rissa, Saris	
*ARCHY	Chary			ARSON	Roans, Sonar	
ARCUS	Carus, Scaur			ARTAL	Altar, Ratal	
ARDEA	Aread			ARTEL	Alert, Alter, Later, Ratel, Telar	
ARDEB	Bader, Barde, Bared, Beard, Bread, Debar					
				ARTSY	Satyr, Stray, Trays	
ARDES	Dares, Rased, Reads			ARUMS	Ramus, Rusma	
AREAD	Ardea			ASCII	Isiac	
ARECA	Acera			ASCOT	Coast, Coats, Costa, Scoat	
AREDD	Adder, Dared, Dread, Dreda, Readd					

ASCUS Casus
ASHEN Hanse
ASHES He-ass, Seahs, Sesha,
      Sheas
ASHET Haets, Haste, Hates,
      Heast, Heats
ASIDE Aides, Ideas, Sadie
ASKER Eskar, Kesar, Rakes,
      Saker
ASKEW Wakes
ASPEN Napes, Neaps, Panes,
      Peans, Snape, Sneap,
      Spane, Spean
ASPER Apers, Pares, Parse,
      Pears, Prase, Presa,
      Rapes, Reaps, Spaer,
      Spare, Spear
ASPIC Picas, Scapi, Spica
*ASSAM Amass, Massa
ASSER Arses, Rases, Rasse,
      Sarse, Sears
ASSES Sasse, Sessa
ASSET Easts, Sates, Seats,
      Tasse, Tessa
ASSOT Oasts, Stoas, Tasso
ASTEL Least, Leats, Slate,
      Stale, Steal, Stela,
      Taels, Tales, Teals,
      Tesla
ASTER Arets, Earst, Rates,
      Reast, Resat, Stare,
      Strae, Tares, Tarse,
      Tears, Teras
ASTIR Airts, Sitar, Stair,
      Stria, Tarsi, Trias
*ASTOR Roast, Rotas, Taros,
      Toras, Troas
ATCHI Aitch
*ATHOL Loath, Lotah
*ATHOS Hoast, Hosta, Oaths,
      Shoat
ATIMY Amity
ATMAN Manta
ATOLL Allot, All-to
ATOMS Moats, Stoma
ATONE Oaten
ATONY Ayont
ATRIA Riata, Taira, Tiara
ATRIP Tapir

ATTAR Tatar
ATTIC Tacit
AUBIN Nubia
AUGER Argue
AUGHT Ghaut
AUMIL Miaul
AUNTS Saunt
AURAL Laura
AURIC Curia
AVENS Evans, Naves, Vanes
AVERS Raves, Saver, Vares
AVERT Tarve, Taver, Trave
AVILE Alive, Velia
AWING Wigan
AWNED Dewan, Waned
AXILS Salix
AYONT Atony
AZOTE Toaze

BACON Banco
*BADER Ardeb, Barde, Bared,
      Beard, Bread, Debar
BADGE Begad, Debag
BAGEL Belga, Gabel, Gable
BAGRE Barge, Garbe
BAILS Basil, Labis
*BAILY Bialy
BAIRN Abrin, Brain, Brian
BAITS Absit
BAKER Brake, Break, Kebar
BALAS Balsa, Basal, Sabal
BALED Blade
BALER Abler, Blare, Blear
BALES Basel, Basle, Blaes,
      Bleas, Blase, Sable
BALSA Balas, Basal, Sabal
BANAL Alban, Laban
BANCO Bacon
BANDS S-band
BARDE Ardeb, Bader, Bared,
      Beard, Bread, Debar
BARDY Darby
BARED Ardeb, Bader, Barde,
      Beard, Bread, Debar
BARES Baser, Bears, Braes,
      Saber, Sabre
BARET Bater, Berta, Taber
BARGE Bagre, Garbe

BARIC	Carib, Rabic
BARKY	Braky
BARMY	Ambry
BASAL	Balas, Balsa, Sabal
BASED	Beads
BASEL	Bales, Basle, Blaes, Bleas, Blase, Sable
BASER	Bares, Bears, Braes, Saber, Sabre
BASES	Basse
BASIL	Bails, Labis
BASIN	Sabin
*BASLE	Bales, Basel, Blaes, Bleas, Blase, Sable
BASSE	Bases
BASSY	Abyss
BASTE	Abets, Bates, Beast, Beats, Esbat, Sebat, Tabes
BASTO	Boast, Boats, Sabot, Tobas
BATER	Baret, Berta, Taber
BATES	Abets, Baste, Beast, Beats, Esbat, Sebat, Tabes
BATHE	Beath
BAYED	Beady
*BAYER	Yerba
BAZAR	Braza, Zabra
BEADS	Based
BEADY	Bayed
BE-ALL	All-be, Bella, Label
BEAMY	Embay, Maybe
BEARD	Ardeb, Bader, Barde, Bared, Bread, Debar
BEARS	Bares, Baser, Braes, Saber, Sabre
BEAST	Abets, Baste, Bates, Beats, Esbat, Sebat, Tabes
BEATH	Bathe
BEATS	Abets, Bates, Beast, Beast, Esbat, Sebat, Tabes
BECHE	Beech
BEDEL	Beeld, Bleed, Debel
BEDIM	Imbed
BEECH	Beche
BEELD	Bedel, Bleed, Debel

BEELE	Belee
BEETS	Beset, Betes
BEGAD!	Badge, Debag
BEGIN	Being, Binge
BEING	Begin, Binge
BELEE	Beele
BELGA	Bagel, Gabel, Gable
BELIT	Blite
*BELLA	All-be, Be-all, Label
BELOW	Bowel, Elbow
BELTS	Blest, Blets
BENDY	By-end
BENTY	Tenby
BEROE	Boree
*BERTA	Baret, Bater, Taber
BESET	Beets, Betes
BESIT	Bites
BESOM	Mebos
BESOT	Betso, Botes
BETES	Beets, Beset
BETID	Bidet, Debit
BETSO	Besot, Botes
BEVER	Breve
BIALY	Baily
BIDER	Bride, Debir, Rebid
BIDET	Betid, Debit
BIERS	Birse, Bries, Ribes
BIGLY	Bilgy
BILES	Eblis
BILGE	Gibel
BILGY	Bigly
BINGE	Begin, Being
BIRLE	Liber
BIRSE	Biers, Bries, Ribes
BITER	Brite, Tiber, Tribe
BITES	Besit
BLADE	Baled
BLAES	Bales, Basel, Basle, Bleas, Blase, Sable
BLAIN	Albin
*BLAKE	Bleak
BLAME	Amble, Embla, Mabel
BLAND	L-band
BLARE	Abler, Baler, Blear
BLASE	Bales, Basel, Basle, Blaes, Bleas, Sable
BLAST	Blats
BLATE	Ablet, Bleat, Table

BLATS	Blast		
BLEAK	Blake		
BLEAR	Abler, Baler, Blare		
BLEAS	Bales, Basel, Basle,		
	Blaes, Blase, Sable		
BLEAT	Ablet, Blate, Table		
BLEED	Bedel, Beeld, Debel		
BLEST	Belts, Blets		
BLETS	Belts, Blest		
BLITE	Belit		
BLORE	Roble		
BLUER	Ruble		
BLUES	Bulse		
BLURS	Burls, Slurb		
BLUSH	Buhls		
BOARD	Abord, Broad, Dobra,		
	Dorab		
BOART	Abort, Rabot, Tabor		
BOAST	Basto, Boats, Sabot,		
	Tobas		
BOATS	Basto, Boast, Sabot,		
	Tobas		
BODHI	Dhobi		
BODLE	Lobed		
*BOERS	Bores, Brose, Robes,		
	Sober		
BOGLE	Globe		
BOHEA	Obeah		
BOLAR	Labor, Lobar		
BOLOS	Lobos, Obols, Sobol		
BOMAS	Ambos, Moabs, Sambo		
BONER	Borne		
BONEY	Boyne, Ebony		
BONUS	Bosun, Bouns		
BOOMS	Bosom		
BOONS	Boson		
BOORD	Brood, Dobro		
BOORS	Sorbo		
BOOSE	Oboes		
BOOST	Boots		
BOOTS	Boost		
BORED	Brode, Orbed, Robed		
BOREE	Beroe		
BORES	Boers, Brose, Robes,		
	Sober		
BORNE	Boner		
BORTS	Strob		
BOSOM	Booms		
BOSON	Boons		

BOSUN	Bonus, Bouns		
BOTES	Besot, Betso		
BOUNS	Bonus, Bosun		
BOURN	Bruno		
BOUSY	Buoys, Byous		
BOUTS	Tsubo		
BOWEL	Below, Elbow		
*BOYNE	Boney, Ebony		
BRACE	Acerb, Caber, Cabre		
BRAES	Bears, Bares, Baser,		
	Saber, Sabre		
BRAID	Rabid		
BRAIL	Libra		
BRAIN	Abrin, Bairn, Brian		
BRAKE	Baker, Break, Kebar		
BRAKY	Barky		
BRAME	Amber, Bream, Embar		
BRASH	Shrab		
BRAST	Brats		
BRATS	Brast		
BRAUL	Lubra		
BRAZA	Bazar, Zabra		
BRAZE	Zebra		
BREAD	Ardeb, Bader, Barde,		
	Bared, Beard, Debar		
BREAK	Baker, Brake, Kebar		
BREAM	Amber, Brame, Embar		
BREDE	Breed		
BREED	Brede		
BREEM	Breme, Ember		
BREER	Brere		
BREME	Breem, Ember		
BRERE	Breer		
BREVE	Bever		
*BRIAN	Abrin, Bairn, Brain		
BRIDE	Bider, Debir, Rebid		
BRIEF	Fiber, Fibre		
BRIES	Biers, Birse, Ribes		
BRITE	Biter, Tiber, Tribe		
BROAD	Abord, Board, Dobra,		
	Dorab		
BRODE	Bored, Orbed, Robed		
BROME	Omber, Ombre		
BROMO	Broom, Ombro		
BROOD	Boord, Dobro		
BROOM	Bromo, Ombro		
BROSE	Boers, Bores, Robes,		
	Sober		
BROTH	Throb		

BRUIN	Burin, Rubin		CALKS	Lacks, Slack
BRUME	Umber, Umbre		CALLS	Scall
*BRUNO	Bourn		*CALOR	Carol, Claro, Coral
BRUNT	Burnt		CALPS	Claps, Clasp, Scalp
BRUSH	Buhrs, Burhs, Bursh,		CALVE	Cavel, Clave
	Shrub		CAMEL	Macle
BRUST	Burst, Strub		CAMPS	Scamp
BRUTE	Buret, Rebut, Tuber		CANED	Dance
BUGLE	Bulge		CANEH	Hence
BUHLS	Blush		CANER	Carne, Crane, Crena,
BUHRS	Brush, Burhs, Bursh,			Nacre, Rance
	Shrub		CANES	Scena
BULGE	Bugle		CANIS	Cains
BULSE	Blues		CANNY	Nancy
BUNKS	Knubs		CANOE	Ocean
BUOYS	Bousy, Byous		CANON	Ancon
BURAN	Unbar, Urban		CANST	Cants, Scant
BURET	Brute, Rebut, Tuber		CANTO	Acton
BURHS	Brush, Buhrs, Bursh,		CANTS	Canst, Scant
	Shrub		CAPED	Paced
BURIN	Bruin, Rubin		CAPEL	Caple, Place
BURLS	Blurs, Slurb		CAPER	Crape, Pacer, Perca,
*BURMA	Rumba, Umbra			Recap
BURNT	Brunt		CAPES	Paces, Scape, Space
BURSA	Abrus		CAPLE	Capel, Place
BURSE	Rebus, Suber		*CAPRI	Picra
BURST	Brust, Strub		CARDS	Scard
BUSED	Debus		CARED	Acred, Arced, Cadre,
BWANA	Nawab			Cedar, Dacre, Raced
BY-END	Bendy		CARER	Crare, Racer
BYOUS	Bousy, Buoys		CARES	Acers, Acres, Carse,
				Races, Sacre, Scare,
				Scrae, Serac
CABER	Acerb, Brace, Cabre		CARET	Carte, Cater, Crate,
CABLE	Caleb			React, Recta, Trace
CABRE	Acerb, Brace, Caber		*CARIB	Baric, Rabic
CACHE	Chace		CARLE	Clare, Clear
CADES	Cased, Daces		*CARNE	Caner, Crane, Crena,
CADET	Acted, Ectad			Nacre, Rance
CADGE	Caged		CAROB	Coarb, Cobra
CADRE	Acred, Arced, Cared,		CAROL	Calor, Claro, Coral
	Cedar, Dacre, Raced		CAROM	Marco
CAESE	Cease		CARPS	Craps, Scarp, Scrap
CAGED	Cadge		CARSE	Acers, Acres, Cares,
CAGER	Grace			Races, Sacre, Scare,
CAINS	Canis			Scrae, Serac
CAIRD	Acrid, Daric		CARTE	Caret, Cater, Crate,
*CALEB	Cable			React, Recta, Trace
CALIN	Linac		CARTS	Scart, Scrat

CARUS	Arcus, Scaur			
CARVE	Crave, Varec			
CASAL	Scala			
CASCO	Cocas			
CASED	Cades, Daces			
CASES	Casse			
CASSE	Cases			
CASTE	Cates, Scate, Sceat, Taces			
CASUS	Ascus			
CATER	Caret, Carte, Crate, React, Recta, Trace			
CATES	Caste, Scate, Sceat, Taces			
*CATHY	Yacht			
CAULD	Claud, Ducal			
CAUSE	Sauce			
CAVEL	Calve, Clave			
CAVIN	Vinca			
CEASE	Caese			
CEBUS	Cubes			
CEDAR	Acred, Arced, Cadre, Cared, Dacre, Raced			
CEDER	Cered, Creed			
CEILS	Ciels, Slice			
CENSE	Scene			
CENTO	Conte			
CENTS	Scent			
*CERAM	Crame, Cream, Macer			
CERED	Ceder, Creed			
*CERES	Crees, Scree			
CERIN	Crine, Nicer			
CERTS	Crest			
CHACE	Cache			
CHACO	Coach			
CHAIN	Chian, China			
CHAMS	Chasm			
CHANT	Natch			
CHAOS	Oshac			
CHAPE	Cheap, Peach			
CHAPS	Pasch			
CHAPT	Patch			
CHARD	Darch			
CHARE	Rache, Reach			
CHARM	March			
CHARS	Crash			
CHART	Ratch			
CHARY	Archy			
CHASE	Aches			
CHASM	Chams			
CHATS	Scath			
CHEAP	Chape, Peach			
CHEAT	Tache, Teach, Theca			
CHEEK	Keech			
CHEER	Reech			
CHELA	Leach			
CHERT	Retch			
CHEST	Stech			
*CHIAN	Chain, China			
CHIEF	Fiche			
CHIEL	Elchi			
CHIEN	Chine, Niche			
CHIME	Hemic, Miche			
CHINA	Chain, Chian			
CHINE	Chien, Niche			
CHIRT	Crith, Richt			
CHITS	Stich			
CHOIR	Ichor			
CHORE	Ocher, Ochre, Roche			
CHOUT	Couth, Touch			
CHUET	Chute, Teuch			
CHURL	Lurch			
CHURN	Runch			
CHUTE	Chuet, Teuch			
CIDER	Cried, Dicer			
CIELS	Ceils, Slice			
CIGAR	Craig			
CILIA	Iliac			
*CILLA	Lilac			
CITED	Edict, Ticed			
CIVES	Vices			
CIVET	Evict			
CLADE	Laced			
CLAES	Alces, Laces, Scale			
CLAIM	Malic			
CLAPS	Calps, Clasp, Scalp			
CLARE	Carle, Clear			
CLARO	Calor, Carol, Coral			
CLASP	Calps, Claps, Scalp			
*CLAUD	Cauld, Ducal			
CLAVE	Calve, Cavel			
CLAYS	Scaly			
CLEAN	Ancle, Lance, Lenca			
CLEAR	Carle, Clare			
CLEAT	Eclat, Ectal, Lacet			
CLIME	Melic			
CLODS	Colds, Scold			
CLOSE	Coles, Socle			

CLOUD	Could	COSTA	Ascot, Coats, Coast, Scoat	
CLUED	Dulce			
COACH	Chaco	COTES	Escot, Estoc, Scote	
COARB	Carob, Cobra	COULD	Cloud	
COAST	Ascot, Coats, Costa, Scoat	COUPS	Scoup	
		COURT	Crout, Turco	
COATS	Ascot, Coast, Costa, Scoat	COUTH	Chout, Touch	
		COVES	Scove, Voces	
COBRA	Carob, Coarb	COWLS	Scowl	
COCAS	Casco	CRABS	Scrab	
CODER	Cored, Credo, Decor	CRAFT	Fract	
CODES	Coeds, Cosed	CRAGS	Scrag	
CODLE	Dolce	CRAIG	Cigar	
COEDS	Codes, Cosed	CRAKE	Creak	
COFFS	Scoff	CRAME	Ceram, Cream, Macer	
COGON	Congo	CRAMS	Scram	
COIGN	Incog	CRANE	Caner, Carne, Crena, Nacre, Rance	
COINS	Icons, Scion, Sonic			
COLDS	Clods, Scold	CRANS	Scran	
COLES	Close, Socle	CRAPE	Caper, Pacer, Perca, Recap	
COLIN	Nicol			
COLOR	Crool	CRAPS	Carps, Scarp, Scrap	
COMER	Crome	CRARE	Carer, Racer	
CONES	Cosen, Scone, Sonce	CRASH	Chars	
*CONGO	Cogon	CRASS	Scars	
CONNE	Nonce	CRATE	Caret, Carte, Cater, React, Recta, Trace	
CONTE	Cento			
COONS	Scoon	CRAVE	Carve, Varec	
COOPS	Copos, Scoop	CRAWS	Scraw	
COOST	Coots, Scoot	CREAK	Crake	
COOTS	Coost, Scoot	CREAM	Ceram, Crame, Macer	
COPER	Crope	CREDO	Coder, Cored, Decor	
COPES	Copse, Pecos, Scope	CREED	Cared, Ceder	
COPOS	Coops, Scoop	CREEP	Crepe	
COPSE	Copes, Pecos, Scope	*CREES	Ceres, Scree	
CORAL	Calor, Carol, Claro	CRENA	Caner, Carne, Crane, Nacre, Rance	
CORDS	Scrod			
CORED	Coder, Credo, Decor	CREPE	Creep	
CORER	Crore	CREST	Certs	
CORES	Corse, Score	*CRETE	Erect, Terce	
CORKY	Rocky	CREWS	Screw	
CORNO	Croon	CRIED	Cider, Dicer	
CORNS	Scorn	CRIER	Ricer	
CORNY	Crony	CRIES	Seric	
CORPS	Crops	CRINE	Cerin, Nicer	
CORSE	Cores, Score	CRISP	Scrip	
COSEC	Secco	CRITH	Chirt, Richt	
COSED	Codes, Coeds	CROAT	Actor, Rocta, Taroc	
COSEN	Cones, Scone, Sonce	CROME	Comer	

CRONE	Oncer, Recon
CRONY	Corny
CROOL	Color
CROON	Corno
CROPE	Coper
CROPS	Corps
CRORE	Corer
CROUT	Court, Turco
CROWS	Scrow
CRUDE	Cured
CRUEL	Lucre, Ulcer
CRUET	Cuter, Eruct, Recut, Truce
CRUSE	Cures, Curse, Sucre
CRUST	Cruts, Curst
CRUTS	Crust, Curst
CRUVE	Curve
CUBES	Cebus
CUFFS	Scuff
CULLS	Scull
CUMIN	Mucin
CUPID	Pudic
CURBS	Scrub
CURED	Crude
CURER	Curre, Recur
CURES	Cruse, Curse, Sucre
CURIA	Auric
CURRE	Curer, Recur
CURSE	Cruse, Cures, Sucre
CURST	Crust, Cruts
CURVE	Cruve
CUTER	Cruet, Eruct, Recut, Truce
CUT-IN	Incut, Tunic
CUTIS	Ictus
CYARS	Scary, Scray
CYLIX	Xylic
*CYRIL	Lyric
DACES	Cades, Cased
*DACRE	Acred, Arced, Cadre, Cared, Cedar, Raced
*DAGON	Donga, Gonad
DAGOS	Gadso, Goads
*DAIRI	Radii
DAIRY	Diary
DAISY	Sayid
DAKER	Drake, Raked

DALED	Addle, Dedal, Laded
DALER	Alder
DALES	Deals, Lades, Leads, Slade
DALLE	Ladle
DALTS	Stal'd
DAMAN	Adman
DAMAR	Drama
DAMES	Demas, Desma, Meads
DANCE	Caned
*DANES	Andes, Deans, Sedan, Snead
DARBY	Bardy
*DARCH	Chard
DARED	Adder, Aredd, Dread, Dreda, Readd
DARER	Drear
DARES	Ardes, Rased, Reads
DARGA	Garda
DARIC	Acrid, Caird
DARTS	Drats, Strad
DASHY	Hyads, Shady
DATER	Rated, Tared, Trade, Tread
DATES	Sated, Stade, Stead, Teads, Tsade
DAUKS	Sudak
DAUTS	Adust
DEALS	Dales, Lades, Leads, Slade
DEALT	Delta, Lated
DEANS	Andes, Danes, Sedan, Snead
DEARN	Redan
DEARY	Deray, Rayed, Ready, Yeard
DEATH	Hated
DEAVE	Evade
DEBAG	Badge, Begad
DEBAR	Ardeb, Bader, Bared, Barde, Beard, Bread
DEBEL	Bedel, Beeld, Bleed
*DEBIR	Bider, Bride, Rebid
DEBIT	Betid, Bidet
DEBUS	Bused
DEBUT	Tubed
DECOR	Coder, Cored, Credo
DEDAL	Addle, Daled, Laded
DEENS	Denes, Dense, Edens, Needs

DEEPS	Speed			DICER	Cider, Cried	
DEFER	Freed, Refed			DICHT	Ditch	
DEIFY	Edify			DICTA	Diact	
DEIGN	Dinge, Nidge			DIETS	Deist, Edits, Sited,	
DE-INK	Inked				Stied, Tides	
DEISM	Dimes, Disme			DIKES	Skied	
DEIST	Diets, Edits, Sited,			DILLY	Idyll	
	Stied, Tides			DIMER	Mired, Rimed	
DELAY	Leady			DIMES	Deism, Disme	
*DELOS	Doles, Dosel, Lodes,			DINAR	Drain, Indra, Nadir	
	Solde, Soled			DINER	Rined	
DELTA	Dealt, Lated			DINES	Denis, Enids, Nides,	
DELVE	Devel				Sdein, Snide	
*DEMAS	Dames, Desma, Meads			DINGE	Deign, Nidge	
DEMIT	Timed			DINGO	Doing, Gondi	
DEMON	Monde			DINGY	Dying	
DEMOS	Domes, Modes			DINIC	Indic	
DEMUR	Mured			DIRER	Drier, Reird, Rider	
DENAY	Nayed			DIRGE	Gride, Ridge	
DENES	Deens, Dense, Edens,			DIRTS	Strid	
	Needs			DISME	Deism, Dimes	
DENGU	Nudge			DITAL	Tidal	
DENIM	Mined			DITCH	Dicht	
*DENIS	Dines, Enids, Nides,			DIVAN	Viand	
	Sdein, Snide			DIVER	Drive, Rived, Verdi	
DENSE	Deens, Denes, Edens,			DOBRA	Abord, Board, Broad,	
	Needs				Dorab	
DENTS	Stend, Tends			*DOBRO	Boord, Brood	
DE-OIL	Oiled			DOERS	Dorse, Doser, Rodes,	
DEPOD	Doped				Rosed	
DEPOT	Opted, Toped			DOEST	Dotes	
DERAY	Deary, Rayed, Ready,			DOGIE	Geoid	
	Yeard			DOING	Dingo, Gondi	
DERMA	Armed, Dream, Madre,			DOITS	Odist	
	Ramed			DOLCE	Codle	
DERRY	Dryer, Redry, Ryder			DOLER	Older	
*DESMA	Dames, Demas, Meads			DOLES	Delos, Dosel, Lodes,	
DETER	Treed				Solde, Soled	
DEUCE	Educe			DOLIA	Idola, Iodal	
DEVAS	Saved, Vades, Vedas			DOLOR	Drool, Loord	
DEVEL	Delve			DOMAL	Modal	
DEVIL	Lived, Vilde			DOMES	Demos, Modes	
DEWAN	Awned, Waned			DONEE	Enode	
DHOBI	Bodhi			DONET	Noted, Toned	
DHOLE	Holed			DONGA	Dagon, Gonad	
DIACT	Dicta			DONOR	Doorn, Rondo	
DIALS	Slaid			DOOLE	Looed	
*DIANA	Naiad			DOOLS	Soldo	
DIARY	Dairy			DOOMS	Dsomo, Moods	

DOORN	Donor, Rondo	
DOORS	Roods, Sordo	
DOPED	De-pod	
DOPER	Pedro, Pored, Repro, Roped	
DOPES	Posed, Spode	
DORAB	Abord, Board, Broad, Dobra	
*DORAS	Roads, Sorda	
DOREE	Erode	
DORPS	Drops, Prods, Sprod	
DORSE	Doers, Doser, Rodes, Rosed	
DOSEH	Hosed, Shoed	
DOSEL	Delos, Doles, Lodes, Solde, Soled	
DOSER	Doers, Dorse, Rodes, Rosed	
DOTED	Todde	
DOTES	Doest	
DOUAR	Doura	
DOURA	Douar	
DOVER	Drove, Roved, Vedro	
DOWEL	Dowle, Lowed, Owled	
DOWER	Rowed	
DOWLE	Dowel, Lowed, Owled	
DOWNS	Sownd	
DOWRY	Rowdy, Wordy	
DOWSE	Sowed	
*DOYLE	Odyle, Yodel, Yodle	
DOZEN	Zoned	
DRAIL	Laird, Liard	
DRAIN	Dinar, Indra, Nadir	
DRAKE	Daker, Raked	
DRAMA	Damar	
DRAPE	Padre, Pared, Raped, Repad	
DRATS	Darts, Strad	
DRAVE	Raved	
DRAWS	Sward, Wards	
DREAD	Adder, Aredd, Dared, Dreda, Readd	
DREAM	Armed, Derma, Madre, Ramed	
DREAR	Darer	
*DREDA	Adder, Aredd, Dared, Dread, Readd	
DRENT	Trend	
DREUL	Lured, Ruled	

DRIED	Redid	
DRIER	Direr, Reird, Rider	
DRIES	Rides, Sider, Sired	
DRILY	Lyrid	
D-RING	Grind	
DRIVE	Diver, Rived, Verdi	
DROME	Moder	
DRONE	Endor, Roden, Ronde	
DROOL	Dolor, Loord	
DROPS	Dorps, Prods, Sprod	
DROSS	Sords	
DROVE	Dover, Roved, Vedro	
DROWS	Sword, Words	
DRUPE	Duper, Perdu, Prude	
DRYAD	Ydrad	
DRYER	Derry, Redry, Ryder	
DSOMO	Dooms, Moods	
DUCAL	Cauld, Claud	
DUELS	Dules, Dulse, Leuds, Slued	
DULCE	Clued	
DULES	Duels, Dulse, Leuds, Slued	
DULSE	Duels, Dules, Leuds, Slued	
*DUMAS	Adsum, Mauds	
DUPER	Drupe, Perdu, Prude	
DUPLE	Puled	
DURAS	Rudas	
DURED	Udder	
DURGA	Guard	
DUSTY	Study	
DWALE	Waled, Weald	
DWINE	Edwin, Widen, Wined	
DYING	Dingy	
DYNAM	Mandy	
EAGER	Aeger, Agree, Eagre, Ragee	
EAGLE	Aglee	
EAGRE	Aeger, Agree, Eager, Ragee	
EARED	Arede, Areed, Reeda	
EARLS	Arles, Lares, Laser, Lears, Rales, Reals, Seral	
EARLY	Layer, Leary, Rayle, Relay	

EARNS	Nares, Nears, Saner, Snare			ELERS	Leers, Leres, Reels, Sleer		
EARST	Arets, Aster, Rates, Reast, Resat, Stare, Strae, Tares, Tarse, Tears, Teras			ELEVE	Levee		
				*ELGAR	Alger, Glare, Lager, Large, Regal		
				ELGIN	Ingle, Nigel		
EARTH	Hater, Heart, Herat, Rathe, Thrae			ELIAD	Ailed, Ideal		
				ELIDE	Edile		
EASEL	Easle, Lease			*ELLIS	Lisle		
EASES	Sease			ELOIN	Olein		
EASLE	Easel, Lease			EELOPS	Lopes, Olpes, Poles, Slope, Spole		
EASTS	Asset, Sates, Seats, Tasse, Tessa						
				*ELSIE	Eisel		
EATEN	Enate			ELSIN	Liens, Lines, Nelis		
EATER	Arete, Reate			ELVAN	Navel, Venal		
EAT-IN	Teian, Tenia, Tinea			ELVAS	Laves, Salve, Selva, Slave, Vales, Valse, Veals		
EAVES	Seave						
*EBLIS	Biles						
EBONY	Boney, Boyne			ELVER	Lever, Revel		
ECLAT	Cleat, Ectal, Lacet			*ELVIS	Evils, Levis, Lives, Slive, Veils, Vleis		
ECTAD	Acted, Cadet						
ECTAL	Cleat, Eclat, Lacet			EMBAR	Amber, Brame, Bream		
*EDENS	Deens, Denes, Dense, Needs			EMBAY	Beamy, Maybe		
				EMBER	Breem, Breme		
*EDGAR	Grade, Radge, Raged			*EMBLA	Amble, Blame, Mabel		
EDGES	Sedge			EMIRS	Meris, Mires, Miser, Reims, Riems, Rimes		
EDICT	Cited, Ticed						
EDIFY	Deify			EMITS	Items, Meist, Metis, Mites, Smite, Stime, Times		
EDILE	Elide						
EDITS	Deist, Diets, Sited, Stied, Tides						
				EMONG	Gnome		
EDUCE	Deuce			EMONY	Money		
*EDWIN	Dwine, Widen, Wined			ENATE	Eaten		
EGEST	Geest, Geste			*ENDOR	Drone, Roden, Ronde		
EGGAR	Gager			ENDOW	Nowed, Owned, Woden, Woned		
EGRET	Greet, Reget						
EIGNE	Genie			ENDUE	Undee		
EIKON	Koine			ENEMA	Amene, Meane		
EISEL	Elsie			ENEMY	Yemen		
ELAIN	Alien, Aline, Anile, Laine, Liane			ENGLE	Glene		
				*ENIDS	Denis, Dines, Nides, Sdein, Snide		
ELAND	Laden, Lande, Laned						
ELAPS	Lapse, Leaps, Pales, Peals, Pleas, Salep, Sepal, Slape, Spale, Speal			*ENNIS	Innes, Nines		
				ENODE	Donee		
				ENORM	Morne, Moner		
				ENROL	Loner, Loren		
ELATE	Telae			ENSEW	Sewen, Weens		
ELBOW	Below, Bowel			ENTAL	Leant		
ELCHI	Chiel			ENTER	Etern, Rente, Terne, Treen		

EOSIN	Noise		
EPHAS	Heaps, Phase, Shape		
EPHOD	Hoped		
EPICS	Sepic, Spice		
EPSOM	Mopes, Poems, Pomes		
EPURE	Puree, Rupee		
EQUIP	Pique		
ERASE	Saree		
ERECT	Crete, Terce		
ERGOS	Goers, Gores, Gorse, Ogres, Soger		
ERNES	Renes, Sneer		
*ERNIE	Irene		
*ERNST	Rents, Stern, Terns		
ERODE	Doree		
ERUCT	Cruet, Cuter, Recut, Truce		
ERVEN	Nerve, Never		
ERVIL	Liver, Livre, Rivel, Viler		
ESBAT	Abets, Baste, Bates, Beast, Beats, Sebat, Tabes		
ESCOT	Cotes, Estoc, Scote		
ESKAR	Asker, Kesar, Rakes, Saker		
ESKER	Reeks, Reesk		
*ESSEN	Sense		
ESTER	Reest, Reset, Retes, Steer, Stere, Teers, Teres, Terse, Trees		
ESTOC	Cotes, Escot, Scote		
ESTOP	Poets, Stoep, Stope, Topes		
ETERN	Enter, Rente, Terne, Treen		
ETHAL	Lathe		
ETHER	There, Three		
ETHIC	Theic		
ETHOS	Shote, Those		
*ETONS	Notes, Onset, Seton, Steno, Stone, Tones		
ETUIS	Suite		
EURUS	Usure		
EUSOL	Louse, Ousel		
EVADE	Deave		
*EVANS	Avens, Naves, Vanes		
EVENS	Seven		
EVERT	Revet		

EVERY	Veery		
EVICT	Civet		
EVILS	Elvis, Levis, Lives, Slive, Veils, Vleis		
EWERS	Resew, Sewer, Sweer		
EWEST	Sweet		
EXALT	Latex, Taxel		
EXERT	Retex		
EXILE	Lexie		
EXIST	Exits, Sixte		
EXITS	Exist, Sixte		
EXORS	Oxers, Sorex		
EXTRA	Retax, Taxer		
EYETI	Eytie		
EYTIE	Eyeti		
FACER	Farce		
FADER	Fared, Freda		
FAINT	Fanti		
FAIRS	Farsi, Fiars		
FAKER	Freak		
FAKIR	Kafir		
FALSE	Fleas		
FANTI	Faint		
FARCE	Facer		
FARED	Fader, Freda		
FARES	Farse, Fears, Safer		
FARLE	Feral, Flare		
FARSE	Fares, Fears, Safer		
FARSI	Fairs, Fiars		
FASTI	Fiats		
*FATES	Feast, Feats		
FAUNS	Snafu		
*FAUST	Stufa, Tufas		
FEARS	Fares, Farse, Safer		
FEAST	Fates, Feats		
FEATS	Fates, Feast		
FELID	Field, Filed, Flied		
FELIS	Files, Flies, S'life		
FELTY	Flyte, Lefty		
FEMUR	Fumer		
FERAL	Farle, Flare		
FERIA	Afire		
FERLY	Flyer		
FERRY	Fryer, Refry		
FETOR	Foret, Forte		
FEUDS	Fused		
FIARS	Fairs, Farsi		

FIATS	Fasti	FOSSA	Sofas
FIBER	Brief, Fibre	FOUND	Fondu
FIBRE	Brief, Fiber	FRACT	Craft
FICHE	Chief	FRAIL	Filar, Flair
FIELD	Felid, Filed, Flied	FRATI	Afrit
FIEND	Fined	FREAK	Faker
FIERY	Reify	*FREDA	Fader, Fared
FILAR	Flair, Frail	FREED	Defer, Refed
FILED	Felid, Field, Flied	FREER	Frere, Refer
FILER	Flier, Lifer, Rifle	FREIT	Refit
FILES	Felis, Flies, S'life	FRERE	Freer, Refer
FILET	Flite	FRIED	Fired
FINED	Fiend	FRIER	Firer
FINER	Infer	FRIES	Fires, Serif
FIRED	Fried	FRIST	First, Frits, Rifts
FIRER	Frier	FRITH	Firth
FIRES	Fries, Serif	FRITS	First, Frist, Rifts
FIRST	Frist, Frits, Rifts	*FROME	Forme
FIRTH	Frith	FROST	Forts
FIXER	Refix	FROTH	Forth
FLAIR	Filar, Frail	FRYER	Ferry, Refry
FLAKE	Fleak	FUELS	Flues, Fusel
FLAME	Fleam	FUMER	Femur
FLARE	Farle, Feral	FURAN	Unfar
FLEAK	Flake	FUSED	Feuds
FLEAM	Flame	FUSEL	Flues, Fuels
FLEAS	False	FUSTY	Yufts
FLEER	Refel		
FLESH	Shelf		
FLIED	Felid, Field, Filed	GABEL	Bagel, Belga, Gable
FLIER	Filer, Lifer, Rifle	GABLE	Bagel, Belga, Gabel
FLIES	Felis, Files, S'life	GADGE	Gaged
FLITE	Filet	GADSO	Dagos, Goads
FLOAT	Aloft, Flota	GADUS	Gauds
FLOOK	Kloof	GAGED	Gadge
FLOTA	Aloft, Float	GAGER	Eggar
FLOUR	Fluor	GAITS	Agist, Staig
FLUES	Fuels, Fusel	GALEA	Algae
FLUOR	Flour	GALED	Glade, Glead
FLYER	Ferly	GALLY	Gyall
FLYTE	Felty, Lefty	GAMED	Madge
FOALS	Loafs, Solfa	GAMER	Grame, Marge, Regma
FONDU	Found	GAMIC	Magic
FORET	Fetor, Forte	GAMMA	Magma
FORGE	Gofer	GANTS	Angst, Gnats, Stang,
FORME	Frome		Tangs
FORTE	Fetor, Foret	GAPED	Padge, Paged
FORTH	Froth	GAPER	Grape, Parge
FORTS	Frost	GARBE	Bagre, Barge

*GARDA	Darga
GASES	Sages
GATER	Grate, Great, Greta, Targe
GATES	Geats, Stage
GAUDS	Gadus
GAUMS	Sagum
GAUPS	Pagus
GAVEL	Glave
GAZEL	Glaze
GAZER	Graze
GEARS	Rages, Sager, Segar
GEATS	Gates, Stage
GEEST	Egest, Geste
GEIST	Gites, Tiges
GELID	Glide
GENIE	Eigne
GENRE	Green, Negre
GENRO	Goner, Negro
GENUS	Negus
GEODE	Ogeed
GEOID	Dogie
GERBE	Grebe
GESSO	Segos
GESTE	Egest, Geest
GHAST	Ghats
GHATS	Ghast
GHAUT	Aught
GHOST	Goths
GHOUL	Lough
GIBEL	Bilge
GIRON	Groin, Ringo
GIRTH	Grith, Right
GIRTS	Grist, Grits, Strig, Trigs
GITES	Geist, Tiges
GLADE	Galed, Glead
GLAIR	Argil, Grail
GLANS	Langs, Slang
GLARE	Alger, Elgar, Lager, Large, Regal
GLARY	Gyral
GLASS	Slags
GLAUM	Algum, Almug, Mulga
GLAUR	Gular
GLAVE	Gavel
GLAZE	Gazel
GLEAD	Galed, Glade
GLEAN	Agnel, Angel, Angle
GLEDE	Gleed, Ledge
GLEED	Glede, Ledge
GLEES	Leges
GLENE	Engle
GLIDE	Gelid
GLOBE	Bogle
GLCDE	Lodge, Ogled
GLOSS	Slogs
GLUER	Gruel, Luger
GLUES	Gules, Gusle, Luges
GNASH	Hangs
GNATS	Angst, Gants, Stang, Tangs
GNAWS	Swang, Wangs
GNOME	Emong
GOADS	Dagos, Gadso
GOERS	Ergos, Gores, Gorse, Ogres, Orges, Soger
GOFER	Forge
GONAD	Dagon, Donga
*GONDI	Dingo, Doing
GONER	Genro, Negro
GORAL	Largo, Orgal
GORED	Rodge
GORER	Roger
GORES	Ergos, Goers, Gcrse, Ogres, Soger
GORGE	Grego
GORSE	Ergos, Goers, Gores, Ogres, Soger
*GOTHS	Ghost
GOUTS	Gusto
GOWAN	Wagon
GRACE	Cager
GRADE	Edgar, Radge, Raged
GRAIL	Argil, Glair
GRAIN	Agrin
GRAMA	Magar
GRAME	Gamer, Marge, Regma
GRAPE	Gaper, Parge
GRASP	Sprag
GRATE	Gater, Great, Greta, Targe
GRAZE	Gazer
GREAT	Gater, Grate, Greta, Targe
GREBE	Gerbe
GREEN	Genre, Negre
GREES	Grese

GREET	Egret, Reget		
GREGO	Gorge		
GREIN	Niger, Reign, Renig,		
	Ringe		
GREIT	Tiger		
GRESE	Grees		
*GRETA	Gater, Grate, Great,		
	Targe		
GRIDE	Dirge, Ridge		
GRIND	D-ring		
GRIPS	Prigs, Sprig		
GRIST	Girts, Grits, Strig,		
	Trigs		
GRITH	Girth, Right		
GRITS	Girts, Grist, Strig,		
	Trigs		
GROAN	Angor, Argon, Nagor,		
	Orang, Organ		
GROAT	Argot		
GROIN	Giron, Ringo		
GROWN	Wrong		
GRUEL	Gluer, Luger		
GUARD	Durga		
GULAR	Glaur		
GULES	Glues, Gusle, Luges		
GUSLE	Glues, Gules, Luges		
GUSTO	Gouts		
GYALL	Gally		
GYRAL	Glary		
GYRUS	Surgy		
HACKS	Shack		
HADES	Heads, Sadhe, Shade		
HADJI	Jihad		
HAETS	Ashet, Haste, Hates,		
	Heast, Heats		
HAFTS	Shaft		
HAILS	Alish		
HAIRS	Arish		
HAITS	Saith, Taish		
HAKES	Shake		
HALED	Heald		
HALES	Halse, Heals, Leash,		
	Selah, Shale, Sheal		
HALLO	Holla		
HALLS	Shall		
HALMA	Almah, Hamal		
HALMS	Shalm		

HALOS	Shoal, Shola, Solah
HALSE	Hales, Heals, Leash,
	Selah, Shale, Sheal
HALTS	Laths, Shalt
HAMAL	Almah, Halma
HAMES	Ahems, Heams, Shame
HANCE	Caneh
HANDS	Shand
HANDY	Haydn
HANGS	Gnash
HANKS	Khans, Shank
HANSE	Ashen
HAPLY	Phyla
HARDS	Shard
HARDY	Hydra
HARED	Heard
HAREM	Herma
HARES	Hears, Share, Shear
HARKS	Shark
HARMS	Marsh, Shram
HARNS	Sharn
HARPS	Sharp
HARST	Harts, Raths, Tahrs,
	Thars, Trash
HARTS	Harst, Raths, Tahrs,
	Thars, Trash
HASPS	Shaps
HASTE	Ashet, Haets, Hates,
	Heast, Heats
HASTY	Yasht
HATED	Death
HATER	Earth, Heart, Herat,
	Tathe, Thrae
HATES	Ashet, Haets, Haste,
	Heast, Heats
HAUNT	Unhat
HAVES	Shave, Sheva
HAWMS	Shawm, Whams
*HAYDN	Handy
HEADS	Hades, Sadhe, Shade
HEALD	Haled
HEALS	Hales, Halse, Leash,
	Selah, Shale, Sheal
HEAMS	Ahems, Hames, Shame
HEAPS	Ephas, Phase, Shape
HEARD	Hared
HEARS	Hares, Share, Shear
HEART	Earth, Hater, Herat,
	Rathe, Thrae

HE-ASS	Ashes, Seahs, Sesha, Sheas			HOPED	Ephod	
HEAST	Ashet, Haets, Haste, Hates, Heats			HORDE	Herod	
				HORME	Homer	
HEATS	Ashet, Haets, Haste, Hates, Heast			HORNS	Shorn	
				HORSE	Heros, Shoer, Shore	
HEELS	Sheel			HORST	Short	
HEIRS	Hires, Shier, Shire			*HORUS	Hours	
HELLS	Shell			HOSED	Doseh, Shoed	
HELOT	Hotel, Thole			HOSEN	Hones, Shone	
HELPS	Plesh			HOSTA	Athos, Hoast, Oaths, Shoat	
HE-MAN	Maneh					
HEMIC	Chime, Miche			HOSTS	Shots, Stosh	
HENDS	Shend			HOTEL	Helot, Thole	
HENRY	Rhyne			HOURS	Horus	
HEPAR	Phare, Raphe			HOVES	Shove	
*HERAT	Earth, Hater, Heart, Rathe, Thrae			HOWES	Whose	
				HOWRE	Whore	
HERDS	Sherd, Shred			HOWSO	Whoso	
HERES	Herse, Sheer			HSIEN	Shine	
HERMA	Harem			HUCKS	Shuck	
HEROD	Horde			HUMOR	Mohur	
HEROS	Horse, Shoer, Shore			HUMPS	Sumph	
HERSE	Heres, **Sheer**			HUNTS	Shunt	
HEWER	Where			HURST	Hurts	
HIDER	Hired, Rehid			HURTS	Hurst	
HIDES	Shide, Shied			HYADS	Dashy, Shady	
HIGHT	Thigh			HYDRA	Hardy	
HIKES	Sheik			*HYLAS	Shaly	
*HINDU	Unhid					
HINGE	Neigh			ICHOR	Choir	
HIRED	Hider, Rehid			ICONS	Coins, Scion, Sonic	
HIRES	Heirs, Shier, Shire			ICTUS	Cutis	
HIVES	Shive			IDEAL	Ailed, Eliad	
HOARD	Rhoda			IDEAS	Aides, Aside, Sadie	
HOARS	Saroh			IDIOM	Imido	
HOAST	Athos, Hosta, Oaths, Shoat			IDLER	Riled	
				IDLES	Sidle, Sield, Slide	
HOCKS	Shock			IDOLA	Dolia, Iodal	
HOIKS	Shiko			IDOLS	Silo'd, Sloid, Soldi, Solid	
HOLED	Dhole					
HOLES	Sheol, Shole			IDYLL	Dilly	
HOLLA	Hallo			ILEAC	Alice	
HOLTS	Sloth			ILEUS	Lieus	
HOMER	Horme			ILIAC	Cilia	
HONER	Rhone			ILIAN	Inial	
HONES	Hosen, Shone			ILLTH	Thill	
HOOKS	Shook			IMAGO	Amigo	
HOOTS	Shoot, Sooth, Sotho			IMAMS	Maims, Miasm	

IMBED	Bedim	ITEMS	Emits, Meist, Metis,	
IMIDO	Idiom		Mites, Smite, Stime,	
IMINE	Minie		Times	
INANE	Annie	ITHER	Rithe	
INAPT	Paint, Patin, Pinta	IVIES	Visie	
INARM	Minar			
IN-CAP	Panic			
INCOG	Coign	JANES	Jeans	
INCUR	Runic	JANTU	Jaunt, Junta	
INCUT	Cut-in, Tunic	JAPES	Jaspe	
*INDIC	Dinic	JASPE	Japes	
*INDRA	Dinar, Drain, Nadir	JAUNT	Jantu, Junta	
INDUE	Nudie	JEANS	Janes	
INERM	Miner	JIHAD	Hadji	
INERT	Inter, Niter, Nitre,	*JOANS	Jonas	
	Retin, Trine	*JOHAN	Jonah	
INFER	Finer	*JONAH	Johan	
INGLE	Elgin, Nigel	*JONAS	Joans	
INGOT	Tigon, Toing	JORAM	Major	
INIAL	Ilian	JOTUN	Junto	
INKED	De-ink	JUNTA	Jantu, Jaunt	
INKER	Re-ink	JUNTO	Jotun	
INKLE	Liken			
*INNES	Ennis, Nines			
INORB	Robin	KAFIR	Fakir	
INSET	Neist, Nesti, Senti,	KAILS	Kalis, Skail	
	Set-in, Stein, Tines	KAINS	Kisan, Skain	
INTER	Inert, Niter, Nitre,	KALES	Lakes, Leaks, Slake	
	Retin, Trine	KALIS	Kails, Skail	
INTRA	Riant, Tarin, Train	KANES	Skean, Snake, Sneak	
INURE	Urine	KARST	Stark	
INURN	Run-in	*KATES	Keats, Skate, Steak,	
INUST	Suint, Tunis, Units		Stake, Takes, Teaks	
INVAR	Ravin	KAYLE	Leaky	
IODAL	Dolia, Idola	*KEATS	Kates, Skate, Steak,	
IOTAS	Ostia, Stoai		Stake, Takes, Teaks	
IRADE	Aider, Aired, Redia	KEBAR	Baker, Brake, Break	
IRATE	Terai	KEECH	Cheek	
*IRENE	Ernie	KEELS	Leeks, Skeel, Sleek	
*IRISH	Rishi, Sirih	KEEPS	Peeks, Pekes, Speke	
IRONS	Ornis, Roins, Rosin	KELPS	Skelp, Spelk	
*ISIAC	Ascii	KENOS	Snoek, Snoke	
*ISLAM	Mails, Salmi, Simla	KEPIS	Kipes, Pikes, Spike	
ISLES	Lisse, Siles	KESAR	Asker, Eskar, Rakes,	
ISLET	Istle, Steil, Stile,		Saker	
	Teils, Tiles	KHANS	Hanks, Shank	
ISTLE	Islet, Steil, Stile,	KILEY	Kylie	
	Teils, Tiles	KILLS	Skill	
*ITALY	Laity	KILNS	Links, Slink	

KINKS	Skink		LAIRD	Drail, Liard	
KIPES	Kepis, Pikes, Spike		LAITY	Italy	
KISAN	Kains, Skain		LAKES	Kales, Leaks, Slake	
KITES	Skite, Tikes		LAMAS	Almas	
KLOOF	Flook		LAMED	Medal	
KNARS	Krans, Narks, Ranks,		LAMER	Realm	
	Skran, Snark		LAMES	Almes, Amsel, Leams,	
KNEAD	Naked			Males, Meals, Melas,	
KNEES	Skene			Mesal, Salem, Samel	
KNIPS	Pinks, Spink		LAMPS	Palms, Plasm, Psalm	
KNITS	Stink, Tinks		*LANAS	Nasal	
KNOPS	Knosp		LANCE	Ancle, Clean, Lenca	
KNOSP	Knops		LANDE	Eland, Laden, Laned	
KNOTE	Token		LANED	Eland, Laden, Lande	
KNOWE	Woken		LANES	Leans, Neals, Senal,	
KNOWS	Snowk			Slane	
KNUBS	Bunks		LANGS	Glans, Slang	
KOFFS	Skoff		LAPIN	Plain	
KOINE	Eikon		LAPIS	Pails, Spail, Spial	
KOLAS	Skoal		LAPSE	Elaps, Leaps, Pales,	
KORAN	Krona			Peals, Pleas, Salep,	
KOROS	Rooks			Sepal, Slape, Spale,	
KOTOS	Stook, Tokos			Speal	
KRAIT	Traik		LARDY	Lyard	
KRANS	Knars, Narks, Ranks,		LARES	Arles, Earls, Laser,	
	Skran, Snark			Lears, Rales, Reals,	
KRONA	Koran			Seral	
KYLIE	Kiley		LARGE	Alger, Elgar, Glare,	
				Lager, Regal	
			LARGO	Goral, Orgal	
*LABAN	Alban, Banal		*LARNE	Learn, Lerna, Renal ·	
LABEL	All-be, Be-all, Bella		LARUM	Mural, Rumal	
LABIS	Bails, Basil		LARUS	Sural	
LABOR	Bolar, Lobar		LASER	Arles, Earls, Lares,	
LACED	Clade			Lears, Rales, Reals,	
LACES	Alces, Claes, Scale			Seral	
LACET	Cleat, Eclat, Ectal		LASSO	Solas	
LACKS	Calks, Slack		LATED	Dealt, Delta	
LADAS	Salad, Salda		LATER	Alert, Alter, Artel,	
LADED	Addle, Daled, Dedal			Ratel, Telar	
LADEN	Eland, Lande, Laned		LATEX	Exalt, Taxel	
LADES	Dales, Deals, Leads,		LATHE	Ethal	
	Slade		LATHS	Halts, Shalt	
LADLE	Dalle		LAUND	Ulnad	
LAGER	Alger, Elgar, Glare,		LAURA	Aural	
	Large, Regal		LAVAS	Vasal	
LAICS	Aclis, Salic, Scail		LAVED	Valed	
LAINE	Alien, Aline, Anile,		LAVER	Ravel, Velar	
	Elain, Liane		LAVES	Elvas, Salve, Selva,	

	Slave, Vales, Valse, Veals
LAWNY	Wanly
LAYER	Early, Leary, Rayle, Relay
LAY-UP	Uplay
L-BAND	Bland
LEACH	Chela
LEADS	Dales, Deals, Lades, Slade
LEADY	Delay
LEAKS	Kales, Lakes, Slake
LEAKY	Kayle
LEAMS	Almes, Amsel, Lames, Males, Meals, Melas, Mesal, Salem, Samel
LEANS	Lanes, Neals, Senal, Slane
LEANT	Ental
LEAPS	Elaps, Lapse, Pales, Peals, Pleas, Salep, Sepal, Slape, Spale, Speal
LEAPT	Lepta, Pelta, Petal, Plate, Pleat, Tepal
LEARE	Leear,
LEARN	Larne, Lerna, Renal
LEARS	Arles, Earls, Lares, Laser, Rales, Reals, Seral
LEARY	Early, Layer, Rayle, Relay
LEASE	Easel, Easle
LEASH	Hales, Halse, Heals, Selah, Shale, Sheal
LEAST	Astel, Leats, Slate, Stale, Steal, Stela, Taels, Tales, Teals, Tesla
LEATS	Astel, Leats, Slate, Stale, Steal, Stela, Taels, Tales, Teals, Tesla
LEAVY	Vealy
LEDGE	Glede, Gleed
LEEAR	Leare
LEEKS	Keels, Skeel, Sleek
LEERS	Leres, Reels, Sleer
LEETS	Sleet, Steel, Stele, Teels

LEFTY	Felty, Flyte
LEGER	Regel, Regle
LEGES	Glees
*LEITH	Lieth, Lithe
LEMAN	Lemna
LEMNA	Leman
LEMON	Melon, Monel
LENCA	Ancle, Clean, Lance
*LENIN	Linen
LENOS	Solen
LENTO	Olent
LEPER	Repel
LEPID	Piel'd, Piled, Plied
LEPIS	Piles, Plies, Slipe, Spiel, Spile
LEPRA	Paler, Parle, Pearl, Repla
LEPTA	Leapt, Pelta, Petal, Plate, Pleat, Tepal
LERES	Leers, Reels, Sleer
LERNA	Larne, Learn, Renal
LEUDS	Duels, Dules, Dulse, Slued
LEVEE	Eleve
LEVER	Elver, Revel
LEVIN	Liven
*LEVIS	Elvis, Evils, Lives, Slive, Veils, Vleis
LEWIS	Wiles
*LEXIE	Exile
LEXIS	Silex
LIANE	Alien, Aline, Anile, Elain, Laine
LIANG	Algin, Align, Ligan, Linga
LIARD	Drail, Laird
LIART	Trail, Trial
LIBER	Birle
*LIBRA	Brail
LICKS	Slick
LIENS	Elsin, Lines, Nelis
LIERS	Riles, Risel, Slier
LIETH	Leith, Lithe
LIEUS	Ileus
LIFER	Filer, Flier, Rifle
LIGAN	Algin, Align, Liang, Linga
LIKEN	Inkle
LILAC	Cilla

LILTS	Still, Tills		
LIMES	Miles, Misle, Slime, Smile		
LIMSY	Misly, Slimy		
LINAC	Calin		
LINEN	Lenin		
LINES	Elsin, Liens, Nelis		
LINGA	Algin, Align, Liang, Ligan		
LINGS	Sling		
LINGY	Lying		
LINKS	Kilns, Slink		
LISLE	Ellis		
LISPS	Slips		
LISSE	Isles, Siles		
LITAS	Tails		
LITER	Litre, Relit, Tiler		
LITHE	Leith, Lieth		
LITRE	Liter, Relit, Tiler		
LIVED	Devil, Vilde		
LIVEN	Levin		
LIVER	Ervil, Livre, Rivel, Viler		
LIVES	Elvis, Evils, Levis, Slive, Veils, Vleis		
LIVRE	Ervil, Liver, Rivel, Viler		
LOAFS	Foals, Sol-fa		
LOAMS	Lomas, Salmo, Sloam		
LOANS	Salon, Sloan		
LOATH	Athol, Lotah		
LOBAR	Bolar, Labor		
LOBED	Bodle		
LOBOS	Bolos, Obols, Sobol		
LODES	Delos, Doles, Dosel, Solde, Soled		
LODGE	Glode, Ogled		
LOESS	Loses, Sloes, Soles		
LOGAN	Along		
*LOIRE	Oiler, Oriel, Reoil		
LOMAS	Loams, Salmo, Sloam		
LONER	Enrol, Loren		
LOOED	Doole		
LOOES	Loose, Soole		
LOOFA	Aloof		
LOOKS	Sokol		
LOOMS	Sloom		
LOONS	Snool, Solon		
LOOPS	Pools, Sloop, Spool		
LOORD	Dolor, Drool		
LOOSE	Looes, Soole		
LOOTS	Lotos, Sloot, Sotol, Stool, Tools		
LOPED	Poled		
LOPES	Elops, Olpes, Poles, Slope, Spole		
LOPPY	Polyp		
*LOREN	Enrol, Loner		
LORES	Loser, Orles, Roles, Soler, Sorel		
LORIS	Roils		
LOSER	Lores, Orles, Roles, Soler, Sorel		
LOSES	Loess, Sloes, Soles		
LOTAH	Athol, Loath		
LOTES	Stole, Toles		
LOTOS	Loots, Sloot, Sotol, Stool, Tools		
LOTUS	Louts		
LOUGH	Ghoul		
LOUND	Nould		
LOUSE	Eusol, Ousel		
LOUTS	Lotus		
LOVAT	Volta		
LOVED	Voled		
LOVES	Slove, Solve, Voles		
LOWED	Dowel, Dowle, Owled		
LOWER	Owler, Rowel		
LOWNE	Nowel		
LOWNS	Swoln		
LOWSE	Sowle		
LOYAL	Alloy		
LUBRA	Braul		
LUCRE	Cruel, Ulcer		
LUGER	Gluer, Gruel		
LUGES	Glues, Gules, Gusle		
LUMPS	Plums, Slump		
LUMPY	Plumy		
LUNAR	Ulnar, Urnal		
LUNGS	Slung		
LUPPA	Pupal		
LUPUS	Pulus		
LURCH	Churl		
LURED	Dreul, Ruled		
LURER	Ruler		
LYARD	Lardy		
LYING	Lingy		
LYRIC	Cyril		
LYRID	Drily		

*MABEL	Amble, Blame, Embla	
MACER	Ceram, Crame, Cream	
MACKS	Smack	
MACLE	Camel	
MADGE	Gamed	
MADRE	Armed, Derma, Dream, Ramed	
MAGAR	Grama	
MAGIC	Gamic	
MAGMA	Gamma	
MAIDS	Midas	
MAILS	Islam, Salmi, Simla	
MAIMS	Imams, Miasm	
MAINS	Manis, Minas	
MAIST	Tamis	
MAJOR	Joram	
MALAR	Alarm, Ramal	
MALES	Almes, Amsel, Lames, Leams, Meals, Melas, Mesal, Salem, Samel	
MALIC	Claim	
MALLS	Small	
*MALTA	Talma, Tamal	
MALTS	Smalt	
MANDE	Admen, Amend, Maned, Menad, Named	
*MANDY	Dynam	
MANED	Admen, Amend, Menad, Named	
MANEH	He-man	
MANES	Amens, Manse, Means, Mensa, Names, Samen	
MANET	Ament, Meant	
MANGE	Megan	
MANGO	Among	
MANIA	Amain, Amnia, Anima	
MANIS	Mains, Minas	
MANNA	Naman	
MANOR	Norma, Ramon, Roman	
MANSE	Amens, Manes, Means, Mensa, Names, Samen	
MANTA	Atman	
MANUS	Mauns	
MAPLE	Ample, Pelma	
MARCH	Charm	
*MARCO	Carom	
MARES	Maser, Mears, Reams, Smear	
MARGE	Gamer, Grame, Regma	

*MARIE	Aimer, Ramie, Rimae
MARLY	Almay
*MAROS	Osram, Roams
MARSH	Harms, Shram
MARTS	Smart, Trams
MARYS	Symar
MASER	Mares, Mears, Reams, Smear
MASON	Moans, Monas, Osman
MASSA	Amass, Assam
MASSE	Seasm
MASTY	Mayst
MATED	Tamed
MATER	Armet, Metra, Tamer, Terma, Trema
MATES	Meats, Satem, Steam, Tames, Teams
MATEY	Meaty
MATIN	Tamin
MAUDS	Adsum, Dumas
MAUND	Munda, Undam, Unmad
MAUNS	Manus
MAYBE	Beamy, Embay
MAYOR	Moray
MAYST	Masty
MEADS	Dames, Demas, Desma
MEALS	Almes, Amsel, Lames, Leams, Males, Melas, Mesal, Salem, Samel
MEANE	Amene, Enema
MEANS	Amens, Manse, Manes, Mensa, Names, Samen
MEANT	Ament, Manet
MEANY	Yamen
MEARS	Mares, Maser, Reams, Smear
*MEATH	Thame, Thema
MEATS	Mates, Satem, Steam, Tames, Teams
MEATY	Matey
MEBOS	Besom
MEDAL	Lamed
MEDIA	Aimed, Amide
MEETS	Metes, Steem, Steme, Teems, Temes, Temse
*MEGAN	Mange
MEISM	Mimes
MEIST	Emits, Items, Metis, Mites, Smite, Stime, Times

MELAS	Almes, Amsel, Lames, Leams, Males, Meals, Mesal, Salem, Samel	
MELIC	Clime	
MELLS	Smell	
MELON	Lemon, Monel	
*MELOS	Moles	
MELTS	Smelt	
MENAD	Admen, Amend, Mande, Maned, Named	
MENSA	Amens, Manse, Manes, Means, Names, Samen	
MENSE	Mesne, Neems, Semen	
MERIL	Miler	
*MERIS	Emirs, Mires, Miser, Reims, Riems, Rimes	
MERIT	Miter, Mitre, Remit, Timer	
MESAL	Almes, Amsel, Lames, Leams, Males, Meals, Melas, Salem, Samel	
MESNE	Mense, Neems, Semen	
MESON	Nomes, Omens	
MESTO	Motes, Smote, Tomes	
METED	Temed	
METER	Metre, Retem	
METES	Meets, Steem, Steme, Teems, Temes, Temse	
METIS	Emits, Items, Meist, Mites, Smite, Stime, Times	
METOL	Motel	
METRA	Armet, Mater, Tamer, Terma, Trema	
METRE	Meter, Retem	
MIASM	Imams, Maims	
MIAUL	Aumil	
MICHE	Chime, Hemic	
*MIDAS	Maids	
MILER	Meril	
MILES	Limes, Misle, Slime, Smile	
MILKS	Sklim	
MIMES	Meism	
MINAR	Inarm	
MINAS	Manis, Mains	
MINED	Denim	
MINER	Inerm	
*MINIE	Imine	

*MINOS	Simon
MIRED	Dimer, Rimed
MIRES	Emirs, Meris, Miser, Reims, Riems, Rimes
MISDO	Odism
MISER	Emirs, Meris, Mires, Reims, Riems, Rimes
MISES	Seism, Semis
MISLE	Limes, Miles, Slime, Smile
MISLY	Limsy, Slimy
MISSY	Mysis
MISTY	Stimy
MITER	Merit, Mitre, Remit, Timer
MITES	Emits, Items, Meist, Metis, Smite, Stime, Times
MITRE	Merit, Miter, Remit, Timer
MITTS	Smitt
MIXER	Re-mix
*MOABS	Ambos, Bomas, Sambo
MOANS	Mason, Monas, Osman
MOATS	Atoms, Stoma
MOCKS	Smock
MODAL	Domal
MODEL	Moled
MODER	Drome
MODES	Demos, Domes
MOHUR	Humor
MOKES	Smoke
MOLAR	Moral, Romal
MOLED	Model
MOLES	Melos
MOLLA	Ollam
MONAD	Nomad
*MONAS	Mason, Moans, Osman
MONDE	Demon
MONEL	Lemon, Melon
MONER	Enorm, Morne
*MONET	Monte, Moten
MONEY	Emony
MONTE	Monet, Moten
MOODS	Dooms, Dsomo
MOONS	Nomos
MOORY	Roomy
MOOTS	Smoot, Stoom, Tooms
MOPER	Proem

MOPES	Epsom, Poems, Pomes	
MOPSY	Myops	
MORAL	Molar, Romal	
MORAT	Amort	
MORAY	Mayor	
MORES	Omers, Smore	
MORNE	Enorm, Moner	
MORRA	Armor	
MORTS	Storm	
MOTEL	Metol	
MOTEN	Monet, Monte	
MOTES	Mesto, Smote, Tomes	
MOTET	Motte, Totem	
MOTHY	Y-moth	
MOTTE	Motet, Totem	
MOUES	Mouse	
MOUNT	Muton, Notum	
MOURN	Munro	
MOUSE	Moues	
MOVER	Vomer	
MOWER	Remow, Rowme	
MUCIN	Cumin	
MUCKS	Smuck	
MUCOR	Mucro	
MUCRO	Mucor	
MULES	Mulse	
MULGA	Algum, Almug, Glaum	
MULSE	Mules	
MUNDA	Maund, Undam, Unmad	
*MUNRO	Mourn	
MURAL	Larum, Rumal	
MURED	Demur	
MURES	Muser, Remus, Serum	
MUREX	Rumex	
MUSCA	Sumac	
MUSCI	Music	
MUSED	Sedum	
MUSER	Mures, Remus, Serum	
MUSET	Mutes	
MUSIC	Musci	
MUTES	Muset	
MUTON	Mount, Notum	
MVULE	Velum	
MYOPS	Mopsy	
MYSIS	Missy	
NACRE	Caner, Carne, Crane, Crena, Rance	

NADIR	Dinar, Drain, Indra
NAEVI	Naive
NAGOR	Angor, Argon, Groan, Orang, Organ
NAIAD	Diana
NAILS	Anils, Salin, Slain, Snail
NAIVE	Naevi
NAKED	Knead
NAKER	Anker
NAMAN	Manna
NAMED	Admen, Amend, Mande, Maned, Menad
NAMER	Reman
NAMES	Amens, Manse, Manes, Means, Mensa, Samen
*NANCY	Canny
NAPES	Aspen, Neaps, Panes, Peans, Snape, Sneap, Spane, Spean
NARES	Earns, Nears, Saner, Snare
NARIS	Rains, Ranis
NARKS	Knars, Krans, Ranks, Skran, Snark
NASAL	Lanas
NASTY	Tansy
NATCH	Chant
NATES	Nesta, Stean
NATTY	Tanty
NAVEL	Elvan, Venal
NAVES	Avens, Evans, Vanes
NAWAB	Bwana
NAYED	Denay
NAZES	Senza
*NEALS	Lanes, Leans, Senal, Slane
NEAPS	Aspen, Napes, Panes, Peans, Snape, Sneap, Spane, Spean
NEARS	Earns, Nares, Saner, Snare
NEATH	Thane
NECKS	Sneck
NEEDS	Deens, Denes, Dense, Edens
NEEMS	Mense, Mesne, Semen
NEGRE	Genre, Green
NEGRO	Goner, Genro

NEGUS	Genus	NOOKS	Snook	
NEIGH	Hinge	NOOPS	Poons, Snoop, Spoon	
NEIST	Inset, Nesti, Senti,	NO-PAR	Apron	
	Set-in, Stein, Tines	NORAH	Rohan	
NELIS	Elsin, Liens, Lines	NORMA	Manor, Ramon, Roman	
NEPER	Preen, Repen	NORSE	Noser, Rones, Senor,	
NERVE	Erven, Never		Seron, Snore	
NESKI	Skein	NORTH	Thorn	
*NESTA	Nates, Stean	NOSED	Nodes, Sonde	
NESTI	Inset, Neist, Senti,	NOSER	Norse, Rones, Senor,	
	Set-in, Stein, Tines		Seron, Snore	
NEVER	Erven, Nerve	NOTAL	Alton, Talon, Tolan,	
*NEVIS	Sevin, Venis, Veins,		Tonal	
	Vines, Visne	NOTED	Donet, Toned	
NEVUS	Venus	NOTER	Tenor, Toner, Trone	
NEWER	Renew	NOTES	Etons, Onset, Seton,	
NEXUS	Unsex		Steno, Stone, Tones	
NICER	Cerin, Crine	NOTUM	Mount, Muton	
NICHE	Chien, Chine	NOTUS	Snout, Stoun, Tonus	
NICKS	Snick	NOULD	Lound	
NICOL	Colin	NOUNS	Unson	
NIDES	Denis, Dines, Enids,	NOWED	Endow, Owned, Woden,	
	Sdein, Snide		Woned	
NIDGE	Deign, Dinge	NOWEL	Lowne	
*NIGEL	Elgin, Ingle	NUBIA	Aubin	
*NIGER	Grein, Reign, Renig,	NUDGE	Dengu	
	Ringe	NUDIE	Indue	
NIGHT	Thing	NURSE	Runes	
NINES	Ennis, Innes	NYULA	Yulan	
NISSE	Sines			
NISUS	Sinus			
NITER	Inert, Inter, Nitre,	OARED	Adore, Oread	
	Retin, Trine	OASTS	Assot, Stoas, Tasso	
NITON	Noint	OATEN	Atone	
NITRE	Inert, Inter, Niter,	OATHS	Athos, Hoast, Hosta,	
	Retin, Trine		Shoat	
NITTY	Tinty	OBEAH	Bohea	
*NOBEL	Noble	OBEYS	Syboe	
NOBLE	Nobel	OBOES	Boose	
NODES	Nosed, Sonde	OBOLS	Bolos, Lobos, Sobol	
NODUS	Sound	OCEAN	Canoe	
NOINT	Niton	OCHER	Chore, Ochre, Roche	
NOISE	Eosin	OCHRE	Chore, Ocher, Roche	
NOKES	Soken	ODISM	Misdo	
NOMAD	Monad	ODIST	Doits	
NOMES	Meson, Omens	ODYLE	Doyle, Yodel, Yodle	
*NOMOS	Moons	ODYLS	Sloyd	
NONCE	Conne	OFFER	Reffo	
NONET	Tenon, Tonne	OGEED	Geode	

OGIVE	Vogie		
OGLED	Glode, Lodge		
OGRES	Ergos, Goers, Gores,		
	Gorse, Soger		
OILED	De-oil		
OILER	Loire, Oriel, Re-oil		
OLDER	Doler		
OLEIN	Eloin		
OLENT	Lento		
OLIVE	Viole, Voile		
OLLAM	Molla		
OLPES	Elops, Lopes, Poles,		
	Slope, Spole		
OMBER	Brome, Ombre		
OMBRE	Brome, Omber		
OMBRO	Bromo, Broom		
OMENS	Meson, Nomes		
OMERS	Mores, Smore		
ONCER	Crone, Recon		
ONSET	Etons, Notes, Seton,		
	Steno, Stone, Tones		
OPALS	Salop		
OPENS	Peons, Pones, Posen		
OPTED	Depot, Toped		
OPTIC	Picot, Topic		
ORACH	Achor, Roach		
ORALS	Solar, Soral		
ORANG	Angor, Argon, Groan		
	Nagor, Organ		
ORANT	Arnot, Toran, Trona		
ORATE	Roate		
ORBED	Bored, Brode, Robed		
OREAD	Adore, Oared		
ORGAL	Goral, Largo		
ORGAN	Angor, Argon, Groan,		
	Nagor, Orang		
ORGUE	Rogue, Rouge		
ORIEL	Loire, Oiler, Re-oil		
ORLES	Lores, Loser, Roles,		
	Soler, Sorel		
ORNIS	Irons, Roins, Rosin		
ORPIN	Proin		
OSHAC	Chaos		
OSIER	Rosie		
*OSMAN	Mason, Moans, Monas		
OSRAM	Maros, Roams		
OSTIA	Iotas, Stoai		
OTHER	Throe		
OTTER	Toter		

OUGHT	Tough
OUSEL	Eusol, Louse
*OUSES	Souse
OUTER	Outre, Route
OUTRE	Outer, Route
OVALS	Salvo, Volas
OVERS	Roves, Servo, Verso
OVERT	Trove, Voter
OVIST	Visto
OWLED	Dowel, Dowle, Lowed
OWLER	Lower, Rowel
OWLET	Towel
OWNED	Endow, Nowed, Woden, Woned
OWNER	Rewon, Rowen
OWSER	Resow, Serow, Sower, Swore, Worse
OXERS	Exors, Sorex
PACED	Caped
PACER	Caper, Crape, Perca, Recap
PACES	Capes, Scape, Space
PADAR	Padra
PADGE	Gaped, Paged
PADLE	Paled, Pedal, Plead
PADRA	Padar
PADRE	Drape, Pared, Raped, Repad
PAEAN	Apnea
PAGED	Gaped, Padge
PAGLE	Plage
PAGUS	Gaups
PAILS	Lapis, Spail, Spial
PAINS	Spain, Spina
PAINT	Inapt, Patin, Pinta
PAIRS	Paris, Parsi
PALAS	Salpa
PALED	Padle, Pedal, Plead
PALER	Lepra, Parle, Pearl, Repla
PALES	Elaps, Lapse, Leaps, Peals, Pleas, Salep, Sepal, Slape, Spale, Speal
PALLS	Spall
PALMS	Lamps, Plasm, Psalm
PALMY	Amply

PALPI	Pipal		
PALSY	Plays, Splay, Spyal		
PANEL	Alpen, Pelan, Penal, Plane		
PANES	Aspen, Napes, Neaps, Peans, Snape, Sneap, Spane, Spean		
PANGS	Spang		
PANIC	In-cap		
PANNE	Penna		
PANTO	Paton		
PAPAL	Appal		
PARDI	Rapid		
PARDS	Prads, Sprad		
PARED	Drape, Padre, Raped, Repad		
PARES	Apers, Asper, Parse, Pears, Prase, Rapes, Reaps, Spaer, Spare, Spear		
PARGE	Gaper, Grape		
*PARIS	Pairs, Parsi		
PARKS	Spark		
PARLE	Lepra, Paler, Pearl, Repla		
PAROL	Polar, Poral		
PARSE	Apers, Asper, Pares, Pears, Prase, Presa, Rapes, Reaps, Spaer, Spare, Spear		
*PARSI	Pairs, Paris		
PARTS	Spart, Sprat, Strap, Traps		
PARTY	Praty, Yrapt		
*PASCH	Chaps		
PASTE	Apest, Pates, Peats, Septa, Spate, Speat, Tapes		
PASTY	Patsy		
PATCH	Chapt		
PATED	Adept, Taped		
PATEN	Tapen		
PATER	Apert, Peart, Petar, Petra, Prate, Taper, Trape		
PATES	Apest, Paste, Peats, Septa, Spate, Speat, Tapes		
PATIN	Inapt, Paint, Pinta		

PATIO	Topia		
PATLY	Aptly, Typal		
*PATON	Panto		
PATSY	Pasty		
*PAULS	Pulas, Spaul		
PAVES	Spave, Vespa		
PAVID	Vapid		
PAWLS	Spawl		
PAWNS	Spawn		
PAYER	Apery, Repay		
PEACH	Chape, Cheap		
PEAKS	Spake, Speak		
PEALS	Elaps, Lapse, Leaps, Pales, Pleas, Salep, Sepal, Slape, Spale, Speal		
PEANS	Aspen, Napes, Neaps, Panes, Snape, Sneap, Spane, Spean		
PEARL	Lepra, Paler, Parle, Repla		
PEARS	Apers, Asper, Pares, Parse, Prase, Presa, Rapes, Reaps, Spaer, Spare, Spear		
PEART	Apert, Pater, Petar, Petra, Prate, Taper, Trape		
PEATS	Apest, Paste, Pates, Septa, Spate, Speat, Tapes		
PECKS	Speck		
*PECOS	Copes, Copse, Scope		
PEDAL	Padle, Paled, Plead		
*PEDRO	Doper, Pored, Repro, Roped		
PEEKS	Keeps, Pekes, Speke		
PEELS	Sleep, Speel		
PEERS	Perse, Prees, Speer, Spree		
PEKES	Keeps, Peeks, Speke		
*PELAN	Alpen, Panel, Penal, Plane		
PELLS	Spell		
PELMA	Ample, Maple		
PELTA	Leapt, Lepta, Petal, Plate, Pleat, Tepal		
PELTS	Slept, Spelt		
PENAL	Alpen, Panel, Pelan, Plane		

PENDS	Spend		PIERT	Petri, Tripe
PENIS	Pines, Snipe, Spine		PIETS	Piste, Spite, Stipe
PENNA	Panne		PIKES	Kepis, Kipes, Spike
PENTS	Spent		PILAR	April
PEONS	Opens, Pones, Posen		PILED	Lepid, Piel'd, Plied
PERCA	Caper, Crape, Pacer,		PILER	Peril, Plier
	Recap		PILES	Lepis, Plies, Slipe,
PERDU	Drupe, Duper, Prude			Spiel, Spile
PERDY	Predy		PILLS	Spill
PERIL	Piler, Plier		PINED	Piend
PERIS	Piers, Pries, Prise,		PINER	Repin, Ripen
	Ripes, Speir, Spier,		PINES	Penis, Snipe, Spine
	Spire		PINKS	Knips, Spink
PERMS	Sperm		PINTA	Inapt, Paint, Patin
*PERON	Prone		PINTO	Piton, Point, Potin
PERRY	Pryer, Ryper		PIPAL	Palpi
PERSE	Peers, Prees, Speer,		PIPUL	Pupil
	Spree		PIQUE	Equip
PERTS	Prest		PISTE	Piets, Spite, Stipe
PESOS	Poses, Posse, Speos		PITAS	Spait, Stipa, Tapis
PETAL	Leapt, Lepta, Pelta,		PITON	Pinto, Point, Potin
	Plate, Pleat, Tepal		PLACE	Capel, Caple
PETAR	Apert, Pater, Peart,		PLAGE	Pagle
	Petra, Prate, Taper,		PLAIN	Lapin
	Trape		PLANE	Alpen, Panel, Pelan,
PETER	Petre, Ptere, Repet			Penal
PETRA	Apert, Pater, Peart,		PLASM	Lamps, Palms, Psalm
	Petar, Prate, Taper,		PLATE	Leapt, Lepta, Pelta,
	Trape			Petal, Pleat, Tepal
PETRE	Peter, Ptere, Repet		PLATS	Spalt, Splat
PETRI	Piert, Tripe		PLAYS	Palsy, Splay, Spyal
PETTO	Topet		PLEAD	Padle, Paled, Pedal
PEYSE	Seepy		PLEAS	Elaps, Lapse, Leaps,
PHARE	Hepar, Raphe			Plaes, Peals, Salep,
PHASE	Ephas, Heaps, Shape			Sepal, Slape, Spale,
PHEON	Phone			Speal
PHESE	Sheep		PLEAT	Leapt, Lepta, Pelta,
PHOCA	Poach			Petal, Plate, Tepal
PHONE	Pheon		PLESH	Helps
PHYLA	Haply		PLIED	Lepid, Piel'd, Piled
PICAS	Aspic, Scapi, Spica		PLIER	Peril, Piler
PICKS	Spick		PLIES	Lepis, Piles, Slipe,
PICOT	Optic, Topic			Spiel, Spile
PICRA	Capri		PLUMS	Lumps, Slump
PIEL'D	Lepid, Piled, Plied		PLUMY	Lumpy
PIEND	Pined		PLYER	Reply
PIERS	Peris, Pries, Prise,		POACH	Phoca
	Ripes, Speir, Spier,		POEMS	Epsom, Mopes, Pomes
	Spire		POESY	Sepoy

POETS	Estop, Stoep, Stope, Topes		PREEN	Neper, Repen	
POINT	Pinto, Piton, Potin		PREES	Peers, Perse, Speer, Spree	
POKAL	Polka		PRESA	Apers, Asper, Pares, Parse, Pears, Prase, Rapes, Reaps, Spaer, Spare, Spear	
POKES	Spoke				
POLAR	Parol, Poral				
POLED	Loped				
POLES	Elops, Lopes, Olpes, Slope, Spole		PRESS	Spers	
			PREST	Perts	
POLIS	Spoil		PREYS	Pryse, Pyres, Rypes, Spyre	
POLKA	Pokal				
POLYP	Loppy		PRIDE	Pried, Redip, Riped	
POMES	Epsom, Mopes, Poems		PRIED	Pride, Redip, Riped	
PONES	Opens, Peons, Posen		PRIER	Riper	
POOFS	Spoof		PRIES	Peris, Piers, Prise, Ripes, Speir, Spier, Spire	
POOLS	Loops, Sloop, Spool				
POONS	Noops, Snoop, Spoon				
POPSY	Psyop, Soppy		PRIGS	Grips, Sprig	
PORAL	Parol, Polar		PRIMS	Prism	
PORED	Doper, Pedro, Repro, Roped		PRISE	Peris, Piers, Pries, Ripes, Speir, Spier, Spire	
PORER	Prore, Roper				
PORES	Poser, Prose, Ropes, Spore		PRISM	Prims	
			PROAS	Psora, Sapor, Spora	
PORTA	Aport		PRODS	Dorps, Drops, Sprod	
*PORTE	Repot, Retop, Tepor, Toper, Trope		PROEM	Moper	
			PROIN	Orpin	
PORTS	Sport, Strop		PRONE	Peron	
POSED	Dopes, Spode		PRORE	Porer, Roper	
*POSEN	Opens, Peons, Pones		PROSE	Pores, Poser, Ropes, Spore	
POSER	Pores, Prose, Ropes, Spore				
			PRUDE	Drups, Duper, Perdu	
POSES	Pesos, Posse, Speos		PRYER	Perry, Ryper	
POSIT	Topis		PRYSE	Preys, Pyres, Rypes, Spyre	
POSSE	Pesos, Poses, Speos				
POTIN	Pinto, Piton, Point		PSALM	Lamps, Palms, Plasm	
POTTY	Typto		PSOAS	Apsos, Soaps	
POUTS	Spout, Stoup, Toups		PSORA	Proas, Sapor, Spora	
PRADS	Pards, Sprad		PSYOP	Popsy, Soppy	
PRASE	Apers, Asper, Pares, Parse, Pears, Presa, Rapes, Reaps, Spaer, Spare, Spear		PTERE	Peter, Petre, Repet	
			PUDIC	Cupid	
			*PULAS	Pauls, Spaul	
			PULED	Duple	
PRATE	Apert, Pater, Peart, Petar, Petra, Taper, Trape		PULES	Pulse	
			PULSE	Pules	
			PULUS	Lupus	
PRATY	Party, Yrapt		PUNKS	Spunk	
PRAYS	Raspy, Spray		PUNTO	Unpot, Untop	
PREDY	Perdy		PUPAL	Luppa	

PUPIL	Pipul		
PUREE	Epure, Rupee		
PURER	Purre		
PURIN	Unrip		
PURLS	Slurp		
PURRE	Purer		
PURSE	Sprue, Super		
PURSY	Pyrus, Syrup		
PUT-ON	Ton-up		
PYRES	Preys, Pryse, Rypes,		
	Spyre		
PYRUS	Pursy, Syrup		
QUABS	Squab		
QUADS	Squad		
QUATS	Squat		
QUIBS	Squib		
QUIDS	Squid		
QUIET	Quite		
QUIST	Quits, Squit		
QUITE	Quiet		
QUITS	Quist, Squit		
QUOTE	Toque		
RABIC	Baric, Carib		
RABID	Braid		
RABOT	Abort, Boart, Tabor		
RACED	Acred, Arced, Cadre,		
	Cared, Cedar, Dacre		
RACER	Carer, Crare		
RACES	Acers, Acres, Cares,		
	Carse, Sacre, Scare,		
	Scrae, Serac		
RACHE	Chare, Reach		
RADGE	Edgar, Grade, Raged		
RADII	Dairi		
RADIO	Aroid		
RADON	Adorn, Andro		
RAGED	Edgar, Grade, Radge		
RAGEE	Aeger, Agree, Eager,		
	Eagre		
RAGES	Gears, Sager, Segar		
RAINS	Naris, Ranis		
RAISE	Aesir, Aries, Arise,		
	Resai, Serai		
RAKED	Daker, Drake		
RAKES	Asker, Eskar, Kesar,		
	Saker		

RALES	Arles, Earls, Lares,		
	Laser, Lears, Reals,		
	Seral		
RAMAL	Alarm, Malar		
RAMED	Armed, Derma, Dream		
	Madre		
RAMEE	Ameer		
RAMIE	Aimer, Marie, Rimae		
RAMON	Manor, Norma, Roman		
RAMUS	Arums, Rusma		
RANCE	Caner, Carne, Crane,		
	Crena, Nacre		
RANEE	Arnee		
RANGE	Anger, Areng, Renga		
RANGY	Angry		
RANIS	Naris, Rains		
RANKS	Knars, Krans, Narks,		
	Skran, Snark		
RANTS	Starn, Tarns		
RANTY	Tyran		
RAPED	Drape, Padre, Pared,		
	Repad		
RAPES	Apers, Asper, Pares,		
	Parse, Pears, Prase,		
	Presa, Reaps, Spaer,		
	Spare		
RAPHE	Hepar, Phare		
RAPID	Pardi		
RASED	Ardes, Dares, Reads		
RASES	Arses, Asser, Rasse,		
	Sarse, Sears		
RASPY	Prays, Spray		
RASSE	Arses, Asser, Rases,		
	Sarse, Sears		
RATAL	Altar, Artal		
RATCH	Chart		
RATED	Dater, Tared, Trade,		
	Tread		
RATEL	Alert, Alter, Artel,		
	Later, Telar		
RATER	Arret, Retar, Tarre,		
	Terra		
RATES	Arets, Aster, Earst,		
	Reast, Resat, Stare,		
	Strae, Tares, Tarse,		
	Tears, Teras		
RATHE	Earth, Hater, Heart,		
	Herat, Thrae		
RATHS	Harst, Harts, Tahrs,		
	Thars, Trash		

RATIO	Ariot			REDIA	Aider,	Aired,	Irade
RAVED	Drave			REDID	Dried		
RAVEL	Laver,	Velar		REDIP	Pride,	Pried,	Riped
RAVES	Avers,	Saver,	Vares	REDRY	Derry,	Dryer,	Ryder
RAVIN	Invar			REDYE	Reedy		
RAYED	Deary,	Deray,	Ready,	REECH	Cheer		
	Yeard			*REEDA	Arede,	Areed,	Eared
RAYLE	Early,	Layer,	Leary,	REEDY	Redye		
	Relay			REEKS	Esker,	Reesk	
*RAYNE	Yearn			REELS	Leers,	Leres,	Sleer
RAZED	Zerda			REESK	Esker,	Reeks	
REACH	Chare,	Rache		REEST	Ester,	Reset,	Retes,
REACT	Caret,	Carte,	Cater,		Steer,	Stere,	Teers,
	Crate,	Recta,	Trace		Teres,	Terse,	Trees
READD	Adder,	Aredd,	Dared,	REFED	Defer,	Freed	
	Dread			REFEL	Fleer		
READS	Ardes,	Dares,	Rased	REFER	Freer,	Frere	
READY	Deary,	Deray,	Rayed,	REFFO	Offer		
	Yeard			REFIT	Freit		
REALM	Lamer			REFIX	Fixer		
REALS	Arles,	Earls,	Lares,	REFRY	Ferry,	Fryer	
	Laser,	Lears,	Rales,	REGAL	Alger,	Elgar,	Glare,
	Seral				Lager,	Large	
REAMS	Mares,	Maser,	Mears,	REGEL	Leger,	Regle	
	Smear			REGET	Egret,	Greet	
REAPS	Apers,	Asper,	Pares,	REGLE	Leger,	Regel	
	Parse,	Pears,	Prase,	REGMA	Gamer,	Marge	
	Presa,	Rapes,	Spaer,	REHID	Hider,	Hired	
	Spare,	Spear		*REICH	Rheic		
RE-ARM	Armer			REIFY	Fiery		
REARS	Serra			REIGN	Grein,	Niger,	Renig,
REAST	Arets,	Aster,	Earst,		Ringe		
	Rates,	Resat,	Stare,	*REIMS	Emirs,	Meris,	Mires,
	Strae,	Tares,	Tarse,		Miser,	Riems,	Rimes
	Tears,	Teras		REINK	Inker		
REATE	Arete,	Eater		REINS	Resin,	Rinse,	Risen,
REBID	Bider,	Bride,	Debir		Serin,	Siren	
REBUS	Burse,	Suber		REIRD	Direr,	Drier,	Rider
REBUT	Buret,	Brute,	Tuber	REIST	Resit,	Rites,	Tiers,
RECAP	Caper,	Crape,	Pacer,		Tires,	Tries	
	Perca			RELAY	Early,	Layer,	Leary,
RECON	Crone,	Oncer			Rayle		
RECTA	Caret,	Carte,	Cater,	RELIT	Liter,	Litre,	Tiler
	Crate,	React,	Trace	REMAN	Namer		
RECTI	Trice			REMIT	Merit,	Miter,	Mitre,
RECUR	Curer,	Curre			Timer		
RECUT	Cruet,	Cuter,	Eruct,	REMIX	Mixer		
	Truce			REMOW	Mower,	Rowme	
REDAN	Dearn			*REMUS	Mures,	Muser,	Serum

RENAL	Larne, Learn, Lerna	RETCH	Chert
RENES	Ernes, Sneer	RETEM	Meter, Metre
RENEW	Newer	RETES	Ester, Reest, Reset,
RENGA	Anger, Areng, Range		Steer, Stere, Teers,
RENIG	Grein, Niger, Reign,		Teres, Terse, Trees
	Ringe	RETEX	Exert
RENTE	Enter, Etern, Terne,	RETIN	Inert, Inter, Niter,
	Treen		Nitre, Trine
RENTS	Ernst, Stern, Terns	RETOP	Porte, Repot, Tepor,
REOIL	Loire, Oiler, Oriel		Toper, Trope
REPAD	Drape, Padre, Pared,	RETRY	Terry, Tryer
	Raped	*REUSS	Ruses, Users
REPAY	Apery, Payer	REVEL	Elver, Lever
REPEL	Leper	REVET	Evert
REPEN	Neper, Preen	REVIE	Rieve
REPET	Peter, Petre, Ptere	REWAX	Waxer
REPIN	Piner, Ripen	REWET	Tweer, Twere
REPLA	Lepra, Paler, Parle,	REWON	Owner, Rowen
	Pearl	RHEIC	Reich
REPLY	Plyer	RHEIN	Rhine
REPOT	Porte, Retop, Tepor,	RHINE	Rhein
	Toper, Trope	*RHODA	Hoard
REPRO	Doper, Pedro, Pored,	RHONE	Honer
	Roped	RHYNE	Henry
RESAI	Aesir, Aries, Arise,	RIANT	Intra, Tarin, Train
	Raise, Serai	RIATA	Atria, Taira, Tiara
RESAT	Arets, Aster, Earst,	RIBES	Biers, Birse, Bries
	Rates, Reast, Stare,	RICER	Crier
	Strae, Tares, Tarse,	RICHT	Chirt, Crith
	Tears, Teras	RIDER	Direr, Drier, Reird
RESAW	Sawer, Sware, Swear,	RIDES	Dries, Sider, Sired
	Wares, Wears	RIDGE	Dirge, Gride
RESAY	Sayer	RIEMS	Emirs, Meris, Mires,
RESET	Ester, Reest, Retes,		Miser, Reims, Rimes
	Steer, Stere, Teers,	RIEVE	Revie
	Teres, Terse, Trees	RIFLE	Filer, Flier, Lifer
RESEW	Ewers, Sewer, Sweer	RIFTS	First, Frist, Frits
RESIN	Reins, Rinse, Risen,	RIGHT	Girth, Grith
	Serin, Siren	RILED	Idler
RESIT	Reist, Rites, Tiers,	RILES	Liers, Risel, Slier
	Tires, Tries	RIMAE	Aimer, Marie, Ramie
RESOW	Owser, Serow, Sower,	RIMED	Dimer, Mired
	Swore, Worse	RIMES	Emirs, Meris, Mires,
RESTS	Tress		Miser, Reims, Riems
RESTY	Styre, Treys, Tyres	RINED	Diner
RETAN	Antre	RINGE	Grein, Niger, Reign,
RETAR	Arret, Rater, Tarre,		Renig
	Terra	RINGO	Giron, Groin
RETAX	Extra, Taxer	RINSE	Reins, Resin, Risen,
			Serin, Siren

RIOTS	Roist, Rosit, Tiros, Torsi, Trios	
RIPED	Pride, Pried, Redip	
RIPEN	Piner, Repin	
RIPER	Prier	
RIPES	Peris, Piers, Pries, Prise, Speir, Spier, Spire	
RISEL	Liers, Riles, Slier	
RISEN	Reins, Resin, Rinse, Serin, Siren	
RISHI	Irish, Sirih	
RISSA	Arsis, Saris	
RITES	Reist, Resit, Tiers, Tires, Tries	
RITHE	Ither	
RIVAL	Viral	
RIVED	Diver, Drive, Verdi	
RIVEL	Ervil, Liver, Livre, Viler	
RIVEN	Viner	
RIVES	Siver	
RIVET	Tiver	
ROACH	Achor, Orach	
ROADS	Doras, Sorda	
ROAMS	Maros, Osram	
ROANS	Arson, Sonar	
ROAST	Astor, Rotas, Taros, Toras, Troas	
ROATE	Orate	
ROBED	Bored, Brode, Orbed	
ROBES	Boers, Bores, Brose, Sober	
ROBIN	Inorb	
ROBLE	Blore	
ROCHE	Chore, Ocher, Ochre	
ROCKY	Corky	
ROCTA	Actor, Croat, Taroc	
*RODEN	Drone, Endor, Ronde	
RODES	Doers, Dorse, Doser, Rosed	
RODGE	Gored	
ROGER	Gorer	
ROGUE	Orgue, Rouge	
ROHAN	Norah	
ROILS	Loris	
ROINS	Irons, Ornis, Rosin	
ROIST	Riots, Rosit, Tiros, Torsi, Trios	
ROLES	Lores, Loser, Orles, Soler, Sorel	
ROMAL	Molar, Moral	
ROMAN	Manor, Norma, Ramon	
RONDE	Drone, Endor, Roden	
RONDO	Donor, Doorn	
RONES	Norse, Noser, Senor, Seron, Snore	
RONTS	Snort, Trons	
ROODS	Doors, Sordo	
ROOKS	Koros	
ROOMY	Moory	
ROOST	Roots, Stoor, Torso	
ROOTS	Roost, Stoor, Torso	
ROPED	Doper, Pedro, Pored, Repro	
ROPER	Porer, Prore	
ROPES	Pores, Poser, Prose, Spore	
ROSED	Doers, Dorse, Doser, Rodes	
ROSET	Store, Tores, Torse	
*ROSIE	Osier	
ROSIN	Irons, Ornis, Roins	
ROSIT	Riots, Roist, Tiros, Torsi, Trios	
ROTAS	Astor, Roast, Taros, Toras, Troas	
ROTCH	Torch	
ROUGE	Orgue, Rogue	
ROUST	Routs, Stour, Sutor, Torus, Tours	
ROUTE	Outer, Outre	
ROUTS	Roust, Stour, Sutor, Torus, Tours	
ROVED	Dover, Drove, Vedro	
ROVES	Overs, Servo, Verso	
ROWDY	Dowry, Wordy	
ROWED	Dower	
ROWEL	Lower, Owler	
ROWEN	Owner, Rewon	
ROWME	Mower, Remow	
ROWTE	Tower, Twoer, Wrote	
ROWTH	Throw, Whort, Worth, Wroth	
ROYST	Ryots, Story, Stroy, Tyros	
RUBIN	Bruin, Burin	
RUBLE	Bluer	

RUDAS	Duras			SAKER	Asker, Eskar, Kesar,	
RUING	Unrig				Rakes	
RULED	Dreul, Lured			SALAD	Ladas, Salda	
RULER	Lurer			SALDA	Ladas, Salad	
RUMAL	Larum, Mural			*SALEM	Almes, Amsel, Lames,	
RUMBA	Burma, Umbra				Leams, Males, Meals,	
RUMEX	Murex				Melas, Mesal, Samel	
RUNCH	Churn			SALEP	Elaps, Lapse, Leaps,	
RUNED	Under, Unred, Urned				Pales, Peals, Pleas,	
RUNES	Nurse				Sepal, Slape, Spale,	
RUNIC	Incur				Speal	
RUN-IN	Inurn			SALES	Salse, Seals	
RUPEE	Epure, Puree			SALIC	Aclis, Laics, Scail	
RUSES	Reuss, Users			SALIN	Anils, Nails, Slain,	
RUSMA	Arums, Ramus				Snail	
RUSTS	Truss			SALIX	Axils	
*RYDER	Derry, Dryer, Redry			SALMI	Islam, Mails, Simla	
RYOTS	Royst, Story, Stroy,			SALMO	Loams, Lomas, Sloam	
	Tyros			SALON	Loans, Sloan	
RYPER	Perry, Pryer			SALOP	Opals	
RYPES	Preys, Pryse, Pyres,			SALPA	Palas	
	Spyre			SALSE	Sales, Seals	
				SALTY	Slaty	
				SALVE	Elvas, Laves, Selva,	
SABAL	Balas, Balsa, Sabal				Slave, Vales, Valse,	
SABER	Bares, Baser, Bears,				Veals	
	Braes, Sabre			SALVO	Ovals, Volas	
SABIN	Basin			SAMBO	Ambos, Bomas, Moabs	
SABLE	Bales, Basel, Basle,			SAMEL	Almes, Amsel, Lames,	
	Blaes, Bleas, Blase				Leams, Males, Meals,	
SABOT	Basto, Boats, Boast,				Melas, Mesal, Salem	
	Tobas			SAMEN	Amens, Manse, Manes,	
SABRE	Bares, Baser, Bears,				Means, Mensa, Names	
	Braes, Saber			SAMPS	Spasm	
SACRA	Arcas			SANDY	Sdayn	
SACRE	Acers, Acres, Cares,			SANER	Earns, Nares, Nears,	
	Carse, Races, Scare,				Snare	
	Scrae, Serac			SAPOR	Proas, Psora, Sopra	
SADHE	Hades, Heads, Shade			SAREE	Erase	
*SADIE	Aides, Aside, Ideas			SARIS	Arsis, Rissa	
SAFER	Fares, Farse, Fears			SAROH	Hoars	
SAGER	Gears, Rages, Segar			SAROS	Soars	
SAGES	Gases			SARSE	Arses, Asser, Rases,	
SAGUM	Gaums				Rasse, Sears	
SAILS	Silas, Sisal			SASIN	Sains	
SAINS	Sasin			SASSE	Asses, Sessa	
SAINT	Antis, Satin, Stain,			SATED	Dates, Stade, Stead,	
	Tains, Tanis				Teads, Tsade	
SAITH	Haits, Taish			SATEM	Mates, Meats, Steam,	
					Tames, Reams	

SATES	Easts,	Asset,	Seats,			Costa	
	Tasse,	Tessa		SCOFF	Coffs		
SATIN	Antis,	Saint,	Stain,	SCOLD	Colds,	Clods	
	Tains,	Tanis		SCONE	Cones,	Cosen,	Sonce
SATYR	Artsy,	Stray,	Trays	SCOON	Coons		
SAUCE	Cause			SCOOP	Coops,	Copos	
SAULT	Talus			SCOOT	Coost,	Coots	
SAUNT	Aunts			SCOPE	Copes,	Copse,	Pecos
SAURY	Surya			SCORE	Cores,	Corse	
SAVED	Devas,	Vades,	Vedas	SCORN	Corns		
SAVER	Avers,	Raves,	Vares	SCOTE	Cotes,	Escot,	Estoc
SAVIN	Sivan,	Vinas		SCOUP	Coups		
SAWED	Wades			SCOVE	Coves,	Voces	
SAWER	Resaw,	Sware,	Swear,	SCOWL	Cowls		
	Wares,	Wears		SCRAE	Acers,	Acres,	Cares,
SAWNY	Yawns				Carse,	Races,	Sacre,
SAYER	Resay				Scare,	Serac	
SAYID	Daisy			SCRAB	Crabs		
SAYNE	Yeans			SCRAG	Crags		
SAYST	Stays			SCRAM	Crams		
S-BAND	Bands			SCRAN	Crans		
SCAIL	Aclis,	Laics,	Salic	SCRAP	Carps,	Craps,	Scarp
SCALA	Casal			SCRAT	Carts,	Scart	
SCALE	Alces,	Claes,	Laces	SCRAW	Craws		
SCALL	Calls			SCRAY	Cyars,	Scary	
SCALP	Calps,	Claps,	Clasp	SCREE	Ceres,	Crees	
SCALY	Clays			SCREW	Crews		
SCAMP	Camps			SCRIP	Crisp		
SCANT	Canst,	Cants		SCROD	Cords		
SCAPE	Capes,	Paces,	Space	SCROW	Crows		
SCAPI	Aspic,	Picas,	Spica	SCRUB	Curbs		
SCARD	Cards			SCUFF	Cuffs		
SCARE	Acers,	Acres,	Cares,	SCULL	Culls		
	Carse,	Races,	Sacre,	SDAYN	Sandy		
	Scrae,	Serac		SDEIN	Denis,	Dines,	Enids,
SCARP	Carps,	Craps,	Scrap		Nides,	Snide	
SCARS	Crass			SEAHS	Ashes,	He-ass,	Sesha,
SCART	Carts,	Scrat			Sheas		
SCARY	Cyars,	Scray		SEALS	Sales,	Salse	
SCATE	Caste,	Cates,	Sceat,	SEAMS	Masse		
	Taces			SEARS	Arses,	Asser,	Rases,
SCATH	Chats				Rasse,	Sarse	
SCAUR	Arcus,	Carus		SEASE	Eases		
SCEAT	Caste,	Cates,	Scate,	SEATS	Asset,	Easts,	Sates,
	Taces				Tasse,	Tessa	
SCENA	Canes			SEAVE	Eaves		
SCENE	Cense			SEBAT	Abets,	Baste,	Bates,
SCENT	Cents				Beast,	Beats,	Esbat,
SCION	Coins,	Icons,	Sonic		Tabes		
SCOAT	Ascot,	Coast,	Coats,	SECCO	Cosec		

SEDAN	Andes, Danes, Deans, Snead		SEROW	Owser, Resow, Sower, Swore, Worse
SEDGE	Edges		SERRA	Rears
SEDUM	Mused		SERUM	Mures, Muser, Remus
SEEPY	Peyse		SERVE	Sever, Veers, Verse
SEGAR	Gears, Rages, Sager		SERVO	Overs, Roves, Verso
SEGOS	Gesso		SESHA	Ashes, He-ass, Seahs, Sheas
SEISM	Mises, Semis		SESSA	Asses, Sasse
SEKOS	Sokes		SETAE	Tease
SELAH	Hales, Halse, Heals, Leash, Shale, Sheal		SET-IN	Inset, Neist, Nesti, Senti, Stein, Tines
SELVA	Elvas, Laves, Salve, Slave, Vales, Valse, Veals		SETON	Etons, Notes, Onset, Steno, Stone, Tones
SEMEN	Mense, Mesne, Neems		SET-TO	Totes
SEMIS	Mises, Seism		SET-UP	Stupe, Upset
SENAL	Lanes, Leans, Neals, Slane		SEVEN	Evens
			SEVER	Serve, Veers, Verse
SENNA	Annes		SEVIN	Nevis, Veins, Venis, Vines, Visne
SENOR	Norse, Noser, Rones, Seron, Snore			
SENSE	Essen		SEWAN	Wanes, Weans
SENTI	Inset, Neist, Nesti, Set-in, Stein, Tines		SEWED	Swede, Weeds
			SEWEL	Weels
SENZA	Nazes		SEWEN	Ensew, Weens
SEPAD	Adeps, Spade		SEWER	Ewers, Resew, Sweer
SEPAL	Elaps, Lapse, Leaps, Pales, Peals, Pleas, Salep, Slape, Spale, Speal		SEWIN	Sinew, Swine, Wines
			SHACK	Hacks
			SHADE	Hades, Heads, Sadhe
			SHADY	Dashy, Hyads
SEPIC	Epics, Spice		SHAFT	Hafts
SEPOY	Poesy		SHAHI	Shiah
SEPTA	Apest, Paste, Pates, Peats, Spate, Speat, Tapes		SHAKE	Hakes
			SHALE	Hales, Halse, Heals, Leash, Selah, Sheal
SERAC	Acers, Acres, Cares, Carse, Races, Sacre, Scare, Screa		SHALL	Halls
			SHALM	Halms
			SHALT	Halts, Laths
SERAI	Aesir, Aries, Arise, Raise, Resai		SHALY	Hylas
			SHAME	Ahems, Hames, Heams
SERAL	Arles, Earls, Lares, Laser, Lears, Rales, Reals		SHAMS	Smash
			SHAND	Hands
			SHANK	Hanks, Khans
SERIC	Cries		*SHANS	Snash
SERIF	Fires, Fries		SHAN'T	Snath
SERIN	Reins, Resin, Rinse, Risen, Siren		SHAPE	Ephas, Heaps, Phase
			SHAPS	Hasps
			SHARD	Hards
SERON	Norse, Noser, Rones, Senor, Snore		SHARE	Hares, Hears, Shear
			SHARK	Harks

SHARN	Harns
SHARP	Harps
SHAVE	Haves, Sheva
SHAWM	Hawms, Whams
SHAWS	Swash
SHEAL	Hales, Halse, Heals, Leash, Selah, Shale
SHEAR	Hares, Hears, Share
SHEAS	Ashes, He-ass, Seahs, Sesha
SHEEL	Heels
SHEEP	Phese
SHEER	Heres, Herse
SHEET	Thees, These
SHEIK	Hikes
SHELF	Flesh
SHELL	Hells
SHEND	Hends
SHEOL	Holes, Shole
SHERD	Herds, Shred
SHEVA	Haves, Shave
SHIAH	Shahi
SHIDE	Hides, Shied
SHIED	Hides, Shide
SHIER	Heirs, Hires, Shire
SHIKO	Hoiks
SHINE	Hsien
SHIRE	Heirs, Hires, Shier
SHIVE	Hives
SHOAL	Halos, Shola, Solah
SHOAT	Athos, Hoast, Hosta, Oaths
SHOCK	Hocks
SHOED	Doseh, Hosed
SHOER	Heros, Horse, Shore
SHOLA	Halos, Shoal, Solah
SHOLE	Holes, Sheol
SHONE	Hones, Hosen
SHOOK	Hooks
SHOOT	Hoots, Sooth, Sotho
SHOPS	Sposh
SHORE	Heros, Horse, Shoer
SHORN	Horns
SHORT	Horst
SHOTE	Ethos, Those
SHOTS	Hosts, Stosh
SHOUT	South, Thous
SHOVE	Hoves
SHRAB	Brash

SHRAM	Harms, Marsh
SHRED	Herds, Sherd
SHREW	Wersh
SHRUB	Brush, Buhrs, Burhs, Bursh
SHUCK	Hucks
SHUNS	Snush
SHUNT	Hunts
SHURE	Usher
*SIBYL	Sybil
SIDER	Dries, Rides, Sired
SIDLE	Idles, Sield, Slide
SIELD	Idles, Sidle, Slide
SIGHT	Thigs
SIKER	Skier
*SILAS	Sails, Sisal
SILES	Isles, Lisse
SILEX	Lexis
SILLY	Slily, Yills
SILO'D	Idols, Sloid, Soldi, Solid
SILVA	Vails, Vials
*SIMLA	Islam, Mails, Salmi
*SIMON	Minos
SINES	Nisse
SINEW	Sewin, Swine, Wines
SINUS	Nisus
SIPED	Spied
SIRED	Dries, Rides, Sider
SIREN	Reins, Resin, Rinse, Risen, Serin
SIRIH	Irish, Rishi
SISAL	Sails, Silas
SITAR	Airts, Astir, Stair, Stria, Tarsi, Trias
SITED	Deist, Diets, Edits, Stied, Tides
SITTA	Taits
SITUS	Suist, Suits
SIVAN	Savin, Vinas
*SIVAS	Visas
SIVER	Rives
SIXTE	Exist, Exits
SKAIL	Kails, Kalis
SKAIN	Kains, Kisan
SKATE	Kates, Keats, Stake, Steak, Takes, Teaks
SKEAN	Kanes, Snake, Sneak
SKEEL	Keels, Leeks, Sleek

SKEIN	Neski
SKELP	Kelps, Spelk
SKENE	Knees
SKIED	Dikes
SKIER	Siker
SKILL	Kills
SKINK	Kinks
SKIRT	Stirk
SKITE	Kites, Tikes
SKLIM	Milks
SKOAL	Kolas
SKOFF	Koffs
SKRAN	Knars, Krans, Narks, Ranks, Snark
SKYTE	Tykes
SLACK	Calks, Lacks
SLADE	Dales, Deals, Lades, Leads
SLAGS	Glass
SLAID	Dials
SLAIE	Aisle
SLAIN	Anils, Nails, Salin, Snail
SLAKE	Kales, Lakes, Leaks
SLANE	Lanes, Leans, Neals, Senal
SLANG	Glans, Langs
SLAPE	Elaps, Lapse, Leaps, Pales, Peals, Pleas, Salep, Sepal, Spale, Speal
SLATE	Astel, Least, Leats, Stale, Steal, Stela, Taels, Tales, Teals, Tesla
SLATY	Salty
SLAVE	Elvas, Laves, Salve, Selva, Vales, Valse, Veals
SLEEK	Keels, Leeks, Skeel
SLEEP	Peels, Speel
SLEER	Leers, Leres, Reels
SLEET	Leets, Steel, Stele, Teels
SLEPT	Pelts, Spelt
SLICE	Ceils, Ciels
SLICK	Licks
SLIDE	Idles, Sield, Sidle
SLIER	Liers, Riles, Risel

S'LIFE	Felis, Files, Flies
SLILY	Silly, Yills
SLIME	Limes, Miles, Misle, Smile
SLIMY	Limsy, Misly
SLING	Lings
SLINK	Kilns, Links
SLIPE	Lepis, Piles, Plies, Spiel, Spile
SLIPS	Lisps
SLIPT	Spilt, Split, Stilp
SLIVE	Elvis, Evils, Levis, Lives, Veils, Vleis
SLOAM	Loams, Lomas, Salmo
SLOAN	Loans, Salon
SLOAT	Altos, Stola, Tolas
SLOES	Loess, Loses, Soles
SLOGS	Gloss
SLOID	Idols, Silo'd, Soldi, Solid
SLOOM	Looms
SLOOP	Loops, Pools, Spool
SLOOT	Loots, Lotos, Stool, Tools
SLOPE	Elops, Lopes, Olpes, Poles, Spole
SLOTH	Holts
SLOVE	Loves, Solve, Voles
SLOYD	Odyls
SLUED	Duels, Dules, Dulse, Leuds
SLUMP	Lumps, Plums
SLUNG	Lungs
SLURB	Blurs, Burls
SLURP	Purls
SLYPE	Yelps
SMACK	Macks
SMALL	Malls
SMALT	Malts
SMART	Marts, Trams
SMASH	Shams
SMEAR	Mares, Maser, Mears, Reams
SMELL	Mells
SMELT	Melts
SMILE	Limes, Miles, Misle, Slime
SMITE	Emits, Items, Meist, Metis, Mites, Stime, Times

SMITT	Mitts		
SMOCK	Mocks		
SMOKE	Mokes		
SMOOT	Moots, Stoom, Tooms		
SMORE	Mores, Omers		
SMOTE	Mesto, Motes, Tomes		
SMUCK	Mucks		
SNAFU	Fauns		
SNAIL	Anils, Nails, Salin, Slain		
SNAKE	Kanes, Skean, Sneak		
SNAKY	Yanks		
SNAPE	Aspen, Napes, Neaps, Panes, Peans, Sneap, Spane, Spean		
SNARE	Earns, Nares, Nears, Saner		
SNARK	Knars, Krans, Narks, Ranks, Skran		
SNARY	Yarns		
SNASH	Shans		
SNATH	Shan't		
SNEAD	Andes, Danes, Deans, Sedan		
SNEAK	Kanes, Skean, Snake		
SNEAP	Aspen, Napes, Neaps, Panes, Peans, Snape, Spane, Spean		
SNECK	Necks		
SNEER	Ernes, Renes		
SNICK	Nicks		
SNIDE	Denis, Dines, Enids, Nides, Sdein		
SNIPE	Penis, Pines, Spine		
SNOEK	Kenos, Snoke		
SNOKE	Kenos, Snoek		
SNOOK	Nooks		
SNOOL	Loons, Solon		
SNOOP	Noops, Poons, Spoon		
SNORE	Norse, Noser, Rones, Senor, Seron		
SNORT	Ronts, Trons		
SNOUT	Notus, Stoun, Tonus		
SNOWK	Knows		
SNUSH	Shuns		
SOAPS	Apsos, Psoas		
SOARS	Saros		
SOBER	Boers, Bores, Brose, Robes		

SOBOL	Bolos, Lobos, Obols		
SOCLE	Close, Coles		
SOFAS	Fossa		
SOGER	Ergos, Goers, Gores, Gorse, Ogres		
SOKEN	Nokes		
SOKES	Sekos		
SOKOL	Looks		
SOLAH	Halos, Shoal, Shola		
SOLAR	Orals, Soral		
SOLAS	Lasso		
SOLDE	Delos, Doles, Dosel, Lodes, Soled		
SOLDI	Idols, Silo'd, Sloid, Solid		
SOLDO	Dools		
SOLED	Delos, Doles, Dosel, Lodes, Solde		
SOLEN	Lenos		
SOLER	Lores, Loser, Orles, Roles, Sorel		
SOLES	Loess, Loses, Sloes		
SOL-FA	Foals, Loafs		
SOLID	Idols, Silo'd, Sloid, Soldi		
SOLON	Loons, Snool		
SOLUS	Souls		
SOLVE	Loves, Slove, Voles		
SONAR	Arson, Roans		
SONCE	Cones, Cosen, Scone		
SONDE	Nodes, Nosed		
SONIC	Coins, Icons, Scion		
SONTY	Stony		
SOOLE	Looes, Loose		
SOOTH	Hoots, Shoot, Sotho		
SOPOR	Spoor		
SOPPY	Popsy, Psyop		
SOPRA	Proas, Psora, Sapor		
SORAL	Orals, Solar		
SORBO	Boors		
SORDA	Doras, Roads		
SORDO	Doors, Roods		
SORDS	Dross		
SOREL	Lores, Loser, Orles, Roles, Soler		
SOREX	Exors, Oxers		
SORUS	Sours		
SOTHO	Hoots, Shoot, Sooth		
SOTOL	Loots, Lotos, Sloot, Stool, Tools		

SOULS	Solus
SOUND	Nodus
SOURS	Sorus
SOUSE	Ouses
SOUTH	Shout, Thous
SOWED	Dowse
SOWER	Owser, Resow, Serow, Swore, Worse
SOWLE	Lowse
SOWND	Downs
SPACE	Capes, Paces, Scape
SPADE	Adeps, Sepad
SPAER	Apers, Asper, Pares, Parse, Pears, Prase, Presa, Rapes, Reaps, Spare, Spear
SPAHI	Aphis, Apish
SPAIL	Lapis, Pails, Spial
*SPAIN	Pains, Spina
SPAIT	Pitas, Stipa, Tapis
SPAKE	Peaks, Speak
SPALE	Elaps, Lapse, Leaps, Pales, Peals, Pleas, Salep, Sepal, Slape, Speal
SPALL	Palls
SPALT	Plats, Splat
SPANE	Aspen, Napes, Neaps, Panes, Peans, Snape, Sneap, Spean
SPANG	Pangs
SPARE	Apers, Asper, Pares, Parse, Pears, Prase, Presa, Rapes, Reaps, Spaer, Spear
SPARK	Parks
SPART	Parts, Sprat, Strap, Traps
SPASM	Samps
SPATE	Apest, Paste, Pates, Peats, Septa, Speat, Tapes
SPAUL	Pauls, Pulas
SPAVE	Paves, Vespa
SPAWL	Pawls
SPAWN	Pawns
SPEAK	Peaks, Spake
SPEAL	Elaps, Lapse, Leaps, Pales, Peals, Pleas,

	Salep, Sepal, Slape, Spale
SPEAN	Aspen, Napes, Neaps, Panes, Peans, Snape, Sneap, Spane
SPEAR	Apers, Asper, Pares, Parse, Pears, Prase, Presa, Rapes, Reaps, Spaer, Spare
SPEAT	Apest, Paste, Pates, Peats, Septa, Spate, Tapes
SPECK	Pecks
SPEED	Deeps
SPEEL	Peels, Sleep
SPEER	Peers, Perse, Prees, Spree
SPEIR	Peris, Piers, Pries, Prise, Ripes, Spier, Spire
*SPEKE	Keeps, Peeks, Pekes
SPELK	Kelps, Skelp
SPELL	Pells
SPELT	Pelts, Slept
SPEND	Pends
SPENT	Pents
SPEOS	Pesos, Poses, Posse
SPERM	Perms
SPERS	Press
SPIAL	Lapis, Pails, Spail
SPICA	Aspic, Picas, Scapi
SPICE	Epics, Sepic
SPICK	Picks
SPIED	Siped
SPIEL	Lepis, Piles, Plies, Slipe, Spile
SPIER	Peris, Piers, Pries, Prise, Ripes, Speir, Spire
SPIKE	Kepis, Kipes, Pikes
SPILE	Lepis, Piles, Plies, Slipe, Spiel
SPILL	Pills
SPLIT	Slipt, Spilt, Stilp
SPINA	Pains, Spain
SPINE	Penis, Pines, Snipe
SPINK	Knips, Pinks
SPIRE	Peris, Piers, Pries, Prise, Ripes, Speir, Spier

SPIRT	Sprit, Stirp, Strip, Trips		STAIG	Agist, Gaits	
SPITE	Piets, Piste, Stipe		STAIN	Antis, Saint, Satin, Tains, Tanis	
SPLAT	Plats, Spalt		STAIR	Airts, Astir, Sitar, Stria, Tarsi, Trias	
SPLAY	Palsy, Plays, Spyal				
SPLIT	Slipt, Spilt, Stilp		STAKE	Kates, Keats, Skate, Steak, Takes, Teaks	
SPODE	Dopes, Posed				
SPOIL	Polis		STAL'D	Dalts	
SPOKE	Pokes		STALE	Astel, Least, Leats, Slate, Steal, Stela, Taels, Tales, Teals, Tesla	
SPOLE	Elops, Lopes, Olpes, Poles, Slope				
SPOOF	Poofs				
SPOOL	Loops, Pools, Sloop		STALK	Talks	
SPOON	Noops, Poons, Snoop		STAMP	Tamps	
SPOOR	Sopor		STANG	Angst, Gants, Gnats, Tangs	
SPORE	Pores, Poser, Prose, Ropes				
			STANK	Tanks	
SPORT	Ports, Strop		STARE	Arets, Aster, Earst, Rates, Reast, Resat, Strae, Tares, Tarse, Tears, Teras	
SPOSH	Shops				
SPOUT	Pouts, Stoup, Toups				
SPRAD	Pards, Prads				
SPRAG	Grasp		STARK	Karst	
SPRAT	Parts, Spart, Strap, Traps		STARN	Rants, Tarns	
			STARS	Trass	
SPRAY	Prays, Raspy		START	Tarts	
SPREE	Peers, Perse, Prees, Speer		STATE	Taste, Tates, Teats, Testa	
SPRIG	Grips, Prigs		STAVE	Vesta	
SPRIT	Spirt, Stirp, Strip, Trips		STAYS	Sayst	
			STEAD	Dates, Sated, Stade, Teads, Tsade	
SPROD	Dorps, Drops, Prods				
SPRUE	Purse, Super		STEAK	Kates, Keats, Skate, Stake, Takes	
SPUNK	Punks				
SPURT	Turps		STEAL	Astel, Least, Leats, Slate, Stale, Stela, Taels, Tales, Teals, Tesla	
SPUTA	Stupa, Tapus				
SPYAL	Palsy, Plays, Splay				
SPYRE	Preys, Pryse, Pyres, Rypes		STEAM	Mates, Meats, Satem, Tames, Teams	
			STEAN	Nates, Nesta	
SQUAB	Quabs		STECH	Chest	
SQUAD	Quads		STEED	Tedes	
SQUAT	Quats		STEEL	Leets, Sleet, Stele, Teels	
SQUIB	Quibs				
SQUID	Quids		STEEM	Meets, Metes, Steme, Teems, Temes, Temse	
SQUIT	Quist, Quits				
STACK	Tacks		*STEEN	Teens, Tense	
STADE	Dates, Sated, Stead, Teads, Tsade		STEER	Ester, Reest, Reset, Retes, Stere, Teers, Teres, Terse, Trees	
STAGE	Gates, Geats				
STAID	Adits				

STEIL	Islet, Istle, Stile, Teils, Tiles	
STEIN	Inset, Nesti, Neist, Senti, Set-in, Tines	
STELA	Astel, Least, Leats, Slate, Stale, Steal, Taels, Tales, Teals, Tesla	
STELE	Leets, Sleet, Steel, Teels	
STELL	Tells	
STEME	Meets, Metes, Steem, Teems, Temes, Temse	
STEND	Dents, Tends	
STENO	Etons, Notes, Onset, Seton, Stone, Tones	
STENT	Tents	
STERE	Ester, Reest, Reset, Retes, Steer, Teers, Teres, Terse, Trees	
STERN	Ernst, Rents, Terns	
STICH	Chits	
STICK	Ticks	
STIED	Deist, Diets, Edits, Sited, Tides	
STIFF	Tiffs	
STILE	Islet, Istle, Steil, Teils, Tiles	
STILL	Lilts, Tills	
STILP	Slipt, Spilt, Split	
STILT	Tilts	
STIME	Emits, Items, Meist, Metis, Mites, Smite, Times	
STIMY	Misty	
STING	Tings	
STINK	Knits, Tinks	
STINT	Tints, 'Tisn't	
STIPA	Pitas, Spait, Tapis	
STIPE	Piets, Piste, Spite	
STIRK	Skirt	
STIRP	Spirt, Sprit, Strip, Trips	
STOAI	Iotas, Ostia	
STOAS	Assot, Oasts, Tasso	
STOAT	Toast	
STOEP	Estop, Poets, Stope, Topes	
STOIT	Toits	

STOLA	Altos, Sloat, Tolas
STOLE	Lotes, Toles
STOMA	Atoms, Moats
STONE	Etons, Notes, Onset, Seton, Steno, Tones
STONY	Sonty
STOOD	To-dos
STOOK	Kotos, Tokos
STOOL	Loots, Lotos, Sloot, Sotol, Tools
STOOM	Moots, Smoot, Tooms
STOOP	Topos
STOOR	Roost, Roots, Torso
STOPE	Estop, Poets, Stoep, Topes
STORE	Roset, Tores, Torse
STORK	Torsk
STORM	Morts
STORY	Royst, Ryots, Stroy, Tyros
STOSH	Hosts, Shots
STOUN	Notus, Snout, Tonus
STOUP	Pouts, Spout, Toups
STOUR	Roust, Routs, Sutor, Torus, Tours
STOUT	Touts
STOVE	Votes
STOWN	Towns
*STRAD	Darts, Drats
STRAE	Arets, Aster, Earst, Rates, Reast, Resat, Stare, Tares, Tarse, Tears, Teras
STRAP	Parts, Spart, Sprat, Traps
STRAW	Swart, Warst, Warts, Wrast
STRAY	Artsy, Satyr, Trays
STREW	Trews, Werts, Wrest
STRIA	Airts, Astir, Sitar, Stair, Tarsi, Trias
STRID	Dirts
STRIG	Girts, Grist, Grits, Trigs
STRIP	Spirt, Sprit, Stirp Trips
STROB	Borts
STROP	Ports, Sport
STROW	Trows, Worst, Worts

STROY	Royst, Ryots, Story, Tyros			
STRUB	Brust, Burst			
STRUM	Turms			
STRUT	Sturt, Trust			
STUCK	Tucks			
STUDY	Dusty			
STUFA	Faust, Tufas			
STUFF	Tuffs			
STUMP	Tumps			
STUPA	Sputa, Tapus			
STUPE	Set-up, Upset			
STURE	Trues			
STURT	Strut, Trust,			
STYRE	Resty, Treys, Tyres			
SUAGE	Usage			
SUAVE	Uveas			
SUBER	Burse, Rebus			
SUCRE	Cruse, Cures, Curse			
SUDAK	Dauks			
SUENT	Tunes, Unset, Usen't			
SUGAR	Argus			
SUING	Using			
SUINT	Inust, Tunis, Units			
SUIST	Situs, Suits			
SUITE	Etuis			
SUITS	Situs, Suist			
SUMAC	Musca			
SUMPH	Humps			
SUPER	Purse, Sprue			
SURAL	Larus			
SURAT	Sutra			
SURGE	Urges			
SURGY	Gyrus			
SURYA	Saury			
SUTOR	Roust, Routs, Stour, Torus, Tours			
SUTRA	Surat			
SWAGE	Wages			
SWAIN	Wains			
SWALE	Sweal, Wales, Weals			
SWANG	Gnaws, Wangs			
SWARD	Draws, Wards			
SWARE	Resaw, Sawer, Swear, Wares, Wears			
SWARM	Warms			
SWART	Straw, Warst, Warts, Wrast			
SWASH	Shaws			
SWATH	Thaws			
SWEAL	Swale, Wales, Weals			
SWEAR	Resaw, Sawer, Sware, Wares, Wears			
SWEAT	Tawse, Waste			
SWEDE	Sewed, Weeds			
SWEEP	Weeps			
SWEER	Ewers, Sewer			
SWEET	Ewest			
SWEIR	Swire, Weirs, Wires, Wiser			
SWELL	Wells			
SWELT	Welts			
SWILL	Wills			
SWINE	Sewin, Sinew, Wines			
SWING	Wings			
SWINK	Winks			
SWIPE	Wipes			
SWIRE	Sweir, Weirs, Wires, Wiser			
SWITH	Whist, Whits, Withs			
SWIVE	Wives			
SWOLN	Lowns			
SWOON	Woons			
SWORD	Drows, Words			
SWORE	Owser, Resow, Serow, Sower, Worse			
*SYBIL	Sibyl			
SYBOE	Obeys			
SYKER	Yerks			
SYMAR	Marys			
SYRUP	Pursy, Pyrus			
SYTHE	Theys			
TABER	Baret, Bater, Berta			
TABES	Abets, Baste, Bates, Beast, Beats, Esbat, Sebat			
TABLE	Ablet, Blate, Bleat			
TABOR	Abort, Boart, Rabot			
TABUS	Abuts, Tsuba, Tubas			
TACES	Caste, Cates, Scate, Sceat			
TACHE	Cheat, Teach, Theca			
TACIT	Attic			
TACKS	Stack			
TAELS	Astel, Least, Leats, Slate, Stale, Steal,			

	Stela, Tales, Teals,	TAPIR	Atrip
	Tesla	TAPIS	Pitas, Spait, Stipa
TAHRS	Harst, Harts, Raths,	TAPUS	Sputa, Stupa
	Thars, Trash	TARDO	Troad
TAIGA	Agait	TARED	Dater, Rated, Trade,
TAILS	Litas		Tread
TAINS	Antis, Saint, Satin,	TARES	Arets, Aster, Earst,
	Stain, Tanis		Rates, Reast, Resat,
TAIRA	Atria, Riata, Tiara		Stare, Strae, Tarse,
TAISH	Haits, Saith		Tears, Teras
TAITS	Sitta	TARGE	Gater, Grate, Great,
TAKER	Terka		Greta
TAKES	Kates, Keats, Skate,	TARIN	Intra, Riant, Train
	Steak, Stake, Teaks	TARNS	Rants, Starn
TALES	Astel, Least, Leats,	TAROC	Actor, Croat, Rocta
	Slate, Stale, Steal,	TAROS	Astor, Roast, Rotas,
	Stela, Taels, Teals,		Toras, Troas
	Tesla	TAROT	Troat
TALKS	Stalk	TARRE	Arret, Rater, Retar,
TALMA	Malta, Tamal		Terra
TALON	Alton, Notal, Tolan,	TARSE	Arets, Aster, Earst,
	Tonal		Rates, Reast, Resat,
TALUS	Sault		Stare, Strae, Tares,
TAMAL	Malta, Talma		Tears, Teras
TAMED	Mated	TARSI	Airts, Astir, Sitar,
TAMER	Armet, Mater, Metra,		Stair, Stria, Trias
	Terma, Trema	TARTS	Start
TAMES	Mates, Meats, Satem,	TARVE	Avert, Taver, Trave
	Steam, Teams	TASSE	Asset, Easts, Sates,
TAMIN	Matin		Seats, Tessa
TAMIS	Maist	TASSO	Assot, Oasts, Stoas
TAMPS	Stamp	TASTE	State, Tates, Teats,
TANGO	Tonga		Testa
TANGS	Angst, Gants, Gnats,	*TATAR	Attar
	Stang	TATER	Arett, Tetra, Treat
*TANIS	Antis, Saint, Satin,	TATES	State, Taste, Teats,
	Stain, Tains		Testa
TANKS	Stank	TAUBE	Tubae
TANNA	Annat	TAULD	Adult
TANSY	Nasty	TAVER	Avert, Tarve, Trave
TANTY	Natty	TAWER	Water, Wrate
TAPED	Adept, Pated	TAWNY	Wanty
TAPEN	Paten	TAWSE	Sweat, Waste
TAPER	Apert, Pater, Peart,	TAXEL	Exalt, Latex
	Petar, Petra, Prate,	TAXER	Extra, Retax
	Trape	TAXES	Texas
TAPES	Apest, Paste, Pates,	TEACH	Cheat, Tache, Theca
	Peats, Septa, Spate,	TEADS	Dates, Sated, Stade,
	Speat		Stead, Tsade

TEAKS	Kates, Keats, Skate,	*TERAI	Irate
	Steak, Stake, Takes	TERAS	Arets, Aster, Earst,
TEALS	Astel, Least, Leats,		Rates, Reast, Resat,
	Slate, Stale, Steal,		Stare, Strae, Tares,
	Stela, Taels, Tales,		Tarse, Tears
	Tesla	TERCE	Crete, Erect
TEAMS	Mates, Meats, Satem,	TERES	Ester, Reest, Reset,
	Steam		Retes, Steer, Stere,
TEARS	Arets, Aster, Earst,		Teers, Terse, Trees
	Rates, Reast, Resat,	*TERKA	Taker
	Stare, Strae, Tares,	TERMA	Armet, Mater, Metra,
	Tarse, Teras		Tamer, Trema
TEASE	Setae	TERNE	Enter, Etern, Rente,
TEATS	State, Taste, Tates,		Treen
	Testa	TERNS	Ernst, Rents, Stern
TECHY	Tyche	TERRA	Arret, Rater, Retar,
TEDES	Steed		Tarre
TEELS	Leets, Sleet, Steel,	TERRY	Retry, Tryer
	Stele	TERSE	Ester, Reest, Reset,
TEEMS	Meets, Metes, Steem,		Retes, Steer, Stere,
	Steme, Temes, Temse		Teers, Teres, Trees
TEENS	Steen, Tense	TESLA	Astel, Least, Leats,
TEERS	Ester, Reest, Retes,		Slate, Stale, Steal,
	Reset, Steer, Stere,		Stela, Taels, Tales,
	Teres, Terse, Trees		Teals
TEETH	Thete	*TESSA	Asset, Easts, Sates,
*TEIAN	Eat-in, Tenia, Tinea		Seats, Tasse
TEILS	Islet, Istle, Steil,	TESTA	State, Taste, Tates,
	Stile, Tiles		Teats
TEIND	Tined	TETRA	Arett, Tater, Treat
TELAE	Elate	TEUCH	Chuet, Chute
TELAR	Alert, Alter, Artel,	TEWED	Tweed
	Later, Ratel	TEWEL	Tweel
TELLS	Stell	TEWIT	Twite
TEMED	Meted	*TEXAS	Taxes
TEMES	Meets, Metes, Steem,	*THAME	Meath, Thema
	Steme, Teems, Temse	THANE	Neath
TEMSE	Meets, Metes, Steem,	THARS	Harst, Harts, Raths,
	Steme, Teems, Temes		Tahrs, Trash
*TENBY	Benty	THAWS	Swath
TENDS	Dents, Stend	THECA	Cheat, Tache, Teach
TENIA	Eat-in, Teian, Tinea	THEES	Sheet, These
TENON	Nonet, Tonne	THEIC	Ethic
TENOR	Noter, Toner, Trone	THEMA	Meath, Thame
TENSE	Steen, Teens	THERE	Ether, Three
TENTS	Stent	THESE	Sheet, Thees
TEPAL	Leapt, Lepta, Pelta,	THETE	Teeth
	Petal, Plate, Pleat	THEYS	Sythe
TEPOR	Porte, Repot, Retop,	THIGH	Hight
	Toper, Trope		

THIGS	Sight	TINEA	Eat-in, Teian, Tenia
THILL	Illth	TINED	Teind
THING	Night	TINES	Inset, Neist, Nesti, Senti, Set-in, Stein
THIRD	Thrid		
THOLE	Helot, Hotel	TINGS	Sting
*THORA	Torah	TINKS	Knits, Stink
THORN	North	TINTS	Stint, 'Tisn't
THOSE	Ethos, Shote	TINTY	Nitty
THOUS	Shout, South	TIRED	Tride, Tried
THRAE	Earth, Hater, Heart, Herat, Rathe	TIRES	Reist, Resit, Rites, Tiers, Tries
THRAW	Warth, Wrath	TIROS	Riots, Roist, Rosit, Torsi, Trios
THREE	Ether, There		
THRID	Third	'TISN'T	Stint, Tints
THROB	Broth	TITER	Titre, Trite
THROE	Other	TITRE	Titer, Trite
THROW	Rowth, Whort, Worth, Wroth	TIVER	Rivet
		TOADY	Today
THRUM	Thurm	TOAST	Stoat
THURM	Thrum	TOAZE	Azote
TIARA	Atria, Riata, Taira	TOBAS	Basto, Boats, Boast, Sabot
*TIBER	Biter, Brite, Tribe		
TICED	Cited, Edict	TODAY	Toady
TICKS	Stick	TODDE	Doted
TIDAL	Dital	TO-DOS	Stood
TIDES	Deist, Diets, Edits, Sited, Stied	TOING	Ingot, Tigon
TIERS	Reist, Resit, Rites, Tires, Tries	TOITS	Stoit
		TOKEN	Knote
TIE-UP	Uptie	TOKOS	Kotos, Stook
TIFFS	Stiff	TOLAN	Alton, Notal, Talon, Tonal
TIGER	Greit		
TIGES	Geist, Gites	TOLAS	Altos, Sloat, Stola
TIGON	Ingot, Toing	TOLES	Lotes, Stole
TIKES	Kites, Skite	TOLLY	Tolyl
TILDE	Tiled	TOLYL	Tolly
TILED	Tilde	TOMES	Mesto, Motes, Smote
TILER	Liter, Litre, Relit	TOMIN	Timon
TILES	Islet, Istle, Steil, Stile, Teils	TONAL	Alton, Notal, Talon, Tolan
TILLS	Lilts, Still	TONED	Donet, Noted
TILTS	Stilt	TONER	Noter, Tenor, Trone
TIMED	Demit	TONES	Etons, Notes, Onset, Seton, Steno, Stone
TIMER	Merit, Miter, Mitre, Remit	TONGA	Tango
		TONNE	Nonet, Tenon
TIMES	Emits, Items, Meist, Metis, Mites, Smite, Stime	TON-UP	Put-on
		TONUS	Notus, Snout, Stoun
TIMON	Tomin	TOOLS	Loots, Lotos, Sloot, Sotol, Stool

TOOMS	Moots,	Smoot,	Stoom
TOPED	Depot,	Opted	
TOPER	Porte,	Repot,	Retop,
	Tepor,	Trope	
TOPES	Estop,	Poets,	Stoep,
	Stope		
TOPET	Petto		
TOPIA	Patio		
TOPIC	Optic,	Picot	
TOPIS	Posit		
TOPOS	Stoop		
TOQUE	Quote		
TORAH	Thora		
TORAN	Arnot,	Orant,	Trona
TORAS	Astor,	Roost,	Rotas,
	Taros,	Troas	
TORCH	Rotch		
TORES	Roset,	Store,	Torse
TORIC	Troic		
TORSE	Roset,	Store,	Tores
TORSI	Riots,	Roist,	Rosit,
	Tiros,	Trios	
TORSK	Stork		
TORSO	Roots,	Roost,	Stoor
TORUS	Roust,	Routs,	Stour,
	Sutor,	Tours	
TOTEM	Motet,	Motte	
TOTER	Otter		
TOTES	Set-to		
TOUCH	Chout,	Couth	
TOUGH	Ought		
TOUPS	Pouts,	Spout,	Stoup
TOURS	Roust,	Routs,	Stour,
	Sutor,	Torus	
TOUTS	Stout		
TOWEL	Owlet		
TOWER	Rowte,	Twoer,	Wrote
TOWNS	Stown		
TOWNY	Towyn		
*TOWYN	Towny		
TRACE	Caret,	Carte,	Cater,
	Crate,	React,	Recta
TRADE	Dater,	Rated,	Tared,
	Tread		
TRAIK	Krait		
TRAIL	Liart,	Trial	
TRAIN	Intra,	Riant,	Tarin
TRAMS	Marts,	Smart	
TRAPA	Apart		

TRAPE	Apert,	Pater,	Peart,
	Petar,	Petra,	Prate,
	Taper		
TRAPS	Parts,	Spart,	Sprat,
	Strap		
TRASH	Harst,	Harts,	Raths,
	Tahrs,	Thars	
TRASS	Stars		
TRAVE	Avert,	Tarve,	Taver
TRAYS	Artsy,	Satyr,	Stray
TREAD	Dater,	Rated,	Tared,
	Trade		
TREAT	Arett,	Tater,	Tetra
TREED	Deter		
TREEN	Enter,	Etern,	Rente,
	Terne		
TREES	Ester,	Reest,	Reset,
	Retes,	Steer,	Stere,
	Teers,	Teres,	Terse
TREND	Drent		
TRESS	Rests		
TREWS	Strew,	Werts,	Wrest
TREYS	Resty,	Styre,	Tyres
TRIAL	Liart,	Trail	
TRIAS	Airts,	Astir,	Sitar,
	Stair,	Stria,	Tarsi
TRIBE	Biter,	Brite,	Tiber
TRICE	Recti		
TRIDE	Tired,	Tried	
TRIED	Tired,	Tride	
TRIES	Reist,	Resit,	Rites,
	Tiers,	Tires	
TRIGS	Girts,	Grist,	Grits,
	Strig		
TRINE	Inert,	Inter,	Niter,
	Nitre,	Retin	
TRIOS	Riots,	Roist,	Rosit,
	Tiros,	Torsi	
TRIPE	Petri,	Piert	
TRIPS	Spirt,	Sprit,	Stirp,
	Strip		
TRITE	Titer,	Titre	
TROAD	Tardo		
TROAS	Astor,	Roast,	Rotas,
	Taros,	Toras	
TROAT	Tarot		
TROIC	Toric		
TRONA	Arnot,	Orant,	Toran
TRONE	Noter,	Tenor,	Toner

TRONS	Ronts, Snort			TYRAN	Ranty	
TROPE	Porte, Repot, Retop,			TYRES	Resty, Styre, Treys	
	Tepor, Toper			TYROS	Royst, Ryots, Story,	
TROUT	Tutor				Stroy	
TROVE	Overt, Voter					
TROWS	Strow, Worst, Worts					
TRUCE	Cruet, Cuter, Eruct,			U-BOAT	About	
	Recut			UDDER	Dured	
TRUES	Sture			ULCER	Cruel, Lucre	
TRUSS	Rusts			ULNAD	Laund	
TRUST	Strut, Sturt			ULNAR	Lunar, Urnal	
TRYER	Retry, Terry			UMBER	Brume, Umbre	
TSADE	Dates, Sated, Stade,			UMBRA	Burma, Rumba	
	Stead, Teads			UMBRE	Brume, Umber	
TSUBA	Abuts, Tabus, Tubas			UNARM	Urman	
TSUBO	Bouts			UNBAR	Buran, Urban	
TUBAE	Taube			UNDAM	Maund, Munda, Unmad	
TUBAS	Abuts, Tabus, Tsuba			UNDEE	Endue	
TUBED	Debut			UNDER	Runed, Unred, Urned	
TUBER	Brute, Buret, Rebut			UNFAR	Furan	
TUCKS	Stuck			UNHAT	Haunt	
TUFAS	Faust, Stufa			UNHID	Hindu	
TUFFS	Stuff			UNITE	Untie	
TUMPS	Stump			UNITS	Inust, Suint, Tunis	
TUNER	Urent			UNLIT	Until	
TUNES	Suent, Unset, Usen't			UNMAD	Maund, Munda, Undam	
TUNIC	Cut-in, Incut			UNPOT	Punto, Untop	
*TUNIS	Inust, Suint, Units			UNRED	Runed, Under, Urned	
TURCO	Court, Crout			UNRIG	Ruing	
TURMS	Strum			UNRIP	Purin	
TURPS	Spurt			UNSET	Suent, Tunes, Usen't	
TUTOR	Trout			UNSEX	Nexus	
TWAIN	Witan			UNSON	Nouns	
TWEED	Tewed			UNTIE	Unite	
TWEEL	Tewel			UNTIL	Unlit	
TWEER	Rewet, Twere			UNTOP	Punto, Unpot	
TWERE	Rewet, Tweer			UPLAY	Lay-up	
TWIER	Twire, Write			UPSET	Set-up, Stupe	
TWIRE	Twier, Write			UPTIE	Tie-up	
TWIST	Twits			URALI	Urial	
TWITE	Tewit			URBAN	Buran, Unbar	
TWITS	Twist			UREAL	Alure	
TWOER	Rowte, Tower, Wrote			URENT	Tuner	
TYCHE	Techy			URGES	Surge	
TYKES	Skyte			URIAL	Urali	
TYNDE	Tyned			URINE	Inure	
TYNED	Tynde			URITE	Uteri	
TYPAL	Aptly, Patly			URMAN	Unarm	
TYPTO	Potty			URNAL	Lunar, Ulnar	

URNED	Runed,	Under,	Unred	VERSO	Overs,	Roves,	Servo
USAGE	Suage			VERST	Verts		
USEN'T	Suent,	Tunes,	Unset	VERTS	Verst		
USERS	Reuss,	Ruses		VESPA	Paves,	Spave	
USHER	Shure			VESTA	Stave		
USING	Suing			VIALS	Silva,	Vails	
USURE	Eurus			VIAND	Divan		
UTERI	Urite			VICAR	Vraic		
UVEAL	Value			VICES	Cives		
UVEAS	Suave			VILDE	Devil,	Lived	
				VILER	Ervil,	Liver,	Livre,
					Rivel		
VADES	Devas,	Saved,	Vedas	VINAL	Anvil		
VAILS	Silva,	Vials		VINAS	Savin,	Sivan	
VALED	Laved			VINCA	Cavin		
VALES	Elvas,	Laves,	Salve,	VINER	Riven		
	Selva,	Slave,	Valse,	VINES	Nevis,	Sevin,	Veins,
	Veals				Venis,	Visne	
VALSE	Elvas,	Laves,	Salve,	VIOLE	Olive,	Voile	
	Selva,	Slave,	Vales,	VIRAL	Rival		
	Veals			VISAS	Sivas		
VALUE	Uveal			VISIE	Ivies		
VANES	Avens,	Evans,	Naves	VISIT	Vitis		
VAPID	Pavid			VISNE	Nevis,	Sevin,	Veins,
VAREC	Carve,	Crave			Venis,	Vines	
VARES	Avers,	Raves,	Saver	VISTO	Ovist		
VASAL	Lavas			VITIS	Visit		
VEALS	Elvas,	Laves,	Salve,	VLEIS	Elvis,	Evils,	Levis,
	Selva,	Slave,	Vales,		Lives,	Slive,	Veils
	Valse			VOCES	Coves,	Scove	
VEALY	Leavy			VOGIE	Ogive		
VEDAS	Devas,	Saved,	Vades	VOILE	Olive,	Viole	
VEDRO	Dover,	Drove,	Roved	VOLAS	Ovals,	Salvo	
VEERS	Serve,	Sever,	Verse	VOLED	Loved		
VEERY	Every			VOLES	Loves,	Slove,	Solve
VEILS	Elvis,	Evils,	Levis,	VOLET	Volte		
	Lives,	Slive,	Vleis	VOLTA	Lovat		
VEINS	Nevis,	Sevin,	Venis,	VOLTE	Volet		
	Vines,	Visne		VOMER	Mover		
VELAR	Laver,	Ravel		VOTER	Overt,	Trove	
VELIA	Alive,	Avile		VOTES	Stove		
VELUM	Mvule			VRAIC	Vicar		
VENAL	Elvan,	Navel					
VENEY	Yeven						
*VENIS	Nevis,	Sevin,	Veins,	WADES	Sawed		
	Vines,	Visne		WAGES	Swage		
*VENUS	Nevus			WAGON	Gowan		
*VERDI	Diver,	Drive,	Rived	WAINS	Swain		
VERSE	Serve,	Sever,	Veers	WAIST	Waits		

WAITS	Waist		
WAKER	Wreak		
WAKES	Askew		
WALED	Dwale, Weald		
WALES	Swale, Sweal, Weals		
WANED	Awned, Dewan		
WANES	Sewan, Weans		
WANGS	Gnaws, Swang		
WANLY	Lawny		
WANTY	Tawny		
WARDS	Draws, Sward		
WARES	Resaw, Sawer, Sware, Swear, Wears		
WARMS	Swarm		
WARST	Straw, Swart, Warts, Wrast		
WARTH	Thraw, Wrath		
WARTS	Straw, Swart, Warst, Wrast		
WASPY	Yawps		
WASTE	Sweat, Tawse		
WATER	Tawer, Wrate		
WAXER	Rewax		
WEALD	Dwale, Waled		
WEALS	Swale, Sweal, Wales		
WEANS	Sewan, Wanes		
WEARS	Resaw, Sawer, Sware, Swear, Wares		
WEEDS	Sewed, Swede		
WEELS	Sewel		
WEENS	Ensew, Sewen		
WEEPS	Sweep		
WEIRD	Wider, Wired		
WEIRS	Sweir, Swire, Wires, Wiser		
*WEISS	Wises		
WELLS	Swell		
WELTS	Swelt		
WERSH	Shrew		
WERTS	Strew, Trews, Wrest		
WHALE	Wheal		
WHAMS	Hawms, Shawm		
WHEAL	Whale		
WHERE	Hewer		
WHIST	Swith, Whits, Withs		
WHITE	Withe		
WHITS	Swith, Whist, Withs		
WHORE	Howre		
WHORT	Rowth, Throw, Worth, Wroth		
WHOSE	Howes		
WHOSO	Howso		
WIDEN	Dwine, Edwin, Wined		
WIDER	Weird, Wired		
WIELD	Wiled		
WIGAN	Awing		
WILED	Wield		
WILES	Lewis		
WILLS	Swill		
WINED	Dwine, Edwin, Widen		
WINES	Sewin, Sinew, Swine		
WINGS	Swing		
WINKS	Swink		
WINZE	Wizen		
WIPES	Swipe		
WIRED	Weird, Wider		
WIRER	Wrier		
WIRES	Sweir, Swire, Weirs, Wiser		
WISER	Sweir, Swire, Weirs, Wires		
WISES	Weiss		
WITAN	Twain		
WITHE	White		
WITHS	Swith, Whist, Whits		
WIVES	Swive		
WIZEN	Winze		
WODEN	Endow, Owned, Nowed, Woned		
WOKEN	Knowe		
WONED	Endow, Owned, Nowed, Woden		
WOONS	Swoon		
WORDS	Drows, Sword		
WORDY	Dowry, Rowdy		
WORSE	Owser, Resow, Serow, Sower, Swore		
WORST	Strow, Trows, Worts		
WORTH	Rowth, Throw, Whort, Wroth		
WORTS	Strow, Trows, Worst		
WRAST	Straw, Swart, Warst, Warts		
WRATE	Tawer, Water		
WRATH	Thraw, Warth		
WREAK	Waker		
WREST	Strew, Trews, Werts		
WRIER	Wirer		
WRIST	Writs		

WRITE	Twier, Twire			YEARN	Rayne		
WRITS	Wrist			YELPS	Slype		
WRONG	Grown			*YEMEN	Enemy		
WROTE	Rowte, Tower, Twoer			YERBA	Bayer		
WROTH	Rowth, Throw, Whort, Worth			YERKS	Syker		
				YEVEN	Veney		
				YILLS	Silly, Slily		
				Y-MOTH	Mothy		
XYLIC	Cylix			YODEL	Doyle, Odyle, Yodle		
				YODLE	Doyle, Odyle, Yodel		
				YRAPT	Party, Praty		
YACHT	Cathy			YUFTS	Fusty		
YAMEN	Meany			YULAN	Nyula		
YANKS	Snaky						
YARNS	Snary						
YASHT	Hasty			ZABRA	Bazar, Braza		
YAWNS	Sawny			ZEBRA	Braze		
YAWPS	Waspy			ZERDA	Razed		
YDRAD	Dryad			ZONED	Dozen		
YEANS	Sayne						
YEARD	Deary, Deray, Rayed, Ready						

Six letters

ABACAS — Casaba
ABATER — Rabate, Trabea
ABATES — Sea-bat
ABATOR — Rabato
ABDEST — Basted
*ABDIEL — Bailed, Bidale, Deblai
ABIDER — Air-bed
ABIENT — Binate
ABLAUT — Tabula
ABLEST — Ablets, Bleats, Stable, Tables
ABLETS — Ablest, Bleats, Stable, Tables
ABLINS — Blains
ABOARD — Aborad, Abroad,
ABORAD — Aboard, Abroad
ABORDS — Adsorb, Boards, Broads, Dobras
ABRADE — Abread
ABREAD — Abrade
ABRINS — Bairns, Brains, Brians, Risban
ABROAD — Aboard, Aborad
ABSENT — Basnet, Besant
ACCITE — Acetic
ACETIC — Accite
ACNODE — Canoed, Deacon
ACTION — Atonic, Cation
ACTORS — Castor, Castro, Co-star, Croats
ACUTES — Cuesta
ADAMIC — Cadmia
ADDERS — Dreads, Readds, Sadder

ADDLED — Daddle
ADDLES — Saddle
ADHERE — Header, Hedera, Rehead
ADMITS — Amidst
ADORED — Deodar, Roaded
ADORER — Roared
ADORES — Oreads, Soared, Sea-rod
ADSORB — Abords, Boards, Broads, Dobras
ADVERB — Braved
ADVIEW — Waived
ADVISE — Avised, Davies
AERIAL — Realia
AERIES — Easier
AFFAIR — Raffia
AFFEER — Raffee
AFIELD — Failed
AFROED — Fedora
AFTERS — Faster, Strafe
AGEISM — Images
AGNISE — Easing
AGREED — Dragee, Geared
AGREES — Eagres, Grease
AIDERS — Irades, Raised
AIGLET — Ligate, Taigle
AIGRET — Gaiter, Triage
AILING — Nilgai
AIR-BED — Abider
AIRCAV — Caviar
AIRMAN — Marian, Marina
AIRMEN — Marine, Remain
AISLED — Deasil, Ideals, Ladies, Sailed

53

AISLES	Lassie
ALBATA	Atabal, Balata
ALBEDO	Doable
ALBEIT	Albite, Betail
*ALBERT	Labret, Tabler
ALBINO	Albion
*ALBION	Albino
ALBITE	Albeit, Betail
*ALCAIC	Cicala
ALCEDO	Coaled
ALCOVE	Coeval
ALDERN	Darnel, Enlard, Lander, Randle, Reland
ALDERS	Dalers, Sardel
ALDINE	Alined, Daniel, Delian, Denial, Lead-in, Nailed
ALEGAR	Laager
ALEGER	Regale
ALERCE	Cereal, Relace
ALERTS	Alters, Artels, Laster, Ratels, Resalt, Salter, Slater, Staler, Tarsel
ALEVIN	Alvine, Venial
ALEXIN	Xenial
*ALFRED	Fardel, Flared
ALIBLE	Belial, Labile, Liable
ALIENS	Alines, Saline, Selina
ALIGNS	Ganils, Liangs, Ligans, Lingas, Signal
ALINED	Aldine, Daniel, Delian, Denial, Lead-in, Nailed
ALINES	Aliens, Saline, Selina
ALIPED	Elapid, Paidle, Pailed, Pleiad
ALLIES	Sallie
ALLOWS	Sallow
ALLUDE	Aludel
ALLURE	Laurel
ALMAIN	Animal, Lamina, Manila
ALMOIN	Monial, Oilman
ALMOND	Dolman
ALMOST	Maltos, Smalto
ALMUCE	Macule
ALNAGE	Angela, Galena, Lagena
ALPINE	Penial, Pineal
ALPIST	Pastil, Plaits, Spital
ALTARS	Astral, Ratals, Tarsal
ALTERN	Antler, Learnt, Rental, Ternal
ALTERS	Alerts, Artels, Laster, Ratels, Resalt, Salter, Slater, Staler, Tarsel
ALUDEL	Allude
ALUMNI	Lumina
ALVINE	Alevin, Venial
AMBLED	Balmed, Bedlam, Beldam, Blamed, Lambed
AMBLER	Blamer, Lamber, Marble, Ramble
AMEERS	Ameres, Ramees, Seamer
AMENDE	Amened, Demean
AMENDS	Desman
AMENED	Amende, Demean
AMENTA	Teaman
AMENTS	Manets, Stamen
AMERCE	Careme, Raceme
AMERES,	Ameers, Ramees, Seamer
AMICES	Camise, Macies
AMIDST	Admits
AMMINE	Immane
AMREET	Remate
AMUSED	Medusa, Sea-mud
AMUSES	Assume
ANADEM	Maenad
ANCHOR	Archon, Charon, Rancho
ANCLES	Cleans, Lances, Lencas, Senlac
*ANDREW	Darwen, Rawden, Warned, Wander, Warden

ANELED	Leaden, Leaned		Debars, Sabred,
ANEMIC	Cinema, Iceman		Serdab
*ANGELA	Alnage, Galena,	ARDENT	Ranted
	Lagena	ARETES	Asteer, Easter,
ANGERS	Ranges, Serang		Eaters, Reseat,
ANGLED	Dangle, Lagend		Saeter, Seater,
ANGLER	Largen, Rangle,		Staree, Steare,
	Regnal		Teaser, Teresa
ANGORA	Aragon, Arango	ARGALI	Garial
ANGORS	Argons, Groans,	ARGENT	Garnet, Gerant,
	Nagors, Orangs,		Gretna
	Organs, Sarong	*ARGIVE	Rivage
ANIMAL	Almain, Lamina,	ARGONS	Angors, Groans,
	Manila		Nagors, Orangs,
ANIONS	Nasion		Organs, Sarong
ANISES	Sanies, Sasine	ARGUES	Augers, Sauger
*ANNIES	Insane, Sienna	ARGUTE	Rugate, Tuareg
ANNULI	Unnail	ARIELS	Israel, Relais,
ANOINT	Nation		Resail, Sailer,
*ANSELM	Lemans, Mensal		Serail, Serial
ANSWER	Resawn	ARIGHT	Graith
ANTHEM	Hetman	ARISES	Raises, Sisera
ANTHER	Tehran, Thenar	ARISTA	Riatas, Tarsia,
ANTICS	Incast, Nastic		Tiaras
ANTLER	Altern, Learnt,	*ARMAGH	Graham
	Rental, Ternal	ARMEST	Armets, Master,
ANTRES	Astern, Retans		Maters, Remast,
*ANTRIM	Martin		Stream, Tamers,
ANVILS	Silvan		Tremas
AORIST	Ratios	ARMETS	Armest, Master,
APPEND	Napped		Maters, Remast,
APRONS	Parson		Stream, Tamers,
APTERA	Patera, Petara		Tremas
APTOTE	Tea-pot	ARMFUL	Fulmar
ARABLE	Arbela	ARMING	Ingmar, Ingram,
*ARAGON	Angora, Arango		Margin
ARANGO	Angora, Aragon	ARMLET	Martel
*ARBELA	Arable	ARMPIT	Impart, Partim
ARCHED	Chared	*ARNHEM	Herman
ARCHES	Chares, Chaser,	ARNICA	Carina, Crania
	Eschar, Raches,	AROINT	Ration
	Search	AROMAS	Masora
*ARCHIE	Cahier	AROUND	Arundo
ARCHON	Anchor, Charon,	AROURA	Aurora
	Rancho	AROYNT	Notary
ARCING	Caring, Racing	ARPENT	Enrapt, Entrap,
ARCKED	Carked, Craked,		Panter, Parent,
	Dacker, Racked		Pterna, Trepan
ARDEBS	Beards, Breads,	ARRECT	Carter, Crater,
			Tracer

ARREST	Arrets, Rarest,		Staree, Steare,
	Raster, Raters,		Teaser, Teresa
	Retars, Sartre,	ASTERN	Antres, Retans
	Starer, Tarres	ASTERS	Assert, Stares
ARRETS	Arrest, Rarest,	ASTERT	Stater, Taster,
	Raster, Raters,		Taters, Treats
	Retars, Sartre,	ASTRAL	Altars, Ratals,
	Starer, Tarres		Tarsal
ARRIDE	Raider	*ASTRID	Triads
ARRIVE	Varier	ASTUTE	Statue
ARROWY	Yarrow	ASWING	Sawing
ARSENO	Reason, Senora	ATABAL	Albata, Balata
ARTELS	Alerts, Alters,	*ATHENS	Hasten, Snathe,
	Laster, Ratels,		Thanes
	Resalt, Salter,	ATONED	Donate
	Slater, Staler,	ATONER	Ornate, Tenora
	Tarsel	ATONES	Seaton
ARTIST	Strait, Traits	ATONIC	Action, Cation
ARUNDO	Around	*ATREUS	Urates
ASCEND	Dances	ATRIAL	Lariat, Latria
ASCENT	Enacts, Secant,	ATTACH	Chatta
	Stance	ATTARS	Astart, Strata
ASH-FLY	Flashy	ATTICS	Static
ASHLER	Halser	ATTIRE	Ratite
ASHMAN	Shaman	ATTORN	Ratton
ASHORE	Hoarse, Shorea	ATTUNE	Nutate, Tauten
ASIDES	Dassie, Sadies	AUGEND	Unaged
ASKING	Gaskin, Kiangs	AUGERS	Argues, Sauger
ASLEEP	Elapse, Please,	AULICS	Caulis, Clusia
	Sapele	AURATE	Aureat
ASPECT	Epacts	AUREAT	Aurate
ASPERS	Parses, Passer,	AURORA	Aroura
	Prases, Repass	*AUSTEN	Nasute, Unseat
	Spaers, Spares,	AVENGE	Geneva, Vangee
	Spears, Sparse	AVERTS	Ravest, Starve,
ASPIRE	Paries, Persia,		Staver, Tarves,
	Praise, Spirae,		Tavers, Traves,
	Spirea		Vaster
ASPORT	Pastor, Portas,	AVISED	Advise, Davies
	Sap-rot	AVOCET	Octave
ASSENT	Steans	AVOWER	Reavow
ASSERT	Asters, Stares	AVULSE	Values
ASSIGN	Signas	AWLESS	Swales, Sweals
ASSIST	Stasis	AWNING	Waning
ASSUME	Amuses		
ASTART	Attars, Strata		
ASTEER	Aretes, Easter,	BACKER	Reback
	Eaters, Reseat,	BADGER	Barged, Garbed
	Saeter, Seater,	BAGNIO	Gabion

BAILED	Abdiel, Belaid, Bidale, Deblai		BASNET	Absent, Besant
BAIRNS	Abrins, Brains, Brians, Risban		BASSET	Bastes, Beasts
			BASTED	Abdest
BAITER	Barite, Rebait, Terbia		BASTER	Barest, Breast
			BASTES	Basset, Beasts
BAKING	Ink-bag		BASTON	Batons
BALATA	Albata, Atabal		BASYLE	Basely
BALDED	Bladed		BATHER	Bareth, Bertha, Breath
*BALDER	Bedral, Blared		BATHES	Shebat
BALEEN	Enable		BATLET	Battel, Battle, Tablet
BALMED	Ambled, Bedlam, Beldam, Blamed, Lambed		BATMAN	Bantam
			BATONS	Baston
BANGER	Graben		BATTEL	Batlet, Battle, Tablet
BANGLE	Bengal		
BANKER	Barken, Rebank		BATTER	Tabret
BANTAM	Batman		BATTLE	Batlet, Battel, Tablet
BANTED	Tan-bed		
BANTER	Barnet		BATTUE	Tubate
BARBED	Dabber, Debarb		BAWBLE	Wabble
BARBEL	Barble, Rabble		BAWLER	Warble
BARBET	Rabbet		BEAKED	Debeak
BARBLE	Barbel, Rabble		BEAKER	Rebake
BAREGE	Bargee		BEARDS	Ardebs, Breads, Debars, Sabred, Serdab
BARELY	Barley, Bleary, Brayle		
			BEASTS	Basset, Bastes
BAREST	Baster, Breast		BEATER	Berate, Rebate
BARETH	Bather, Bertha, Breath		BEAT-UP	Upbeat
			BECAME	Embace
BARGED	Badger, Garbed		BECKED	Bedeck
BARGEE	Barege		BEDASH	Bashed
BARITE	Baiter, Rebait, Terbia		BEDECK	Becked
			BEDELL	Belled
BARKED	Braked, Debark		BEDLAM	Ambled, Balmed, Beldam, Blamed, Lambed
BARKEN	Banker, Rebank		
BARKER	Braker		
BARLEY	Barely, Bleary, Brayle		BEDRAL	Balder, Blared
			BEDRID	Bidder, Birded
*BARNET	Banter		BEDROP	Probed
BARNEY	Near-by		BEDSIT	Bidets, Debits
BARONG	Brogan		BEDUCK	Bucked
BARONY	Baryon		BEDUST	Bestud, Busted, Debuts
BARRET	Barter		
BARSAC	Scarab		BEGILD	Bilged
BARTER	Barret		BEGINS	Beings, Besing, Binges
BARYON	Barony		
BASELY	Basyle		
BASHED	Bedash		BEGIRD	Bridge

BEGONE	Engobe	
BEHEST	Thebes	
BEINGS	Begins, Besing,	
	Binges	
BELATE	Let-a-be	
BELDAM	Ambled, Balmed,	
	Bedlam, Blamed,	
	Lambed	
*BELIAL	Alible, Labile,	
	Liable	
BELIED	Debile, Edible	
BELIES	Iblees	
BELIVE	Bevile	
BELLED	Bedell	
BEMEAN	Bename	
BEMIRE	Bireme	
BEMOIL	Emboil, Mobile	
BENAME	Bemean	
BENDER	Rebend	
*BENGAL	Bangle	
BEPATS	Bespat	
BERATE	Beater, Rebate	
BERETS	Bester	
BERTHA	Bareth, Bather,	
	Breath	
*BERTIE	Rebite	
BESANT	Absent, Basnet	
BESING	Begins, Beings,	
	Binges	
BESOMS	Emboss	
BESORT	Sorbet	
BESOTS	Betoss	
BESPAT	Bepats	
BESTER	Berets	
BESTIR	Bister, Bistre,	
	Biters, Brites,	
	Tribes	
BESTUD	Bedust, Busted,	
	Debuts	
BETAIL	Albeit, Albite	
BETORN	Breton	
BETOSS	Besots	
BETRIM	Timber, Timbre	
BETROD	Debtor	
BEVILE	Belive	
BICORN	Bicron	
BICRON	Bicorn	
BIDALE	Abdiel, Bailed,	
	Deblai	

BIDDER	Bedrid, Birded	
BIDERS	Brides, Debris,	
	Rebids	
BIDETS	Bedsit, Debits	
BIGGIN	Gibing	
BILGED	Begild	
BILLER	Rebill	
BINARY	Brainy	
BINATE	Abient	
BINDER	Brined, Inbred,	
	Rebind	
BINGES	Begins, Beings,	
	Besing	
BIRDED	Bedrid, Bidder	
BIREME	Bemire	
BIRLES	Birsle	
BIRSLE	Birles	
BISTER	Bestir, Bistre,	
	Biters, Brites,	
	Tribes	
BISTRE	Bestir, Bister,	
	Biters, Brites,	
	Tribes	
BITERS	Bestir, Bister,	
	Bistre, Brites,	
	Tribes	
BLADED	Balded	
BLADES	Sabled	
BLAINS	Ablins	
BLAMED	Ambled, Balmed,	
	Bedlam, Beldam,	
	Lambed	
BLAMER	Ambler, Lamber,	
	Marble, Ramble	
BLARED	Balder, Bedral	
BLEARY	Barely, Barley,	
	Brayle	
BLEATS	Ablest, Ablets,	
	Stable, Tables	
BLITHE	Thible	
BLONDE	Bolden	
BLOUSE	Boules, Obelus	
BLOWER	Bowler	
BLOWSE	Bowels, Elbows	
BLUEST	Bustle, Sublet,	
	Subtle	
BLUING	Unglib	
BLUNGE	Bungle	
BOARDS	Abords, Adsorb,	
	Broads, Dobras	

BOATEL	Lobate, Oblate	
BOATER	Borate, Orbate,	
	Rebato	
BOGLET	Goblet	
BOILED	Bolide	
BOILER	Reboil	
BOLDEN	Blonde	
BOLDER	Bordel	
BOLIDE	Boiled	
BOLTER	Rebolt	
BOMBED	Mobbed	
BONNET	Bonten	
BONTEN	Bonnet	
BONZER	Bronze	
BOOERS	Booser, Broose,	
	Reboso	
BORATE	Boater, Orbate,	
	Rebato	
BORDEL	Bolder	
BORDER	Roberd	
BORERS	Resorb	
BORING	Orbing, Robing	
*BORNEO	Oberon	
BOSSES	Obsess	
BO-TREE	Rebote	
BOULES	Blouse, Obelus	
BOURNE	Unrobe	
BOURNS	Suborn	
*BOURSE	Bouser	
BOUSER	Bourse	
BOWELS	Blowse, Elbows	
BOWERS	Bowser, Browse	
BOWERY	Bowyer	
BOWLER	Blower	
BOWSER	Bowers, Browse	
BOWYER	Bowery	
BRACER	Craber	
BRAIDS	Disbar	
BRAILS	Brasil	
BRAINS	Abrins, Bairns,	
	Brians, Risban	
BRAINY	Binary	
BRAISE	Rabies	
BRAKED	Barked, Debark	
BRAKER	Barker	
BRASIL	Brails	
BRASSE	Sabers, Sabres	
BRAVED	Adverb	
BRAYLE	Barely, Barley,	
	Bleary	

BREADS	Ardebs, Beards,
	Debars, Sabred,
	Serdab
BREAST	Barest, Baster
BREATH	Bareth, Bather,
	Bertha
BREHON	Hebron
*BRETON	Betorn
BREWER	Rebrew
*BRIANS	Abrins, Bairns,
	Brains, Risban
BRIBED	Dibber, Ribbed
BRIBER	Ribber
BRIDAL	Ribald
BRIDES	Biders, Debris,
	Rebids
BRIDGE	Begird
BRINED	Binder, Inbred,
	Rebind
BRINES	Nebris
BRITES	Bestir, Bister,
	Bistre, Biters,
	Tribes
BROADS	Abords, Adsorb,
	Boards, Dobras
BROGAN	Barong
BROMES	Ombers, Ombres,
	Somber, Sombre
BRONZE	Bonzer
BROOMS	Ombros
BROOSE	Booers, Reboso
BROWSE	Bowers, Bowser
BRUISE	Buries, Busier,
	Rubies
BRUMAL	Labrum, Lumbar,
	Umbral
*BRUNEI	Rubine
BRUNET	Bunter, Burnet
BRUTES	Buster, Rebuts,
	Subter, Surbet,
	Tubers
BUCKED	Beduck
BUDDER	Redbud
BUFFER	Rebuff
BUGLED	Bulged
BUGLER	Bulger, Burgle
BUILDS	Sub-lid
BULGED	Bugled
BULGER	Bugler, Burgle

BUNDER	Burden, Burned,		CALIFS	Fiscal
	Unbred		CALKER	Lacker, Rackle,
BUNDLE	Unbled			Recalk
BUNGLE	Blunge		CALLER	Cellar, Recall
BUNKED	Debunk		CALMED	Macled
BUNTER	Brunet, Burnet		CALMER	Marcel
BURBLE	Lubber, Rubble		CALQUE	Claque
BURDEN	Bunder, Burned,		CALVER	Carvel, Claver
	Unbred		CALVES	Cavels, Claves,
BURGEE	Gueber, Guebre			Sclave
BURGLE	Bugler, Bulger		CAMARA	Maraca
BURIED	Rubied		CAMBER	Crambe
BURIES	Bruise, Busier,		CAMELS	Macles, Mascle,
	Rubies			Mescal, Scamel
BURKES	Busker		CAMION	Manioc
BURLED	Deblur		CAMISE	Amices, Macies
BURLER	Burrel		CAMPED	Decamp
BURNED	Bunder, Burden,		CANDIE	Decani
	Unbred		CANDLE	Lanced
BURNER	Reburn		CANEHS	Encash
BURNET	Brunet, Bunter		CANERS	Casern, Cranes,
BURRED	Deburr			Crenas, Rances,
BURREL	Burler			Sarcen
BUSIER	Bruise, Buries,		CANGUE	Uncage
	Rubies		CANINE	Encina
BUSKER	Burkes		CANNOT	Canton
BUSMAN	Subman		CANOED	Acnode, Deacon
BUSMEN	Submen		CANTED	Cadent, Decant
BUSTED	Bedust, Bestud,		CANTER	Carnet, Centra,
	Debuts			Creant, Nectar,
BUSTER	Brutes, Rebuts,			Recant, Tanrec,
	Subter, Surbet,			Trance
	Tubers		CANTLE	Cental, Lancet
BUSTIC	Cubist, Cubits		CANTON	Cannot
BUSTLE	Bluest, Sublet,		CANTOR	Carton, Contra
	Subtle		CANTOS	Cotans, Octans,
BUTTON	Nobbut			Snacot
BY-BLOW	Wobbly		CANTUS	Tucans, Tuscan,
				Uncast
			*CANUTE	Uncate
CADENT	Canted, Decant		CAPERS	Crapes, Escarp,
CADETS	Casted, Ectads			Pacers, Parsec,
CADGER	Graced			Recaps, Secpar,
CADMIA	Adamic			Scrape, Spacer
CADRES	Cedars, Sacred,		CAPOTE	Toecap
	Scared		CARDER	Redcar
CAHIER	Archie		CAREEN	Enrace, Recane
CAIMAN	Maniac		CAREME	Amerce, Raceme
CAISON	Casino		CARESS	Carses, Crases,

	Escars,	Scares,		Cresta,	Reacts,
	Scraes,	Seracs		Recast,	Traces
CARETS	Cartes,	Caster,	CASTLE	Cleats,	Eclats
	Caters,	Crates,	CASTOR	Actors,	Castro,
	Cresta,	Reacts,		Co-star,	Croats,
	Recast,	Traces		Roctas	
CARIES	Cerias,	Serica	*CASTRO	Actors,	Castor,
CARINA	Arnica,	Crania		Co-star,	Croats,
CARING	Arcing,	Racing		Roctas	
CARKED	Arcked,	Craked,	CASUAL	Casula,	Causal
	Dacker,	Racked	CASULA	Casual	Causal
CARLES	Clears,	Sarcel,	CATERS	Carets,	Cartes,
	Scaler,	Sclera		Caster,	Crates,
CARNET	Canter,	Centra,		Cresta,	Reacts,
	Creant,	Nectar,		Recast,	Traces
	Recant,	Tanrec,	CATION	Action,	Atonic
	Trance		CATRIG	Tragic	
CARPED	Craped,	Redcap	CATSUP	Upcast	
CARPEL	Parcel,	Placer	CAUDLE	Cedula	
CARPET	Pre-act		CAULIS	Aulics,	Clusia
CARROT	Trocar		CAUSAL	Casual,	Casula
CARSES	Caress,	Crases,	CAUSED	Sauced	
	Escars,	Scares,	CAUSER	Cesura,	Erucas,
	Scraes,	Seracs		Saucer	
CARTED	Cedrat,	Crated,	CAUSEY	Cayuse	
	Redact,	Traced	CAUTER	Curate	
CARTEL	Claret,	Rectal	CAVEAT	Vacate	
CARTER	Arrect,	Crater,	CAVELS	Calves,	Claves,
	Tracer			Sclave	
CARTES	Carets,	Caster,	CAVERN	Carven,	Craven
	Caters,	Crates,	CAVIAR	Aircav	
	Cresta,	Reacts,	CAVIES	Vesica	
	Recast,	Traces	CAVILS	Clavis,	Slavic
CARTON	Cantor,	Contra	CAYUSE	Causey	
CARVED	Craved		CEASER	Crease,	Recase,
CARVEL	Calver,	Claver		Searce	
CARVEN	Cavern,	Craven	CEDARN	Craned,	Dancer
CARVER	Craver		CEDARS	Cadres,	Sacred,
CASABA	Abacas			Scared	
CASEIN	Incase		CEDERS	Creeds,	Screed
CASERN	Caners,	Cranes,	CEDRAT	Carted,	Crated,
	Crenas,	Rances,		Redact,	Traced
	Sarcen		CEDULA	Caudle	
CASINO	Caison		CEILED	Decile	
CASKED	Sacked		CELLAR	Caller,	Recall
CASQUE	Sacque		CENSER	Screen,	Secern
CASTED	Cadets,	Ectads	CENSOR	Crones,	Oncers,
CASTER	Carets,	Cartes,		Recons	
	Caters,	Crates	CENTAL	Cantle,	Lancet

CENTER	Centre, Recent, Tenrec	
CENTRA	Canter, Carnet, Creant, Nectar, Recant, Tanrec, Trance	
CENTRE	Center, Recent, Tenrec	
CEORLS	Closer, Cresol	
CERATE	Create, Ecarte	
CEREAL	Alerce, Relace	
CEREUS	Ceruse, Cesure, Recuse, Rescue, Secure	
CERIAS	Caries, Serica	
CERING	Cringe	
CERIPH	Cipher	
CERISE	Re-ices	
CERITE	Certie, Recite, Tierce	
CEROUS	Course, Crusoe, Source, Crouse	
CERRIS	Criers, Ricers	
CERTES	Erects, Resect, Secret	
CERTIE	Cerite, Recite, Tierce	
CERUSE	Cereus, Cesure, Recuse, Rescue, Secure	
CESIUM	Miscue	
CESSER	Recess, Screes	
CESTUI	Cuties	
CESTUS	Scutes	
CESURA	Causer, Erucas, Saucer	
CESURE	Cereus, Ceruse, Recuse, Rescue, Secure	
CETANE	Tenace	
CETINE	Entice	
CHAIRS	Rachis	
CHALET	Thecal, Thecla	
CHALKY	Hackly	
CHANTS	Snatch, Stanch	
CHAPEL	Lepcha, Pleach	
CHARED	Arched	
CHARES	Arches, Chaser, Eschar, Raches, Search	

CHARON	Anchor, Archon, Rancho	
CHARTS	Starch	
CHASER	Arches, Chares, Eschar, Raches, Search	
CHASES	Chasse	
CHASSE	Chases	
CHASTE	Cheats, Sachet, Scathe, Taches	
CHATTA	Attach	
CHEATS	Chaste, Sachet, Scathe, Taches	
CHEEPS	Speech	
CHEERS	Creesh	
CHEERY	Reechy	
CHEIRO	Coheir, Heroic	
CHELAS	Laches, Sachel	
*CHEOPS	Epochs	
CHESIL	Chiels, Chisel, Elchis	
CHESTY	Scythe	
CHICLE	Cliche	
CHIDER	Dreich, Herdic	
CHIELD	Childe	
CHIELS	Chesil, Chisel Elchis	
CHILDE	Chield	
CHIMED	Miched	
CHIMER	Micher	
CHINED	Inched, Niched	
CHINES	Chinse, Inches, Niches	
CHINSE	Chines, Inches, Niches	
CHIN-UP	Punchi	
CHIRKS	Kirsch, Schrik	
CHIRMS	Chrism, Smirch	
CHISEL	Chesil, Chiels, Elchis	
CHOICE	Echoic	
CHOIRS	Ichors, Orchis	
CHOKED	Hocked	
CHOKER	Hocker	
CHOKEY	Hockey	
CHOPIN	Phonic	
CHORAL	Lorcha, Orchal	
CHOREA	Ochrea, Orache, Rochea	

CHOREE	Cohere, Echoer, Re-echo	COCKER	Recock
CHORES	Cosher, Ochres	CODDER	Corded
CHOUTS	Schout	COEVAL	Alcove
CHRISM	Chirms, Smirch	COHEIR	Cheiro, Heroic
CHYPRE	Cypher	COHERE	Choree, Echoer, Re-echo
CICALA	Alcaic	COILED	Docile
CIGALE	Gaelic	COINER	Enrico, Orcein, Orcine, Recoin
CILICE	Icicle		
CINDER	Crined	COLEUS	Oscule
CINEMA	Anemic, Iceman	COLLIE	Ocelli
CINQUE	Quince	COLONS	Consol
CINTRE	Cretin	COLTER	Lector
CIPHER	Ceriph	COMBAT	Tombac
CIRCLE	Cleric	COMBER	Recomb
CITHER	Thrice	COME-ON	Oncome
CITIES	Iciest	COMICS	Cosmic
CITING	Ticing	COMING	Gnomic
CITRAL	Rictal	COMITY	Myotic
CITRIC	Critic	COMSAT	Mascot, Satcom
CITRIN	Nitric	CONDER	Corned
CITRUS	Rictus, Rustic	CONDOR	Cordon
CLAQUE	Calque	CONGAS	Gascon
CLARET	Cartel, Rectal	CONIES	Cosine, Oscine, Soncie
CLAVER	Calver, Carvel		
CLAVES	Calves, Cavels, Sclave	CONKER	Reckon
		CONSOL	Colons
CLAVIS	Cavils, Slavic	CONSUL	Clonus
CLEANS	Ancles, Lances, Lencas, Senlac	CONTOS	Nostoc, Oncost
		CONTRA	Cantor, Carton
CLEARS	Carles, Sarcel, Scaler, Sclera	COOKER	Recook
		COOLER	Recool
CLEATS	Castle, Eclats	COONTY	Tycoon
CLEEKS	Seckel	COPERS	Corpse, Cropes, Proces
CLERIC	Circle		
CLICHE	Chicle	COPIED	Epodic
CLONUS	Consul	COPPIN	Pin-cop
CLOSED	Dolces	COPULA	Cupola
CLOSER	Ceorls, Cresol	CORDED	Codder
CLOUTS	Locust	CORDON	Condor
CLOVER	Velcro	CORERS	Crores, Scorer
CLOVES	Scovel	CORKED	Docker, Redock, Rocked
CLUSIA	Aulics, Caulis		
CLUTCH	Cultch	CORKER	Recork, Rocker
COALED	Alcedo	CORNED	Conder
COALER	Oracle, Recoal	CORNET	Cronet
COARSE	Rosace	CORONA	Racoon
COATIS	Scotia	CORPSE	Copers, Cropes, Proces
COBRES	Scrobe		

CORPUS	Croups
CORRIE	Orrice
CORSES	Crosse, Scores, Scorse
CORSET	Cortes, Coster, Escort, Recost, Rectos, Scoter, Sector
CORTES	Corset, Coster, Escort, Recost, Rectos, Scoter, Sector
CORVET	Covert, Vector
COSHER	Chores, Ochres
COSINE	Conies, Oscine, Soncie
COSMIC	Comics
CO-STAR	Actors, Castor, Castro, Croats, Roctas
COSTER	Corset, Cortes, Escort, Recost, Rectos, Scoter, Sector
COTANS	Cantos, Octons, Snacot
COUPER	Croupe, Cuerpo, Recoup
COUPON	Uncoop
COURSE	Cerous, Crouse, Crusoe, Source
COURTS	Crouts, Scruto, Turcos
COVERT	Corvet, Vector
COWERS	Escrow
COYOTE	Oocyte
CRABER	Bracer
CRAKED	Arcked, Carked, Dacker, Racked
CRAKES	Creaks, Sacker, Screak
CRAMBE	Camber
CRAMES	Creams, Macers, Scream
CRAMPS	Scramp
CRANED	Cedarn, Dancer
CRANES	Caners, Casern, Crenas, Rances, Sarcen
CRANIA	Arnica, Carina
CRAPED	Carped, Redcap
CRAPES	Capers, Escarp, Racers, Parsec, Recaps, Secpar, Scrape, Spacer
CRASES	Caress, Carses, Escars, Scares, Scraes, Seracs
CRATED	Carted, Cedrat, Redact, Traced
CRATER	Arrect, Carter, Tracer
CRATES	Carets, Cartes, Caster, Caters, Cresta, Reacts, Recast, Traces
CRAVED	Carved
CRAVEN	Carven, Cavern
CRAVER	Carver
CRAWLS	Scrawl
CREAKS	Crakes, Sacker, Screak
CREAMS	Crames, Macers, Scream
CREANT	Canter, Carnet, Centra, Nectar, Recant, Tanrec, Trance
CREASE	Ceaser, Recase, Searce
CREATE	Cerate, Ecarte
CREDIT	Direct, Triced
CREEDS	Ceders, Screed
CREEPS	Crepes, Preces
CREESH	Cheers
CREMOR	Cromer
CRENAS	Caners, Casern, Cranes, Rances, Sarcen
CREPES	Creeps, Preces
CRESOL	Ceorls, Closer
*CRESTA	Carets, Cartes, Caster, Caters, Crates, Reacts, Recast, Traces
CRETIN	Cintre
CREWED	Decrew
CRIERS	Cerris, Ricers

CRIKEY	Rickey	CUMBER	Recumb
CRIMED	Dermic	CUNEAL	Launce, Unlace
CRIMES	Scrime	CUPIDS	Cuspid, Sidcup
CRIMPS	Scrimp	CUPOLA	Copula
CRINED	Cinder	CURATE	Cauter
CRINES	Scrine	CURDLE	Curled
CRINGE	Cering	CURERS	Curser, Recurs
CRISTA	Racist	CURLED	Curdle
CRITIC	Citric	CURRED	Cruder
*CROATS	Actors, Castor,	CURSER	Curers, Recurs
	Castor, Co-star	CURSUS	Ruscus
CROCUS	Occurs, Roccus,	CURTSY	Crusty
	Succor	CUSCUS	Succus
*CROMER	Cremor	CUSPID	Cupids, Sidcup
CRONES	Censor, Oncers,	CUTIES	Cestui
	Recons	CUTLER	Culter, Reluct
CRONET	Cornet	CUTLET	Cuttle
CROPES	Copers, Corpse,	CUT-OFF	Off-cut
	Proces	CUT-OUT	Outcut
CRORES	Corers, Scorer	CUTTLE	Cutlet
CROSSE	Corses, Scores,	CYPHER	Chypre
	Scorse		
CROUPE	Couper, Cuerpo,		
	Recoup	DABBER	Barbed, Debarb
CROUPS	Corpus	DACKER	Arcted, Carked,
CROUSE	Cerous, Course,		Craked, Racked
	Crusoe, Source	DADDLE	Addled
CROUTS	Courts, Scruto,	DAEMON	Moaned, Modena,
	Turcos		Nomade
CRUDER	Curred	DAGGER	Ragged
CRUETS	Cruset, Eructs,	DAGGLE	Lagged
	Rectus, Recuts,	DAIMEN	Demain, Maiden,
	Truces		Mained, Median,
CRUISE	Crusie		Medina
CRUNTS	Scrunt	DAIMON	Domain
CRUSET	Cruets, Eructs,	DALERS	Alders, Sardel
	Rectus, Recuts,	DAMMER	Rammed
	Truces	DAMNED	Demand, Madden
CRUSIE	Cruise	DAMPER	Ramped
*CRUSOE	Cerous, Course,	DAMSEL	Medals
	Crouse, Source	DAMSON	Monads, Nomads
CRUSTY	Curtsy	DANCER	Cedarn, Craned
CUBIST	Bustic, Cubits	DANCES	Ascend
CUBITS	Bustic, Cubist	DANDER	Darned
CUERPO	Couper, Croupe,	DANDLE	Landed
	Recoup	DANGER	Gander, Garden,
CUESTA	Acutes		Grande, Ranged
CULTCH	Clutch	DANGLE	Angled, Lagend
CULTER	Cutler, Reluct	*DANIEL	Aldine, Alined,

	Delian, Denial,	DEBARS	Ardebs, Beards,
	Lead-in, Nailed		Breads, Sabred,
DAPPER	Rapped		Serdab
DAPPLE	Lapped, Palped	DEBEAK	Beaked
DARETH	Dearth, Hatred,	DEBILE	Belied, Edible
	Red-hat, Thread	DEBITS	Bedsit, Bidets
DARGER	Grader, Regard	DEBLAI	Abdiel, Bailed,
DARING	Gradin		Bidale
DARKEN	Ranked	DEBLUR	Burled
DARNED	Dander	DEBRIS	Biders, Brides,
DARNEL	Aldern, Enlard,		Rebids
	Lander, Randle,	DEBTOR	Betrod
	Reland	DEBUNK	Bunked
DARNER	Errand, Redarn,	DEBURR	Burred
	Renard	DEBUTS	Bedust, Bestud,
DARTED	Traded		Busted
DARTER	Dartre, Retard,	DECAMP	Camped
	Retrad, Tarred,	DECANI	Candie
	Trader	DECANT	Cadent, Canted
DARTRE	Darter, Retard,	DECIDE	De-iced
	Retrad, Tarred,	DECILE	Ceiled
	Trader	DECKER	Recked
*DARWEN	Andrew, Rawden,	DECREE	Recede
	Wander, Warden,	DECREW	Crewed
	Warned	DEDANS	Sadden, Sanded
*DARWIN	Inward	DEDUCE	Deuced, Educed
DASHED	Shaded	DEEPER	Peered
DASHER	Rashed, Shader,	DEFANG	Fag-end, Fanged
	Shared	DEFEAT	Feated
DASHES	Sashed, Shades	DEFEND	Fended
DASSIE	Asides, Sadies	DEFINE	Feed-in
DATERS	Desart, Stared,	DEFLEX	Flexed
	Trades, Treads	DEFLUX	Fluxed
DAUNER	Undear, Unread	DEFORM	Formed
*DAVIES	Advise, Avised	DEFOUL	Fouled
DAWDLE	Waddle	DEFRAY	Frayed
DEACON	Acnode, Canoed	DEGUMS	Smudge
DEAFLY	Flayed	DEGUST	Gusted
DEALER	Leader, Redeal,	DEHORN	Horned
	Relead	DEHORS	Herods, Hordes,
DEARER	Reader, Reared,		Horsed, Reshod,
	Redare, Reread		Rhodes, Shoder,
DEARTH	Dareth, Hatred,		Shored
	Red-hat, Thread	DEHORT	Red-hot
DEASIL	Aisled, Ideals,	DE-ICED	Decide
	Ladies, Sailed	DEIGNS	Design, Dinges,
DEATHS	Hasted, 'Sdeath		Nidges, Sdeign,
DEBARB	Barbed, Dabber		Signed, Singed
DEBARK	Barked, Braked	DEISTS	Desist, Sisted

DELATE	Elated	DEPORT	Ported, Red-top
DELEAD	Leaded	DEPOSE	Epodes, Speedo
DELIAN	Aldine, Alined,	DEPOTS	Despot, Posted,
	Daniel, Denial,		Stoped
	Lead-in, Nailed	DERAIL	Railed, Relaid
DELIST	Listed, Silted,	DERAIN	Rained, Randie
	Tildes	DERATE	Redate, Teared
DELTAS	Lasted, Salted,	DERHAM	Harmed
	Slated, Stadle,	DERIVE	Reived
	Staled	DERMAL	Marled, Medlar
DELUDE	Eluded	DERMIC	Crimed
DEMAIN	Daimen, Maiden,	DERNED	Redden
	Mained, Median,	DERRIS	Driers, Reirds,
	Medina		Riders
DEMAND	Damned, Madden	DERVIS	Divers, Drives
DEMARK	Marked	DESART	Daters, Stared,
DEMEAN	Amende, Amened		Trades, Treads
DEMISS	Missed	DESERT	Deters, Rested
DEMONS	Esmond	DESIGN	Deigns, Dinges,
DEMOTE	Emoted		Nidges, Sdeign,
DEMOTH	Mothed		Signed, Singed
DEMURE	Emured	DESINE	Denies, Denise
DENARY	Yarned	DESIRE	Eiders, Reside
DENGUE	Unedge	DESIST	Deists, Sisted
DENIAL	Aldine, Alined,	DESMAN	Amends
	Daniel, Delian,	DESPIN	Piends, Sniped
	Lead-in, Nailed		Spined
DENIED	Indeed	DESPOT	Depots, Posted,
DENIER	Edirne, Nereid,		Stoped
	Reined	DETAIL	Dietal, Dilate,
DENIES	Denise, Desine		Tailed
*DENISE	Denies, Desine	DETENT	Netted, Tented
*DENNIS	Sinned	DETERS	Desert, Rested
DENSER	Enders, Resend,	DETEST	Tested
	Sender	DETORT	Dotter, Rotted
DENTED	Tended	DETOUR	Douter, Redout,
DENTEX	Extend		Routed, Toured
DENTIN	Indent, Intend,	DEUCED	Deduce, Educed
	Tinned	DEUCES	Educes, Seduce
DENUDE	Dudeen, Duende,	DEVEST	Vested
	Dundee, Endued	DEVISE	Sieved
DEODAR	Adored, Roaded	DEVOID	Voided
DEPART	Drapet, Parted,	DEVOIR	Voider
	Petard, Prated,	DEVOTE	Vetoed
	Traped	DEWANI	Edwina, Wained
DEPEND	Pended	DEWING	Winged
DEPERM	Permed, Premed	DEWITT	Witted
DEPLOY	Ployed	DEWLAP	Pawled
DEPONE	Opened	DIALED	Laddie

DIAMYL	Milady	DITONE	Intoed
DIAPER	Paired, Pardie,	DIURNA	Durian
	Repaid	DIVERS	Dervis, Drives
DIBBER	Bribed, Ribbed	DIVEST	Stived
DICKER	Ricked	DOABLE	Albedo
DIDDLE	Lidded	DOBRAS	Abords, Adsorb,
DIESEL	Ediles, Elides,		Boards, Broads
	Sedile, Seidel	DOCILE	Coiled
DIETAL	Detail, Dilate,	DOCKER	Corked, Redock,
	Tailed		Rocked
DIETED	Edited	DODDER	Rodded
DIETER	Re-edit, Retied,	DODGER	Red-dog
	Tiered	DOESN'T	Donets, Ostend,
DIGEST	Gisted		Stoned
DIGGER	Rigged	DOGATE	Dotage, Togaed
DILATE	Detail, Dietal,	DOGGER	Gorged
	Tailed	DOGLEG	Logged
DIMMER	Rimmed	DOINGS	Dosing
DIMPLE	Limped	DOLCES	Closed
DINNLE	Linden	DOLIUM	Idolum
DINGES	Deigns, Design,	DOLMAN	Almond
	Nidges, Sdeign,	DOLOSE	Loosed, Oodles
	Signed, Singed	DOMAIN	Daimon
DINGEY	Dyeing	DOMIFY	Modify
DINGLE	Ingled	DOMINE	Monied
DINING	Indign, Niding	DONATE	Atoned
DINKEY	Kidney	*DONETS	Doesn't, Ostend,
*DIONES	Donsie, Nidose,		Stoned
	Noised, No-side,	DONSIE	Diones, Nidose,
	Onside, Side-on		Noised, No-side,
DIPLOE	Dipole, Peloid		Onside, Side-on
DIPOLE	Diploe, Peloid	DOOVER	Overdo
DIPPER	Ripped	DOPING	Pongid
DIRECT	Credit, Triced	DOPPER	Proped
DIREST	Driest, Ridest,	*DORCAS	Dracos
	Stride	DORIAN	Inroad, Ordain
DIRKED	Kidder	DORING	Roding
DISARM	Marids	DORSEL	Resold, Solder
DISBAR	Braids	DORSES	Dosers, Dosser,
DISHED	Eddish		Sordes
DISHES	Hissed	*DORSET	Doters, Sordet,
DISPEL	Disple, Lisped,		Sorted, Stored,
	Sliped, Spiled		Strode, Trodes
DISPLE	Dispel, Lisped,	DOSAGE	Sea-dog, Sea-god
	Sliped, Spiled	DOSERS	Dorses, Dosser,
DISTAL	Ditals		Sordes
DISUSE	Issued	DOSING	Doings
DITALS	Distal	DOSSER	Dorses, Dosers,
DITHER	Rideth		Sordes

DOSSIL	Sloids, Solids	
DOTAGE	Dogate, Togaed	
DOTERS	Dorset, Sordet,	
	Sorted, Stored,	
	Strode, Trodes	
DOTTER	Detort, Rotted	
DOUCHE	Ouched	
DOUSES	Soused	
DOUTER	Detour, Redout,	
	Routed, Toured	
DOWELS	Slowed	
DOWNER	Wonder	
DOWSER	Drowse	
DOWSES	Sowsed	
DRACOS	Dorcas	
DRAGEE	Agreed, Geared	
DRAGON	Gardon	
DRAMAS	Madras	
DRAPED	Padder	
DRAPES	Padres, Parsed,	
	Rasped, Repads,	
	Spader, Spared,	
	Spread	
DRAPET	Depart, Parted,	
	Petard, Prated,	
	Traped	
DRAWED	Edward, Warded	
DRAWER	Redraw, Reward,	
	Warder, Warred	
DRAYED	Yarded	
DREADS	Adders, Readds,	
	Sadder	
DREARY	Yarred	
DREICH	Chider, Herdic	
DRIERS	Derris, Reirds,	
	Riders	
DRIEST	Direst, Ridest,	
	Stride	
DRIVEN	Verdin	
DRIVES	Dervis, Divers	
DROGUE	Drouge, Gourde,	
	Rogued, Rouged	
DROICH	Orchid, Rhodic	
DROLLY	Lordly	
DRONED	Nodder	
DRONES	Snored, Sorned	
DROUGE	Drogue, Gourde,	
	Rogued, Rouged	
DROWSE	Dowser	

DRUIDS	Siddur	
DRUPEL	Purled	
*DRUSES	Duress	
DUALIN	Unlaid	
DUBBER	Rubbed	
DUCKER	Rucked	
DUDEEN	Denude, Duende,	
	Dundee, Endued	
DUENDE	Denude, Dudeen,	
	Dundee, Endued	
DUFFEL	Duffle, Luffed	
DUFFER	Ruffed	
DUFFLE	Duffel, Luffed	
DUKERY	Duyker	
DULIAS	Lusiad	
DUMOSE	Moused	
DUMPLE	Lumped, Plumed	
DUNCES	Secund	
*DUNDEE	Denude, Dudeen,	
	Duende, Endued	
DUNDER	Durden	
DUNGED	Nudged	
DUNNER	Undern	
DURDEN	Dunder	
DURESS	Druses	
DURIAN	Diurna	
DURING	Ungird	
DUSTER	Redust, Rudest,	
	Rusted	
DUYKER	Dukery	
DWALES	Swaled, Wealds	
DYEING	Dingey	
DYNAMO	Monday	
EAGLET	Legate, Teagle,	
	Telega	
EAGRES	Agrees, Grease	
*EALING	Genial, Linage	
EARFUL	Ferula	
EARING	Gainer, Graine,	
	Regain, Regian,	
	Regina	
EARNED	Endear, Neared	
EARNER	Nearer, Re-earn	
EARTHS	Haters, Hearts,	
	Rathes, Sarthe	
EARTHY	Hearty	
EASELS	Easles, Eassel,	
	Leases	

EASIER	Aeries	ELANET	Lateen
EASING	Agnise	ELAPID	Aliped, Paidle,
EASLES	Easels, Eassel,		Pailed, Pleiad
	Leases	ELAPSE	Asleep, Please,
EASSEL	Easels, Easles,		Sapele
	Leases	ELATED	Delate
EASTER	Aretes, Asteer,	ELATER	Relate
	Eaters, Reseat,	ELBOWS	Blowse, Bowels
	Saeter, Seater,	ELCHIS	Chesil, Chiels,
	Steare, Staree,		Chisel
	Teaser, Teresa	ELDING	Engild
EATERS	Aretes, Asteer,	ELECTS	Select
	Easter, Reseat,	ELIDES	Diesel, Ediles,
	Saeter, Seater,		Sedile, Seidel
	Steare, Staree,	ELISOR	Oilers, Oriels,
	Teaser, Teresa		Reoils, Soiler
EATEST	Estate, Teaset,	ELOIGN	Legion
	Testae	ELOINS	Esloin, Insole,
EATING	Ingate, Tangie,		Lesion, Oleins,
	Teaing		Solein
ECARTE	Cerate, Create	ELUANT	Lunate
ECHOER	Choree, Cohere,	ELUDED	Delude
	Re-echo	ELURES	Saurel
ECHOIC	Choice	ELWAND	Wandle
ECLATS	Castle, Cleats	ELYTRA	Lyrate, Raylet,
ECTADS	Cadets, Casted		Realty, Telary
EDDISH	Dished	EMBACE	Became
EDIBLE	Belied, Debile	EMBOIL	Bemoil, Mobile
EDILES	Diesel, Elides,	EMBOSS	Besoms
	Sedile, Seidel	EMEERS	Seemer
*EDIRNE	Denier, Nereid,	EMERGE	Mergee
	Reined	EMESIS	Missee
EDITED	Dieted	E-METER	Meeter
EDITOR	Rioted, Tie-rod,	EMIGRE	Regime
	Triode	EMOTED	Demote
EDUCED	Deduce, Deuced	EMPIRE	E-prime
EDUCES	Deuces, Seduce	EMURED	Demure
*EDWARD	Drawed, Warded	EMURES	Resume
*EDWINA	Dewani, Wained	ENABLE	Baleen
EGERAN	Enrage, Genera	ENACTS	Ascent, Secant,
EGGLER	Legger		Stance
EGOIST	Stogie	ENCASE	Seance, Seneca
EGRESS	Serges	ENCASH	Canehs
EGRETS	Greets, Regest,	ENCINA	Canine
	Regets	ENDEAR	Earned, Neared
EIDERS	Desire, Reside	ENDERS	Denser, Resend,
EIGHTH	Height		Sender
ELANCE	Enlace	ENDEST	Nested, Sedent,
ELANDS	Ladens, Landes,		Tensed
	Sendal		

ENDING	Ginned	ENTAIL	Tenail
ENDIVE	Envied, Veined	ENTERA	Neater, Rateen,
ENDOWS	Snowed		Renate
ENDUED	Denude, Dudeen,	ENTERS	Ernest, Nester,
	Duende, Dundee		Rentes, Resent,
ENDUES	Ensued		Strene, Tenser,
ENDURE	Enured		Ternes
ENDURO	Undoer	ENTICE	Cetina
ENERGY	Greeny	ENTIRE	Nerite
ENERVE	Evener, Veneer	ENTOIL	Lionet
ENFIRE	Ferine, Fineer,	ENTRAP	Arpent, Enrapt,
	Refine		Panter, Parent,
ENFOLD	Fondle		Pterna, Trepan
ENGILD	Elding	ENTREE	Eterne, Retene
ENGIRD	Ringed	ENURED	Endure
ENGLUT	Gluten	ENURES	Ensure, Unsere
ENGOBE	Begone	ENVIED	Endive, Veined
ENGRAM	German, Manger,	ENWRAP	Pawner, Repawn
	Ragmen	EOSINS	Enosis, Essoin,
ENISLE	Ensile, Senile,		Noesis, Noises,
	Silene		Ossein, Seison,
ENLACE	Elance		Sonsie
ENLARD	Aldern, Darnel,	EOSTRE	Retose, Stereo
	Lander, Randle,	EPACTS	Aspect
	Reland	EPARCH	Preach
ENLIST	Inlets, Listen,	EPICAL	Plaice, Plicae
	Silent, Tinsel	EPOCHS	Cheops
ENODAL	Loaden	EPODES	Depose, Speedo
ENOSIS	Eosins, Essoin,	EPODIC	Copied
	Noesis, Noises,	*EPPING	Pig-pen
	Ossein, Seison,	E-PRIME	Empire
	Sonsie	EQUALS	Lasque, Quesal,
ENRACE	Careen, Recane		Squeal
ENRAGE	Egeran, Genera	ERASED	Reseda, Seared
ENRAIL	Linear, Nailer,	ERBIUM	Imbrue
	Renail	ERECTS	Certes, Resect,
ENRAPT	Arpent, Entrap,		Secret
	Panter, Parent,	ERINGO	Ignore, Region
	Pterna, Trepan	*ERNEST	Enters, Nester,
ENRICH	Nicher, Richen		Rentes, Resent,
*ENRICO	Coiner, Orcein,		Strene, Tenser,
	Orcine, Recoin		Ternes
ENSATE	Sateen, Senate	ERRAND	Darner, Redarn,
ENSEAM	Seamen		Renard
ENSEAR	Serena	ERRANT	Ranter
ENSILE	Enisle, Senile,	ERRING	Ringer
	Silene	*ERROLL	Reroll, Roller
ENSOUL	Nousle, Unsole	ERUCAS	Causer, Cerusa,
ENSUED	Endues		Saucer
ENSURE	Enures, Unsere	ERUCTS	Cruets, Cruset,

	Rectus,	Recuts,	
	Truces		
ERYNGO	Groyne		
ESCAPE	Peaces		
ESCARP	Capers,	Crapes,	
	Pacers,	Parsec,	
	Recaps,	Scrape,	
	Secpar,	Spacer	
ESCARS	Caress,	Carses,	
	Crases,	Scares,	
	Scraes,	Seracs	
ESCHAR	Arches,	Chares,	
	Chaser,	Raches,	
	Search		
ESCORT	Corset,	Cortes,	
	Coster,	Recost,	
	Rectos,	Scoter,	
	Sector		
ESCROW	Cowers		
ESLOIN	Eloins,	Insole,	
	Lesion,	Oleins,	
	Solein		
*ESMOND	Demons		
ESPIAL	Lipase,	Plaise	
ESPRIT	Priest,	Pteris,	
	Ripest,	Sitrep,	
	Sprite,	Stripe	
ESSOIN	Enosis,	Noesis,	
	Noises,	Ossein,	
	Seison,	Sonsie	
ESTATE	Eatest,	Teaset,	
	Testae		
ESTEEM	Mestee		
*ESTHER	Hester,	Threes	
ESTOPS	Posset,	Stoeps,	
	Stopes		
ESTRAY	Stayer,	Stayre	
ETAPES	Peseta		
ETERNE	Entree,	Retene	
ETHICS	Itches	.	
ETHYLS	Shelty		
ETRIER	Retire		
ETTLES	Settle		
ETYMON	Toymen		
EUNOMY	Euonym		
EUONYM	Eunomy		
EVADER	Reaved,	Veader	
EVANID	Invade		
*EVELYN	Evenly		

EVENER	Enerve,	Veneer	
EVENLY	Evelyn		
EVENTS	Steven		
EVERTS	Revest,	Revets,	
	Sterve,	Treves,	
	Verset,	Vester	
EVILLY	Lively,	Vilely	
EXCEPT	Expect		
EXERTS	Exsert		
EXILES	Ilexes		
Exists	Sexist		
EXPECT	Except		
EXSERT	Exerts		
EXTEND	Dentex		
FACIAS	Fascia		
FACILE	Fecial		
FACULA	Faucal		
FADETH	Hafted		
FAERIE	Feriae		
FAG-END	Defang,	Fanged	
FAILED	Afield		
FAKERY	Freaky		
FALCON	Flacon		
FAMINE	Infame		
FANGED	Defang,	Fag-end	
FANGLE	Flange		
FARDEL	Alfred,	Flared	
FARING	Grafin		
FARMED	Framed		
FARMER	Framer		
FASCIA	Facias		
FASTEN	Nefast		
FASTER	Afters,	Strafe	
FATHER	Freath		
FAUCAL	Facula		
FAULTS	Flatus		
FEALTY	Featly		
FEATED	Defeat		
FEATLY	Fealty		
FECIAL	Facile		
FEDORA	Afroed		
FEEDER	Refeed		
FEED-IN	Define		
FEELER	Refeel		
FEINTS	Finest,	Infest	
FELTER	Feltre,	Refelt,	
	Reflet,	Trefle	

FELTRE	Felter, Refelt, Reflet, Trefle	FLUENT	Netful, Unfelt, Unleft
FENDED	Defend	FLUXED	Deflux
FEODAL	Foaled, Loafed	FOALED	Feodal, Loafed
FERIAE	Faerie	FODDER	Forded
FERIAS	Fraise, Sea-fir	FOETAL	Folate
FERINE	Enfire, Fineer, Refine	FOETOR	Footer, Refoot, Tofore
FERULA	Earful	FOILER	Folier
FERULE	Fueler, Refuel	FOLATE	Foetal
FESTER	Freest, Freets	FOLDER	Refold
FETORS	Fortes, Forest, Foster, Softer	FOLIER	Foiler
		FONDER	Fronde
FETTER	Frette	FONDLE	Enfold
FIDGET	Gifted	FOOTER	Foetor, Refoot, Tofore
FILETS	Flites, Itself, Stifle		
		FORAYS	Forsay
FILLER	Refill	FORBYE	Fore-by
FILTER	Lifter, Trifle	FORCES	Fresco
FINDER	Friend, Redfin, Re-find	FORDED	Fodder
		FORE-BY	Forbye
FINEER	Enfire, Ferine, Refine	FOREDO	Roofed
		FOREST	Fetors, Fortes, Foster, Softer
FINEST	Feints, Infest		
FINGER	Fringe	FORMED	Deform
FINISH	Fish-in	FORMER	Reform
FINLET	Infelt	FORSAY	Forays
FIREST	Freits, Refits, Resift, Rifest, Sifter, Strife	FORTES	Fetors, Forest, Foster, Softer
		FORTHY	Frothy
FISCAL	Califs	FOSTER	Fetors, Forest, Fortes, Softer
FISHER	Sherif		
FISH-IN	Finish	FOULED	Defoul
FISTED	Sifted	FOUNTS	Unsoft
FLACON	Falcon	FOUTER	Foutre
FLANGE	Fangle	FOUTRE	Fouter
FLARED	Alfred, Fardel	FOWLER	Flower, Reflow, Wolfer
FLASHY	Ash-fly		
FLATUS	Faults	FRAISE	Ferias, Sea-fir
FLAUNT	Unflat	FRAMED	Farmed
FLAYED	Deafly	FRAMER	Farmer
FLECHE	Fleech	FRATER	Rafter
FLEECH	Fleche	FRAYED	Defray
FLESHY	Shelfy	FREAKY	Fakery
FLEXED	Deflex	FREATH	Father
FLITES	Filets, Itself, Stifle	FREEST	Fester, Freets,
		FREETS	Fester, Freest
FLORET	Lofter	FREITS	Firest, Refits, Resift, Rifest, Sifter, Strife
FLOWER	Fowler, Reflow, Wolfer		

FRESCO	Forces	
FRETTE	Fetter	
FRIEND	Finder,	Redfin,
	Refind	
FRINGE	Finger	
FRINGY	Frying	
FRONDE	Fonder	
FROTHY	Forthy	
FRYING	Fringy	
FUELER	Ferule,	Refuel
FULMAR	Armful	
FUTTER	Tufter	
GABION	Bagnio	
GADDER	Graded	
GADGES	Sagged	
GADGET	Tagged	
GADINE	Gained	
GAELIC	Cigale	
GAGERS	Sagger,	Seggar
GAINED	Gadine	
GAINER	Earing,	Graine,
	Retain,	Regain,
	Regina	
GAINLY	Laying	
GAINST	Giants,	Sating
GAITER	Aigret,	Triage
GALENA	Alnage,	Angela,
	Lagena	
GALING	Gingal,	Laggin
GALOON	Lagoon	
GALORE	Gaoler,	Regalo
GAMELY	Gleamy,	Mygale
GAMETE	Metage	
GAMING	Gigman	
GAMMER	Gramme	
GANDER	Danger,	Garden,
	Grande,	Ranged
GANGER	Grange,	Gregan,
	Nagger	
GANGLE	Laggen	
GAOLER	Galore,	Regalo
GAPERS	Gasper,	Grapes,
	Parges,	Sparge
GAPING	Paging	
GARBED	Badger,	Barged
GARDEN	Danger,	Gander,
	Grande,	Ranged

GARDON	Dragon	
GARGET	Tagger	
GARGLE	Gregal,	Lagger,
	Raggle	
GARIAL	Argali	
GARNER	Ranger	
GARNET	Argent,	Gerant,
	Gretna	
GAROUS	Rugosa	
GARRET	Garter,	Grater
GARTER	Garret,	Grater
GASCON	Congas	
GASKIN	Asking,	Kiangs
GASMEN	Manges,	Megans
GASPER	Gapers,	Grapes
	Parges,	Sparge
GATHER	Rageth	
GAUCHO	Guacho	
GEARED	Agreed,	Dragee
GEIGER	Greige,	Reggie
GENERA	Egeran,	Enrage
GENEVA	Avenge,	Vangee
GENIAL	Ealing,	Linage
GENIES	Seeing	
GENIUS	Sueing	
GENUAL	Lagune,	Langue
GERANT	Argent,	Garnet,
	Gretna	
GERENT	Regent	
GERMAN	Engram,	Manger,
	Ragmen	
GERMED	Merged	
GERMON	Monger,	Morgen
*GERONA	Onager,	Orange
GERUND	Nudger	
GERVAS	Graves	
GHEBER	Ghebre	
GHEBRE	Gheber	
GHOULS	Loughs,	Slough
GIANTS	Gainst,	Sating
GIBING	Biggin	
GIFTED	Fidget	
GIGMAN	Gaming	
GILDED	Glided	
GILDER	Girdle,	Glider,
	Regild,	Ridgel
GILPIN	Piling	
GIMMER	Megrim	
GINETE	Teeing	

GINGAL	Galing, Laggin		GRADIN	Daring	
GINGER	Nigger		GRADUS	Guards	
GINGKO	Ginkgo		GRAFIN	Faring	
GINKGO	Gingko		*GRAHAM	Armagh	
GINNED	Ending		GRAINE	Earing, Gainer,	
GIRDED	Ridged			Regain, Regian,	
GIRDER	Regird			Regina	
GIRDLE	Gilder, Glider,		GRAINS	Rasing, Sangir	
	Regild, Ridgel		GRAINY	Raying	
GIRNEL	Linger		GRAITH	Aright	
GIRONS	Grison, Groins,		GRAMME	Gammer	
	Rosing, Signor		*GRANDE	Danger, Gander,	
*GIRVAN	Raving			Garden, Gnared,	
GISTED	Digest			Ranged	
GLEAMY	Gamely, Mygale		GRANGE	Ganger, Gregan,	
GLEDES	Gleeds, Ledges,			Nagger	
	Sledge		GRAPES	Gapers, Gasper,	
GLEEDS	Gledes, Ledges,			Parges, Sparge	
	Sledge		GRATER	Garter, Garret	
GLIDED	Gilded		GRATES	Greats, Ragest,	
GLIDER	Gilder, Girdle,			Stager, Targes	
	Regild, Ridgel		GRATIN	Rating, Taring,	
GLOBIN	Goblin			Tringa	
GLOVER	Grovel		GRATIS	Strige	
GLOWER	Reglow		GRAVES	Gervas	
GLUING	Luging		GREASE	Agrees, Eagres	
GLUTEN	Englut		GREASY	Yagers	
GLUTIN	Luting, Ungilt		GREATS	Grates, Ragest,	
GNEISS	Singes			Stager, Targes	
GNOMIC	Coming		GREAVE	Regave	
GOBLET	Boglet		GREENY	Energy	
GOBLIN	Globin		GREETS	Egrets, Regest,	
GOGLET	Logget, Toggle			Regets	
GOIDEL	Goldie		GREEVE	Verges	
GOITER	Goitre		GREGAL	Gargle, Lagger,	
GOITRE	Goiter			Raggle	
GOLDEN	Longed		*GREGAN	Ganger, Grange,	
*GOLDIE	Goidel			Nagger	
*GONVIL	Loving		GREIGE	Geiger, Reggie	
GORGED	Dogger		*GRETNA	Argent, Garnet,	
GORING	Gringo			Gerant	
GORSES	Ogress		GREVES	Verges	
GO-STOP	Stop-go		GRIEVE	Regive	
GOURDE	Drogue, Drouge,		GRINGO	Goring	
	Rogued, Rouged		GRIPER	Regrip	
GRABEN	Banger		GRISON	Girons, Groins,	
GRACED	Cadger			Rosing, Signor	
GRADED	Gadder		GROANS	Angors, Argons,	
GRADER	Darger, Regard			Nagors, Orangs,	
				Organs, Sarong	

GROINS	Girons, Grison, Rosing, Signor
GROOVE	Overgo
GROPER	Porger
GROUSE	Orgues, Rogues, Rouges, Rugose
GROVEL	Glover
GROWER	Regrow
GROYNE	Eryngo
GRUDGE	Rugged
GRUNTS	Strung
GUACHO	Gaucho
GUARDS	Gradus
GUEBER	Burgee, Guebre
GUEBRE	Burgee, Gueber
GUESTS	Gusset
*GUIANA	Iguana
GUILER	Ligure, Reguli, Uglier
GUISER	Regius
GULDEN	Lunged
GUNTER	Gurnet, Urgent
GURGLE	Lugger
GURNET	Gunter, Urgent
GUSSET	Guests
GUSTED	Degust
HACKLY	Chalky
HADJIS	Jadish, Jihads
HAERES	Hearse
HAFTED	Fadeth
HAGDEN	Hanged
HALLOO	Holloa
HALSED	Lashed
HALSER	Ashler
HALSES	Hassle, Lashes, Selahs, Shales, Sheals
HALTER	Lather, Thaler
HAMLET	Thelma
HANDER	Harden
HANGED	Hagden
HANGER	Rehang
HANG-UP	Uphang
HANKER	Harken
HANTLE	Lathen, Thenal
HARDEN	Hander
HARD-UP	Purdah

HARELD	Harled, Herald
HARKEN	Hanker
HARLED	Hareld, Herald
HARLOT	Thoral
HARMED	Derham
*HARRIS	Sirrah
HASHER	Rehash
HASLET	Lathes, Shelta
HASPED	Phased, Shaped
HASSLE	Halses, Lashes, Selahs, Shales, Sheals
HASTED	Deaths, 'Sdeath
HASTEN	Athens, Snathe, Thanes
HATERS	Earths, Hearts, Rathes, Sarthe
HATRED	Dareth, Dearth, Red-hat, Thread
HATTER	Threat
HAULER	Rehaul
HAUNTS	Sunhat, Unhats
HAVENS	Hesvan, Shaven
HAVERS	Shaver
HAWSER	Rewash, Washer
HEADER	Adhere, Hedera, Rehead
HEALER	Reheal
HEARER	Rehear
HEARSE	Haeres
HEARTS	Earths, Haters, Rathes, Sarthe
HEARTY	Earthy
HEATER	Hereat, Reheat
HEATHS	Sheath
HEAVES	Sheave
*HEBRON	Brehon
HECTOR	Rochet, Rotche, Tocher, Troche
HEDERA	Adhere, Header, Rehead
HEELER	Reheel
HEIGHT	Eighth
HEISTS	Shiest, Thesis
HELOTS	Hostel, Hotels, Tholes
HELVES	Shelve
HEMINS	Inmesh
HEPARS	Phares, Phrase,

	Raphes, Seraph,		Horsed, Reshod,
	Shaper, Sherpa		Rhodes, Shoder,
HERALD	Hareld, Harled		Shored
HERDIC	Chider, Dreich	HORNED	Dehorn
HEREAT	Heater, Reheat	HORNET	Thorne, Throne
HEREIN	Inhere	HORSED	Dehors, Herods,
HEREON	Rehone		Hordes, Reshod,
*HERMAN	Arnhem		Rhodes, Shoder,
*HERODS	Dehors, Hordes,		Shored
	Horsed, Reshod,	HOSTEL	Helots, Hotels,
	Rhodes, Shoder,		Tholes
	Shored	HOTELS	Helots, Hostel,
HEROIC	Cheiro, Coheir		Tholes
HERONS	Senhor	HOTTER	T'other
HERPES	Hesper, Pheers,	HOUGHS	Shough
	Sphere	HOUNDS	Unshod
HESPER	Herpes, Pheers,	HOUSES	Shouse
	Sphere	HOVELS	Shovel
*HESTER	Esther, Threes	HOVERS	Shover, Shrove
HESVAN	Havens, Shaven	HOWLET	Thowel
HETMAN	Anthem	HOWRES	Reshow, Shower,
HEUCHS	Sheuch		Whores
HEUGHS	Sheugh	HUMINE	Inhume
HEWERS	Reshew, Wheres	HUNGER	Rehung
HEWING	Whinge	HURDLE	Hurled
HIKERS	Shriek, Shrike	HURLED	Hurdle
HILUMS	Mulish	HUSTLE	Sleuth
HINDIS	Sindhi	HYPERS	Sphery, Sypher
HINGES	Neighs, Senghi		
HIRSEL	Hirsle, Relish		
HIRSLE	Hirsel, Relish	*IBLEES	Belies
HISSED	Dishes	ICECAP	Ipecac
HISSER	Shiers, Shires	ICEMAN	Anemic, Cinema
HITMAN	Mithan	ICHORS	Choirs, Orchis
HITTER	Tither	ICICLE	Cilice
HIVERS	Shiver, Shrive	ICIEST	Cities
HOARSE	Ashore, Shorea	ICKERS	Sicker
HOCKED	Choked	IDEALS	Aisled, Deasil,
HOCKER	Choker		Ladies, Sailed
HOCKEY	Chokey	IDIOMS	Iodism
HOGNUT	Nought	IDLERS	Sidler, Slider
HOIDEN	Honied	IDOLUM	Dolium
HOLD-UP	Uphold	IGNARO	Oaring, Origan
HOLLOA	Halloo	IGNITE	Tieing
HOLPEN	Phenol	IGNORE	Eringo, Region
HOMAGE	Ohmage	IGUANA	Guiana
HONERS	Nosher, Rhones	ILEXES	Exiles
HONIED	Hoiden	IMAGER	Maigre, Mirage
HORDES	Dehors, Herods,	IMAGES	Ageism

IMBRUE	Erbium	INMESH	Hemins
*IMELDA	Mailed, Medial	INMOST	Monist
IMMANE	Ammine	INNERS	Sinner
IMPART	Armpit, Partim	INORBS	Robins, Sorbin
IMPELS	Simple	INROAD	Dorian, Ordain
IMPOST	Impots	INSANE	Annies, Sienna
IMPOTS	Impost	INSECT	Incest, Nicest
IMPURE	Umpire	INSERT	Inters, Nitres,
INBRED	Binder, Brined,		Retins, Sinter,
	Rebind		Strine, Trines
INCASE	Casein	INSIDE	Indies
INCAST	Antics, Nastic	INSIST	Sit-ins
INCEPT	Pectin	INSOLE	Eloins, Esloin,
INCEST	Insect, Nicest		Lesion, Oleins,
INCHED	Chined, Niched		Solsin
INCHES	Chines, Chinse,	INSPAN	Pinnas
	Niches	INSTAL	Latins, Stalin
INDEED	Denied	INSTAR	Santir, Strain,
INDENT	Dentin, Intend,		Trains
	Tinned	INSTEP	Spinet, Step-in
*INDIES	Inside	INSTOP	Piston, Pitons,
INDIGN	Dining, Niding		Points, Potins,
INDITE	Tineid		Spin-to
INDUCE	Uniced	INSULT	Sunlit
INFAME	Famine	INSURE	Inures, Rusine,
INFELT	Finlet		Urines, Ursine
INFEST	Feints, Finest	INTAKE	Kinate, Take-in
INGATE	Eating, Tangie,	INTEND	Dentin, Indent,
	Teaing		Tinned
INGEST	Signet, Stinge,	INTERN	Tinner
	Tinges	INTERS	Insert, Nitres,
INGLED	Dingle		Retins, Sinter,
INGLES	Single		Strine, Trines
*INGMAR	Arming, Ingram,	INTOED	Ditone
	Margin	INTORT	Triton
INGOTS	Stingo, Tigons	INTUSE	Tenuis, Unites,
INGRAM	Arming, Ingmar,		Unties
	Margin	INURED	Ruined
*INGRID	Riding	INURES	Insure, Rusine,
INHERE	Herein		Urines, Ursine
INHUME	Humine	INVADE	Evanid
INK-BAG	Baking	INVERT	Virent
INKERS	Kirsen, Reinks,	INWARD	Darwin
	Sinker	INWITH	Within
INKLES	Likens, Silken	IODISM	Idioms
INLETS	Enlist, Listen,	IODOUS	Odious
	Silent, Tinsel	IPECAC	Icecap
INLOCK	Lock-in	IRADES	Aiders, Raised
INMATE	Tamine	IRONER	Renoir

ISLETS	Istles, Sliest, Stiles	
ISOMER	Moires, Rimose	
*ISRAEL	Ariels, Relais, Resail, Sailer, Serail, Serial	
ISSUED	Disuse	
ISTLES	Islets, Sliest, Stiles	
ITCHES	Ethics	
ITSELF	Filets, Flites, Stifle	
JADISH	Hadjis, Jihads	
JAILER	Rejail	
JAPERS	Jasper	
JASPER	Japers	
JERKIN	Jinker	
JIHADS	Hadjis, Jadish	
JINKER	Jerkin	
JOINER	Rejoin	
JOLTER	Rejolt	
JUDAIC	Judica	
JUDICA	Judaic	
KALMIA	Kamila	
KAMILA	Kalmia	
KASHER	Shaker	
KAVASS	Vakass	
KELPIE	Pelike	
KELSON	Sloken	
KELTIC	Tickle	
KEUPER	Peruke	
KIANGS	Asking, Gaskin	
KIDDER	Dirked	
KIDNEY	Dinkey	
KILTER	Kirtle	
KINATE	Intake, Take-in	
KINDLE	Linked	
KIRSCH	Chirks, Schrik	
KIRSEN	Inkers, Reinks, Sinker	
KIRTLE	Kilter	
KISSER	Skiers	
KRAITS	Straik, Traiks	
KREESE	Reseek, Seeker	

LAAGER	Alegar	
LABILE	Alible, Belial, Liable	
LABRET	Albert, Tabler	
LABRUM	Brumal, Lumbar, Umbral	
LACHES	Chelas, Sachel	
LACKER	Calker, Rackle, Recalk	
LADDER	Larded, Raddle	
LADDIE	Dialed	
LADENS	Elands, Landes, Sendal	
LADIES	Aisled, Deasil, Ideals, Sailed	
LAGENA	Alnage, Angela, Galena	
LAGEND	Angled, Dangle	
LAGGED	Daggle	
LAGGEN	Gangle	
LAGGER	Gargle, Gregal, Raggle	
LAGGIN	Galing, Gingal	
LAGOON	Galoon	
LAGUNE	Genual, Langue	
LAMBED	Ambled, Balmed, Bedlam, Beldam, Blamed	
LAMBER	Ambler, Blamer, Marble, Ramble	
LAMELY	Mellay	
LAMENT	Mantel, Mantle, Mental	
LAMIAS	Salami	
LAMINA	Almain, Animal, Manila	
LAMING	Lingam, Malign	
LAMMER	Rammel	
LAMPAS	Palmas, Plasma	
LAMPED	Palmed	
LANCED	Candle	
LANCES	Ancles, Cleans, Lencas, Senlac	
LANCET	Cantle, Cental	
LANDED	Dandle	
LANDER	Aldern, Darnel, Enlard, Randle, Reland	
*LANDES	Elands, Ladens, Sendal	

LANGET	Tangle		Serval, Slaver,
LANGUE	Genual, Lagune		Valser, Velors,
LANUGO	Lugano		Versal
LAPINS	Plains, Spinal	LAVING	Valing
LAPPED	Dapple, Palped	LAWING	Waling
LAPPER	Rappel	LAYERS	Rayles, Relays,
LAPSED	Padles, Pedals,		Slayer
	Pleads	LAYING	Gainly
LARDED	Ladder, Raddle	LAYMEN	Meanly, Namely
LARGEN	Angler, Rangle,	LAY-OUT	Outlay
	Regnal	LEADED	Delead
LARIAT	Atrial, Latria	LEADEN	Aneled, Leaned
LARVAL	Vallar	LEADER	Dealer, Redeal,
LASCAR	Rascal, Sacral,		Relead
	Sarlec, Scaler	LEAD-IN	Aldine, Alined,
LASHED	Halsed		Daniel, Delian,
LASHES	Halses, Hassle,		Denial, Nailed
	Selahs, Shales,	LEALTY	Lately
	Sheals	LEANED	Aneled, Leaden
LASQUE	Equals, Quesal,	LEAN-TO	Tolane
	Squeal	LEAPED	Pealed, Pedale
LASSIE	Aisles	LEAPER	Pealer, Repeal
LASTED	Deltas, Salted,	LEARES	Leaser, Resale,
	Slated, Stadle,		Reseal, Sealer
	Staled	LEARNT	Altern, Antler,
LASTER	Alerts, Alters,		Rental, Ternal
	Artels, Ratels,	LEASED	Sealed
	Resalt, Salter,	LEASER	Leares, Resale,
	Slater, Staler,		Reseal, Sealer
	Tarsel	LEASES	Easels, Easles,
LASTLY	Saltly		Eassel
LATEEN	Elanet	LEAVER	Laveer, Reveal,
LATELY	Lealty		Vealer
LATENT	Latten, Talent	LEAVES	Sleave
LATHEN	Hantle, Thenal	LECTOR	Colter
LATHER	Halter, Thaler	LEDGER	Red-leg
LATHES	Haslet, Shelta	LEDGES	Gledes, Gleeds,
LATIAN	Talian		Sledge
LATINS	Instal, Stalin	LEERED	Reeled
LATRIA	Atrial, Lariat	LEESES	Lessee
LATTEN	Latent, Talent	LEGATE	Eaglet, Teagle,
LATTER	Rattle, Tatler		Telega
LAUNCE	Cuneal, Unlace	LEGGER	Eggler
LAUNCH	Nuchal	LEGION	Eloign
LAUREL	Allure	LEMANS	Anselm, Mensal
LAURIC	Uracil	*LEMNOS	Lemons, Melons,
LAVEER	Leaver, Reveal,		Solemn
	Vealer	LEMONS	Lemnos, Melons,
LAVERS	Ravels, Salver,		Solemn

LENCAS	Ancles, Cleans,	LIMPSY	Simply
	Lances, Senlac	LINAGE	Ealing, Genial
LENDER	Relend	LINDEN	Dinnle
LENSES	Lessen	LINEAR	Enrail, Nailer,
LENTIL	Lintal		Renail
*LEPCHA	Chapel, Pleach	LINERS	Nirles
LEPTUS	Let-ups	LINE-UP	Lupine, Unpile,
LESION	Eloins, Esloin,		Up-line
	Insole, Oleins,	LINGAM	Laming, Malign
	Solein	LINGAS	Aligns, Liangs,
LESSEE	Leeses		Ligans, Signal
LESSEN	Lenses	LINGER	Girnel
LESSOR	Losers, Sorels	LINGUA	Nilgau
LET-A-BE	Belate	LINING	Lignin
LET-OUT	Outlet	LINKED	Kindle
LET-UPS	Leptus	LINTEL	Lentil
LEVEES	Sleeve	LIONEL	Niello
LEVIED	Veiled	LIONET	Entoil
LEVIER	Relive, Revile	LIPASE	Espial, Plaise
LEVINS	Livens, Snivel	LIPOMA	Pimola
LEVITE	Velite	LIPPEN	Nipple
LEYDEN	Needly	LIPPER	Ripple
LIABLE	Alible, Belial,	LISPED	Dispel, Disple,
	Labile		Sliped, Spiled
LIANAS	Salian, Salina	LISPER	Perils, Perlis,
LIANGS	Aligns, Ligans,		Pilers, Pliers
	Lingas, Signal	LISTED	Delist, Silted,
LICKER	Rickle		Tildes
LIDDED	Diddle	LISTEN	Enlist, Inlets,
LIEDER	Relide, Relied		Silent, Tinsel
LIERNE	Reline	LISTER	Litres, Relist,
LIFTER	Filter, Trifle		Tilers
LIGANS	Aligns, Ganils,	LITCHI	Lithic
	Liangs, Lingas,	LITHIC	Litchi
	Signal	LITMUS	Tilmus
LIGATE	Aiglet, Taigle	LITRES	Lister, Relist,
LIGGER	Riggle		Tilers
LIGHTS	Slight	LITTER	Tilter, Titler
LIGNIN	Lining	LIVELY	Evilly, Vilely
LIGURE	Guiler, Reguli,	LIVENS	Levins, Snivel
	Uglier	LIVERS	Livres, Silver,
LIKENS	Inkles, Silken		Sliver
LILACS	Scilla	LIVERY	Verily
LILTED	Tilled	LIVEST	Vilest
LIMENS	Meslin, Simnel	LIVRES	Livers, Silver,
LIMNER	Merlin		Sliver
LIMPED	Dimple	LOADEN	Enodal
LIMPER	Prelim, Rempli,	LOADER	Ordeal, Reload
	Rimple	LOAFED	Feodal, Foaled

LOANER	Reloan	
LOBATE	Boatel,	Oblate
LOCKER	Relock,	Rockel
LOCK-IN	Inlock	
LOCK-UP	Uplock	
LOCUST	Clouts	
LOFTER	Floret	
LOGANS	Slogan	
LOGGED	Dogleg	
LOGGER	Roggle	
LOGGET	Goglet,	Toggle
LOITER	Toiler,	Triole
LOMENT	Melton,	Molten
LONGED	Golden	
LOOKER	Rookle	
LOOPED	Poodle,	Pooled
LOOPER	Pooler	
LOOSED	Dolose,	Oodles
LOOTED	Toledo,	Tooled
LOOTER	Rootle,	Tooler
LOPING	Poling	
LOPPER	Propel	
LORCHA	Choral,	Orchal
LORDLY	Drolly	
LOSERS	Lessor,	Sorels
LOSING	Soling	
LOSSES	Sossle	
LOUDEN	Nodule	
LOUDER	Loured	
LOUGHS	Ghouls,	Slough
LOURED	Louder	
LOUSED	Souled	
LOUVAR	Ovular,	Valour
LOUVER	Louvre,	Velour
LOUVRE	Louver,	Velour
LOVELY	Volley	
LOVERS	Solver	
LOVING	Gonvil	
LOWERS	Owlers,	Rowels,
	Slower	
LOWERY	Owlery	
LOWEST	Owlets,	Towels
LOWING	Owling	
LOWISH	Owlish	
*LOXIAS	Oxalis	
LUBBER	Burble,	Rubble
LUFFED	Duffel,	Duffle
LUFFER	Ruffle	
*LUGANO	Lanugo	

LUGGER	Gurgle	
LUGING	Gluing	
LUMBAR	Brumal,	Labrum,
	Umbral	
LUMBER	Rumble	
LUMINA	Alumni	
LUMPED	Dumple,	Plumed
LUMPER	Replum,	Rumple
LUNATE	Eluant	
LUNGED	Gulden	
LUPINE	Line-up,	Unpile,
	Up-line	
LUREST	Luster,	Lustre,
	Result,	Rulest,
	Rustle,	Sutler,
	Ulster	
LURING	Ruling	
LUSIAD	Dulias	
LUSTER	Lurest,	Lustre,
	Result,	Rulest,
	Rustle,	Sutler,
	Ulster	
LUSTRE	Lurest,	Luster,
	Result,	Rulest,
	Rustle,	Sutler,
	Ulster	
LUTEIN	Lutine,	Untile
LUTINE	Lutein,	Untile
LUTING	Glutin,	Ungilt
LYINGS	Singly	
LYRATE	Elytra,	Raylet,
	Realty,	Telary
MACERS	Crames,	Creams,
	Scream	
MACIES	Amices,	Camise
MACLED	Calmed	
MACLES	Camels,	Mascle,
	Mescal,	Scamel
MACULE	Almuce	
MADDEN	Damned,	Demand
MADRAS	Dramas	
MAENAD	Anadem	
*MAGYAR	Margay	
MAHSIR	Marish	
MAIDEN	Daimen,	Demain,
	Mained,	Median,
	Medina	

MAIGRE	Imager, Mirage		MARIDS	Disarm
MAILED	Imelda, Medial		MARINA	Airman, Marian
MAILER	Remail		MARINE	Airmen, Remain
MAIMER	Remaim		MARISH	Mahsir
MAINED	Daimen, Demain,		MARKED	Demark
	Maiden, Median,		MARKER	Remark
	Medina		MARLED	Dermal, Medlar
MAKERS	Masker		MAROON	Ramoon
MALATE	Tamale		MARTEL	Armlet
MALEIC	Malice		MARTEN	Rament
MALICE	Maleic		MARTIN	Antrim
MALIGN	Laming, Lingam		MASCLE	Camels, Macles,
MALTOS	Almost, Smalto			Mescal, Scamel
MANEGE	Menage		MASCOT	Comsat, Satcom
MANETS	Aments, Stamen		MASHED	Shamed
MANGEL	Mangle		MASKER	Makers
MANGER	Engram, German,		MASONS	Samson
	Ragmen		MASORA	Aromas
MANGES	Gasmen, Megans		MASTER	Armest, Armets,
MANGLE	Mangel			Maters, Remast,
MANIAC	Caiman			Stream, Tamers,
MANIAS	Samian			Tremas
MANILA	Almain, Animal,		MATERS	Armest, Armets,
	Lamina			Master, Remast,
MANIOC	Camion			Stream, Tamers,
MANNED	Mennad			Tremas
MANORS	Normas, Ramson,		MATIES	Samite, Semita,
	Ransom, Romans			Tamise
MANRED	Randem, Redman,		MATING	Taming
	Remand		MATINS	Mantis, Stamin,
MANSES	Messan			Tamins
MANTEL	Lament, Mantle,		MAUGER	Maugre, Murage
	Mental		MAUGRE	Mauger, Murage
MANTIS	Matins, Stamin,		MAULER	Ramule
	Tamins		MEAGER	Meagre
MANTLE	Lament, Mantel,		MEAGRE	Meager
	Mental		MEANER	Rename
MANTUA	Tamanu		MEANLY	Laymen, Namely
MANURE	Menura		MEASES	Seames, Sesame
*MAOIST	Taoism		MEASLY	Samely
MAPLES	Pelmas, Sample		MEDALS	Damsel
MAPPER	Pamper		MEDDLE	Melded
MARACA	Camara		MEDIAL	Imelda, Mailed
MARBLE	Ambler, Blamer,		MEDIAN	Daimen, Demain,
	Lamber, Ramble			Maiden, Mained,
MARCEL	Calmer			Medina
MARGAY	Magyar		*MEDINA	Daimen, Demain,
MARGIN	Arming, Ingmar,			Maiden, Mained,
	Ingram			Median
*MARIAN	Airman, Marina		MEDLAR	Dermal, Marled

MEDUSA	Amused, Sea-mud		MILTER	Rimlet
MEETER	E-meter		MIMERS	Simmer
*MEGANS	Gasmen, Manges		MINDED	Midden
MEGERG	Megger		MINDER	Remind
MEGGER	Megerg		MINTER	Remint
MEGRIM	Gimmer		MINUET	Minute, Munite
MEITHS	Theism, Themis		MINUTE	Minuet, Munite
MELDED	Meddle		MIRAGE	Imager, Maigre
MELEES	Semele		MIRING	Riming
MELLAY	Lamely		MISCUE	Cesium
MELONS	Lemnos, Lemons,		MISERE	Remise
	Solemn		MISERS	Remiss
MELTER	Remelt		MISHAP	Pashim
MELTON	Loment, Molten		MISLED	Slimed, Smiled
MENAGE	Manege		MISSAL	Salmis
MENDER	Remend		MISSED	Demiss
MENNAD	Manned		MISSEE	Emesis
MENSAL	Anselm, Lemans		MISSEL	Slimes, Smiles
MENTAL	Lament, Mantel,		MIS-SET	Smites, Stimes,
	Mantle			Tmesis
MENTOR	Montre		MISTER	Merits, Miters,
MENURA	Manure			Mitres, Remits,
MERGED	Germed			Smiter, Timers
MERGEE	Emerge		MISTLE	Smilet
MERITS	Mister, Miters,		MITHAN	Hitman
	Mitres, Remits,		MITERS	Merits, Mister,
	Smiter, Timers			Mitres, Remits,
MERLIN	Limner			Smiter, Timers
*MEROPS	Mopers, Proems		MITRAL	Ramtil
MESAIL	Mesial, Samiel		MITRES	Merits, Mister,
MESCAL	Camels, Macles,			Miters, Remits,
	Mascle, Scamel			Smiter, Timers
MESIAL	Mesail, Samiel		MOANED	Daemon, Modena,
MESLIN	Limens, Simnel			Nomade
MESSAN	Manses		MOANER	Monera
MESTEE	Esteem		MOBBED	Bombed
METAGE	Gamete		MOBILE	Bemoil, Emboil
METALS	Samlet		MODELS	Seldom
METEOR	Remote		MODENA	Daemon, Moaned,
METERS	Metres, Restem,			Nomade
	Termes		MODERN	Morned, Nemrod,
METIER	Re-emit, Retime			Normed
METRES	Meters, Restem,		MODIFY	Domify
	Termes		MOIRES	Isomer, Rimose
MICHED	Chimed		MOLARS	Morals, Morsal
MICHER	Chimer		MOLDER	Remold
MIDDEN	Minded		MOLEST	Motels
MILADY	Diamyl		MOLINE	Oilmen
MILERS	Smiler		MOLLAH	Ollamh
MILLER	Remill		MOLTEN	Loment, Melton

MOMENT	Montem		NAGGER	Ganger, Grange,
MONADS	Damson, Nomads			Gregan
MONDAY	Dynamo		NAGORS	Angors, Argons,
MONERA	Moaner			Groans, Orangs,
MONGER	Germon, Morgen			Organs, Sarong
MONIAL	Almoin, Oilman		NAILED	Aldine, Alined,
MONIED	Domine			Daniel, Delian,
MONISM	Nomism			Denial, Lead-in
MONIST	Inmost		NAILER	Enrail, Linear,
MONTEM	Moment			Renail
*MONTES	Ostmen		NAMELY	Laymen, Meanly
MONTRE	Mentor		*NAPLES	Panels, Planes
MOONER	Morone		NAPPED	Append
MOORED	Roomed		NAPPER	Rappen
MOPERS	Merops, Proems		NASARD	Sandra
MORALS	Molars, Morsal		NASION	Anions
MORATS	Stroam, Stroma		*NASSER	Sarsen, Snares
MORELS	Morsel		NASTIC	Antics, Incast
MORGEN	Germon, Monger		NASUTE	Austen, Unseat
MORNED	Modern, Nemrod,		NATION	Anoint
	Normed		NATTER	Ratten
MORNES	Sermon		NATURE	Tea-urn
MORONE	Mooner		NEARBY	Barney
MORSAL	Molars, Morals		NEARED	Earned, Endear
MORSEL	Morels		NEARER	Earner, Re-earn
MOTELS	Molest		NEATER	Entera, Rateen,
MOTHED	Demoth			Renate
MOT-MOT	Tomtom		NEBRIS	Brines
MOUNDS	Osmund		NEBULA	Unable, Unbale
MOUSED	Dumose		NECTAR	Canter, Carnet,
MOUSES	Mousse, Smouse			Centra, Creant,
MOUSSE	Mouses, Smouse			Recant, Tanrec,
MULISH	Hilums			Trance
MUNITE	Minuet, Minute		NEEDER	Reeden
MURAGE	Mauger, Maugre		NEEDLY	Leyden
MURINE	Nerium		NEFAST	Fasten
MUSCAT	Mustac		NEIGHS	Hinges, Senghi
MUSHER	Rheums		NELIES	Nelsie
MUSLIN	Unslim		*NELSIE	Nelies
MUSMON	Summon		*NEMROD	Modern, Morned,
MUSTAC	Muscat			Normed
MUSTER	Stumer		*NEPALI	Plaint, Pliant
MUTUAL	Umlaut		NEPMAN	Penman
MUTISM	Summit		NEPMEN	Penmen
MYGALE	Gamely, Gleamy		NEREID	Denier, Edirne,
MYOSIN	Simony			Reined
MYOTIC	Comity		NEREIS	Seiner, Serein,
MYRTLE	Termly			Serine
MYTHIC	Thymic		NERITE	Entire
MYTHUS	Thymus			

NERIUM	Murine
NERVAL	Vernal
NERVED	Revend, Vender
NERVES	Nevers, Severn
NESTED	Endest, Sedent, Tensed
NESTER	Enters, Ernest, Rentes, Resent, Strene, Tenser, Ternes
*NESTON	Nonets, Sonnet, Tenons, Tenson, Tonnes
NESTOR	Noters, Stoner, Strone, Tenors, Tensor, Toners, Trones
NETFUL	Fluent, Unfelt, Unleft
NETHER	Threne
NETTED	Detent, Tented
NETTER	Retent, Tenter
NEURAL	Ulnare, Unreal
NEUTER	Retune, Tenure, Tureen
*NEVERS	Nerves, Severn
NICEST	Incest, Insect
NICHED	Chined, Inched
NICHER	Enrich, Richen
NICHES	Chines, Chinse, Inches
NIDDER	Ridden, Rinded
NIDGES	Deigns, Design, Dinges, Sdeign, Signed, Singed
NIDGET	Tinged
NIDING	Dining, Indign
NIDOSE	Diones, Donsie, Noised, No-side, Onside, Side-on
NIELLO	Lionel
NIGGER	Ginger
NILGAI	Ailing
NILGAU	Lingua
NIPPLE	Lippen
NIRLES	Liners
NITRES	Insert, Inters, Retins, Sinter, Strine, Trines

NITRIC	Citrin
NITTER	Retint, Tinter
NIVOSE	Vinose
NOBBUT	Button
NOCTUA	Toucan, Uncoat
NODDER	Droned
NODOSE	Noosed
NODULE	Louden
NOESIS	Enosis, Eosins, Essoin, Noises, Ossein, Seison, Sonsie
NOETIC	Notice
NOISED	Diones, Donsie, Nidose, No-side, Onside, Side-on
NOISES	Enosis, Eosins, Essoin, Noesis, Ossein, Seison, Sonsie
NOMADE	Daemon, Moaned, Modena
NOMADS	Damson, Monads
NOMISM	Monism
NONETS	Neston, Sonnet, Tenons, Tenson, Tonnes
NONIUS	Unions, Unison
NOOSED	Nodose
*NORMAS	Manors, Ramson, Ransom, Romans
NORMED	Modern, Morned, Nemrod
NOSERS	Senors, Sensor, Snores
NOSHER	Honers, Rhones
NO-SIDE	Diones, Donsie, Nidose, Noised, Onside, Side-on
NOSTOC	Contos, Oncost
NOTARY	Aroynt
NOTERS	Nestor, Stoner, Strone, Tenors, Tensor, Toners, Trones
NOTICE	Noetic
NOTING	Toning
NOTOUR	Unroot
NOUGHT	Hognut

NOUSLE	Ensoul, Unsole	
NOVELS	Sloven	
NUBIAS	Unbias	
NUBILE	Unible	
NUCHAL	Launch	
NUDGED	Dunged	
NUDGER	Gerund	
NUDGES	Snudge	
NUDITY	Untidy	
NUNCIO	Uncoin	
NURSED	Sunder, Unders,	
	Unreds	
NURSER	Runers	
NUTATE	Attune, Tauten	
NUTRIA	Taurin	
OAKERS	Resoak, Soaker	
OARING	Ignaro, Origan	
OBELUS	Blouse, Boules	
OBERON	Borneo	
OBLATE	Boatel, Lobate	
OBSESS	Bosses	
OCCURS	Crocus, Roccus,	
	Succor	
OCELLI	Collie	
OCHREA	Chorea, Orache,	
	Rochea	
OCHRES	Chores, Cosher	
OCTANS	Cantos, Cotans,	
	Snacot	
OCTAVE	Avocet	
ODIUMS	Sodium	
ODIOUS	Iodous	
OFF-CUT	Cut-off	
OFFPUT	Put-off	
OFFSET	Set-off	
OGRESS	Gorses	
OHMAGE	Homage	
OILERS	Elisor, Oriels,	
	Reoils, Soiler	
OILMAN	Almoin, Monial	
OILMEN	Moline	
OLEINS	Eloins, Esloin,	
	Insole, Lesion,	
	Solein	
OLIVES	Solive, Voiles	
OLIVET	Violet	
OLIVIN	Violin	

OLLAMH	Mollah	
OMBERS	Bromes, Ombres,	
	Somber, Sombre	
OMBRES	Bromes, Ombers,	
	Somber, Sombre	
OMBROS	Brooms	
ONAGER	Gerona, Orange	
ONCERS	Censor, Crones,	
	Recons	
ONCOME	Come-on	
ONCOST	Contos, Nostoc	
ONEYER	Oneyre	
ONEYRE	Oneyer	
ON-SIDE	Diones, Donsie,	
	Nidose, Noised,	
	No-side, Side-on	
OOCYTE	Coyote	
OODLES	Dolose, Loosed	
OPENED	Depone	
OPENER	Reopen	
OPINED	Pioned	
OPINES	Ponies	
OPPUGN	Popgun	
OPSTER	Poster, Presto,	
	Repost, Repots,	
	Retops, Stoper,	
	Topers, Tropes	
OPTICS	Picots, Topics	
OPTING	Toping	
OPTION	Potion	
ORACHE	Chores, Ochrea,	
	Rochea	
ORACLE	Coaler, Recoal	
ORANGE	Gerona, Onager	
ORANGS	Angors, Argons,	
	Groans, Nagors,	
	Organs, Sarong	
ORBATE	Boater, Borate,	
	Rebato	
ORBING	Boring, Robing	
ORCEIN	Coiner, Enrico	
	Orcine, Recoin	
ORCHAL	Choral, Lorcha	
ORCHID	Droich, Rhodic	
ORCHIS	Choirs, Ichors	
ORCINE	Coiner, Enrico,	
	Orcein, Recoin	
ORDAIN	Dorian, Inroad	
ORDEAL	Loader, Reload	

OREADS	Adores,	Sea-rod
	Soared	
ORGANS	Angors,	Argons,
	Groans,	Nagors,
	Orangs,	Sarong
ORGUES	Grouse,	Rogues,
	Rouges,	Rugose
ORIELS	Elisor,	Oilers,
	Reoils,	Soiler
ORIGAN	Ignaro,	Oaring
*ORIONS	Orison	
ORISON	Orions	
ORNATE	Atoner,	Tenora
ORPINS	Prison,	Proins,
	Ripons	
ORRICE	Corrie	
OSCINE	Conies,	Cosine,
	Soncie	
OSCULE	Coleus	
OSMUND	Mounds	
OSSEIN	Enosis,	Eosins
	Essoin,	Noesis,
	Noises,	Seison,
	Sonsie	
*OSTEND	Doesn't,	Donets,
	Stoned	
OSTLER	Relost,	Rostel,
	Sterol,	Torsel
OSTMEN	Montes	
OTHERS	Throes	
OUCHED	Douche	
OUGHTS	Sought,	Toughs
OUSTED	Toused	
OUSTER	Outers,	Routes,
	Souter,	Touser,
	Trouse	
OUTBAR	Rubato,	Tabour
OUTCUT	Cut-out	
OUTERS	Ouster,	Routes,
	Souter,	Touser,
	Trouse	
OUTLAY	Lay-out	
OUTLET	Let-out	
OUTPOP	Popout	
OUTPUT	Put-out	
OUTRIG	Rig-out	
OUTRUN	Run-out	
OUTSET	Set-out	
OUTTOP	Puttoo	

OVERDO	Doover	
OVERGO	Groove	
OVERLY	Volery	
OVULAR	Louvar,	Valour
OWLERS	Lowers,	Rowels,
	Slower	
OWLERY	Lowery	
OWLETS	Lowest,	Towels
OWLING	Lowing	
OWLISH	Lowish	
OWNERS	Resown,	Rowens,
	Worsen	
OWNING	Woning	
OXALIS	Loxias	
OYSTER	Storey,	Troyes
OZONES	Snooze	

PACERS	Capers,	Crapes,
	Escarp,	Parsec,
	Recaps,	Scrape,
	Secpar,	Spacer
PACKER	Repack	
PADANG	Padnag	
PADDER	Draped	
PADLES	Lapsed,	Pedals,
	Pleads	
PADNAG	Padang	
PADRES	Drapes,	Parsed,
	Rasped,	Repads,
	Spader,	Spared,
	Spread	
PAELLA	Pallae	
PAEONS	Peason	
PAGING	Gaping	
PAIDLE	Aliped,	Elapid,
	Pailed,	Pleiad
PAILED	Aliped,	Elapid,
	Paidle,	Pleiad
PAINTS	Patins,	Pintas,
	Ptisan	
PAIRED	Diaper,	Pardie,
	Repaid	
PALEST	Pastel,	Peltas,
	Petals,	Plates,
	Pleats,	Septal,
	Staple,	Tepals
PALISH	Phials,	Silpha

PALLAE	Paella		PARSEE	Serape
*PALMAS	Lampas, Plasma		PARSER	Parers, Rasper,
PALMED	Lamped			Sparer, Sparre
PALPED	Dapple, Lapped		PARSES	Aspers, Passer,
PALPUS	Slap-up			Prases, Repass,
PALTER	Plater			Spaers, Spares,
PALTRY	Partly			Sparse, Spears
PAMPER	Mapper		PARSON	Aprons
PANDER	Repand		PARTAN	Tarpan, Trapan
PANELS	Naples, Planes		PARTED	Depart, Drapet,
PANICS	Panisc			Petard, Prated,
PANISC	Panics			Traped
PANNEL	Pennal		PARTER	Prater, Repart
PANNUS	Sannup, Unsnap,		PARTIM	Armpit, Impart
	Unspan		PARTLY	Paltry
PANTED	Pedant, Pentad		PARTON	Patron, Tarpon
PANTER	Arpent, Enrapt,		PARURE	Uprear
	Entrap, Parent,		PASHIM	Mishap
	Pterna, Trepan		PASSED	Sepads, Spades
PAPERS	Sapper		PASSER	Aspers, Parses,
PAPERY	Prepay, Yapper			Prases, Repass,
PARCEL	Carpel, Placer			Spaers, Spares,
PARDIE	Diaper, Paired,			Sparse, Spears
	Repaid		PASSIM	Sampis
PARENT	Arpent, Enrapt,		PASTEL	Palest, Peltas,
	Entrap, Panter,			Petals, Plates,
	Pterna, Trepan			Pleats, Septal,
PARERS	Parser, Rasper,			Staple, Tepals
	Sparer, Sparre		PASTER	Paters, Petars,
PARGES	Gapers, Gasper,			Prates, Repast,
	Grapes, Sparge			Tapers, Trapes
PARIAH	Raphia		PASTES	Spates, Speats,
PARIES	Aspire, Persia,			Stapes
	Praise, Spirae,		PASTIL	Alpist, Plaits,
	Spirea			Spital
PARING	Raping		PASTOR	Asport, Portas,
PARISH	Raphis			Sap-rot
PARKER	Repark		PATENS	Septan
PARLED	Pedlar, Predal		PATENT	Patten
PARLEY	Pearly, Player,		PATERA	Aptera, Petara
	Replay		PATERS	Paster, Petars,
PARROT	Pro-art, Raptor			Prates, Repast,
PARSEC	Capers, Crapes,			Tapers, Trapes
	Escarp, Pacers,		PATHOS	Potash
	Recaps, Scrape,		PATINS	Paints, Pintas,
	Secpar, Spacer			Ptisan
PARSED	Drapes, Padres,		PATIOS	Patois
	Rasped, Repads,		PATOIS	Patios
	Spader, Spared,		PATROL	Portal
	Spread			

PATRON	Parton, Tarpon		PERONE	Repone
PATTEN	Patent		PERSES	Preses, Speers,
PAVERS	Sparve			Sperse, Sprees
PAVINS	Spavin		*PERSIA	Aspire, Paries,
PAWLED	Dewlap			Praise, Spirae,
PAWNER	Enwrap, Repawn			Spirea
PEACES	Escape		PERSIC	Precis, Prices,
PEALED	Leaped, Pedale			Spicer
PEALER	Leaper, Repeal		PERSON	Prones
PEARLY	Parley, Player,		PERSUE	Peruse
	Replay		PERTLY	Peltry
PEASON	Paeons		PERUKE	Keuper
PECTIN	Incept		PERUSE	Persue
PEDALE	Leaped, Pealed		PESETA	Etapes
PEDALS	Lapsed, Padles,		PESTER	Peters, Petres,
	Pleads			Pre-set, Pteres,
PEDANT	Panted, Pentad			Serpet
PEDLAR	Parled, Predal		PETALS	Palest, Pastel,
PEERED	Deeper			Peltas, Plates,
PELIKE	Kelpie			Pleats, Septal,
*PELION	Pinole			Staple, Tepals
PELMAS	Maples, Sample		PETARA	Aptera, Patera
PELMET	Temple		PETARD	Depart, Drapet,
PELOID	Diploe, Dipole			Parted, Prated,
PELOTA	Pot-ale			Traped
PELTAS	Palest, Pastel,		*PETARS	Paster, Paters,
	Petals, Plates,			Prates, Repast,
	Pleats, Septal,			Tapers, Trapes
	Staple, Tepals		PETERS	Pester, Petres,
PELTER	Petrel			Pteres, Preset,
PELTRY	Pertly			Serpet
PENDED	Depend		PETREA	Repeat, Retape
PENGOS	Sponge		PETREL	Pelter
PENIAL	Alpine, Pineal		PETRES	Pester, Peters,
PENMAN	Nepman			Pteres, Preset,
PENMEN	Nepmen			Serpet
PENNAL	Pannel		PETROL	Replot
PENSIL	Spelin, Spinel,		PHARES	Hepars, Phrase,
	Spline			Raphes, Seraph,
PENTAD	Panted, Pedant			Shaper, Sherpa
PERILS	Lisper, Perlis,		PHASED	Hasped, Shaped
	Pilers, Pliers		PHASIS	Spahis
PERISH	Reship, Seriph		PHEERS	Herpes, Hesper,
PERKIN	Pinker			Sphere
*PERLIS	Lisper, Perils,		PHENOL	Holpen
	Pilers, Pliers		PHIALS	Palish, Silpha
PERMED	Deperm, Premed		PHONIC	Chopin
PERMIT	Primet		PHRASE	Hepars, Phares,
PERNIS	Repins, Ripens,			Raphes, Seraph,
	Sniper			Shaper, Sherpa

PHYTON	Python, Typhon	
PICENE	Piecen	
PICKER	Repick	
PICOTS	Optics, Topics	
PIECEN	Picene	
PIECER	Pierce, Recipe	
PIECES	Specie	
PIENDS	Despin, Sniped, Spined	
PIERCE	Piecer, Recipe	
PIGHTS	Spight	
PIG-PEN	Epping	
PILERS	Lisper, Perils, Perlis, Pliers	
PILE-UP	Up-pile	
PILING	Gilpin	
PILOTS	Pistol, Postil, Spoilt	
PILOUS	Poilus	
PIMOLA	Lipoma	
PINCER	Prince	
PINCOP	Coppin	
PINEAL	Alpine, Penial	
PINKER	Perkin	
PINNAS	Inspan	
PINOLE	Pelion	
PINTAS	Paints, Patins, Ptisan	
PIOLET	Polite	
PIONED	Opined	
PIPERS	Sipper	
PIPULS	Pupils, Slip-up	
PIRATE	Pteria	
*PIRENE	Repine	
PISCES	Spices	
PISSES	Sepsis, Speiss	
PISTOL	Pilots, Postil, Spoilt	
PISTON	Instop, Pitons, Points, Potins, Spin-to	
PITONS	Instop, Piston, Points, Potins, Spin-to	
PITSAW	Sawpit	
PLACER	Carpel, Parcel	
PLAICE	Epical, Plicae	
PLAINS	Lapins, Spinal	
PLAINT	Nepali, Pliant	
PLAISE	Espial, Lipase	
PLAITS	Alpist, Pastil, Spital	
PLANER	Replan	
PLANES	Naples, Panels	
PLANET	Platen	
PLASMA	Lampas, Palmas	
PLATEN	Planet	
PLATER	Palter	
PLATES	Palest, Pastel, Peltas, Petals, Pleats, Septal, Staple, Tepals	
PLAYER	Parley, Pearly, Replay	
PLEACH	Chapel, Lepcha	
PLEADS	Lapsed, Padles, Pedals	
PLEASE	Asleep, Elapse, Sapele	
PLEATS	Palest, Pastel, Peltas, Petals, Plates, Septal, Staple, Tepals	
PLEIAD	Aliped, Elapid, Paidle, Pailed	
PLIANT	Nepali, Plaint	
PLICAE	Epical, Plaice	
PLIERS	Lisper, Perils, Perlis, Pilers	
PLISSE	Slipes, Spiels, Spiles	
PLOWER	Replow	
PLOYED	Deploy	
PLUMED	Dumple, Lumped	
POILUS	Pilous	
POINTS	Instop, Piston, Pitons, Potins, Spin-to	
POLERS	Splore	
POLING	Loping	
POLITE	Piolet	
POLYPS	Sloppy	
PONGID	Doping	
PONIES	Opines	
PONTEE	Poteen	
POODLE	Looped, Pooled	
POOLED	Looped, Poodle	
POOLER	Looper	

POPERY	Pyrope		Passer, Repass,
POPGUN	Oppugn		Spaers, Spares,
POPOUT	Out-pop		Sparse, Spears
PORERS	Prores, Proser,	PRATED	Depart, Drapet,
	Ropers		Parted, Petard,
PORGER	Groper		Traped
PORING	Roping	PRATER	Parter, Repart
PORKER	Proker	PRATES	Paster, Paters,
PORRET	Porter, Pretor,		Petars, Repast,
	Report		Tapers, Trapes
PORTAL	Patrol	PREACH	Eparch
PORTAS	Asport, Pastor,	PRE-ACT	Carpet
	Sap-rot	PRE-ARM	Ramper
PORTED	Deport, Red-top	PRECES	Creeps, Crepes
PORTER	Porret, Pretor,	PRECIS	Persic, Prices,
	Report		Spicer
PORTLY	Protyl	PREDAL	Parled, Pedlar
POSEUR	Uprose	PRELIM	Limper, Rempli,
POSITS	Ptosis		Rimple
POSSET	Estops, Stoeps,	PREMED	Deperm, Permed
	Stopes	PREPAY	Papery, Yapper
POSTED	Depots, Despot,	PRESES	Perses, Speers,
	Stoped		Sperse, Sprees
POSTER	Opster, Presto,	PRESET	Pester, Peters,
	Repost, Repots,		Petres, Pteres,
	Retops, Stoper,		Serpet
	Topers, Tropes	PRESTO	Opster, Poster,
POSTIL	Pilots, Pistol,		Repost, Repots,
	Spoilt		Retops, Stopes,
POT-ALE	Pelota		Topers, Tropes
POTASH	Pathos	PRETOR	Porret, Porter,
POTEEN	Pontee		Report
POTFUL	Topful	PRE-WAR	Rewrap, Warper
POTHAT	Top-hat	PRICES	Persic, Precis,
POTHER	Thorpe		Spicer
POTINS	Instop, Piston,	PRIDES	Prised, Redips
	Pitons, Points,		Spider, Spired
	Spin-to	PRIERS	Sprier
POTION	Option	PRIEST	Esprit, Pteris,
POTMAN	Tampon, Topman		Ripest, Sitrep,
POTMEN	Topmen		Sprite, Stripe
POUNCE	Uncope	PRIMES	Simper
POURED	Rouped	PRIMET	Permit
POURER	Repour	PRIMUS	Purims, Purism
POUSSE	Spouse	PRINCE	Pincer
POUTER	Roupet, Troupe	PRINTS	Sprint
PRAISE	Aspire, Paries,	PRISED	Prides, Redips,
	Persia, Spirae,		Spider, Spired
	Spirea	PRISES	Speirs, Spires
PRANGS	Sprang	PRISON	Orpins, Proins,
PRASES	Aspers, Parses,		Ripons

PRO-ART	Parrot, Raptor		PURPLE	Pulper, Repulp
PROBED	Bedrop		PUSHTO	Tophus, Upshot
PROCES	Copers, Corpse,		PUSHTU	Shut-up
	Cropes		PUT-OFF	Offput
PROEMS	Merops, Mopers		PUT-ONS	Ton-ups, Unstop
PROINS	Orpins, Prison,		PUT-OUT	Output
	Ripons		PUTTOO	Outtop
PROKER	Porker		PUZZEL	Puzzle
PRONES	Person		PUZZLE	Puzzel
PRONGS	Sprong		PYROPE	Popery
PRONTO	Proton		PYTHON	Phyton, Typhon
PROPED	Dopper			
PROPEL	Lopper			
PRORES	Porers, Proser,		QUAILS	Squail
	Ropers		QUAKES	Squeak
PROSER	Porers, Prores,		QUARTE	Quatre
	Ropers		QUATRE	Quarte
PROSIT	Tripos		QUEEST	Queets
PROTON	Pronto		QUEETS	Queest
PROTYL	Portly		QUESAL	Equals, Lasque,
PRUNES	Spurne			Squeal
PTERES	Pester, Peters,		QUILLS	Squill
	Petres, Preset,		QUINCE	Cinque
	Serpet		QUINTS	Squint
PTERIA	Pirate		QUIRES	Risque, Squire
PTERIS	Esprit, Priest,		QUIRTS	Squirt
	Ripest, Sitrep,		QUOTER	Roquet, Torque
	Sprite, Stripe			
PTERNA	Arpent, Enrapt,			
	Entrap, Panter,		RABATE	Abater, Trabea
	Parent, Trepan		RABATO	Abator
PTISAN	Paints, Patins,		RABBET	Barbet
	Pintas		RABBLE	Barbel, Barble
PTOSIS	Posits		RABIES	Braise
PUISNE	Supine		RACEME	Amerce, Careme
PULPER	Purple, Repulp		RACHES	Arches, Chares,
PUMPER	Repump			Chaser, Eschar,
PUNCHI	Chin-up			Search
PUNIER	Purine, Unripe		RACHIS	Chairs
PUNISH	Unship		RACING	Arcing, Caring
PUPILS	Pipuls, Slip-up		RACIST	Crista
PURDAH	Hard-up		RACKED	Arcked, Carked,
PURGES	Spurge			Craked, Dacker
*PURIMS	Primus, Purism		RACKET	Retack, Tacker
PURINE	Punier, Unripe		RACKLE	Calker, Lacker,
PURISM	Primus, Purims			Recalk
PURIST	Spruit, Stir-up,		RACOON	Corona
	Uprist, Upstir		RADDLE	Ladder, Larded
PURLED	Drupel		RAFFEE	Affeer

RAFFIA	Affair	
RAFTER	Frater	
RAGEST	Grates,	Greats,
	Stager,	Targes
RAGETH	Gather	
RAGGED	Dagger	
RAGGLE	Gargle,	Gregal,
	Lagger	
RAGMEN	Engram,	German,
	Manger	
RAG-TAG	Tag-rag	
RAIDER	Arride	
RAILED	Derail,	Relaid
RAILER	Rerail	
RAINED	Derain,	Randie
*RAINER	Renira	
RAISED	Aiders,	Irades
RAISER	Sierra	
RAISES	Arises,	Sisera
RAITED	Tirade	
RAKISH	Shikar	
RAMBLE	Ambler,	Blamer,
	Lamber,	Marble
RAMEES	Ameers,	Ameres,
	Seamer	
RAMENT	Marten	
RAMMED	Dammer	
RAMMEL	Lammer	
RAMOON	Maroon	
RAMPED	Damper	
RAMPER	Pre-arm	
RAMSON	Manors,	Normas,
	Ransom,	Romans
RAMTIL	Mitral	
RAMULE	Mauler	
RANCES	Caners,	Casern,
	Cranes,	Crenas,
	Sarcen	
RANCHO	Anchor,	Archon,
	Charon	
RANDEM	Manred,	Redman,
	Remend	
RANDIE	Derain,	Rained
RANDLE	Aldern,	Darnel,
	En ard,	Lander,
	Reland	
RANDOM	Rodman	
RANGED	Danger,	Gander,
	Garden,	Gnared,
	Grande	

RANGER	Garner	
RANGES	Angers,	Serang
RANGLE	Angler,	Largen,
	Regnal	
RANKED	Darken	
RANKER	Rerank	
RANSOM	Manors,	Normas,
	Ramson,	Romans
RANTED	Ardent	
RANTER	Errant	
RAPHES	Hepars,	Phares,
	Phrase,	Seraph,
	Shaper,	Sherpa
RAPHIA	Pariah	
RAPHIS	Parish	
RAPIER	Repair	
RAPING	Paring	
RAPPED	Dapper	
RAPPEL	Lapper	
RAPPEN	Napper	
RAPTOR	Parrot,	Pro-art
RAREST	Arrest,	Arrets,
	Raster,	Raters,
	Retars,	Sartre,
	Starer,	Tarres
RASANT	Ratans	
RASCAL	Lascar,	Sacral,
	Sarlac,	Scalar
RASHED	Dasher,	Shader,
	Shared	
RASHER	Sharer	
RASHES	Shares,	Shears
RASING	Grains,	Sangir
RASPED	Drapes,	Padres,
	Parsed,	Repads,
	Spader,	Spared,
	Spread	
RASPER	Parers,	Parser,
	Sparer,	Sparre
RASTER	Arrest,	Arrets,
	Rarest,	Raters,
	Retars,	Sartre,
	Starer,	Tarres
RATALS	Altars,	Astral
	Tarsal	
RATANS	Rasant	
RATEEN	Entera,	Neater,
	Renate	
RATELS	Alerts,	Alters,

	Artels,	Laster,	READDS	Adders,	Dreads,
	Resalt,	Salter,		Sadder	
	Slater,	Staler,	READER	Dearer,	Reared,
	Tarsel			Redare,	Reread
RATERS	Arrest,	Arrets,	REALIA	Aerial	
	Rarest,	Raster,	REALTY	Elytra,	Lyrate,
	Retars,	Sartre,		Raylet,	Telary
	Starer,	Tarres	REAMED	Remade	
RATHES	Earths,	Haters,	REARED	Dearer,	Reader,
	Hearts,	Sarthe		Redare,	Reread
RATINE	Retain,	Retina	REASON	Arseno,	Senora
RATING	Gratin,	Taring,	REAVED	Evader,	Veader
	Tringa		REAVOW	Avower	
RATION	Aroint		REBACK	Backer	
RATIOS	Aorist		REBAIT	Baiter,	Barite,
RATITE	Attire			Terbia	
RATLIN	Trinal		REBAKE	Beaker	
RATTAN	Tantra,	Tartan	REBANK	Banker,	Barken
RATTED	Tetrad		REBATE	Beater,	Berate
RATTEN	Natter		REBATO	Boater,	Borate,
RATTLE	Latter,	Tatler		Orbate	
RATTLY	Tartly		REBEND	Bender	
RATTON	Attorn		REBIDS	Biders,	Brides,
RAVE-IN	Ravine,	Vainer		Debris	
RAVELS	Lavers,	Salver,	REBILL	Biller	
	Serval,	Slaver,	REBIND	Binder,	Brined,
	Valser,	Velars,		Inbred	
	Versal		REBITE	Bertie	
RAVEST	Averts,	Starve,	REBOIL	Boiler	
	Staver,	Tarves,	REBOLT	Bolter	
	Tavers,	Traves,	REBOSO	Booers,	Broose
	Vaster		REBOTE	Bo-tree	
RAVETH	Thrave		REBREW	Brewer	
RAVINE	Rave-in,	Vainer	REBUFF	Buffer	
RAVING	Girvan		REBURN	Burner	
*RAWDEN	Andrew,	Darwen,	REBUTS	Buster,	Brutes,
	Wander,	Warden,		Subter,	Surbet,
	Warned			Tubers	
RAYING	Grainy		RECALK	Calker,	Lacker,
RAYLES	Layers,	Relays,		Rackle	
	Slayer		RECALL	Caller,	Cellar
RAYLET	Elytra,	Lyrate,	RECANE	Careen,	Enrace
	Realty,	Telary	RECANT	Canter,	Carnet,
*RAYNER	Yarner			Centra,	Creant,
RAYNES	Senary,	Yearns		Nectar,	Tanrec,
REACTS	Carets,	Cartes,		Trance	
	Caster,	Caters,	RECAPS	Capers,	Crapes,
	Crates,	Cresta,		Escarp,	Pacers,
	Recast,	Traces		Parsec,	Secpar,
				Scrape,	Spacer

RECASE	Ceaser, Crease, Searce	REDANS	Sander, Snared
RECAST	Carets, Cartes, Caster, Caters, Crates, Cresta, Reacts, Traces	REDARE	Dearer, Reader, Reared, Reread
		REDARN	Darner, Errand, Renard
RECEDE	Decree	REDATE	Derate, Teared
RECENT	Center, Centre, Tenrec	REDBUD	Budder
		REDCAP	Carped, Craped
RECESS	Cesser, Screes	*REDCAR	Carder
RECIPE	Piecer, Pierce	REDDEN	Derned
RECITE	Cerite, Certie, Tierce	RED-DOG	Dodger
		REDFIN	Finder, Friend, Re-find
RECKED	Decker	REDEAL	Dealer, Leader, Relead
RECKON	Conker		
RECOAL	Coaler, Oracle	RED-HAT	Dareth, Dearth, Hatred, Thread
RECOCK	Cocker		
RECOIN	Coiner, Enrico, Orcien, Orcine	RED-HOT	Dehort
		REDIPS	Prides, Prised, Spider, Spired
RECOMB	Comber		
RECONS	Censor, Crones, Oncers	*REDLEG	Ledger
		REDMAN	Manred, Random, Remand
RECOOK	Cooker		
RECOOL	Cooler	REDOCK	Corked, Docker, Rocked
RECORK	Corker, Rocker		
RECOST	Corset, Cortes, Coster, Escort, Rectos, Scoter, Sector	REDOUT	Detour, Douter, Routed, Toured
		REDRAW	Drawer, Reward, Warder, Warred
RECOUP	Couper, Croupe, Cuerpo	RED-TOP	Deport, Ported
		REDUST	Duster, Rudest, Rusted
RECTAL	Cartel, Claret		
RECTOS	Corset, Cortes, Coster, Escort, Recost, Scoter, Sector	RE-EARN	Earner, Nearer
		RE-ECHO	Chores, Cohere, Echoer
		REECHY	Cheery
RECTUS	Cruets, Cruset, Eructs, Recuts, Truces	REEDEN	Needer
		RE-EDIT	Dieter, Retied, Tiered
		REELED	Leered
RECUMB	Cumber	REELER	Re-reel
RECURS	Curers, Curser	RE-EMIT	Metier, Retime
RECUSE	Cereus, Ceruse, Cesure, Rescue, Secure	REEVED	Veered
		REEVES	Severe
		REFEED	Feeder
RECUTS	Cruets, Cruset, Eructs, Rectus, Truces	REFEEL	Feeler
		REFELT	Felter, Feltre, Reflet, Trefle
REDACT	Carted, Cedrat, Crated, Traced	REFILE	Ferile, Relief

REFILL	Filler	REGULI	Guiler, Ligure,
RE-FIND	Finder, Friend,		Uglier
	Redfin	REHANG	Hanger
REFINE	Enfire, Ferine,	REHASH	Hasher
	Fineer	REHAUL	Hauler
REFITS	Firest, Freits,	REHEAD	Adhere, Header,
	Resift, Rifest,		Hedera
	Sifter, Strife	RE-HEAL	Healer
REFLET	Felter, Feltre,	REHEAR	Hearer
	Refelt, Trefle	REHEAT	Heater, Hereat
REFLOW	Flower, Fowler,	REHEEL	Heeler
	Wolfer	REHONE	Hereon
REFOLD	Folder	REHUNG	Hunger
REFOOT	Foetor, Footer,	RE-ICES	Cerise
	Tofore	REIGNS	Resign, Ringes,
REFORM	Former		Signer, Singer
REFUEL	Ferule, Fueler	REINED	Denier, Edirne,
REGAIN	Earing, Gainer,		Nereid
	Graine, Regian,	REINKS	Inkers, Kirsen,
	Regina		Sinker
REGALE	Aleger	REIRDS	Derris, Driers,
REGALO	Galore, Gaoler		Riders
REGARD	Darger, Grader	REIVED	Derive
REGAVE	Greave	REIVER	Riever
REGENT	Gerent	REJAIL	Jailer
REGEST	Egrets, Greets,	REJOIN	Joiner
	Regets	REJOLT	Jolter
REGETS	Egrets, Greets,	REKNIT	Tinker
	Regest	RELACE	Alerce, Cereal
*REGGIE	Geiger, Greige	RELAID	Derail, Railed
REGIAN	Earing, Gainer,	RELAIS	Ariels, Israel,
	Graine, Regain,		Resail, Sailer,
	Regina		Serail, Serial
REGILD	Gilder, Girdle,	RELAND	Aldern, Darnel,
	Glider, Ridgel		Enlard, Lander,
REGILT	Riglet		Randle
REGIME	Emigre	RELATE	Elater
REGINA	Earing, Gainer,	RELAYS	Layers, Rayles,
	Graine, Regain,		Slayer
	Regian	RELEAD	Dealer, Leader,
REGION	Eringo, Ignore		Redeal
REGIRD	Girder	RELEND	Lender, Rendle
REGIUS	Guiser	RELICS	Slicer
REGIVE	Grieve	RELIDE	Lieder, Relied
REGLOW	Glower	RELIED	Lieder, Relide
REGNAL	Angler, Largen,	RELIEF	Refile
	Rangle	RELIES	Resile
REGRIP	Griper	RELINE	Lierne
REGROW	Grower	RELISH	Hirsel, Hirsle

RELIST	Lister, Litres, Tilers	RENTED	Tender
		RENTER	Rerent
RELIVE	Levier, Revile	RENTES	Enters, Ernest, Nester, Resent, Strene, Ternes, Tenser
RELOAD	Loader, Ordeal		
RELOAN	Loaner		
RELOCK	Locker, Rockel		
RELOSE	Resole	RENULE	Unreel
RELOST	Ostler, Rostel, Sterol, Torsel	RE-OILS	Elisor, Oilers, Oilers, Soiler
RELUCT	Culter, Cutler	RE-OPEN	Opener
REMADE	Reamed	REPACK	Packer
REMAIL	Mailer	REPADS	Drapes, Padres, Parsed, Rasped, Spader, Spared, Spread
REMAIM	Maimer		
REMAIN	Airmen, Marine		
REMAND	Manred, Randem, Redman		
		REPAID	Diaper, Paired, Pardie
REMARK	Marker		
REMAST	Armest, Armets, Master, Maters, Stream, Tamers, Tremas	REPAIR	Rapier
		REPAND	Pander
		REPARK	Parker
		RE-PART	Parter, Prater
REMATE	Amreet	REPASS	Aspers, Parses, Passer, Prases, Spaers, Spares, Sparse, Spears
REMELT	Melter		
REMEND	Mender		
REMILL	Miller		
REMIND	Minder	REPAST	Paster, Paters, Petars, Prates, Tapers, Trapes
REMINT	Minter		
REMISE	Misere		
REMISS	Misers	REPAWN	Enwrap, Pawner
REMITS	Merits, Mister, Miters, Mitres, Smiter, Timers	REPEAL	Leaper, Pealer
		REPEAT	Petrea, Retape
		REPICK	Picker
REMOLD	Molder	REPINE	Pirene
REMORA	Roamer	REPINS	Pernis, Ripens, Sniper
REMOTE	Meteor		
REMPLI	Limper, Prelim, Rimple	REPLAN	Planer
		REPLAY	Parley, Pearly, Player
RENAIL	Enrail, Linear, Nailer		
		REPLOT	Petrol
RENAME	Meaner	REPLOW	Plower
RENARD	Darner, Errand, Redarn	REPLUM	Lumper, Rumple
		REPONE	Perone
RENATE	Entera, Neater, Rateen	REPORT	Porret, Porter, Pretor
*RENIRA	Rainer	REPOST	Opster, Poster, Presto, Repots, Retops, Stoper, Topers, Tropes
RENNET	Tenner		
*RENOIR	Ironer		
RENOWN	Wonner		
RENTAL	Altern, Antler, Learnt, Ternal	REPOTS	Opster, Poster,

	Presto, Repost,		RESETS	Steers, Steres
	Retops, Stoper,		RESHEW	Hewers, Wheres
	Topers, Tropes		RESHIP	Perish, Seriph
REPOUR	Pourer		RESHOD	Dehors, Herods,
REPULP	Pulper, Purple			Hordes, Horsed,
REPUMP	Pumper			Rhodes, Shoder,
RE-RAIL	Railer			Shored
RERANK	Ranker		RESHOW	Howres, Shower,
RE-READ	Dearer, Reader,			Whores
	Reared, Redare		RESIDE	Desire, Eiders
REREEL	Reeler		RESIFT	Firest, Freist,
RERENT	Renter			Refits, Rifest,
REROLL	Erroll, Roller			Sifter, Strife
REROOT	Rooter, Torero		RESIGN	Reigns, Ringes,
RESAIL	Ariels, Israel,			Signer, Singer
	Relais, Sailer,		RESILE	Relies
	Serail, Serial		RESIST	Resits, Sister
RESALE	Leares, Leaser,		RESITS	Resist, Sister
	Reseal, Sealer		RESOAK	Oakers, Soaker
RESALT	Alerts, Alters,		RESOLD	Dorsel, Solder
	Artels, Laster,		RESOLE	Relose
	Ratels, Salter,		RESORB	Borers
	Slater, Staler,		RESORT	Roster, Sorter,
	Tarsel			Storer
RESAWN	Answer		RESOWN	Owners, Rowens,
RESAWS	Swears, Wrasse			Worsen
RESCUE	Cereus, Ceruse,		RESOWS	Sowser
	Cesure, Recuse,		RESTED	Desert, Deters
	Secure		RESTEM	Meters, Metres,
RESEAL	Leares, Leaser,			Termes
	Resale, Sealer		RESTIR	Triers
RESEAT	Aretes, Asteer,		RESULT	Lurest, Luster,
	Easter, Eaters,			Lustre, Rulest,
	Saeter, Seater,			Rustle, Sutler,
	Staree, Steare,			Ulster
	Teaser, Teresa		RESUME	Emures
RESEAU	Urease		RETACK	Racket, Tacker
RESECT	Certes, Erects,		RETAIL	Tailer
	Secret		RETAIN	Ratine, Retina
RESEDA	Erased, Seared		RETANS	Antres, Astern
RESEED	Seeder		RETAPE	Petrea, Repeat
RESEEK	Kreese, Seeker		RETARD	Darter, Dartre,
RESELL	Seller			Retrad, Tarred,
RESEND	Denser, Enders,			Trader
	Sender		RETARS	Arrest, Arrets,
RESENT	Enters, Ernest,			Rarest, Raster,
	Nester, Rentes,			Raters, Sartre,
	Strene, Ternes,			Starer, Tarres
	Tenser		RETEAR	Tearer

RETENE	Entree, Eterne		REWARD	Drawer, Redraw,
RETELL	Teller			Warder, Warred
RETENT	Netter, Tenter		REWARM	Warmer
RETEST	Setter, Street,		REWARN	Warner, Warren
	Tester		REWASH	Hawser, Washer
RETHAW	Thawer, Wreath		REWEAR	Wearer
RETIED	Dieter, Re-edit,		REWELD	Welder
	Tiered		REWIND	Winder
RETILL	Rillet, Tiller		REWORK	Worker
RETIME	Metier, Re-emit		REWRAP	Pre-war, Warper
RETINA	Ratine, Retain		RHESUS	Rushes, Ushers
RETINS	Insert, Inters,		RHEUMS	Musher
	Nitres, Sinter,		RHINES	Shiner, Shrine
	Strine, Trines		*RHODES	Dehors, Herods,
RETINT	Nitter, Tinter			Hordes, Horsed,
RETIRE	Etrier			Reshod, Shoder,
RETOPS	Opster, Poster,			Shored
	Presto, Repost,		RHODIC	Droich, Orchid
	Repots, Stoper,		RHONES	Honers, Nosher
	Topers, Tropes		RHYTON	Thorny
RETORT	Rotter		*RIALTO	Tailor
RETOSE	Eostre, Stereo		RIATAS	Arista, Tarsia,
RETOSS	Rosets, Sorest,			Tiaras
	Stores, Torses,		RIBALD	Bridal
	Tosser		RIBBED	Bribed, Dibber
RETOUR	Roture, Router,		RIBBER	Briber
	Tourer		RIBBON	Robbin
RETRAD	Darter, Dartre,		RICERS	Cerris, Criers
	Retard, Tarred,		RICHEN	Enrich, Nicher
	Trader		RICKED	Dicker
RETUNE	Neuter, Tenure,		RICKEY	Crikey
	Tureen		RICKLE	Licker
RETURF	Turfer		RICTAL	Citral
RETURN	Turner		RICTUS	Citrus, Rustic
*REUTER	Ureter		RIDDEL	Riddle
REVAMP	Vamper		RIDDEN	Nidder, Rinded
REVEAL	Laveer, Leaver,		RIDDLE	Riddel
	Vealer		RIDENT	Tinder, Trined
REVEND	Nerved, Vender		RIDERS	Derris, Driers,
REVERS	Server, Verser			Reirds
REVEST	Everts, Revets,		RIDEST	Direst, Driest,
	Sterve, Treves,			Stride
	Verset, Vester		RIDETH	Dither
REVETO	Revote, Vetoer		RIDGED	Girded
REVETS	Everts, Revest,		RIDGEL	Gilder, Girdle,
	Sterve, Treves,			Glided, Regild
	Verset, Vester		RIDING	Ingrid
REVIEW	Viewer		RIEVER	Reiver
REVILE	Levier, Relive		RIFEST	Firest, Freits,
REVOTE	Reveto, Vetoer			

	Refits, Resift, Sifter, Strife	
RIGGED	Digger	
RIGGLE	Ligger	
RIGLET	Regilt	
RIG-OUT	Outrig	
RILLES	Siller	
RILLET	Retill, Tiller	
RIMING	Miring	
RIMLET	Milter	
RIMMED	Dimmer	
RIMOSE	Isomer, Moires	
RIMPLE	Limper, Prelim, Rempli	
RINDED	Nidder, Ridden	
RINGED	Engird	
RINGER	Erring	
RINGES	Reigns, Resign, Signer, Singer	
RIOTED	Editor, Tie-rod, Triode	
RIPENS	Pernis, Repins, Sniper	
RIPEST	Esprit, Priest, Pteris, Sitrep, Sprite, Stripe	
*RIPONS	Orpins, Prison, Proins	
RIPPED	Dipper	
RIPPLE	Lipper	
RISBAN	Abrins, Bairns, Brains, Brians	
RISETH	Rithes, Shrite, Theirs	
RISING	Siring	
RISQUE	Quires, Squire	
RITHES	Riseth, Shrite, Theirs	
RITTER	Territ, Tirret	
RIVAGE	Argive	
RIVETH	Thrive	
RIVETS	Stiver, Strive, Tivers, Trevis, Verist	
RIVING	Virgin	
RIVOSE	Vireos, Virose	
ROADED	Adored, Deodar	
ROAMER	Remora	
ROARED	Adorer	
ROBBIN	Ribbon	
ROBERD	Border	
ROBING	Boring, Orbing	
ROBINS	Inorbs, Sorbin	
ROBUST	Turbos	
ROCCUS	Crocus, Occurs, Succor	
ROCHEA	Chorea, Ochrea, Orache	
ROCHET	Hector, Rotche, Tocher, Troche	
ROCKED	Corked, Docker, Redock	
ROCKEL	Locker, Relock	
ROCKER	Corker, Recork	
RODDED	Dodder	
RODING	Doring	
RODMAN	Random	
ROGGLE	Logger	
ROGUED	Drogue, Drouge, Gourde, Rouged	
ROGUES	Grouse, Orgues, Rogues, Rugose	
ROLLER	Erroll, Reroll	
ROMANS	Manors, Normas, Ramson, Ransom	
ROMERO	Roomer	
RONDEL	Rondle	
RONDLE	Rondel	
RONEOS	Seroon, Sooner	
ROOFED	Foredo	
ROOKLE	Looker	
ROOMED	Moored	
ROOMER	Romero	
ROOSES	Sorose	
ROOTER	Torero	
ROOTLE	Looter, Tooler	
ROPERS	Porers, Prores, Proser	
ROPING	Poring	
ROQUET	Quoter, Torque	
ROSACE	Coarse	
ROSETS	Retoss, Sorest, Stores, Torses, Tosser	
ROSING	Girons, Grison, Groins, Signor	
ROSTEL	Ostler, Relost, Sterol, Torsel	

ROSTER	Resort, Sorter,	
	Storer	
ROSTRA	Sartor	
ROTCHE	Hector, Rochet,	
	Tocher, Troche	
ROTTED	Detort, Dotter	
ROTTER	Retort	
ROTULA	Torula	
ROTUND	Untrod	
ROTURE	Retour, Router,	
	Tourer	
ROUGED	Drogue, Drouge,	
	Gourde, Rogued	
ROUGES	Grouse, Orgues,	
	Rogues, Rugose	
ROUNCE	Uncore	
ROUPED	Poured	
ROUPET	Pouter, Troupe	
ROUSED	Soured	
ROUSES	Serous	
ROUSTS	Stours, Sutors,	
	Tussor	
ROUTED	Detour, Douter,	
	Redout, Toured	
ROUTER	Retour, Roture,	
	Tourer	
ROUTES	Ouster, Outers,	
	Souter, Touser,	
	Trouse	
ROVEST	Stover, Strove,	
	Voters	
ROVETH	Throve	
ROWELS	Lowers, Owlers,	
	Slower	
ROWENS	Owners, Resown,	
	Worsen	
ROWEST	Rowtes, Sowter,	
	Stower, Towers,	
	Towser, Twoers	
ROWTES	Rowest, Sowter,	
	Stower, Towers,	
	Towser, Twoers	
RUBATO	Outbar, Tabour	
RUBBED	Dubber	
RUBBLE	Burble, Lubber	
RUBIED	Buried	
RUBIES	Bruise, Buries,	
	Busier	
RUBINE	Brunei	

RUCKED	Ducker	
RUDEST	Duster, Redust,	
	Rusted	
RUEING	Rugine	
RUFFED	Duffer	
RUFFES	Suffer	
RUFFLE	Luffer	
RUGATE	Argute, Tuareg	
RUGGED	Grudge	
RUGINE	Rueing	
RUGOSA	Garous	
RUGOSE	Grouse, Orgues,	
	Rogues, Rouges	
RUINED	Inured	
RULEST	Lurest, Luster,	
	Lustre, Result,	
	Rustle, Sutler,	
	Ulster	
RULING	Luring	
RUMBAS	Sambur, Umbras	
RUMBLE	Lumber, Umbrel	
RUMPLE	Lumper, Replum	
RUNERS	Nurser	
RUNNET	Tunner, Unrent	
RUN-OUT	Outrun	
RUNWAY	Unwary	
RUSCUS	Cursus	
RUSHES	Rhesus, Shures,	
	Ushers	
RUSINE	Insure, Inures,	
	Urines, Ursine	
RUSSET	Surest, Tusser	
RUSTED	Duster, Redust,	
	Rudest	
RUSTIC	Citrus, Rictus	
RUSTLE	Lurest, Luster,	
	Lustre, Result,	
	Rulest, Sutler,	
	Ulster	
RUTTER	Turret	
RUTTLE	Turtle	
SABERS	Brasse, Sabres	
SABLED	Blades	
SABRED	Ardebs, Beards,	
	Breads, Debars,	
	Serdab	
SABRES	Brasse, Sabers	

SACHEL	Chelas, Laches	SALTIE	Salite
SACHEM	Schema	SALTLY	Lastly
SACHET	Chaste, Cheats,	SALVED	Slaved
	Scathe, Taches	SALVER	Lavers, Ravels,
SACKED	Casked		Serval, Slaver,
SACKER	Crakes, Creaks,		Valser, Velars,
	Screak		Versal
SACQUE	Casque	SALVIA	Saliva
SACRAL	Lascar, Rascal,	SAMBUR	Rumbas, Umbras
	Sarlac, Scalar	SAMELY	Measly
SACRED	Cadres, Cedars,	SAMIAN	Manies
	Scared	SAMIEL	Mesail, Mesial
SADDEN	Dedans, Sanded	SAMITE	Maties, Semita,
SADDER	Adders, Dreads,		Tamise
	Readds	SAMLET	Metals
SADDLE	Addles	SAMPIS	Passim
*SADIES	Asides, Dassie	SAMPLE	Maples, Pelmas
SADIST	Staids	*SAMSON	Masons
SAETER	Aretes, Asteer,	SANDED	Dedans, Sadden
	Easter, Eaters,	SANDER	Redans, Snared
	Reseat, Seater,	*SANDRA	Nasard
	Staree, Steare,	SANGIR	Grains, Rasing
	Teaser, Teresa	SANIES	Anises, Sasine
SAGEST	Stages	SANITY	Satiny, Stay-in
SAGGED	Gadges	SANNUP	Pannus, Unsnap,
SAGGER	Gagers, Seggar		Unspan
SAILED	Aisled, Deasil,	SANTIR	Instar, Strain,
	Ideals, Ladies		Trains
SAILER	Ariels, Israel,	SANTON	Sonant
	Relais, Resail,	SAPELE	Asleep, Elapse,
	Serail, Serial		Please
SALAMI	Lamias	SAPPER	Papers
SALIAN	Lianas, Salina	SAP-ROT	Asport, Pastor,
SALINA	Lianas, Salian		Portas
SALINE	Aliens, Alines,	SARCEL	Carles, Clears,
	Aniles, Selina		Scaler, Sclera
SALITE	Saltie	SARCEN	Caners, Casern,
SALIVA	Salvia		Cranes, Crenas,
*SALLIE	Allies		Rances
SALLOW	Allows	SARDEL	Alders, Dalers
SALMIS	Missal	SARLAC	Lascar, Rascal,
SALTED	Deltas, Lasted,		Sacral, Scalar
	Slated, Stadle,	SARONG	Angors, Argons,
	Staled		Groans, Nagors,
SALTER	Alerts, Alters,		Orangs, Organs
	Artels, Laster,	SARSEN	Nasser, Snares
	Ratels, Resalt,	*SARTHE	Earths, Haters,
	Slater, Staler,		Hearts, Rathes
	Tarsel	SARTOR	Rostra

*SARTRE	Arrest, Arrets, Rarest, Raster, Raters, Retars, Starer, Tarres	SCORES	Corses, Crosse, Scorse
SASHED	Dashes, Shades	SCORSE	Corses, Crosse, Scores
SASHES	She-ass	SCOTER	Corset, Cortes, Coster, Escort, Recost, Rectos, Sector
SASINE	Anises, Sanies		
SATCOM	Comsat, Mascot		
SATEEN	Ensate, Senate	SCOTIA	Coatis
SATING	Gainst, Giants	SCOVEL	Cloves
SATINY	Sanity, Stay-in	SCRAMP	Cramps
SATIRE	Striae	SCRAPE	Capers, Crapes, Escarp, Pacers, Parsec, Recaps, Secpar, Spacer
SATRAP	Sparta		
SAUCED	Caused		
SAUCER	Causer, Cesura, Erucas		
		SCRAWL	Crawls
SAUGER	Argues, Augers	SCREAK	Crakes, Creaks, Sacker
SAUREL	Elures		
SAWDER	Waders	SCREAM	Crames, Creams, Macers
SAWING	Aswing		
SAWN-UP	Supawn	SCREED	Ceders, Creeds
SAW-PIT	Pitsaw	SCREEN	Censer, Secern
SAW-SET	Sweats, Tawses, Wastes	SCREES	Cesser, Recess
		SCRIME	Crimes
SAWYER	Swayer	SCRIMP	Crimps
SCALAR	Lascar, Rascal, Sacral, Sarlac	SCRINE	Crines
		SCROBE	Cobres
SCALER	Carles, Clears, Sarcel, Sclera	SCRUNT	Crunts
		SCRUTO	Courts, Crouts, Turcos
SCAMEL	Camels, Macles, Mascle, Mescal		
		SCUTES	Cestus
SCAPED	Spaced	SCYTHE	Chesty
SCARAB	Barsac	'SDEATH	Deaths, Hasted
SCARED	Cadres, Cedars, Sacred	SDEIGN	Deigns, Design, Dinges, Nidges, Signed, Singed
SCARES	Caress, Carses, Crases, Escars, Scraes, Seracs		
		SEA-BAT	Abates
		SEA-DOG	Dosage, Sea-god
		SEA-FIR	Ferias, Fraise
SCATHE	Chaste, Cheats, Sachet, Taches	SEA-GOD	Dosage, Sea-dog
		SEALED	Leased
SCHEMA	Sachem	SEALER	Leares, Leaser, Resale, Reseal
SCHOUT	Chouts		
SCHRIK	Chirks, Kirsch	SEAMEN	Enseam
SCILLA	Lilacs	SEAMER	Ameers, Ameres, Ramees
SCLAVE	Calves, Cavels, Claves		
		SEAMES	Meases, Sesame
SCLERA	Carles, Clears, Sarcel, Scaler	SEA-MUD	Amused, Medusa
		SEANCE	Encase, Seneca
SCORER	Corers, Crores		

SEARCE	Ceaser, Crease, Recase	SEINER	Nereis, Serein, Serine
SEARCH	Arches, Chares, Chaser, Eschar, Raches	SEISON	Enosis, Eosins, Essoin, Noesis, Noises, Ossein, Sonsie
SEARED	Erased, Reseda		
SEA-ROD	Adores, Oreads, Soared	SELAHS	Halses, Hassle, Lashes, Shales, Sheals
SEATED	Sedate, Teades, Teased	SELDOM	Models
SEATER	Aretes, Asteer, Easter, Eaters, Reseat, Saeter, Staree, Steare, Teaser, Teresa	SELECT	Elects
		*SELINA	Aliens, Alines, Saline
		SELLER	Resell
		SELVES	Vessel
		SEMELE	Melees
*SEATON	Atones	SEMITA	Maties, Samite, Tamise
SECANT	Ascent, Enacts, Stance		
		SENARY	Raynes, Yearns
SECERN	Censer, Screen	SENATE	Ensate, Sateen
SECKEL	Cleeks	SENDAL	Elands, Ladens, Landes
SECPAR	Capers, Crapes, Escarp, Pacers, Parsec, Recaps, Scrape, Spacer	SENDER	Denser, Enders, Resend
		SEND-UP	Upends, Upsend
SECRET	Certes, Erects, Resect	SENECA	Encase, Seance
		SENGHI	Hinges, Neighs
SECTOR	Corset, Cortes, Coster, Escort, Recost, Rectos, Scoter	SENHOR	Herons
		SENILE	Enisle, Ensile, Silene
		*SENLAC	Ancles, Cleans, Lances, Lencas
SECUND	Dunces		
SECURE	Cereus, Ceruse, Cesure, Recuse, Rescue	SENNIT	Sinnet, Tennis
		SENORA	Arseno, Reason
		SENORS	Nosers, Sensor, Snores
SEDATE	Seated, Teades, Teased		
		SENSOR	Nosers, Senors, Snores
SEDENT	Endest, Nested, Tensed		
		SEPADS	Passed, Spades
SEDILE	Diesel, Ediles, Elides, Seidel	SEPSIN	Snipes, Spines
		SEPSIS	Pisses, Speiss
SEDUCE	Deuces, Educes	SEPTAL	Palest, Pastel, Peltas, Petals, Plates, Pleats, Staple, Tepals
SEEDER	Reseed		
SEEING	Genies		
SEEKER	Kreese, Reseek		
SEEMER	Emeers	SEPTAN	Patens
SEETHE	Te-hees	SERACS	Caress, Carses, Crases, Escars, Scares, Scraes
SEGGAR	Gagers, Sagger		
SEIDEL	Diesel, Ediles, Elides, Sedile		

SERAIL	Ariels, Israel, Relais, Resail, Sailer, Serial	*SEVRES	Serves, Severs, Verses
SERANG	Angers, Ranges	SEWING	Swinge
SERAPE	Parsee	SEXIST	Exists
SERAPH	Hepars, Phares, Phrase, Raphes, Shaper, Sherpa	SHADED	Dashed
		SHADER	Dasher, Rashed, Shared
SERDAB	Ardebs, Beards, Breads, Debars, Sabred	SHADES	Dashes, Sashed
		SHAKER	Kasher
		SHALES	Halses, Hassle, Lashes, Selahs, Sheals
SEREIN	Nereis, Seiner, Serine		
		SHAMAN	Ashman
SERENA	Ensear	SHAMED	Mashed
*SERETH	Threes	SHAPED	Hasped, Phased
SERGES	Egress	SHAPER	Hepars, Phares, Phrase, Raphes, Seraph, Sherpa
SERIAL	Ariels, Israel, Relais, Resail, Sailer, Serail		
		SHARED	Dasher, Rashed, Shader
SERICA	Caries, Cerias		
SERINE	Nereis, Seiner, Serein	SHARER	Rasher
		SHARES	Rashes, Shears
SERIPH	Perish, Reship	SHAVEN	Havens, Hesvan
SERMON	Mornes	SHAVER	Havers
SEROON	Roneos, Sooner	SHEALS	Halses, Hassle, Lashes, Selahs, Shales
SEROUS	Rouses		
SERPET	Pester, Peters, Petres, Preset, Pteres		
		SHEARS	Rashes, Shares
		SHE-ASS	Sashes
SERVAL	Lavers, Ravels, Salver, Slaver, Valser, Velars, Versal	SHEATH	Heaths
		SHEAVE	Heaves
		SHEBAT	Bathes
		SHEENS	Sneesh
SERVED	Versed	SHEETS	Theses
SERVER	Revers, Verser	SHELFY	Fleshy
SERVES	Severs, Sevres, Verses	SHELTA	Haslet, Lathes
		SHELTY	Ethyls
SESAME	Meases, Seames	SHELVE	Helves
SESTET	Testes, Tsetse	SHERIF	Fisher
*SESTOS	Tosses	SHERPA	Hepars, Phares, Phrase, Raphes, Seraph, Shaper
SET-OFF	Offset		
SET-OUT	Outset		
SETTER	Retest, Street, Tester	SHEUCH	Heuchs
		SHEUGH	Heughs
SETTLE	Ettles	SHIERS	Hisser, Shires
SEVERE	Reeves	SHIEST	Heists, Thesis
*SEVERN	Nerves, Nevers	SHIKAR	Rakish
SEVERS	Serves, Sevres, Verses	SHINER	Rhines, Shrine
		SHIRES	Hisser, Shiers

SHIVER	Hivers, Shrive	
SHODER	Dehors, Herods, Hordes, Horsed, Reshod, Rhodes, Shored	
SHOREA	Ashore, Hoarse	
SHORED	Dehors, Herods, Hordes, Horsed, Reshod, Rhodes, Shoder	
SHOUGH	Houghs	
SHOUSE	Houses	
SHOVEL	Hovels	
SHOVER	Hovers, Shrove	
SHOWER	Howres, Reshow, Whores	
SHRIEK	Hikers, Shrike	
SHRIKE	Hikers, Shriek	
SHRINE	Rhines, Shiner	
SHRITE	Riseth, Rithes, Theirs	
SHRIVE	Hivers, Shiver	
SHROVE	Hovers, Shover	
SHUT-UP	Pushtu	
SICKER	Ickers	
*SIDCUP	Cupids, Cuspid	
SIDDUR	Druids	
SIDE-ON	Diones, Donsie, Nidose, Noised, No-side, Onside	
SIDLER	Idlers, Slider	
SIENNA	Annies, Insane	
SIERRA	Raiser	
SIESTA	Tassie	
SIEVED	Devise	
SIFTED	Fisted	
SIFTER	Firest, Freits, Refits, Resift, Rifest, Strife	
SIGNAL	Aligns, Liangs, Ligans, Lingas	
SIGNAS	Assign	
SIGNED	Deigns, Design, Dinges, Nidges, Sdeign, Singed	
SIGNER	Reigns, Resign, Ringes, Singer	
SIGNET	Ingest, Stinge, Tinges	

SIGN-IN	Sing-in	
SIGNOR	Girons, Grison, Groins, Rosing	
SILENE	Enisle, Ensile, Senile	
SILENT	Enlist, Inlets, Listen, Tinsel	
SILKEN	Inkles, Likens	
SILLER	Rilles	
SILOED	Soiled	
SILPHA	Palish, Phials	
SILTED	Delist, Listed, Tildes	
SILVAN	Anvils	
SILVER	Livers, Livres, Sliver	
SIMMER	Mimers	
SIMNEL	Limens, Meslin	
SIMONY	Myosin	
SIMPER	Primes	
SIMPLE	Impels	
SIMPLY	Limpsy	
*SINDHI	Hindis	
SINEWY	Winsey	
SINGED	Deigns, Design, Dinges, Nidges, Sdeign, Signed	
SINGER	Reigns, Resign, Ringes, Signer	
SINGES	Gneiss	
SING-IN	Sign-in	
SINGLE	Ingles	
SINGLY	Lyings	
SINKER	Inkers, Kirsen, Reinks	
SINNED	Dennis	
SINNER	Inners	
SINNET	Sennit, Tennis	
SINTER	Insert, Inters, Nitres, Retins, Strine, Trines	
SINTOC	Tocsin, Tonics	
SIPPER	Pipers	
SIRING	Rising	
SIRRAH	Harris	
*SISERA	Arises, Raises	
SISTED	Deists, Desist	
SISTER	Resist, Resits	
SITING	Tingis	

SIT-INS	Insist		SLIVER	Livers, Livres,
SITREP	Esprit, Priest,			Silver
	Pteris, Ripest,		SLOGAN	Logans
	Sprite, Stripe		SLOIDS	Dossil, Solids
SITTER	Titers, Titres,		SLOKEN	Kelson
	Triste		SLOPPY	Polyps
SKATED	Tasked		SLOUGH	Ghouls, Loughs
SKATER	Strake, Streak,		SLOVEN	Novels
	Takers, Tasker		SLOWED	Dowels
SKEELY	Sleeky		SLOWER	Lowers, Owlers,
SKIERS	Kisser			Rowels
SLAP-UP	Palpus		SLYEST	Styles
SLATED	Deltas, Lasted,		SMALTO	Almost, Maltos
	Salted, Stadle,		SMILED	Misled, Slimed
	Staled		SMILER	Milers
SLATER	Alerts, Alters,		SMILES	Missel, Slimes
	Artels, Laster,		SMILET	Mistle
	Ratels, Resalt,		SMIRCH	Chirms, Chrism
	Salter, Staler,		SMITER	Merits, Mister,
	Tarsel			Miters, Mitres,
SLATES	Stales, Steals,			Remits, Timers
	Tassel		SMITES	Misset, Stimes,
SLAVED	Salved			Tmesis
SLAVER	Lavers, Ravels,		SMOUSE	Mouses, Mousse
	Salver, Serval,		SMUDGE	Degums
	Valser, Velars,		SNACOT	Cantos, Cotans,
	Versal			Octans
SLAVIC	Cavils, Clavis		SNARED	Redans, Sander
SLAYER	Layers, Rayles,		SNARES	Nasser, Sarsen
	Relays		SNATCH	Chants, Stanch
SLEAVE	Leaves		SNATHE	Athens, Hasten,
SLEDGE	Gledes, Gleeds,			Thanes
	Ledges		SNEESH	Sheens
SLEEKY	Skeely		SNIPED	Despin, Piends,
SLEETY	Steely			Spined
SLEEVE	Levees		SNIPER	Pernis, Repins,
SLEUTH	Hustle			Ripens
SLICER	Relics		SNIPES	Sepsin, Spines
SLIDER	Idlers, Sidler		SNIVEL	Levins, Livens
SLIEST	Islets, Istles,		SNOOPY	Spoony
	Stiles		SNOOZE	Ozones
SLIGHT	Lights		SNORED	Drones, Sorned
SLIMED	Misled, Smiled		SNORER	Sorner
SLIMES	Missel, Smiles		SNORES	Nosers, Senors,
SLIPED	Dispel, Disple,			Sensor
	Lisped, Spiled		SNOWED	Endows
SLIPES	Plisse, Spiels,		SNUDGE	Nudges
	Spiles		SOAKER	Oakers, Resoak
SLIP-UP	Pipuls, Pupils		SOARED	Adores, Oreads,
				Sea-rod

SOBEIT	Tobies	
SODIUM	Odiums	
SOFTER	Fetors, Forest,	
	Fortes, Foster	
SOILED	Siloed	
SOILER	Elisor, Oilers,	
	Oriels, Reoils	
SOLDER	Dorsel, Resold	
SOLEIN	Eloins, Esloin,	
	Insole, Lesion,	
	Oleins	
SOLEMN	Lemnos, Lemons,	
	Melons	
SOLIDS	Dossil, Sloids	
SOLING	Losing	
SOLIVE	Olives, Voiles	
SOLUTE	Tousle	
SOLVER	Lovers	
SOMBER	Bromes, Ombers,	
	Ombres, Sombre	
SOMBRE	Bromes, Ombers,	
	Ombres, Somber	
SONANT	Santon	
SONCIE	Conies, Cosine,	
	Oscine	
SONNET	Neston, Nonets,	
	Tenons, Tenson,	
	Tonnes	
SONSIE	Enosis, Eosins,	
	Essoin, Noesis,	
	Noises, Ossein,	
	Seison	
SONTAG	Tangos, Tongas,	
	Tsonga	
SOONER	Roneos, Seroon	
SORBET	Besort	
SORBIN	Inorbs, Robins	
SORDES	Dorses, Dosers,	
	Dosser	
SORDET	Dorset, Doters,	
	Sorted, Stored,	
	Strode, Trodes	
SORELS	Lessor, Losers	
SOREST	Retoss, Rosets,	
	Stores, Torses,	
	Tosser	
SORNED	Drones, Snored	
SORNER	Snorer	
SOROSE	Rooses	
SORTED	Dorset, Doters,	

	Sordet, Stored,	
	Strode, Trodes	
SORTER	Resort, Roster,	
	Storer	
SORTIE	Tories	
SOSSLE	Losses	
SOUGHT	Oughts, Toughs	
SOULED	Loused	
SOURCE	Cerous, Course,	
	Crouse, Crusoe	
SOURED	Roused	
SOUSED	Douses	
SOUTER	Ouster, Outers,	
	Routes, Touser,	
	Trouse	
SOWSED	Dowses	
SOWSER	Resows	
SOWTER	Rowest, Rowtes,	
	Stower, Towers,	
	Towser, Twoers	
SPACED	Scaped	
SPACER	Capers, Crapes,	
	Escarp, Pacers,	
	Parsec, Recaps,	
	Scrape, Secpar	
SPADER	Drapes, Padres,	
	Parsed, Rasped,	
	Repads, Spared,	
	Spread	
SPADES	Passed, Sepads	
SPAERS	Aspers, Parses,	
	Passer, Prases,	
	Repass, Spares,	
	Sparse, Spears	
SPAHIS	Phasis	
SPARED	Drapes, Padres,	
	Parsed, Rasped,	
	Repads, Spader,	
	Spread	
SPARER	Parers, Parser,	
	Rasper, Sparre	
SPARES	Aspers, Parses,	
	Passer, Prases,	
	Repass, Spaers,	
	Sparse, Spears	
SPARGE	Gapers, Gasper,	
	Grapes, Parges	
SPARRE	Parers, Parser,	
	Rasper, Sparer	

SPARSE	Aspers,	Parses,
	Passer,	Prases,
	Repass,	Spaers,
	Spares,	Spears
SPARTA	Satrap	
SPARTH	Thraps	
SPARVE	Pavers	
SPATES	Pastes,	Speats,
	Stapes	
SPAVIN	Pavins	
SPEARS	Aspers,	Parses,
	Passer,	Prases,
	Repass,	Spaers,
	Spares,	Sparse
SPEATS	Pastes,	Spates,
	Stapes	
SPECIE	Pieces	
SPEECH	Cheeps	
SPEEDO	Depose,	Epodes
SPEERS	Perses,	Preses,
	Sperse,	Sprees
SPEIRS	Prises,	Spires
SPEISS	Pisses,	Sepsis
SPELIN	Pensil,	Spinel,
	Spline	
SPERSE	Perses,	Preses,
	Speers,	Sprees
SPHERE	Herpes,	Hesper,
	Pheers	
SPHERY	Hypers,	Sypher
SPICER	Persic,	Precis,
	Prices	
SPICES	Pisces	
SPIDER	Prides,	Prised,
	Redips,	Spired
SPIELS	Plisse,	Slipes,
	Spiles	
SPIGHT	Pights	
SPILED	Dispel,	Disple,
	Lisped,	Sliped
SPILES	Plisse,	Slipes,
	Spiels	
SPINAL	Lapins,	Plains
SPINAR	Sprain	
SPINED	Despin,	Piends,
	Sniped	
SPINEL	Pensil,	Spelin,
	Spline	
SPINES	Sepsin,	Snipes

SPINET	Instep,	Step-in
SPIN-TO	Instop,	Piston,
	Pitons,	Points,
	Potins	
SPIRAE	Aspire,	Paries,
	Persia,	Praise,
	Spirea	
SPIREA	Aspire,	Paries,
	Persia,	Praise,
	Spirae	
SPIRED	Prides,	Prised,
	Redips,	Spider
SPIRES	Prises,	Speirs
SPIRTS	Sprits,	Stirps,
	Strips	
SPITAL	Alpist,	Pastil,
	Plaits	
SPITES	Stipes	
SPLINE	Pensil,	Spelin,
	Spinel	
SPLORE	Polers	
SPOILT	Pistol,	Pilots,
	Postil	
SPONGE	Pengos	
SPOONY	Snoopy	
SPOUSE	Pousse	
SPOUTS	Stoups,	Toss-up,
	Uptoss	
SPRAIN	Spinar	
SPRANG	Prangs	
SPREAD	Drapes,	Padres,
	Parsed,	Rasped,
	Repads,	Spader,
	Spared	
SPREES	Perses,	Preses,
	Speers,	Sperse
SPRIER	Priers	
SPRINT	Prints	
SPRITE	Esprit,	Priest,
	Pteris,	Ripest,
	Sitrep,	Stripe
SPRITS	Spirts,	Stirps,
	Strips	
SPRONG	Prongs	
SPROUT	Stupor	
SPRUIT	Purist,	Stir-up,
	Uprist,	Upstir
SPUNGE	Unpegs	
SPURGE	Purges	

SPURNE	Prunes	
SQUAIL	Quails	
SQUEAK	Quakes	
SQUEAL	Equals,	Lasque,
	Quesal	
SQUILL	Quills	
SQUINT	Quints	
SQUIRE	Quires,	Risque
SQUIRT	Quirts	
STABLE	Ablest,	Ablets,
	Bleats,	Tables
STACTE	Tacets	
STADLE	Deltas,	Lasted,
	Salted,	Slated,
	Staled	
STAGER	Grates,	Greats,
	Ragest,	Targes
STAGES	Sagest	
STAIDS	Sadist	
STALED	Deltas,	Lasted,
	Salted,	Slated,
	Stadle	
STALER	Alerts,	Alters,
	Artels,	Laster,
	Ratels,	Resalt,
	Salter,	Slater,
	Tarsel	
STALES	Slates,	Steals,
	Tassel	
*STALIN	Instal,	Latins
STAMEN	Aments,	Manets
STAMIN	Mantis,	Matins,
	Tamins	
STANCE	Ascent,	Enacts,
	Secant	
STANCH	Chants,	Snatch
STAPES	Pastes,	Spates,
	Speats	
STAPLE	Palest,	Pastel,
	Peltas,	Petals,
	Plates,	Pleats,
	Septal,	Tepals
STARCH	Charts	
STARED	Daters,	Desart,
	Trades,	Treads
STAREE	Aretes,	Asteer,
	Easter,	Eaters,
	Reseat,	Saeter,
	Seater,	Steare,
	Teaser,	Teresa

STARER	Arrest,	Arrets,
	Rarest,	Raster,
	Raters,	Retars,
	Sartre,	Tarres
STARES	Assert,	Asters
STARVE	Averts,	Ravest,
	Staver,	Tarves,
	Tavers,	Traves,
	Vaster	
STASIS	Assist	
STATED	Tasted	
STATER	Astart,	Taster,
	Taters,	Treats
STATES	Tasset,	Tastes
STATIC	Attics	
STATOR	Tarots,	Troats
STATUE	Astute	
STAVER	Averts,	Ravest,
	Starve,	Tarves,
	Tavers,	Traves,
	Vaster	
STAWED	Wadset,	Wasted
STAYER	Estray,	Stayre
STAY-IN	Sanity,	Satiny
STAYRE	Estray,	Stayer
STEALS	Slates,	Stales,
	Tassel	
STEANS	Assent	
STEARE	Aretes,	Asteer,
	Easter,	Eaters,
	Reseat,	Saeter,
	Seater,	Staree,
	Teaser,	Teresa
STEELY	Sleety	
STEERS	Resets,	Steres
STEEVE	Vestee	
STELAE	Teasel	
STEP-IN	Instep,	Spinet
STEREO	Eostre,	Retose
STERES	Resets,	Steers,
STERIC	Trices	
STEROL	Ostler,	Relost,
	Rostel,	Torsel
STERVE	Everts,	Revest,
	Revets,	Treves,
	Verset,	Vester
STEVEN	Events	
STEWED	Tweeds,	Wested
STEWER	Wester	

STIFLE	Filets, Flites, Itself	STOUPS	Spouts, Toss-up, Uptoss
STILAR	Trails, Trials	STOURS	Rousts, Sutors, Tussor
STILES	Islets, Istles, Sliest	STOVER	Rovest, Strove, Voters
STIMES	Misset, Smites, Tmesis	STOWER	Rowest, Rowtes, Sowter, Towers, Towser, Twoers
STINGE	Ingest, Signet, Tinges	STRAFE	Afters, Faster
STINGO	Ingots, Tigons	STRAIK	Kraits, Traiks
STINGY	Stying, Tyings	STRAIN	Instar, Santir, Trains
STIPES	Spites	STRAIT	Artist, Traits
STIRPS	Spirts, Sprits, Strips	STRAKE	Skater, Streak, Takers, Tasker
STIR-UP	Purist, Spruit, Uprist, Upstir	STRATA	Astart, Attars
STIVED	Divest	STRAWY	Wastry
STIVER	Rivets, Strive, Tivers, Trevis, Verist	STREAK	Skater, Strake, Takers, Tasker
STOEPS	Estops, Posset, Stopes	STREAM	Armest, Armets, Master, Maters, Remast, Tamers, Tremas
STOGIE	Egoist	STREEK	Tereks
STOKER	Storke, Trokes	STREET	Retest, Setter, Tester
STOLEN	Telson	STRENE	Enters, Ernest, Nester, Rentes, Resent, Tenser, Ternes
STONED	Donets, Doesn't, Ostend		
STONER	Nestor, Noters, Strone, Tenors, Tensor, Toners, Trones	STRIAE	Satire
		STRICK	Tricks
STOPED	Depots, Despot, Posted	STRIDE	Direst, Driest, Ridest
STOPER	Opster, Poster, Presto, Repost, Repots, Retops, Topers, Tropes	STRIFE	Firest, Freits, Refits, Resift, Rifest, Sifter
		STRIGA	Gratis
		STRIKE	Trikes
STOPES	Estops, Posset, Stoeps	STRINE	Insert, Inters, Nitres, Retins, Sinter, Trines
STOP-GO	Go-stop		
STORED	Dorset, Doters, Sordet, Sorted, Strode, Trodes	STRIPE	Esprit, Priest, Pteris, Ripest, Sitrep, Sprite
STORER	Resort, Roster, Sorter	STRIPS	Spirts, Sprits, Stirps
STORES	Retoss, Rosets, Sorest, Torses, Tosser		
STOREY	Oyster, Troyes		

STRIVE	Rivets, Stiver,		SUN-DOG	Sun-god, Ungods
	Tivers, Trevis,		SUN-GOD	Sun-dog, Ungods
	Verist		SUN-HAT	Haunts, Unhats
STROAM	Morats, Stroma		SUNLIT	Insult
STRODE	Dorset, Doters,		SUNSET	Unsets
	Sordet, Sorted,		SUPAWN	Sawn-up
	Stored, Trodes		SUPINE	Puisne
STROKE	Stoker, Trokes		SUPPER	Uppers
STROLL	Trolls		SURBET	Brutes, Buster,
STROMA	Morats, Stroam			Rebuts, Subter,
STRONE	Nestor, Noters,			Tubers
	Stoner, Tenors,		SUREST	Russet, Tusser
	Tensor, Toners,		SUTLER	Lurest, Luster,
	Trones			Lustre, Result,
STROUD	Tudors			Rulest, Rustle,
STROUT	Trouts, Tutors			Ulster
STROVE	Rovest, Stover,		SUTORS	Rousts, Stours,
	Voters			Tussor
STRUCK	Trucks		SUTURE	Uterus
STRUNG	Grunts		SWALED	Dwales, Wealds
STUMER	Muster		SWALES	Awless, Sweals
STUPOR	Sprout		SWARTH	Thraws, Warths,
STYING	Stingy, Tyings			Wraths
STYTHE	Tethys		SWARVE	Wavers
STYLES	Slyest		SWATHE	Wheats
SUABLE	Usable		SWAYER	Sawyer
SUABLY	Usably		SWEALS	Awless, Swales
SUBLET	Bluest, Bustle,		SWEARS	Resaws, Wrasse
	Subtle		SWEATS	Sawset, Tawses,
SUBLID	Builds			Wastes
SUBMAN	Busman		SWINGE	Sewing
SUBMEN	Busmen		SWIPED	Wisped
SUBORN	Bourns		SWIPER	Wipers
SUBTER	Brutes, Buster,		SWITHE	Whites, Withes
	Rebuts, Surbet,		SWOUND	Wounds
	Tubers		SYPHER	Hypers, Sphery
SUBTLE	Bluest, Bustle,			
	Sublet			
SUCCOR	Crocus, Occurs,		TABLER	Albert, Labret
	Roccus		TABLES	Ablest, Ablets,
SUCCUS	Cuscus			Bleats, Stable
SUDDER	Udders		TABLET	Batlet, Battel,
SUEING	Genius			Battle
SUFFER	Ruffes		TABOUR	Outbar, Rubato
SUITES	Tissue		TABRET	Batter
SUMMIT	Mutism		TABULA	Ablaut
SUMMON	Musmon		TACETS	Stacte
SUNDER	Nursed, Unders,		TACHES	Chaste, Cheats,
	Unreds			Sachet, Scathe

TACKER	Racket, Retack	
TAGGED	Gadget	
TAGGER	Garget	
TAG-RAG	Rag-tag	
TAIGLE	Aiglet, Ligate	
TAILED	Detail, Dietal,	
	Dilate	
TAILER	Retail	
TAILOR	Rialto	
TAINTS	Tanist, Titans	
TAKE-IN	Intake, Kinate	
TAKERS	Skater, Strake	
	Streak, Tasker	
TAKE-UP	Uptake	
TALENT	Latent, Latten	
TALIAN	Latian	
TAMALE	Malate	
TAMANU	Mantua	
TAMERS	Armest, Armets,	
	Master, Maters,	
	Remast, Stream,	
	Tremas	
TAMINE	Inmate	
TAMING	Mating	
TAMINS	Mantis, Matins,	
	Stamin	
TAMISE	Maties, Samite,	
	Semita	
TAMPON	Potman, Topman	
TAN-BED	Banted	
TANGIE	Eating, Ingate,	
	Teaing	
TANGLE	Langet	
TANGOS	Sontag, Tongas,	
	Tsonga	
TANIST	Taints, Titans	
TANNIC	Tin-can	
TANREC	Canter, Carnet,	
	Centra, Creant,	
	Nectar, Recant,	
	Trance	
TANTRA	Rattan, Tartan	
*TAOISM	Maoist	
TAPERS	Paster, Paters,	
	Petars, Prates,	
	Repast, Trapes	
TARGES	Grates, Greats,	
	Ragest, Stager	
TARING	Gratin, Rating,	
	Tringa	

TAROTS	Stator, Troats	
TARPAN	Partan, Trapan	
TARPON	Parton, Patron	
TARRED	Darter, Dartre,	
	Retard, Retrad,	
	Trader	
TARRES	Arrest, Arrets,	
	Rarest, Raster,	
	Raters, Retars,	
	Sartre, Starer	
TARSAL	Altars, Astral,	
	Ratals	
TARSEL	Alerts, Alters,	
	Artels, Laster,	
	Ratels, Resalt,	
	Salter, Slater,	
	Staler	
TARSIA	Arista, Riatas,	
	Tiaras	
TARSUS	Tussar	
TARTAN	Rattan, Tantra	
TARTLY	Rattly	
TARVES	Averts, Ravest,	
	Starve, Staver,	
	Tavers, Traves,	
	Vaster	
TASKED	Skated	
TASKER	Skater, Strake,	
	Streak, Takers	
TASSEL	Slates, Stales,	
	Steals	
TASSET	States, Tastes	
TASSIE	Siesta	
TASTED	Stated	
TASTER	Astert, Stater,	
	Taters, Treats	
TASTES	States, Tasset	
TATERS	Astert, Stater,	
	Taster, Treats	
TATLER	Latter, Rattle	
TAUNTS	Tutsan	
TAURIN	Nutria	
TAUTEN	Attune, Nutate	
TAVERS	Averts, Ravest,	
	Starve, Staver,	
	Tarves, Traves,	
	Vaster	
TAWERS	Waster, Waters	
TAWERY	Watery	

TAWSES	Sawset, Sweats,		Trones
	Wastes	TENREC	Center, Centre,
TAXING	Xangti		Recent
TEADES	Seated, Sedate	TENSED	Endest, Nested,
	Teased		Sedent
TEAGLE	Eaglet, Legate,	TENSER	Enters, Ernest,
	Telega		Nester, Rentes,
TEAING	Eating, Ingate,		Resent, Strene,
	Tangie		Ternes
TEAMAN	Amenta	TENSON	Neston, Nonets,
TEA-POT	Aptote		Sonnet, Tenons,
TEARED	Derate, Redate		Tonnes
TEARER	Retear	TENSOR	Nestor, Noters,
TEASED	Seated, Sedate,		Stoner, Strone,
	Teades		Tenors, Toners,
TEASEL	Stelae		Trones
TEASER	Aretes, Asteer,	TENTED	Detent, Netted
	Easter, Eaters,	TENTER	Netter, Retent
	Reseat, Saeter,	TENUIS	Intuse, Unites,
	Seater, Staree,		Unties
	Steare, Teresa	TENURE	Neuter, Retune,
TEA-SET	Eatest, Estate,		Tureen
	Testae	TENUTO	Teuton
TEA-URN	Nature	TEPALS	Palest, Pastel,
TEAZEL	**Teaz**le		Peltas, Petals,
TEAZLE	Teazel		Plates, Pleats,
TEEING	Ginete		Septal, Staple
TEETER	Terete	TERAPH	Threap
TE-HEES	Seethe	TERBIA	Baiter, Barite,
*TEHRAN	Anther, Thenar		Rebait
TELARY	Eyltra, Lyrate,	TEREKS	Streek
	Raylet, Realty	TERESA	Aretes, Asteer,
TELEGA	Eaglet, Legate,		Easter, Eaters,
	Teagle		Reseat, Saeter,
TELLER	Retell		Seater, Staree,
TELSON	Stolen		Steare, Teaser
TEMPLE	Pelmet	TERETE	Teeter
TENACE	Cetane	TERMES	Meters, Metres,
TENAIL	Entail		Restem
TENDED	Dented	TERMLY	Myrtle
TENDER	Rented	TERMOR	Tremor
TENNER	Rennet	TERNAL	Altern, Antler,
TENNIS	Sennit, Sinnet		Learnt, Rental
TENONS	Neston, Nonets,	TERNES	Enters, Ernest,
	Sonnet, Tenson,		Nester, Rentes,
	Tonnes		Resent, Tenser,
TENORA	Atoner, Ornate		Strene
TENORS	Nestor, Noters,	TERRIT	Ritter, Tirret
	Strone, Stoner,	TESTAE	Eatest, Estate,
	Tensor, Toners		Teaset

TESTED	Detest		THRONE	Hornet, Thorne
TESTER	Retest, Setter,		THROVE	Roveth
	Street		THRUST	Truths
TESTES	Sestet, Tsetse		THYMIC	Mythic
*TETHYS	Stythe		THYMUS	Mythus
TETRAD	Ratted		TIARAS	Arista, Riatas,
TEUTON	Tenuto			Tarsia
TEWING	Twinge		TICING	Citing
THALER	Halter, Lather		TICKLE	Keltic
THANES	Athens, Hasten,		TIEING	Ignite
	Snathe		TIERCE	Cerite, Certie
THAWED	Wadeth			Recite
THAWER	Rethaw, Wreath		TIERED	Dieter, Re-edit,
THEBES	Behest			Retied
THECAL	Chalet, Thecla		TIE-ROD	Editor, Rioted,
THECLA	Chalet, Thecal			Triode
THEIRS	Riseth, Rithes,		TIGONS	Ingots, Stingo
	Shrite		TILDES	Delist, Listed,
THEISM	Meiths, Themis			Silted
THEIST	Tithes		TILERS	Lister, Litres,
*THELMA	Hamlet			Relist
THEMIS	Meiths, Theism		TILLED	Lilted
THENAL	Hantle, Lathen		TILLER	Retill, Rillet
THENAR	Anther, Tehran		TILMUS	Litmus
THESES	Sheets		TILTED	Titled
THESIS	Heists, Shiest		TILTER	Litter, Titler
THIBLE	Blithe		TIMBER	Betrim, Timbre
THIRST	Thrist		TIMBRE	Betrim, Timber
THOLES	Helots, Hostel,		TIMERS	Merits, Mister,
	Hotels			Miters, Mitres,
THORAL	Harlot			Remits, Smiter
*THORNE	Hornet, Throne		TIN-CAN	Tannic
THORNY	Rhyton		TINDER	Rident, Trined
THORPE	Pother		TINEID	Indite
THOWEL	Howlet		TINGED	Nidget
THRAPS	Sparth		TINGES	Ingest, Signet,
THRAVE	Raveth			Stinge
THRAWS	Swarth, Warths,		TINGIS	Siting
	Wraths		TINKER	Reknit
THREAD	Dareth, Dearth,		TINNED	Dentin, Indent,
	Hatred, Red-hat			Intend
THREAP	Teraph		TINNER	Intern
THREAT	Hatter		TINSEL	Enlist, Inlets,
THREES	Esther, Hester			Listen, Silent
THRENE	Nether		TINTER	Nitter, Retint
THRICE	Cither		TIRADE	Raited
THRIST	Thirst		TIRRET	Ritter, Territ
THRIVE	Riveth		TISSUE	Suites
THROES	Others		TITANS	Taints, Tanist

TITERS	Sitter, Titres, Triste
TITHER	Hitter
TITHES	Theist
TITLED	Tilted
TITLER	Litter, Tilter
TITRES	Sitter, Titers, Triste
TIVERS	Rivets, Stiver, Strive, Trevis, Verist
TMESIS	Misset, Smites, Stimes
TOBIES	Sobeit
TOCHER	Hector, Rochet, Rotche, Troche
TOCSIN	Sintoc, Tonics
TOE-CAP	Capote
TOFORE	Foetor, Footer, Refoot
TOGAED	Dogate, Dotage
TOGGLE	Goglet, Logget
TOILER	Loiter, Triole
TOLANE	Lean-to
TOLEDO	Looted, Tooled
TOMBAC	Combat
TOMTOM	Mot-mot
TONERS	Nestor, Noters, Stoner, Strone, Tenors, Tensor, Trones
TONGAS	Sontag, Tangos, Tsonga
TONICS	Sintoc, Tocsin
TONING	Noting
TONNES	Neston, Nonets, Sonnet, Tenons, Tenson
TON-UPS	Put-ons, Unstop
TOOLED	Looted, Toledo
TOOLER	Looter, Rootle
TOPERS	Opster, Poster, Presto, Repost, Repots, Retops, Stoper, Tropes
TOPFUL	Potful
TOP-HAT	Pot-hat
TOPHUS	Pushto, Upshot
TOPICS	Optics, Picots
TOPING	Opting

TOPMAN	Potman, Tampon
TOPMEN	Potmen
TORERO	Rooter
TORIES	Sortie
TORPID	Tripod
TORQUE	Quoter, Roquet
TORSEL	Ostler, Relost, Rostel, Sterol
TORSES	Retoss, Rosets, Sorest, Stores, Tosser
TORULA	Rotula
TOSSER	Retoss, Rosets, Sorest, Stores, Torses
TOSSES	Sestos
TOSS-UP	Spouts, Stoups, Uptoss
T'OTHER	Hotter
TOUCAN	Noctua, Uncoat
TOUGHS	Oughts, Sought
TOURED	Detour, Douter, Redout, Routed
TOURER	Retour, Roture, Router
TOUSED	Ousted
TOUSER	Ouster, Outers, Routes, Souter, Trouse
TOUSLE	Solute
TOWELS	Lowest, Owlets
TOWERS	Rowest, Rowtes, Sowter, Stower, Towser, Twoers
TOWING	Wigton
TOWSER	Rowest, Rowtes, Sowter, Stower, Towers, Twoers
TOYMEN	Etymon
TRABEA	Abater, Rabate
TRACED	Carted, Cedrat, Crated, Redact
TRACER	Arrect, Carter, Crater
TRACES	Carets, Cartes, Caster, Caters, Crates, Cresta, Reacts, Recast
TRADED	Darted

TRADER	Darter, Dartre, Retard, Retrad, Tarred	TRIAGE	Aigret, Gaiter
		TRIALS	Stilar, Trails
		TRIBES	Bestir, Bister, Bistre, Biters, Brites
TRADES	Daters, Desart, Stared, Treads		
TRAGIC	Catrig	TRICED	Credit, Direct
TRAIKS	Straik, Kraits	TRICES	Steric
TRAILS	Stilar, Trials	TRICKS	Strick
TRAINS	Instar, Santir, Strain	TRIERS	Restir
		TRIFLE	Filter, Lifter
TRAITS	Artist, Strait	TRIKES	Strike
TRANCE	Canter, Carnet, Centra, Creant, Nectar, Recant, Tanrec	TRINAL	Ratlin
		TRINED	Rident, Tinder
		TRINES	Insert, Inters, Nitres, Retins, Sinter, Strine
TRAPAN	Partan, Tarpan		
TRAPED	Depart, Drapet, Parted, Petard, Prated	TRINGA	Gratin, Rating, Taring
		TRIODE	Editor, Rioted, Tie-rod
TRAPES	Paster, Paters, Petars, Prates, Repast, Tapers	TRIOLE	Loiter, Toiler
		TRIPOD	Torpid
TRAVEL	Varlet	TRIPOS	Prosit
TRAVES	Averts, Ravest, Starve, Staver, Tarves, Tavers, Vaster	TRISTE	Sitter, Titers, Titres
		TRITON	Intort
		TRIUNE	Uniter, Untire
TREADS	Daters, Desart, Stared, Trades	TROATS	Stator, Tarots
		TROCAR	Carrot
TREATS	Astert, Stater, Taster, Taters	TROCHE	Hector, Rochet, Rotche, Tocher
TREFLE	Felter, Feltre, Refelt, Reflet	TRODES	Dorset, Doters, Sordet, Sorted, Stored, Strode
TREMAS	Armest, Armets, Master, Maters, Remast, Stream, Tamers		
		TROKES	Stoker, Stroke
		TROLLS	Stroll
		TRONES	Nestor, Noters, Stoner, Strone, Tenors, Tensor, Toners
TREMOR	Termor		
TREPAN	Arpent, Enrapt, Entrap, Panter, Parent, Pterna		
		TROPES	Opster, Poster, Presto, Repost, Repots, Retops, Stoper, Topers
*TREVES	Everts, Revest, Revets, Sterve, Verset, Vester		
		TROUPE	Pouter, Roupet
TREVET	Vetter	TROUSE	Ouster, Outers, Routes, Souter, Touser
TREVIS	Rivets, Stiver, Strive, Tivers, Verist		
TRIADS	Astrid	TROUTS	Strout, Tutors

*TROYES	Oyster, Storey		TWOERS	Rowest, Rowtes,
TRUCES	Cruets, Cruset,			Sowter, Stower,
	Eructs, Rectus,			Towers, Towser
	Recuts		TYCOON	Coonty
TRUCKS	Struck		TYINGS	Stingy, Stying
TRUEST	Utters		TYPHON	Phyton, Python
TRUTHS	Thrust		TYRING	Trying
TRYING	Tyring			
TSETSE	Sestet, Testes			
TSONGA	Sontag, Tangos,		UDDERS	Sudder
	Tongas		UGLIER	Guiler, Ligure,
TUAREG	Argute, Rugate			Reguli
TUBATE	Battue		UHLANS	Unlash
TUBERS	Brutes, Buster,		ULLING	Ungill
	Rebuts, Subter,		ULNARE	Neural, Unreal
	Surbet		ULSTER	Lurest, Luster,
TUCANS	Cantus, Tuscan,			Lustre, Result,
	Uncast			Rulest, Rustle,
*TUDORS	Stroud			Sutler
TUFTER	Futter		UMBELS	Umbles
TUNERS	Unrest		UMBLES	Umbels
TUNNEL	Unlent		UMBRAL	Brumal, Labrum,
TUNNER	Runnet, Unrent			Lumbar
TURBOS	Robust		UMBRAS	Rumbas, Sambur
TURCOS	Courts, Crouts,		UMLAUT	Mutual
	Scruto		UMPIRE	Impure
TUREEN	Neuter, Retune,		UNABLE	Nebula, Unbale
	Tenure		UNAGED	Augend
TURFER	Returf		UNBALE	Nebula, Unable
TURNER	Return		UNBARE	Unbear, Urbane
TURNIP	Turpin		UNBEAR	Unbare, Urbane
TURN-UP	Upturn		UNBIAS	Nubias
*TURPIN	Turnip		UNBLED	Bundle
TURRET	Rutter		UNBRED	Bunder, Burden,
TURTLE	Ruttle			Burned
TUSCAN	Cantus, Tucans,		UNCAGE	Cangue
	Uncast		UNCASE	Usance
TUSSAR	Tarsus		UNCAST	Cantus, Tucans,
TUSSER	Russet, Surest			Tuscan
TUSSOR	Rousts, Stours,		UNCATE	Canute
	Sutors		UNCOAT	Noctua, Toucan
TUTORS	Strout, Trouts		UNCOIN	Nuncio
TUTSAN	Taunts		UNCOOP	Coupon
TWEEDS	Stewed, Wested		UNCOPE	Pounce
TWIERS	Twires, Wriest,		UNCORE	Rounce
	Writes		UNDEAR	Dauner, Unread
TWINER	Winter		UNDERN	Dunner
TWINGE	Tewing		UNDERS	Nursed, Sunder,
TWIRES	Twiers, Wriest,			Unreds
	Writes			

UNDOER	Enduro		
UNDOES	Undose		
UNDOSE	Undoes		
UNEDGE	Dengue		
UNFELT	Fluent, Netful,		
	Unleft		
UNFIST	Unfits		
UNFITS	Unfist		
UNFLAT	Flaunt		
UNFURL	Urnful		
UNGILL	Ulling		
UNGILT	Glutin, Luting		
UNGIRD	During		
UNGIRT	Untrig		
UNGLIB	Bluing		
UNGODS	Sundog, Sungod		
UNGUAL	Ungula		
UNGULA	Ungual		
UNHATS	Haunts, Sunhat		
UNHURT	Unruth		
UNIBLE	Nubile		
UNICED	Induce		
UNIONS	Nonius, Unison		
UNISON	Nonius, Unions		
UNITED	Untied		
UNITER	Triune, Untire		
UNITES	Intuse, Tenuis,		
	Unties		
UNLACE	Cuneal, Launce		
UNLADE	Unlead		
UNLAID	Dualin		
UNLASH	Uhlans		
UNLEAD	Unlade		
UNLEFT	Fluent, Netful,		
	Unfelt		
UNLENT	Tunnel		
UNLIVE	Unveil		
UNNAIL	Annuli		
UNNEST	Unsent		
UNPEGS	Spunge		
UNPILE	Line-up, Lupine,		
	Up-line		
UNPINS	Unspin		
UNREAD	Dauner, Undear		
UNREAL	Neural, Ulnare		
UNREDS	Nursed, Sunder,		
	Unders		
UNREEL	Renule		
UNRENT	Runnet, Tunner		
UNREST	Tuners		
UNRING	Urning		
UNRIPE	Punier, Purine		
UNROBE	Bourne		
UNROOT	Notour		
UNRUDE	Unrued		
UNRUED	Unrude		
UNRUTH	Unhurt		
UNSEAT	Austen, Nasute		
UNSENT	Unnest		
UNSERE	Ensure, Enures		
UNSETS	Sunset		
UNSHIP	Punish		
UNSHOD	Hounds		
UNSLIM	Muslin		
UNSNAP	Pannus, Sannup,		
	Unspan		
UNSOFT	Founts		
UNSOLE	Ensoul, Nousle		
UNSPAN	Pannus, Sannup,		
	Unsnap		
UNSPIN	Unpins		
UNSTOP	Put-ons, Ton-ups		
UNSUED	Unused		
UNTIDY	Nudity		
UNTIED	United		
UNTIES	Intuse, Tenuis,		
	Unites		
UNTILE	Lutein, Lutine		
UNTIRE	Triune, Uniter		
UNTRIG	Ungirt		
UNTROD	Rotund		
UNUSED	Unsued		
UNVEIL	Unlive		
UNWARP	Unwrap		
UNWARY	Runway		
UNWRAP	Unwarp		
UPBEAT	Beat-up		
UPCAST	Catsup		
UPDRAW	Upward		
UPENDS	Send-up, Upsend		
UPHANG	Hang-up		
UPHOLD	Hold-up		
UP-LINE	Line-up, Lupine,		
	Unpile		
UPLOCK	Lock-up		
UPPERS	Supper		
UP-PILE	Pile-up		
UPRATE	Uptear		

UPREAR	Parure	
UPRIST	Purist, Spruit, Stir-up, Upstir	
UPROSE	Poseur	
UPSEND	Send-up, Upends	
UPSHOT	Pushto, Tophus	
UPSTIR	Purist, Spruit, Stir-up, Uprist	
UPSWAY	Upways	
UPTAKE	Take-up	
UPTEAR	Uprate	
UPTOSS	Spouts, Stoups, Toss-up	
UPTURN	Turn-up	
UPWARD	Updraw	
UPWAYS	Upsway	
UPWIND	Wind-up	
URACIL	Lauric	
URATES	Atreus	
URBANE	Unbare, Unbear	
UREASE	Reseau	
URETER	Reuter	
URGENT	Gunter, Gurnet	
URINES	Insure, Inures, Rusine, Ursine	
URNFUL	Unfurl	
URNING	Unring	
URSINE	Insure, Inures, Rusine, Urines	
USABLE	Suable	
USABLY	Suably	
USANCE	Uncase	
USHERS	Rhesus, Rushes	
UTERUS	Suture	
UTTERS	Truest	
VACATE	Caveat	
VAINER	Rave-in, Ravine	
VAKASS	Kavass	
VALETS	Vestal	
VALING	Laving	
VALLAR	Larval	
VALOUR	Louvar, Ovular	
VALSER	Lavers, Ravels, Salver, Serval, Slaver, Velars, Versal	
VALUES	Avulse	
VAMPER	Revamp	
VANGEE	Avenge, Geneva	
VARIER	Arrive	
VARLET	Travel	
VASTER	Averts, Ravest, Starve, Staver, Tarves, Tavers, Traves	
VEADER	Evader, Reaved	
VEALER	Laveer, Leaver, Reveal	
VECTOR	Corvet, Covert	
VEERED	Reeved	
VEILED	Levied	
VEINED	Endive, Envied	
VELARS	Lavers, Ravels, Salver, Serval, Slaver, Valser, Versal	
VELATE	Veleta	
VELCRO	Clover	
VELETA	Velate	
VELITE	Levite	
VELOUR	Louver, Louvre	
VENDER	Nerved, Revend	
VENEER	Enerve, Evener	
VENIAL	Alevin, Alvine	
VERDIN	Driven	
VERGEE	Greeve	
VERGES	Greves	
VERILY	Livery	
VERISM	Vermis	
VERIST	Rivets, Stiver, Strive, Tivers, Trevis	
VERMIS	Verism	
VERNAL	Nerval	
VERSAL	Lavers, Ravels, Salver, Serval, Slaver, Valser, Velars	
VERSED	Served	
VERSER	Revers, Server	
VERSES	Serves, Severs, Sevres	
VERSET	Everts, Revets, Revest, Sterve, Treves, Vester	
VESICA	Cavies	

VESSEL	Selves	
VESTAL	Valets	
VESTED	Devest	
VESTEE	Steeve	
VESTER	Everts, Revest,	
	Revets, Sterve,	
	Treves, Verset	
VETOED	Devote	
VETOER	Reveto, Revote	
*VETTER	Trevet	
VIEWER	Review	
VIEWLY	Wively	
VILELY	Evilly, Lively	
VILEST	Livest	
VINOSE	Nivose	
VIOLET	Olivet	
VIOLIN	Olivin	
VIRENT	Invert	
VIREOS	Rivose, Virose	
VIRGIN	Riving	
VIROSE	Rivose, Vireos	
VOIDED	Devoid	
VOIDER	Devoir	
VOILES	Olives, Solive	
VOLERY	Overly	
VOLLEY	Lovely	
VOTERS	Rovest, Stover,	
	Strove	
VOWELS	Wolves	
WABBLE	Bawble	
WADDLE	Dawdle	
WADERS	Sawder	
WADETH	Thawed	
WADSET	Stawed, Wasted	
WAGGEL	Waggle	
WAGGLE	Waggel	
WAINED	Dewani, Edwina	
WAIVED	Adview	
WALING	Lawing	
WALRUS	Wrauls	
WANDER	Andrew, Darwen,	
	Rawden, Warden,	
	Warned	
WANDLE	Elwand	
WANING	Awning	
WARBLE	Bawler	
WARDED	Drawed, Edward	

WARDEN	Andrew, Darwen,	
	Rawden, Wander,	
	Warned	
WARDER	Drawer, Redraw,	
	Reward, Warred	
WARDOG	War-god	
WAR-GOD	Wardog	
WARMER	Rewarm	
WARNED	Andrew, Darwen,	
	Rawden, Wander,	
	Warden	
WARNER	Rewarn, Warren	
WARPER	Pre-war, Rewrap	
WARRED	Drawer, Redraw,	
	Reward, Warder	
WARREN	Rewarn, Warner	
WARTHS	Swarth, Thraws,	
	Wraths	
WASHER	Hawser, Rewash	
WASTED	Stawed, Wadset	
WASTER	Tawers, Waters	
WASTES	Sawset, Sweats,	
	Tawses	
WASTRY	Strawy	
WATERS	Tawers, Waster	
WATERY	Tawery	
WAVERS	Swarve	
WEALDS	Dwales, Swaled	
WEARER	Rewear	
WELDER	Reweld	
WELKIN	Winkle	
WESTED	Stewed, Tweeds	
WESTER	Stewer	
WHEATS	Swathe	
WHERES	Hewers, Reshew	
WHINGE	Hewing	
WHITER	Wither, Writhe	
WHITES	Swithe, Withes	
WHORES	Howres, Reshow,	
	Shower	
WIDELY	Wieldy	
WIELDY	Widely	
*WIGTON	Towing	
WINDER	Rewind	
WIND-UP	Upwind	
WINGED	Dewing	
WINKLE	Welkin	
WINSEY	Sinewy	
WINTER	Twiner	

WIPERS	Swiper		WRITES	Twiers, Twires,
WISPED	Swiped			Wriest
WITHER	Whiter, Writhe		WRITHE	Whiter, Wither
WITHES	Swithe, Whites			
WITHIN	Inwith			
WITTED	Dewitt		XANGTI	Taxing
WIVELY	Viewly		XENIAL	Alexin
WOBBLY	By-blow			
WOLFER	Flower, Fowler,			
	Reflow		YAGERS	Greasy
WOLVES	Vowels		YAPPER	Papery, Prepay
WONDER	Downer		YARDED	Drayed
WONING	Owning		YARELY	Yearly
WONNER	Renown		YARNED	Denary
WORKER	Rework		YARNER	Rayner
WORSEN	Owners, Resown,		YARRED	Dreary
	Rowens		YARROW	Arrowy
WOUNDS	Swound		YEARLY	Yarely
WRASSE	Resaws, Swears		YEARNS	Raynes, Senary
WRATHS	Swarth, Thraws,			
	Warths			
WRAULS	Walrus		ZAFFER	Zaffre
WREATH	Rethaw, Thawer		ZAFFRE	Zaffer
WRIEST	Twiers, Twires,			
	Writes			

Seven letters

AARONIC	Ocarina	ADHERER	Reheard
ABACTOR	Acrobat, Boat-car	ADHERES	Headers, Hearsed,
ABATERS	Abreast, Tea-bars		Reheads, Sheared
ABETTOR	Taboret	ADMIRER	Madrier, Married
ABIDERS	Airbeds, Sidebar	ADMIRES	Misread, Sidearm
ABLUENT	Tunable	ADOPTER	Readopt
ABORTED	Borated	ADORERS	Drosera
ABREACT	Bearcat, Cabaret	ADORING	Gordian, Roading
ABREAST	Abaters, Tea-bars	ADORNER	Readorn
ABRIDGE	Brigade	ADVERSE	Evaders
ABSTAIN	Tsabian	ADVERTS	Starved
ABYSMAL	Balsamy	AEDILES	Deiseal
ACARIDS	Ascarid	AEOLIST	Isolate
ACCOMPT	Compact	AEROSOL	Roseola
ACCRUAL	Caracul	AETATIS	Satiate
ACCRUED	Cardecu	AFREETS	Fearest, Feaster
ACCURSE	Accuser	AGELESS	Sealegs
ACCUSED	Succade	AGGRESS	Saggers, Seggars
ACCUSER	Accurse	AGISTER	Aigrets, Gaiters,
ACEROUS	Carouse		Sea-girt
ACETOIN	Aconite, Anoetic	AGNAMED	Managed
ACETOSE	Coatees	AGONIES	Agonise
ACHINGS	Cashing, Chasing	AGONISE	Agonies
ACONITE	Acetoin, Anoetic	AGROUND	Durango
ACORNED	Dracone	AIGRETS	Agister, Gaiters,
ACRILAN	Carinal, Clarain,		Sea-girt
	Cranial	AILERON	Alienor
ACROBAT	Abactor, Boat-car	AILMENT	Aliment
ACROGEN	Cornage	AIMLESS	Melissa, Samiels,
ACTINGS	Casting		Seismal
ACTRESS	Casters, Recasts	*AINTREE	Trainee
ADAMITE	Amidate	AIRBALL	Barilla
ADAPTER	Readapt	AIRBEDS	Abiders, Sidebar
*ADELINE	Delaine	AIRBELL	Braille, Liberal
ADHERED	Redhead		

124

AIRFLUE	Failure	ALTERNE	Eternal
AIRINGS	Arising, Raising,	ALTESSE	Tealess, Teasels
	Sairing	ALTHING	Halting, Lathing
AIRLESS	Resails, Sailers,	ALUMING	Mauling
	Serails, Serials	ALYSSUM	Asylums
*ALAMEIN	Laminae	AMASSER	Reamass
*ALBERTA	Latebra, Ratable	AMBERED	Breamed, Embread
ALBERTS	Blaster, Labrets,	AMBLING	Balming, Blaming,
	Stabler, Tablers		Lambing
ALBINOS	Asbolin	AMBULET	Mutable
ALBUMEN	Balneum	*AMELIAS	Malaise
ALECOST	Lactose, Locates,	AMENDED	Deadmen
	Talcose	AMENDER	Meander, Reamend,
ALEMBIC	Emblica		Renamed
ALERTED	Altered, Delater,	AMENING	Meaning
	Redealt, Related,	AMENITY	Anytime
	Treadle	AMENTIA	Animate
ALGEBAR	Algebra	AMERCED	Creamed, Racemed
ALGEBRA	Algebar	AMERCER	Creamer
*ALGERIA	Regalia	AMIDATE	Adamite
ALIENER	Realine	AMMETER	Metamer
ALIENOR	Aileron	AMMINES	Misname
ALIGNED	Dealing, Leading	AMNIONS	Mansion
ALIGNER	Engrail, Realign,	*AMORETS	Maestro
	Reginal	AMOUNTS	Saumont
ALIMENT	Ailment	ANAPEST	Peasant
ALINING	Nailing	ANCRESS	Caserns
ALIPEDS	Palsied, Pleiads	ANDANTE	Dantean
*ALISTER	Realist, Saltier,	ANELING	Eanling, Leaning
	Saltire, Slatier,	ANETHOL	Athlone
	Tailers	ANGELIC	Anglice, Galenic
ALIUNDE	Unideal	ANGERED	Derange, Enraged,
ALLEDGE	Alleged		Grandee, Grenade
ALLEGED	Alledge	ANGLICE	Angelic, Galenic
ALLERGY	Gallery, Largely,	ANGLIST	Lasting, Salting,
	Regally		Slating, Staling
ALL-HEAL	Heal-all	ANGRIER	Earring, Grainer,
ALL-OVER	Overall		Rangier, Rearing
ALLURED	Udaller	ANGRIES	Earings, Erasing,
*ALMERIC	Claimer, Miracle,		Gainers, Regains,
	Reclaim		Regians, Reginas,
ALMOIGN	Loaming		Searing, Seringa
ALMONDS	Dolmans	ANGUINE	Guanine
ALMONER	Moneral, Nemoral	ANGULAR	Granula
ALMUCES	Macules, Mascule	ANIGHTS	Hasting, Shangti
ALSIRAT	Lariats	ANIMATE	Amentia
ALTERED	Alerted, Delater,	ANIMIST	Intimas
	Redealt, Related,	ANKLETS	Asklent
	Treadle	ANNELID	Lindane
ALTERER	Realter, Relater		

ANNEXER	Reannex	ARTISAN	Antiars, Tsarina
ANOETIC	Acetoin, Aconite	ARTISTE	Attires, Ratites,
ANOSMIC	Camions, Maniocs,		Striate, Tastier
	Masonic	ARTISTS	Straits, Tsarist
ANSWERS	Rawness	ARTLESS	Lasters, Salters,
ANTHERS	Hanster, Thenars		Slaters, Tarsels
ANTIARS	Artisan, Tsarina	*ARUNDEL	Launder, Lurdane,
ANTIGEN	Gentian		Rundale
ANTIQUE	Quinate	ASBOLIN	Albinos
ANTI-RED	Detrain, Tanride,	ASCARID	Acarids
	Trade-in, Trained	ASCITIC	Sciatic
ANTI-SEX	Sextain	ASEPTIC	Spicate
ANTLERS	Rentals, Saltern,	ASKINGS	Gaskins
	Sternal	ASKLENT	Anklets
ANYTIME	Amenity	ASPERSE	Parsees, Serapes
ANUROUS	Uranous	ASPIRED	Despair, Diapers,
APANAGE	Pangaea		Praised
APERTOR	Praetor, Prorate	ASPIRER	Praiser, Rapiers,
APHETIC	Hepatic		Repairs
APLITES	Talipes	ASPIRES	Paresis, Praises,
APOSTIL	Topsail		Serapis, Spireas
APOSTLE	Pelotas, Pot-ales	ASPREAD	Parades, Saperda
APPENDS	Snapped	ASSUAGE	Sausage
APPULSE	Papules	ASSUMER	Masseur
APRICOT	Parotic, Patrico	ASSURER	Rasures
APRONED	Operand, Padrone,	ASTERIA	Aristae, Atresia
	Pandore	ASTERID	Astride, Disrate,
APTNESS	Patness		Staider, Tirades
ARANEID	Ariadne	ASTRIDE	Asterid, Disrate,
ARBITER	Rarebit		Staider, Tirades
ARBORED	Boarder, Broader,	ASYLUMS	Alyssum
	Reboard	ATHEISM	Hamites
ARBORET	Taborer	ATHEIST	Staithe
ARCADES	Sea-card	ATHIRST	Rattish, Tartish
*ARCHIES	Cahiers, Cashier	*ATHLONE	Anethol
ARCHING	Chagrin, Charing	ATINGLE	Elating, Gelatin,
AREFIES	Faeries, Freesia,		Genital, Langite
	Sea-fire	ATOMICS	Somatic
*ARIADNE	Araneid	ATOMIES	Atomise
ARISING	Airings, Raising,	ATOMISE	Atomies
	Sairing	ATONERS	Senator, Treason
ARISTAE	Asteria, Atresia	ATRAZIN	Tzarina
ARNICAS	Carinas, Sarcina	ATRESIA	Aristae, Asteria
ARNOTTO	Otranto, Rattoon	ATTIRES	Artiste, Ratites,
*ARNSIDE	Sardine		Striate, Tastier
ARPENTS	Entraps, Panters,	ATTRITE	Titrate
	Parents, Pastern,	ATTUNED	Nutated, Taunted
	Persant, Trepans	ATTUNES	Nutates, Tautens
ARSENIC	Cerasin, Sarcine		Tetanus, Unstate
ARTICLE	Recital		

AUCTION	Caution		BECHARM	Chamber, Chambre
AUDILES	Deasiul		*BEDALES	Beadles
*AUSTENS	Senatus, Unseats		BEDLESS	Blessed
AUTOCUE	Couteau		BED-ROCK	Brocked
AVARICE	Caviare		BEDROOM	Boredom, Broomed
AVENGER	Engrave, Genevra		BEDTIME	Betimed
AVODIRE	Avoider		BEECHES	Beseech
AVOIDER	Avodire		BELACED	Debacle
AWESOME	Waesome		BELATED	Bleated
AXLE-PIN	Explain		BELGARD	Garbled
			*BELGIAN	Bengali
			BELLIED	Delible
BAALITE	Labiate		BELTANE	Tenable
BABBLED	Blabbed		*BENGALI	Belgian
BABBLER	Blabber, Brabble		BENMOST	Entombs
BACK-OUT	Out-back		BENTEAK	Betaken
BACKSET	Set-back		BERATED	Betread, Debater,
BALDEST	Blasted, Stabled			Rebated
BALDING	Blading		BERRIED	Briered
BALLUTE	Bullate		BESAINT	Bestain
BALMING	Ambling, Blaming,		BESEECH	Beeches
	Lambing		BESHREW	Hebrews
BALNEUM	Albumen		BESTAIN	Besaint
BALSAMY	Abysmal		BESTIAL	Bastile
BANDORE	Broaden		BESTILL	Billets
BANSHEE	Has-been		BESTREW	Webster
BANTAMS	Batsman		BETAKEN	Benteak
BARBELS	Rabbles, Slabber		BETHUMB	Bumpeth
BARBETS	Rabbets, Stabber		BETIDED	Debited
BARGING	Garbing		BETIMED	Bedtime
BARILLA	Air-ball		BETRAYS	Barytes
BARINGS	Sabring		BETREAD	Berated, Debater,
BARLESS	Bra-less			Rebated
BARKING	Braking		BIG-NAME	Beaming
BARONET	Reboant		BILBOES	Lobbies
BARYTES	Betrays		BILLETS	Bestill
BASTARD	Tabards		BILOBED	Lobbied
BASTERS	Brasset, Breasts		BILTONG	Bloting, Bolting
BASTILE	Bestial		BIPOLAR	Parboil
BASTION	Obtains		BIRETTA	Ratbite
BASTING	Batings		BIZARRE	Brazier
BATINGS	Basting		BLABBED	Babbled
BATSMAN	Bantams		BLABBER	Babbler, Brabble
BATTLER	Blatter		BLADING	Balding
BEADLES	Bedales		BLAMING	Ambling, Balming,
BEAMING	Big-name			Lambing
BEARCAT	Abreact, Cabaret		BLARETH	Blather, Halbert
BEARDED	Breaded		BLASTED	Baldest, Stabled
BECALMS	Scamble		BLASTER	Alberts, Labrets,
				Stabler, Tablets

BLASTIE	Stabile		BOSCAGE	Bocages
BLATHER	Blareth, Halbert		BOTTLED	Blotted
BLATTER	Battler		BOTTLER	Blotter
BLEATED	Belated		BOULDER	Doubler
BLEATER	Retable		BOULTED	Doublet
BLENDER	Reblend		BOULTER	Trouble
BLESSED	Bedless		BOUNDEN	Unboned
BLETHER	Herblet		BOUNDER	Rebound, Unbored,
BLINDER	Brindle			Unorbed, Unrobed
BLISTER	Bristle, Riblets		BOWELED	Elbowed
BLOATED	Lobated		BOW-HAND	Handbow
BLOCKER	Reblock		BOWLDER	Low-bred
BLOOMER	Rebloom		BOWLING	Blowing
BLOTING	Biltong, Bolting		BOXWOOD	Wood-box
BLOTTED	Bottled		BOXWORK	Workbox
BLOTTER	Bottler		BRABBLE	Babbler, Blabber
BLOWFLY	Fly-blow		BRACCIO	Boracic
BLOWING	Bowling		BRAILLE	Air-bell, Liberal
BLOW-OUT	Outblow, Outbowl		BRAISED	Darbies, Sea-bird
BLUBBER	Bubbler		BRAISES	Brassie
BLUNDER	Bundler		BRAKING	Barking
BLUNGED	Bungled		BRA-LESS	Barless
BLUNGER	Bungler		BRANDER	Rebrand
BLUSHES	Bushels		BRANKIE	Break-in, Inbreak
BLUSTER	Brustle, Bustler,		BRASSET	Basters, Breasts
	Butlers, Subtler		BRASSIE	Braises
BOARDED	Road-bed		BRAWLED	Warbled
BOARDER	Arbored, Broader,		BRAWLER	Warbler
	Reboard		BRAWLIE	Wirable
BOARING	Grobian		BRAZIER	Bizarre
BOASTER	Boaters, Rebatos,		BREADED	Bearded
	Sorbate		BREAK-IN	Brankie, Inbreak
BOAT-CAR	Abactor, Acrobat		BREAK-UP	Upbreak
BOATERS	Boaster, Rebatos,		BREAMED	Ambered, Embread
	Sorbate		BREASTS	Basters, Brasset
BOAT-FLY	Flyboat		BREEDER	Rebreed
BOCAGES	Boscage		BRIBING	Ribbing
BOLSTER	Bolters, Lobster,		BRICOLE	Corbeil
	Rebolts		BRIEFED	Debrief
BOLTERS	Bolster, Lobster,		BRIERED	Berried
	Rebolts		BRIGADE	Abridge
BOLTING	Biltong, Bloting		BRINDLE	Blinder
BOMBING	Mobbing		BRISTLE	Blister, Riblets
BONDAGE	Dogbane		BRISURE	Bruiser, Buriers
BONE-DRY	Dry-bone		BRITTLE	Triblet
BOOSTED	Deboost		BROADEN	Bandore
BORACIC	Braccio		BROADER	Arbored, Boarder,
BORATED	Aborted			Reboard
BOREDOM	Bedroom, Broomed		BROCHAN	Charbon

BROCKED	Bed-rock
BROGUES	Rose-bug
BROOKED	Red-book
BROOMED	Bedroom, Boredom
BRUCKLE	Buckler
BRUISER	Brisure, Buriers
BRUSHER	Rebrush
BRUSTLE	Bluster, Bustler, Butlers, Subtler
BUBBLER	Blubber
BUCKLER	Bruckle
BUCKSAW	Sawbuck
BUGLING	Bulging
BUILDER	Rebuild
BUILD-UP	Upbuild
BUILT-UP	Upbuilt
BULGING	Bugling
BULLATE	Ballute
BUMPETH	Bethump
BUNDLER	Blunder
BUNGLED	Blunged
BUNGLER	Blunger
BURBLES	Lubbers, Rubbles, Slubber
BURIERS	Brisure, Bruiser
*BURMESE	Embrues
BURN-OUT	Outburn
BURST-UP	Upburst
BURTHEN	Unberth
BURYING	Rubying
BUSHELS	Blushes
BUSKING	Sub-king
BUS-MILE	Sublime
BUSSING	Subsign
BUSTLER	Bluster, Brustle, Butlers, Subtler
BUTANES	Sunbeat
BUTLERS	Bluster, Brustle, Bustler, Subtler
CABARET	Abreact, Bearcat
CACHETS	Catches
CACKLED	Clacked
CACKLER	Clacker, Crackle
CADENUS	Uncased
CAHIERS	Archies, Cashier
CAIMANS	Camansi, Maniacs
CAISSON	Casinos, Cassino

CALCINE	Laccine
CALENDS	Candles
CALIBER	Calibre
CALIBRE	Caliber
CALICHE	Chalice
CALIPER	Replica
CALIVER	Caviler, Clavier, Valeric
CALKERS	Lackers, Recalks, Slacker
CALKING	Lacking
CALLERS	Cellars, Recalls, Scleral
CALLUNA	Lacunal
CALMANT	Clamant
CALORIE	Cariole
*CALVARY	Cavalry
CAMANSI	Caimans, Maniacs
CAMARAS	Maracas, Marasca, Mascara
CAMBREL	Clamber
CAMERAL	Caramel
*CAMERON	Cremona, Menorca, Romance
CAMIONS	Anosmic, Maniocs, Masonic
CAMPERS	Scamper
CANALED	Candela, Decanal
CANDELA	Canaled, Decanal
CANDLES	Calends
CANNERS	Scanner
CANTHUS	Staunch
CANTION	Contain
CANTLES	Centals, Lancets, Scantle
CANTRED	Tancred, Tranced
CAPABLE	Pacable
CAPELIN	Panicle, Pelican
CAPITAN	Captain
CAPITOL	Coal-pit, Optical, Pit-coal, Topical
CAPSULA	Pascual, Scapula
CAPSULE	Lace-ups, Specula
CAPTAIN	Capitan
CAPTION	Paction
CARACUL	Accrual
*CARACAS	Cascara
CARAMEL	Cameral
CARDECU	Accrued

CARDERS	Scarred	CATTILY	Tacitly
CAREERS	Creaser	CAULOME	Leucoma
CARGOES	Socager	CAUSING	Saucing
CARINAL	Acrilan, Clarain,	CAUTION	Auction
	Cranial	CAVALRY	Calvary
CARINAS	Arnicas, Sarcina	◦CAVIARE	Avarice
CARIOLE	Calorie	CAVILER	Caliver, Clavier,
CARIOUS	Curiosa		Valeric
CARKING	Craking, Racking	CEASING	Incages
CARLIST	Citrals	CEDRATE	Catered, Cerated,
CARMART	Tramcar		Created, Reacted
CARNAGE	Cranage	CEDRELA	Cleared, Declare,
CARNOSE	Coarsen, Corneas,		Relaced
	Narcose, Sea-corn	CEILING	Cieling
CAROCHE	Coacher	CELLARS	Callers, Recalls,
CAROLUS	Oculars, Oscular		Scleral
CAROUSE	Acerous	CELSIUS	Sluices
CARPELS	Clasper, Parcels,	CENTALS	Cantles, Lancets,
	Placers, Reclasp,		Scantle
	Scalper	CENTARE	Crenate, Re-enact
CARPERS	Scraper	CENTIMO	Entomic, Metonic
CARPETS	Pre-acts, Precast,	CENTRED	Credent, Red-cent
	Spectra	CERAMET	Cremate
CARPING	Craping	CERAMIC	Racemic
CARTELS	Clarets, Scarlet	CERASIN	Arsenic, Sarcine
CARTING	Crating, Tracing	CERATED	Catered, Cedrate,
CARTOON	Coranto		Created, Reacted
CARVING	Craving	CERATES	Creates, Ecartes,
CASABAS	Cassaba		Secreta
CASCADE	Saccade	CERESIN	Cerines, Sincere
CASCARA	Caracas	CERINES	Ceresin, Sincere
CASEMEN	Menaces	CERIPHS	Ciphers, Spheric
CASERNS	Ancress	CERIUMS	Murices
CASHIER	Archies, Cahiers	CEROTIC	Orectic
CASHING	Achings, Chasing	CERTAIN	Creatin, Crinate
CASINOS	Caisson, Cassino	CERTIFY	Cretify, Rectify
CASKING	Sacking	CERUSED	Reduces, Seducer
CASSABA	Casabas	CESSION	Cosines, Oscines
CASSINO	Caisson, Casinos	CESS-PIT	Septics
CASSOCK	Cossack	CESURAL	Secular
CASTERS	Actress, Recasts	CHAGRIN	Arching, Charing
CASTING	Actings	CHAINED	Echidna
CAST-OFF	Offcast	*CHALDEE	Cheadle, Leached
CATCHES	Cachets	CHALETS	Latches, Satchel
CATERED	Cedrate, Cerated,	CHALICE	Caliche
	Created, Reacted	CHALKED	Hackled
CATERER	Recrate, Retrace	CHALKER	Hackler
	Terrace	CHAMBER	Becharm, Chambre
CATRIGS	Gastric, Tragics	CHAMBRE	Becharm, Chamber

CHANCER	Chancre	CINDERS	Discern, Rescind	
CHANCRE	Chancer	CINEMAS	Emiscan	
CHANGED	Ganched	CIPHERS	Ceriphs, Spheric	
CHANSON	Non-cash	CIRRATE	Erratic	
CHAPTER	Patcher, Repatch	CIRROSE	Corries, Crosier,	
CHARBON	Brochan		Orrices	
CHARING	Arching, Chagrin	CISTERN	Cretins	
CHARIOT	Haricot	CITADEL	Deltaic, Dialect,	
*CHARLES	Larches		Edictal	
CHARMED	Decharm, Marched	CITIZEN	Zincite	
CHARMER	Marcher	CITRALS	Carlist	
CHARTED	Ratched	CITRENE	Enteric, Enticer,	
CHARTER	Rechart		Tercine	
CHASING	Achings, Cashing	CITRINE	Crinite, Inciter	
CHATTED	Datchet	CLACKED	Cackled	
CHATTEL	Latchet	CLACKER	Cackler, Crackle	
CHATTER	Ratchet	CLAIMED	Decimal, Declaim,	
CHAWING	Chinwag		Medical	
*CHEADLE	Chaldee, Leached	CLAIMER	Almeric, Miracle,	
CHEAPER	Peacher		Reclaim	
CHEATER	Hectare, Rechate,	CLAMANT	Calmant	
	Recheat, Reteach,	CLAMBER	Cambrel	
	Teacher	CLANGED	Glanced	
CHECKER	Recheck	CLARAIN	Acrinal, Carinal,	
CHEERLY	Lechery		Cranial	
CHEER-UP	Upcheer	CLARETS	Cartels, Scarlet	
CHELONE	Echelon	CLASPED	Scalped	
*CHELSEA	Selache	CLASPER	Carpels, Parcels,	
CHERMES	Schemer		Placers, Reclasp,	
CHIASMS	Schisma		Scalper	
CHIMING	Miching	CLASSED	Declass	
CHINING	Inching	CLASSER	Reclass, Sarcels,	
CHINWAG	Chawing		Scalers	
CHISELS	S-chisel	CLAVIER	Caliver, Caviler,	
CHOKERS	Shocker		Valeric	
CHOKING	Hocking	CLAYPIT	Typical	
CHOLERA	Chorale	CLEANED	Elanced, Enlaced	
CHOPINE	Phocine	CLEANER	Reclean, Relance	
CHORALE	Cholera	CLEANSE	Elances, Enlaces,	
CHORALS	Scholar		Scalene	
CHOREES	Coheres, Echoers,	CLEAN-UP	Unplace	
	Rechose	CLEARED	Cedrela, Declare,	
CHORIST	Ostrich		Relaced	
CHOROID	Ochroid	CLIENTS	Stencil	
CHOUSED	Douches	CLIMBER	Reclimb	
CHOWDER	Cowherd	CLINGER	Cringle	
CHURNED	Runched	CLINKER	Crinkle	
CIELING	Ceiling	CLIPPER	Cripple	
CIERGES	Grecise	CLOBBER	Cobbler	

CLOCKED	Cockled		COLTERS	Corslet, Costrel,
CLOCKER	Cockler			Croslet, Lectors
CLODDED	Coddled		COLURES	Closure
CLOSE-IN	Inclose		COMBERS	Recombs, Scomber
CLOSEST	Closets		COMMITS	Comtism
CLOSETS	Closest		COMPACT	Accompt
CLOSE-UP	Couples, Opuscle,		COMPARE	Compear
	Upclose		COMPEAR	Compare
CLOSURE	Colures		COMPEER	Compere
CLOTTER	Crottle		COMPERE	Compeer
CLOTURE	Coulter		COMPILE	Polemic
CLUMBER	Crumble		COMTISM	Commits
CLUMPER	Crumple		CONATUS	Toucans, Uncoats
CLUSTER	Culters, Custrel,		CONCENT	Connect
	Cutlers, Relucts		CONDIGN	Conding
COACHER	Caroche		CONDING	Condign
COAGENT	Cognate		CONDITE	Ctenoid, Deontic,
COALERS	Oracles, Recoals,			Noticed
	Solacer		CONDUIT	Noctuid
COAL-PIT	Capitol, Optical,		CONICAL	Laconic
	Pit-coal, Topical		CONIFER	Fir-cone
COARSEN	Carnose, Corneas,		CONKING	Nocking
	Narcose, Sea-corn		CONNECT	Concent
COASTER	Coaters, Recoast,		CONSIST	Tocsins
	Recoats		CONSORT	Crotons
COATERS	Coaster, Recoast,		CONSTER	Cornets
	Recoats		CONSUTE	Contuse
COATEES	Acetose		CONTAIN	Cantion
COATING	Cotinga		CONTOUR	Cornuto, Crouton
COBBLER	Clobber		CONTUSE	Consute
COCAINE	Oceanic		COOLANT	Octonal
COCKLED	Clocked		COOLERS	Creosol, Recools
COCKLER	Clocker		COOLEST	Ocelots
CODDLED	Clodded		COOPERS	Scooper
CODDLES	Scolded		COPINGS	Copsing
CODLING	Lingcod		COPSING	Copings
COEXIST	Exotics		CORANTO	Cartoon
COFFERS	Scoffer		CORBEIL	Bricole
COGNATE	Coagent		CORDATE	Red-coat
COHERES	Chorees, Echoers,		CORKING	Rocking
	Rechose		CORNAGE	Acrogen
COINERS	Cronies, Recoins,		CORNEAS	Carnose, Coarsen,
	Sericon			Narcose, Sea-corn
COLITIS	Solicit		CORNERS	Scorner
COLLIDE	Collied		CORNETS	Conster
COLLIED	Collide		CORNUAL	Courlan
COLLOPS	Scollop		CORNUTE	Counter, Recount,
COLLUMS	Mollusc			Trounce
COLORER	Recolor		CORNUTO	Contour, Crouton

CORONER	Crooner	
CORPSES	Process	
CORRIES	Cirrose, Crosier,	
	Orrices	
CORSITE	Erotics	
CORSLET	Colters, Costrel,	
	Croslet, Lectors	
CORSNED	Scorned	
COSINES	Cession, Oscines	
COSSACK	Cassock	
COSTEAN	Octanes	
COSTING	Gnostic	
COSTREL	Colters, Corslet,	
	Croslet, Lectors	
COTINGA	Coating	
COULTER	Cloture	
COUNSEL	Unclose	
COUNTER	Cornute, Recount,	
	Trounce	
COUPLES	Close-up, Opuscle,	
	Upclose	
COUPLET	Octuple	
COUPONS	Soupcon, Uncoops	
COURLAN	Cornual	
COURSED	Scoured	
COURSER	Scourer	
COURSES	Croesus, Scourse,	
	Scouser, Sources,	
	Sucrose	
COUTEAU	Autocue	
COVERER	Recover	
COWHERD	Chowder	
CRACKLE	Cackler, Clacker	
CRADLES	Scalder	
CRAKING	Carking, Racking	
CRANAGE	Carnage	
CRANIAL	Acrilan, Carinal,	
	Clarain	
CRAPING	Carping	
CRAPPIE	Epicarp	
CRATING	Carting, Tracing	
CRAVING	Carving	
CREAMED	Amerced, Racemed	
CREAMER	Amercer	
CREASED	Decares	
CREASER	Careers	
CREATED	Catered, Cedrate,	
	Cerated, Reacted	
CREATES	Cerates, Ecartes,	
	Secreta	

CREATIN	Certain, Crinate	
CREATOR	Reactor	
CREDENT	Centred, Red-cent	
CREMATE	Ceramet	
CREMONA	Cameron, Menorca,	
	Romance	
CRENATE	Centare, Re-enact	
CREOSOL	Coolers, Recools	
CRESSET	Re-sects, Secrets	
CRETIFY	Certify, Rectify	
CRETINS	Cistern	
CRIMSON	Microns	
CRINATE	Certain, Creatin	
CRINGES	Scringe	
CRINGLE	Clinger	
CRINITE	Citrine, Inciter	
CRINKLE	Clinker	
CRIPPLE	Clipper	
CRISPED	Discerp	
CROCKED	Red-cock	
CROESUS	Courses, Scourse,	
	Scouser, Sources,	
	Sucrose	
CRONIES	Coiners, Recoins,	
	Sericon	
CROOKED	Rock-doe	
CROONER	Coroner	
CROSIER	Corries, Cirrose,	
	Orrices	
CROSLET	Colters, Corslet,	
	Costrel, Lectors	
CROSSER	Recross, Scorers	
CROTONS	Consort	
CROTTLE	Clotter	
CROUPER	Procure	
CROUTON	Contour, Cornuto	
CROWDED	Decrowd	
CROWNED	Decrown	
CROWNER	Recrown	
CRUDEST	Crusted	
CRUELTY	Cutlery	
CRUISED	Discure	
CRUISER	Curries	
CRUIVES	Cursive	
CRUMBLE	Clumber	
CRUMPLE	Clumper	
CRUSTAE	Curates	
CRUSTED	Crudest	
CRYINGS	Scrying	

CTENOID	Condite, Deontic,		DANGLES	Slanged
	Noticed		DANSKER	Darkens
CUDDLER	Curdled		*DANTEAN	Andante
CUDDLES	Scuddle		*DANTIST	Distant
CULDEES	Seclude		DAPPLES	Slapped
CULLERS	Sculler		DARBIES	Braised, Sea-bird
CULTERS	Cluster, Custrel,		DARKENS	Dansker
	Cutlers, Relucts		DARLING	Larding
CUMBERS	Recumbs, Scumber		DARNELS	Enlards, Landers,
CUMMERS	Scummer			Relands, Slander
CUNNERS	Scunner		DARREIN	Drainer
CUPPERS	Scupper		DARTERS	Retards, Traders,
CUPRITE	Picture			Starred
CURACAO	Curacoa		DARTING	Trading
CURACOA	Curacao		DASHING	Shading
CURATES	Crustae		DASYURE	Daysure
CURDLED	Cuddler		*DATCHET	Chatted
CURINGS	Cursing		DAUNTED	Undated
CURIOSA	Carious		DAWDLED	Waddled
CURRIES	Cruiser		DAWDLER	Drawled, Waddler
CURSING	Curings		DAWDLES	Swaddle, Waddles
CURSIVE	Cruives		DAYSURE	Dasyure
CURTAIL	Trucial		DAYWORK	Workday
CURTESY	Curtsey		DEADMEN	Amended
CURTSEY	Curtesy		DEALING	Aligned, Leading
CUSPATE	Teacups		DEANERY	Yearned
CUSTREL	Cluster, Culters,		DEAREST	Derates, Estrade,
	Cutlers, Relucts			Redates
CUTLERS	Cluster, Culters,		DEASIUL	Audiles
	Custrel, Relucts		DEAVING	Evading
CUTLERY	Cruelty		DEBACLE	Belaced
CUTLETS	Cuttles, Scuttle		DEBATER	Berated, Betread,
CUTTERS	Scutter			Rebated
CUTTLES	Cutlets, Scuttle		DEBITED	Betided
CYTASES	Ecstasy		DEBITOR	Deorbit, Orbited
			DEBOOST	Boosted
			DEBRIEF	Briefed
DABBLER	Drabble		DECAMPS	Scamped
DABBLES	Slabbed		DECANAL	Canaled, Candela
DADDLES	Saddled		DECANTS	Descant, Scanted
DAHLINE	Inhaled		DECARES	Creased
DAILIES	Sedilia		DECAYER	Redecay
DAIRIES	Diaries, Diarise		DECHARM	Charmed, Marched
DALLIED	Dialled		DECIMAL	Claimed, Declaim,
DALLIER	Rallied			Medical
DALLIES	Sallied		DECLAIM	Claimed, Decimal,
DAMAGER	Megarad			Medical
DANGLED	Gladden		DECLARE	Cedrela, Cleared,
DANGLER	Gnarled			Relaced

DECLASS	Classed			
DECREED	Receded			
DECREES	Recedes,	Seceder		
DECREWS	Screwed			
DECRIAL	Radicel,	Radicle		
DECROWD	Crowded			
DECROWN	Crowned			
DEDUCES	Seduced			
DEEDING	Deigned			
DEEPEST	Steeped			
DEFACER	Refaced			
DEFAULT	Faulted			
DEFEATS	Feasted			
DEFIANT	Fainted			
DEFILED	Fielded			
DEFILER	Fielder,	Refiled		
DEFINER	Refined			
DEFLOUR	Floured			
DEFORMS	Serfdom			
DEFROCK	Frocked			
DEFROST	Frosted			
DEFUSER	Refused			
DEHORTS	Shorted			
*DEIRDRE	Derider,	Redried,		
	Ridered			
DEIFIED	Edified			
DEIFIER	Edifier			
DEIGNED	Deeding			
DEISEAL	Aediles			
DELAINE	Adeline			
DELATER	Alerted,	Altered,		
	Redealt,	Related,		
	Treadle			
DELAYER	Layered,	Relayed		
DELIBLE	Bellied			
DELIGHT	Lighted			
DELIMIT	Limited			
DELIVER	Livered,	Relived		
	Reviled			
DELTAIC	Citadel,	Dialect,		
	Edictal			
DELUDER	Dreuled			
DEMAINS	Maidens,	Mandies,		
	Medians,	Sideman		
DEMERIT	Dimeter,	Merited,		
	Mitered,	Retimed		
DEMERSE	Emersed,	Redeems		
*DEMETER	Metered			
DEMIREP	Epiderm,	Impeder,		
	Remiped			

DEMOUNT	Mounted
DENSITY	Destiny
DENTALS	Slanted, Standel
DENTELS	Nestled
DENTING	Tending
DENTIST	Distent, Stinted
DENTURE	Retuned, Untreed
DEONTIC	Condite, Ctenoid,
	Noticed
DEORBIT	Debitor, Orbited
DEPAINT	Painted
DEPETER	Petered
DEPICTS	Discept
DEPONES	Spondee
DEPORTS	Red-tops, Sported
DEPOSER	Reposed
DEPOSIT	Posited, Topside
DEPRAVE	Pervade, Repaved
DEPRESS	Pressed
DEPRIVE	Prieved
DERAIGN	Gradine, Grained,
	Reading
DERANGE	Angered, Enraged,
	Grandee, Grenade
DERATES	Dearest, Estrade,
	Redates
DERIDER	Deirdre, Redried,
	Ridered
DERIDES	Desired, Resided
DERIVER	Redrive
DERIVES	Deviser, Diverse,
	Revised
DERRIES	Desirer, Serried
DERVISH	Shrived
DESCANT	Decants, Scanted
DESCENT	Scented
DESERTS	Dessert, Tressed
DESERVE	Severed
DESIRED	Derides, Resided
DESIRER	Derries, Resider,
	Serried
DESKILL	Skilled
DESMANS	Madness
DESPAIR	Aspired, Diapers,
	Praised
DESPISE	Pedesis
DESPOIL	Dilopes, Diploes,
	Dipoles, Soliped,
	Spoiled

DESSERT	Deserts, Tressed		DISCEPT	Depicts
DESTINY	Density		DISCERN	Cinders, Rescind
DETAINS	Instead, Sainted,		DISCERP	Crisped
	Satined, Stained		DISCURE	Cruised
DETERGE	Greeted		DISEASE	Seaside
DETRACT	Tracted		DISHING	Hidings, Shindig
DETRAIN	Anti-red, Tanride,		DISHORN	Dronish
	Trade-in, Trained		DISJUNE	Jundies
DEVISER	Derives, Diverse,		DISNEST	Dissent
	Revised		DISPORT	Torpids, Tripods
DEVISOR	Visored		DISRATE	Asterid, Astride,
DEVOLVE	Evolved			Staider, Tirades
DEVOTER	Revoted		DISROOT	Toroids
DEWATER	Watered		DISSENT	Disnest
DHURRIE	Hurried		DISSERT	Strides
DIALECT	Citadel, Deltaic,		DISTANT	Dantist
	Edictal		DISTENT	Dentist, Stinted
DIALING	Glaidin, Gliadin		DISTOMA	Diatoms, Mastoid
DIALLED	Dallied		DITTIES	Dietist, Tidiest
DIANDER	Drained		DIVERGE	Grieved
DIAPERS	Aspired, Despair,		DIVERSE	Derives, Deviser,
	Praised			Revised
DIARIES	Dairies, Diarise		DIVERTS	Strived
DIARISE	Dairies, Diaries		DIVINER	Drive-in
DIATOMS	Distoma, Mastoid		DOCKETS	Stocked
DIBBLER	Dribble		DOGBANE	Bondage
DICERAS	Sidecar		DOGEARS	Dog's-ear
DICKENS	Snicked		DOG-ENDS	Goddens, God-send
DIDDLER	Riddled		DOG-FISH	Fish-god
DIETING	Editing, Ignited		DOGGREL	Roggled
DIETIST	Ditties, Tidiest		DOGHEAD	Godhead
DIGNITY	Tidying		DOGHOOD	Godhood
DILATER	Red-tail, Trailed		DOGLESS	Godless
DILUENT	Untiled		DOGLIKE	Godlike
DIMETER	Demerit, Merited,		DOG-NAIL	Loading
	Mitered, Retimed		DOG'S-EAR	Dogears
DIMNESS	Missend		DOGSHIP	Godship
DIMPLES	Simpled		DOG'S-RUE	Drogues, Gourdes
DINGING	Nidging		DOGWOOD	Wood-god
DINGLES	Singled		DOILIES	Idolise
DIOPTER	Dioptre, Peridot,		DOLMANS	Almonds
	Proteid		DOMINES	Misdone
DIOPTRE	Diopter, Peridot,		*DOMINGO	Dooming
	Proteid		DONATED	Nodated
DIPLOES	Despoil, Dipoles,		DONATES	Onstead
	Soliped, Spoiled		DONATOR	Tornado
DIPNOAN	Non-paid		DONE-FOR	Fordone
DIPOLES	Despoil, Diploes,		*DONGOLA	Gondola
	Soliped, Spoiled		DOOMING	Domingo

DOORMAN	Madrono
DORMANT	Mordant
DOUBLER	Boulder
DOUBLET	Boulted
DOUBTER	Obtrude, Redoubt
DOUCETS	Scouted
DOUCHES	Choused
DOWAGER	Wordage
DRABBLE	Dabbler
DRACONE	Acorned
DRAFTER	Redraft
DRAGGLE	Gargled, Raggled
DRAGOON	Gadroon
DRAINED	Diander
DRAINER	Darrein
DRAWING	Warding
DRAWLED	Dawdler, Waddler
DRAW-OUT	Outdraw, Outward
DRAYAGE	Yardage
DRAYING	Yarding
DRAYMAN	Yardman
DREAMER	Rearmed
DREEING	Energid, Enridge, Reeding, Reigned
*DRESDEN	Reddens
DRESSER	Redress
DREULED	Deluder
DRIBBLE	Dibbler
DRILLER	Redrill
DRIVE-IN	Diviner
DROGUES	Dog's-rue, Gourdes
DRONISH	Dishorn
DROOPER	Redroop
DROPLET	Pretold
DROP-NET	Portend, Protend
DROSERA	Adorers
DRUMBLE	Rumbled
DRY-BONE	Bone-dry
DULCINE	Include
DUNGING	Nudging
DURAMEN	Manured, Maunder, Unarmed
DURANCE	Uncared, Unraced
*DURANGO	Aground
*DURANTE	Unrated, Untread
DURIANS	Sundari
DURMAST	Mustard
DUSTIER	Studier

EANLING	Aneling, Leaning
EARFULS	Ferulas, Fur-seal, Refusal
EARINGS	Angries, Erasing, Gainers, Regains, Regians, Reginas, Searing, Seringa
EARLESS	Leasers, Resales, Reseals, Sealers
EARNEST	Eastern, Nearest
EARNETH	Earthen, Hearten, Neareth, Teheran
EARNING	Engrain, Grannie, Nearing
EARRING	Angrier, Grainer, Rangier, Rearing
EARTHED	Hearted, Red-heat
EARTHEN	Earneth, Hearten, Neareth, Teheran
EARTHLY	Heartly, Lathery
EAST-END	Standee
EASTERN	Earnest, Nearest
EASTERS	Reseats, Seaters, Teasers, Tessera
EASTING	Genista, Ingates, Ingesta, Seating, Signate, Teasing
ECARTES	Cerates, Creates, Secreta
ECBASIS	Scabies
ECHELON	Chelone
ECHIDNA	Chained
ECHOERS	Chorees, Coheres, Rechose
ECSTASY	Cytases
EDICTAL	Citadel, Deltaic, Dialect
EDIFIED	Deified
EDIFIER	Deifier
EDITING	Dieting, Ignited
EDITION	Tenioid
EDITORS	Steroid, Storied, Tie-rods, Triodes
EDUCRAT	Traduce
EIGHTHS	Heights, Highest
EITHERS	Heister
ELANCED	Cleaned, Enlaced
ELANCES	Cleanse, Enlaces, Scalene

ELAPSED	Pleased	END-USER	Endures
ELASTIC	Latices, Salicet	ENDWISE	Sinewed
ELASTIN	Entails, Salient,	ENERGIC	Generic
	Slainte, Staniel,	ENERGID	Dreeing, Enridge,
	Tenails		Reeding, Reigned
ELATING	Atingle, Gelatin,	ENFRAME	Freeman
	Genital, Langite	ENGINED	Needing
ELATION	Toenail	ENGLISH	Shingle
ELBOWED	Boweled	ENGRAIL	Aligner, Realign,
ELECTOR	Electro		Reginal
ELECTRO	Elector	ENGRAIN	Earning, Grannie,
ELEGIST	Elegits		Nearing
ELEGITS	Elegist	ENGRAVE	Avenger, Genevra
ELF-WORT	Felwort	ENIGMAS	Seaming
ELISION	Lionise	ENISLED	Ensiled, Linseed,
*ELOHIST	Eoliths, Hostile		Nelides
ELOIGNS	Legions, Lignose,	ENISLES	Ensiles, Sensile,
	Lingoes, Sloe-gin		Silenes
ELOPERS	Leprous, Pelorus,	ENJOYER	Re-enjoy
	Perlous, Sporule	ENLACED	Cleaned, Elanced
ELUDING	Indulge	ENLACES	Cleanse, Elances,
EMANATE	Manatee		Scalene
EMANIST	Inmates, Inmeats,	ENLARDS	Darnels, Landers,
	Tamines		Relands, Slander
EMBLICA	Alembic	ENLARGE	General, Gleaner
EMBRAIL	Remblai	ENLIGHT	Lighten
EMBREAD	Ambered, Breamed	ENLOCKS	Slocken
EMBRUES	Burmese	ENRAGED	Angered, Derange,
EMERSED	Demerse, Redeems		Grandee, Grenade
EMIGRES	Regimes, Remiges	ENRIDGE	Dreeing, Energid,
EMISCAN	Cinemas		Reeding, Reigned
EMITTER	Termite	ENROBES	Ensober
EMPALED	Emplead	ENROUGH	Roughen
EMPANEL	Emplane	ENSIGNS	Sensing
EMPIRES	Emprise, Premise,	ENSILED	Enisled, Linseed,
	Spireme		Nelides
EMPLANE	Empanel	ENSILES	Enisles, Sensile,
EMPLEAD	Empaled		Silenes
EMPRISE	Empires, Premise,	ENSLAVE	Leavens
	Spireme	ENSOBER	Enrobes
ENAMOUR	Euroman	ENSTEEP	Steepen
ENCAVED	Vendace	ENTAILS	Elastin, Salient,
ENCLASP	Spancel		Slaite, Staniel,
ENCLAVE	Valence		Tenails
ENCORES	Necrose	ENTASIS	Sestina, Tisanes
ENDINGS	Sending	ENTERER	Re-enter, Terreen,
ENDOWER	Re-endow		Terrene
ENDURES	End-user	ENTERIC	Citrene, Enticer,
ENDUROS	Resound, Sounder,		Tercine
	Undoers, Unrosed		

ENTERON	Tenoner	ESCHEAT	Teaches
ENTHEAL	Lethean	ESPARTO	Pro-east, Seaport
ENTICER	Citrene, Enteric,	ESPINEL	Pensile, Sleep-in
	Tercine	ESQUIRE	Queries
ENTOILS	Lionets, Tonsile	ESSOINS	Session
ENTOMBS	Benmost	ESTOVER	Overset, Revotes,
ENTOMIC	Centimo, Metonic		Setover, Vetoers
ENTRAIL	Latrine, Ratline,	ESTRADE	Dearest, Derates,
	Reliant, Retinal,		Redates
	Trenail	ESTREAT	Restate, Retaste,
ENTRAIN	Trannie		Tearest
ENTRAPS	Arpents, Panters,	ESTRICH	Richest
	Parents, Pastern,	ETAMINE	Matinee
	Persant, Trepans	ETERNAL	Alterne
ENTREAT	Ratteen, Ternate	ETHERIC	Erethic, Heretic
ENVIERS	Inverse, Versine	ETHNICS	Sthenic
ENVIOUS	Niveous	EUCLASE	Sea-luce
ENWRAPS	Pawners, Repawns,	EUROMAN	Enamour
	Spawner	EVADERS	Adverse
EOLITHS	Elohist, Hostile	EVADING	Deaving
EPARCHY	Preachy	EVOLUTE	Veloute
EPHEBOS	Phoebes	EVOLVED	Devolve
*EPHRAIM	Rephaim	EVOLVER	Revolve
EPICARP	Crappie	EXACTER	Excreta
EPIDERM	Demirep, Impeder,	EXCITOR	Xerotic
	Remiped	EXCRETA	Exacter
EPIDOTE	Opetide	EXCURSE	Excuser
EPIGRAM	Primage	EXCUSER	Excurse
EPSILON	Pinoles	EXOTICS	Coexist
ERASING	Angries, Earings,	EXPLAIN	Axle-pin
	Gainers, Regains,	EX-TERNS	Sextern
	Regians, Reginas,	EYEWALL	Walleye
	Searing, Seringa		
ERECTER	Re-erect		
EREPSIN	Repines	FACTURE	Furcate
ERETHIC	Etheric, Heretic	FAERIES	Arefies, Freesia,
EREWHON	Nowhere, Whereon		Sea-fire
ERINGOS	Ignores, Regions,	FAIENCE	Fiancee
	Signore	FAILURE	Air-flue
*ERNESTS	Nesters, Resents,	FAINTED	Defiant
	Streens, Strenes	FALLOUT	Outfall
ERODING	Gironde, Groined,	FANCIES	Fascine, Fiances
	Ignored, Negroid,	FARMING	Framing
	Redoing	FARMOST	Formats
EROTICS	Corsite	FARTING	Ingraft, Rafting
EROTISM	Mortise	FASCINE	Fancies, Fiances
ERRATIC	Cirrate	FASTENS	Fastnet, Fatness
ERUPTED	Reputed	*FASTNET	Fastens, Fatness
ESCAPER	Percase, Respace	FATNESS	Fastens, Fastnet

FAULTED	Default	
FAULTER	Refutal, Tearful	
FAUNIST	Fustian, Infaust	
FEAREST	Afreets, Feaster	
FEARETH	Feather	
FEASTED	Defeats	
FEASTER	Afreets, Fearest	
FEATHER	Feareth	
FEEDING	Feigned	
FEELING	Fleeing	
FEERING	Freeing, Reefing	
FEIGNED	Feeding	
FELWORT	Elf-wort	
FEMINAL	Inflame	
FENGITE	Feteing	
FERRITE	Fir-tree	
FERROUS	Furores	
FERULAS	Earfuls, Fur-seal, Refusal	
FETEING	Fengite	
FIANCEE	Faience	
FIANCES	Fancies, Fascine	
FIELDED	Defiled	
FIELDER	Defiler, Refiled	
FIGHTER	Freight	
FILTERS	Lifters, Stifler, Trifles	
FINAGLE	Leafing	
FIR-CONE	Conifer	
FIREDOG	Firegod	
FIREGOD	Firedog	
FIR-TREE	Ferrite	
FISH-GOD	Dogfish	
FISHNET	Net-fish	
FISTING	Sifting	
FITNESS	Infests	
FIZZING	Gin-fizz	
FLANEUR	Funeral	
FLECKER	Freckle	
FLEEING	Feeling	
FLEMISH	Himself	
FLESHER	Herself	
FLIRTED	Trifled	
FLIRTER	Trifler	
FLOATER	Refloat	
FLOURED	Deflour	
FLOWING	Fowling, Wolfing	
FLUSTER	Fluters, Restful	
FLUTERS	Fluster, Restful	

FLUVIAL	Vialful	
FLY-BLOW	Blowfly	
FLYBOAT	Boatfly	
FLY-OVER	Overfly	
FLY-RAIL	Frailly	
FOALING	Loafing	
FOCUSER	Refocus	
FOG-RING	Forging	
FOOTHOT	Hot-foot	
FORAMEN	Foreman	
FORDONE	Done-for	
FOREMAN	Foramen	
FOREMEN	Formene	
FORGERY	Frogery	
FORGING	Fog-ring	
FORMATS	Farmost	
FORMENE	Foremen	
FORWARD	Froward	
FOUNDER	Refound	
FOWLING	Flowing, Wolfing	
FRAILLY	Fly-rail	
FRAMING	Farming	
FRANTIC	Infarct, Infract	
FRECKLE	Flecker	
FREEING	Feering, Reefing	
FREEMAN	Enframe	
FREESIA	Arefies, Faeries, Sea-fire	
FREIGHT	Fighter	
FRESHER	Refresh	
FRETFUL	Truffle	
FROCKED	Defrock	
FROGERY	Forgery	
FROSTED	Defrost	
FROWARD	Forward	
FULL-PAY	Playful	
FUNERAL	Flaneur	
FUNFAIR	Ruffian	
FURCATE	Facture	
FURORES	Ferrous	
FUR-SEAL	Earfuls, Ferules, Refusal	
FUSTIAN	Faunist, Infaust	
GABBLER	Grabble	
GADROON	Dragoon	
GAHNITE	Heating	
GAINERS	Angries, Erasing,	

	Earings, Regains,
	Regians, Reginas,
	Searing, Seringa
GAITERS	Agister, Aigrets,
	Sea-girt
GALENIC	Angelic, Anglice
GALLERY	Allergy, Largely,
	Regally
GALLING	Gingall
GALL-NUT	Nut-gall
GAMBLER	Gambrel
GAMBREL	Gambler
GANCHED	Changed
GANGERS	Granges, Naggers,
	Snagger
GANGING	Nagging
GARBING	Barging
GARBLED	Belgard
GARGETS	Stagger, Taggers
GARGLED	Draggle, Raggled
GARMENT	Margent
GARNERS	Rangers
GARNETS	Sargent, Strange
GARNISH	Rashing, Sharing
GASKINS	Askings
GASPING	Pagings
GAS-RING	Ragings
GASTRIC	Catrigs, Tragics
GASTRIN	Gratins, Ratings,
	Staring
GATEMAN	Magenta, Magnate
GATEWAY	Getaway
GATINGS	Staging
GAUFFER	Gauffre
GAUFFRE	Gauffer
GAVILAN	Vaginal
GELATIN	Atingle, Elating,
	Genital, Langite
GELDING	Gingled, Niggled
GENERAL	Enlarge, Gleaner
GENERIC	Energic
GENESIS	Seeings
*GENEVRA	Avenger, Engrave
GENISTA	Easting, Ingates,
	Ingesta, Seating,
	Signate, Teasing
GENITAL	Atingle, Elating,
	Gelatin, Langite
GENITOR	Negrito, Trigone
GENTIAN	Antigen

GENUINE	Ingenue
GESTAPO	Postage, Potages
GESTATE	Tagetes
GET-AWAY	Gateway
GIBBONS	Sobbing
GILDING	Gliding
*GINEVRA	Reaving, Vinegar
GIN-FIZZ	Fizzing
GINGALL	Galling
GINGERS	Niggers, Snigger
GINGERY	Greying, Niggery
GINGLED	Gelding, Niggled
GINGLES	Niggles, Sniggle
GINTRAP	Parting, Prating
GIRASOL	Glorias
GIRDING	Griding, Ridging
GIRDLED	Glidder, Griddle
GIRKINS	Griskin, Risking
GIRNELS	Lingers, Singler,
	Slinger
GIRNING	Ringing
*GIRONDE	Eroding, Groined,
	Ignored, Negroid,
	Redoing
GISARME	Imagers, Mirages
GITTERN	Retting
GLACIER	Gracile
GLADDEN	Dangled
GLAIDIN	Dialing, Gliadin
GLANCED	Clanged
GLEANER	Enlarge, General
GLEEING	Neglige
GLEEMAN	Melange
GLIADIN	Dialing, Glaidin
GLIDDER	Girdled, Griddle
GLIDING	Gilding
GLIMPSE	Megilps
GLINTED	Tingled
GLISTEN	Lingets, Singlet,
	Tingles
GLISTER	Gristle
*GLORIAS	Girasol
GLUTINS	Lusting, Lutings,
	Singult, Sutling
GLUTTED	Guttled
GMELINA	Leaming, Mealing
GNARING	Ranging
GNARLED	Dangler
GNAT-NET	Tangent

GNOSTIC	Costing
GOBELIN	Ignoble, Inglobe
GODDENS	Dog-ends, Godsend
GODHEAD	Doghead
GODHOOD	Doghood
GODLESS	Dogless
GODLIKE	Doglike
GODLING	Golding, Lodging
GODSEND	Dog-ends, Goddens
GODSHIP	Dogship
*GOLDING	Godling, Lodging
GONDOLA	Dongola
GORDIAN	Adoring, Roading
GOSLING	Oglings
GOSNICK	Socking
GOURDES	Dog's-rue, Drogues
GRABBLE	Gabbler
GRACILE	Glacier
GRADINE	Deraign, Grained, Reading
GRADING	Niggard
GRAFTER	Regraft
GRAINED	Deraign, Gradine, Reading
GRAINER	Angrier, Earring, Rangier, Rearing
GRANDAM	Grandma
GRANDEE	Angered, Derange, Enraged, Grenade
GRANDMA	Grandam
GRANGES	Gangers, Naggers, Snagger
GRANITE	Ingrate, Tangier, Tearing
GRANNIE	Earning, Engrain, Nearing
GRANTEE	Greaten, Negater, Reagent
GRANTER	Regrant
GRANULA	Angular
GRANULE	Unlarge, Unregal
GRAPHER	Regraph
GRASPED	Sparged
GRASPER	Regrasp, Sparger
GRATINS	Gastrin, Ratings, Staring
GRAUPEL	Plaguer
GRAVELS	Verglas
GREATEN	Grantee, Negater, Reagent

GREATER	Regrate
GREAVES	Servage
GRECISE	Cierges
GREENED	Reneged
GREETED	Deterge
GREETER	Regreet
GREMLIN	Merling, Mingler
GREMMIE	Immerge
GRENADE	Angered, Derange, Enraged, Grandee
GREYING	Gingery, Niggery
GRIDDLE	Girdled, Glidder
GRIDING	Girding, Ridging
GRIEVED	Diverge
GRIFFIN	Riffing
GRINDER	Regrind
GRINNED	Rending
GRISKIN	Girkins, Risking
GRISTLE	Glister
GROBIAN	Boaring
GROINED	Eroding, Gironde, Ignored, Negroid, Redoing
GROUPER	Regroup
GROUPIE	Pirogue
GRUMOSE	Morgues
GUANINE	Anguine
GUELDER	Reglued
GUERDON	Undergo, Ungored
GUNSHIP	Pushing
GUNSHOT	Hognuts, Noughts, Shotgun
GURGLES	Luggers, Slugger
GUTTLED	Glutted
GYRATED	Tragedy
HABITAT	Tabitha
HACKLED	Chalked
HACKLER	Chalker
HACKLES	Shackle
HAFFIRS	Raffish
HAIRNET	Inearth
HALBERT	Blareth, Blather
HALLOWS	Shallow
HALTERS	Harslet, Hastler, Lathers, Slather, Thalers
HALTING	Althing, Lathing

HAMBLES	Shamble	
*HAMITES	Atheism	
HAMMERS	Shammer	
HANDBOW	Bow-hand	
HANDLES	Handsel	
HANDSEL	Handles	
HANKERS	Harkens, Shanker	
HANSTER	Anthers, Thenars	
HARDEST	Hardset, Hatreds,	
	Red-hats, Threads	
HARDIER	Harried	
HARDIES	Shadier	
HARDSET	Hardest, Hatreds,	
	Red-hats, Threads	
HAREING	Hearing	
HARICOT	Chariot	
HARKEES	Reshake	
HARKENS	Hankers, Shanker	
HARKERS	Sharker	
HARPERS	Sharper	
HARRIED	Hardier	
HARSLET	Halters, Hastler,	
	Lathers, Slather,	
	Thalers	
HAS-BEEN	Banshee	
HASLETS	Hatless	
HASPING	Phasing, Shaping	
HASTING	Anights, Shangti	
HASTLER	Halters, Harslet,	
	Lathers, Slather,	
	Thalers	
HATEFUL	Heatful	
HATLESS	Haslets	
HATREDS	Hardest, Hardset,	
	Red-hats, Threads	
HATTERS	Shatter, Stareth,	
	Threats	
HAULING	Laugh-in	
HAUNTER	Unearth, Unheart,	
	Urethan	
HAVINGS	Shaving	
HAWKISM	Mawkish	
HAWSERS	Swasher, Washers	
HEADERS	Adheres, Hearsed,	
	Reheads, Sheared	
HEADPAN	Pan-head	
HEADPIN	Pin-head	
HEAL-ALL	All-heal	
HEARERS	Rehears, Reshare,	
	Shearer	

HEARING	Hareing	
HEARSED	Adheres, Headers,	
	Reheads, Sheared	
HEARTED	Earthed, Red-heat	
HEARTEN	Earneth, Earthen,	
	Neareth, Teheran	
HEARTLY	Earthly, Lathery	
HEATFUL	Hateful	
HEATING	Gahnite	
HEAVERS	Reshave	
*HEBREWS	Bestrew	
HECTARE	Cheater, Rechate,	
	Recheat, Reteach,	
	Teacher	
HECTORS	Rochets, Rotches,	
	Tochers, Torches,	
	Troches	
HEEDERS	Heredes	
HEEDING	Neighed	
HE-GOATS	Hostage, She-goat	
HEIGHTS	Eighths, Highest	
HEINOUS	In-house	
HEIRDOM	Homerid	
HEIRESS	Herisse	
HEISTER	Eithers	
HELLERS	Sheller	
HEPATIC	Aphetic	
HEPTADS	Spathed	
HERBLET	Blether	
HEREDES	Heeders	
HERETIC	Erethic, Etheric	
HERISSE	Heiress	
HERNIAL	Inhaler	
HEROINS	Inshore	
HEROISM	Himeros	
HERSELF	Flesher	
HIDINGS	Dishing, Shindig	
HIGHEST	Eighths, Heights	
*HIMEROS	Heroism	
HIMSELF	Flemish	
HINDERS	Shrined	
HINDGUT	Undight	
HISTORY	Toryish	
*HITLERS	Slither	
HITTING	Tithing	
HOCKING	Choking	
HOGNUTS	Gunshot, Noughts,	
	Shotgun	
HOLIDAY	Hyaloid	

HOLSTER	Hostler	ILL-USED	Sullied
HOMERID	Heirdom	ILL-USES	Sullies
HOODMAN	Manhood	IMAGERS	Gisarme, Mirages
HOOKERS	Reshook	IMBRUES	Imburse
HOOTERS	Reshoot, Shooter,	IMBRUTE	Terbium
	Soother	IMBURSE	Imbrues
HOPPERS	Shopper	IMMERGE	Gremmie
HORMONE	Moorhen	IMPAINT	Timpani
HORNETS	Shorten, Threnos,	IMPALED	Implead, Pelamid
	Thrones	IMPALER	Impearl, Lempira,
HORRENT	Norther		Palmier
HORSING	Shoring	IMPANEL	Maniple
HOSTAGE	He-goats, She-goat	IMPASTE	Pastime
HOSTILE	Elohist, Eoliths	IMPEARL	Impaler, Lempira,
HOSTLER	Holster		Palmier
HOT-FOOT	Foothot	IMPEDER	Epiderm, Impeder,
HOTPOTS	Hot-spot, Pot-shot		Remiped
HOT-SPOT	Hotpots, Pot-shot	IMPEDES	Semiped
HOTTING	To-night	IMPETUS	Imputes
HOWEVER	Whoever	IMPLEAD	Impaled, Pelamid
HUDDLER	Hurdled	IMPONES	Peonism
HUMIDOR	Rhodium	IMPORTS	Tropism
HUNTERS	Shunter	IMPOSER	Promise
HURDLED	Huddler	IMPRESS	Premiss, Simpers
HURRIED	Dhurrie	IMPREST	Permits
HURTFUL	Ruthful	IMPUTES	Impetus
HURTLES	Hustler	INAPTLY	Ptyalin
HUSTLER	Hurtles	INBREAK	Brankie, Break-in
HYALOID	Holiday	INCAGES	Ceasing
HYDRATE	Thready	INCEPTS	Inspect, Pectins
HYDROUS	Shroudy	INCHING	Chining
		INCISED	Indices
		INCISES	Iciness
IATRICS	Satiric	INCITED	Identic
ICEPACK	Pack-ice	INCITER	Citrine, Crinite
ICINESS	Incises	INCLOSE	Close-in
IDENTIC	Incited	INCLUDE	Dulcine
IDOLISE	Doilies	INCUDES	Incused, Induces
IGNAROS	Origans, Signora,	INCUSED	Incudes, Induces
	Soaring	*INDESIT	Indites
IGNITED	Dieting, Editing	INDEXER	Reindex
IGNITER	Nigrite, Tiering,	INDICES	Incised
	Tigrine	INDITER	Nitride
IGNITOR	Rioting	INDITES	Indesit
IGNOBLE	Gobelin, Inglobe	INDOORS	Sordino
IGNORED	Eroding, Gironde,	INDORSE	Rosined, Sordine
	Groined, Negroid,	INDUCER	Uncried
	Redoing	INDUCES	Incudes, Incused
IGNORES	Eringos, Regions,	INDULGE	Eluding
	Signore		

INEARTH	Hairnet		INSULIN	Inulins
INFARCT	Frantic, Infract		INSURES	Serinus, Sunrise
INFAUST	Faunist, Fustian		INTEGER	Retinge, Teering,
INFESTS	Fitness			Treeing
INFIDEL	Infield		INTERIM	Termini
INFIELD	Infidel		INTIMAS	Animist
INFLAME	Feminal		INTONER	Ternion
INFRACT	Frantic, Infarct		INTONES	Sonnite, Tension
INGATES	Easting, Genista,		INTREAT	Iterant, Nitrate,
	Ingesta, Seating,			Tertian
	Signate, Teasing		INTRUDE	Turdine, Untired,
INGENUE	Genuine			Untried
INGESTA	Easting, Genista,		INULINS	Insulin
	Ingates, Seating,		INURING	Ruining
	Signate, Teasing		INVADER	Ravined
INGINES	Seining		INVERSE	Enviers, Versine
INGLOBE	Ignoble, Gobelin		INVERTS	Striven
INGRAFT	Farting, Rafting		IODURET	Outride
INGRAIN	Raining		IRATELY	Reality
INGRATE	Granite, Tangier,		IRKSOME	Smokier
	Tearing		IRONIES	Noisier
INGRESS	Resigns, Signers,		ISOLATE	Aeolist
	Singers		ISSUANT	Sustain
INGROUP	Pouring, Rouping		ITERANT	Intreat, Nitrate,
INHALED	Dahline			Tertian
INHALER	Hernial			
INHERES	Inherse, Reshine			
INHERSE	Inheres, Reshine		JOINTER	Rejoint
IN-HOUSE	Heinous		JOLTERS	Jostler, Rejolts
INKLESS	Kinless		JOSTLER	Jolters, Rejolts
INKLING	Kilning, Linking		JOYANCE	Joycean
INLAYER	Nailery		JOYCEAN	Joyance
INMATES	Emanist, Inmeats,		JUNDIES	Disjune
	Tamines			
INMEATS	Emanist, Inmates,			
	Tamines		KAISERS	Sea-risk
INNERVE	Nervine		KEELERS	Sleeker
INNINGS	Sinning		KEENING	Kneeing
INROADS	Ordains, Sadiron		KELTERS	Skelter
INSCULP	Sculpin, Unclips		KERATIN	Kreatin
INSHORE	Heroins		KESTREL	Skelter
INSOFAR	Snofari		KIDNAPS	Skid-pan
INSOLES	Lesions, Lioness		KILNING	Inkling, Linking
INSPECT	Incepts, Pectins		KILTING	Kitling
INSTATE	Satinet		KIMMERS	Skimmer
INSTEAD	Detains, Sainted,		KING-PIN	Pinking
	Satined, Stained		KINLESS	Inkless
INSTEPS	Spinets, Step-ins		KIPPERS	Skipper
INSULAR	Urinals, Ursinal		*KIRSTEN	Reknits, Stinker,
				Tinkers

KISSING	Skiings	
KITCHEN	Thicken	
KITLING	Kilting	
KITTLES	Skittle	
KNARLED	Rankled	
KNEADER	Reknead	
KNEEING	Keening	
KNITTER	Trinket	
KNOCKER	Reknock	
KNOCK-ON	No-knock	
KREATIN	Keratin	
LABELER	Relabel	
LABIATE	Baalite	
LABOURS	Sub-oral	
LABRETS	Alberts, Blaster,	
	Stabler, Tablers	
LACCINE	Calcine	
LACEMAN	Manacle	
LACE-UPS	Capsule, Specula	
LACKERS	Calkers, Recalks,	
	Slacker	
LACKING	Calking	
LACONIC	Conical	
LACTOSE	Alecost, Locates,	
	Talcose	
LACUNAL	Calluna	
LADDERS	Raddles, Saddler	
LAIRAGE	Railage	
LAIRING	Railing	
LAMBING	Ambling, Balming,	
	Blaming	
LAMINAE	Alamein	
LAMINAL	Manilla	
LAMINAR	Railman	
LAMPATE	Palmate	
LAMPERS	Palmers, Sampler	
LAMPING	Palming	
LAMPREY	Palmery	
LANCETS	Cantles, Centals,	
	Scantle	
LANDERS	Darnels, Enlards,	
	Relands, Slander	
LANGITE	Atingle, Elating,	
	Gelatin, Genital	
LANGUID	Lauding	
LANSING	Linsang	
LANTERN	Trannel	

LAPPERS	Rappels, Slapper	
LAPPING	Palping	
LAPPISH	Palship	
LAPSING	Palings, Sapling,	
	Spaling	
LAPWING	Pawling	
LARCHES	Charles	
LARDING	Darling	
LARGELY	Allergy, Gallery,	
	Regally	
LARIATS	Alsirat	
LASABLE	Sabella, Salable	
LASHERS	Slasher	
LASTERS	Artless, Salters,	
	Slaters, Tarsels	
LASTING	Anglist, Salting,	
	Slating, Staling	
LATCHES	Chalets, Satchel	
LATCHET	Chattel	
LATEBRA	Alberta, Ratable	
LATHERS	Halters, Harslet,	
	Hastler, Slather,	
	Thalers	
LATHERY	Earthly, Heartly	
LATHING	Althing, Halting	
LATICES	Elastic, Salicet	
LATRINE	Entrail, Ratline,	
	Reliant, Retinal,	
	Trenail	
LATTICE	Tactile, Talcite	
*LATVIAN	Valiant	
LAUDING	Languid	
LAUGH-IN	Hauling	
LAUNDER	Arundel, Lurdane,	
	Rundale	
LAVAGES	Salvage	
LAVEERS	Leavers, Reveals,	
	Several, Vealers	
LAYERED	Delayer, Relayed	
LAYINGS	Slaying	
LAYOVER	Overlay	
LEACHED	Chaldee, Cheadle	
LEADING	Aligned, Dealing	
LEAFING	Finagle	
LEAGUER	Regulae	
LEAKING	Linkage	
LEAMING	Gmelina, Mealing	
*LEANDER	Learned	
LEANING	Aneling, Eanling	

LEAPERS	Pealers, Pleaser, Preseal, Relapse, Repeals	LIGHTEN	Enlight
		LIGHTER	Relight
		LIGNITE	Tigline
LEAPING	Pealing	LIGNOSE	Eloigns, Legions, Lingoes, Sloe-gin
LEARNED	Leander		
LEARNER	Relearn	LIGULAS	Lugsail
LEASERS	Earless, Resales, Reseals, Sealers	LILTING	Tilling
		LIMBATE	Timbale
LEASING	Linages, Sealing	LIMITED	Delimit
LEAVENS	Enslave	LIMITER	Leitrim, Relimit
LEAVERS	Laveers, Reveals, Several, Vealers	LIMNERS	Merlins, Smerlin
		LINAGES	Leasing, Sealing
LECHERY	Cheerly	LINDANE	Annelid
LECTORS	Colters, Corslet, Costrel, Croslet	LINEMAN	Melanin
		LINE-OUT	Outline
LEDGERS	Red-legs	LINE-UPS	Lupines, Spinule, Unpiles, Up-lines
LEEMOST	Omelets		
LEERING	Reeling	LINGCOD	Codling
LEGIONS	Eloigns, Lignose, Lingoes, Sloe-gin	LINGERS	Girnels, Singler, Slinger
LEISTER	Retiles, Sterile	LINGETS	Glisten, Singlet, Tingles
LEITRIM	Limiter, Relimit		
LEMPIRA	Impaler, Impearl, Palmier	LINGISM	Smiling
		LINGOES	Eloigns, Legions, Lignose, Sloe-gin
LENDERS	Relends, Slender		
LEPROUS	Elopers, Pelorus, Perlous, Sporule	LINGUAL	Lingula
		LINGULA	Lingual
LESIONS	Insoles, Lioness	LINKAGE	Leaking
LESSONS	Sonless	LINKING	Inkling, Kilning
LETHEAN	Entheal	LINSANG	Lansing
LETTERN	Nettler	LINSEED	Enisled, Ensiled, Nelides
LETTERS	Settler, Sterlet, Trestle		
		LINTERS	Snirtle
LETTISH	Thistle	LIONESS	Insoles, Lesions
LEUCOMA	Caulome	LIONETS	Entoils, Tonsile
LEVELER	Relevel	LIONISE	Elision
LEVIERS	Relives, Reviles, Servile, Veilers	LIPPERS	Ripples, Slipper
		LIP-READ	Predial
*LEVITES	Velites	LISPING	Pilings, Spiling
LIASSIC	Silicas	LISTING	Silting
LIBERAL	Air-bell, Braille	LITERAL	Tallier
LIBRATE	Tablier, Triable, Trilabe	LITOTES	Toilets
		LITTERS	Slitter, Testril, Tilters, Titlers
LICENSE	Selenic, Silence		
LICKERS	Rickles, Sickler, Slicker	LITTERY	Tritely
		LIVE-OUT	Outlive, Ovulite
LIFTERS	Filters, Stifler, Trifles	LIVERED	Deliver, Relived, Reviled
LIGHTED	Delight	LOADING	Dog-nail

LOAFERS	Safrole		Sutling, Singult
LOAFING	Foaling	MACULES	Almuces, Mascule
LOAMING	Almoign	MADNESS	Desmans
LOATHER	Rat-hole	MADRIER	Admirer, Married
LOATHLY	Tally-ho	MADRONO	Doorman
LOBATED	Bloated	MAESTRO	Amorets
LOBBERS	Slobber	MAGENTA	Gateman, Magnate
LOBBIED	Bilobed	MAGNATE	Gateman, Magenta
LOBBIES	Bilboes	MAIDENS	Demains, Mandies
LOBSTER	Bolster, Bolters,		Medians, Sideman
	Rebolts	MAILERS	Realism, Remails
LOBULES	Soluble	MAINTOP	Tampion, Timpano
LOCATES	Alecost, Lactose,	MAISTER	Misrate
	Talcose	MALAISE	Amelias
LOCHIAS	Scholia	MALATES	Maltase, Tamales
LOCOMEN	Monocle	*MALINES	Menials, Seminal
LOCULES	Ocellus	MALISON	Monials, Osmanli,
LOCUSTA	Talcous		Somnial
LODGING	Godling, Golding	MALKINS	Slamkin
LOGGERS	Roggles, Slogger	MALTASE	Malates, Tamales
LOOKOUT	Outlook	MANACLE	Laceman
LOOPING	Pooling	MANAGED	Agnamed
LOOTING	Tooling	MANATEE	Emanate
*LORINDA	Ordinal	*MANDIES	Demains, Maidens,
LOUDENS	Nodules, Unsoled		Medians, Sideman
LOUNDER	Roundel, Roundle	MANDORA	Roadman
LOUSIER	Soilure	MANHOOD	Hoodman
LOUTING	Tung-oil	MANIACS	Caimans, Camansi
LOVABLE	Volable	MANILLA	Laminal
LOVERED	Reloved	MANIOCS	Anosmic, Camions,
LOW-BRED	Bowlder		Masonic
LOWINGS	Slowing	MANIPLE	Impanel
LUBBERS	Burbles, Rubbles,	MANITOU	Tinamou
	Slubber	MANSION	Amnions
LUCARNE	Nuclear, Unclear	MAN-TRAP	Rampant
LUGGERS	Gurgles, Slugger	MANURED	Duramen, Maunder,
LUGSAIL	Ligulas		Unarmed
LUMBERS	Rumbles, Slumber,	MANURES	Surname
	Umbrels	MARACAS	Camaras, Marasca,
LUMPERS	Replums, Rumples,		Mascara
	Slumper	MARASCA	Camaras, Maracas,
LUMPING	Pluming		Mascara
LUNATED	Undealt	MARBLED	Rambled
LUNIEST	Untiles, Utensil	MARBLER	Rambler
LUPINES	Line-ups, Spinule,	MARCHED	Charmed, Decharm
	Unpiles, Up-lines	MARCHER	Charmer
LURDANE	Arundel, Launder,	MARCHES	Schmear
	Rundale	*MARCONI	Minorca, Romanic
LUSTING	Glutins, Lutings,	MARGENT	Garment
	Singult, Sutling	MARINES	Remains, Seminar,
LUTINGS	Glutins, Lusting,		Sirname

MARITAL	Martial
MARLINE	Mineral, Railmen, Ramline
MARRIED	Admirer, Madrier
MARRIES	Simarre
MARTENS	Smarten
MARTIAL	Marital
MARTIAN	Martina
*MARTINA	Martian
MASCARA	Camaras, Maracas, Marasca
MASCULE	Almuces, Macules
MASHERS	Shamers, Smasher
MASHING	Shaming
MASONIC	Anosmic, Camions, Maniocs
MASSEUR	Assumer
MASTERY	Mayster, Streamy
MASTICS	Miscast
MASTOID	Diatoms, Distoma
MATCHER	Rematch
MATINEE	Etamine
MATRONS	Transom
MATTERS	Smatter
MAULING	Aluming
MAUNDER	Duramen, Manured, Unarmed
MAWKISH	Hawkism
MAXI-MIN	Mini-max
MAYSTER	Mastery, Streamy
MEALIES	Sea-mile
MEALING	Gmelins, Leaming
MEANDER	Amender, Reamend, Renamed
MEANETH	Methane
MEANING	Amening
MEDIALS	Misdeal, Mislead
MEDIANS	Demains, Maidens, Mandies, Sideman
MEDICAL	Claimed, Decimal, Declaim
MEDICOS	Miscode
MEETING	Teeming
MEGARAD	Damager
MEGASSE	Message
MEGILPS	Glimpse
MELANGE	Gleeman
MELANIN	Lineman
*MELISSA	Aimless, Samiels, Seismal
MELTERS	Remelts, Smelter
MENACES	Casemen
MENIALS	Malines, Seminal
MENIVER	Minever
*MENORCA	Cameron, Cremona, Romance
MENTORS	Monster, Montres
MERINOS	Mersion
MERITED	Demerit, Dimeter, Mitered, Retimed
MERLING	Gremlin, Mingler
MERLINS	Limners, Smerlin
MERSION	Merinos
MESSAGE	Megasse
MESSINS	Sensism
METAMER	Ammeter
METERED	Demeter
METIERS	Re-emits, Retimes, Triseme
METHANE	Meaneth
METONIC	Centimo, Entomic
METTLES	Stemlet
MICHING	Chiming
MICRONS	Crimson
MID-EAST	Misdate
MIGRATE	Ragtime
MILLETS	Mistell
MIMOSAS	Mosaism
MINARET	Raiment
MINERAL	Marline, Railmen, Ramline
*MINERVA	Vermian
MINEVER	Meniver
MINGLER	Gremlin, Merling
MINIBUS	Minisub
MINI-MAX	Maxi-min
MINIMUS	Minisum, Miniums
MINISUB	Minibus
MINISUM	Minimus, Miniums
MINIUMS	Minimus, Minisum
MINORCA	Marconi, Romanic
MINSTER	Minters, Remints
MINTAGE	Teaming
MINTERS	Minster, Remints
MINTOES	Moisten
MINUEND	Unmined
MINUETS	Minutes, Mistune
MINUTES	Minuets, Mistune
MIRACLE	Almeric, Claimer, Reclaim

MIRAGES	Gisarme, Imagers	MORTISE	Erotism
MISCAST	Mastics	MOSAISM	Mimosas
MISCITE	Semitic	MOTHERS	Smother, Thermos
MISCODE	Medicos	MOTIVED	Vomited
MISDATE	Mid-east	MOULDER	Remould
MISDEAL	Medials, Mislead	MOUNTED	Demount
MISDIET	Stimied	MOUNTER	Monture, Remount
MISDONE	Domines	MOUSERS	Smouser
MISLEAD	Medials, Misdeal	MUNDANE	Unmaned, Unnamed
MISNAME	Ammines	*MUNSTER	Sternum
MISRATE	Maister	MURICES	Ceriums
MISREAD	Admires, Sidearm	MUSLIMS	Slumism
MISSEND	Dimness	MUSTARD	Durmast
MISSILE	Similes	MUSTILY	Mytilus
MISTELL	Millets	MUTABLE	Ambulet
MISTERY	Smytrie	MYTILUS	Mustily
MISTICO	Somitic		
MISTING	Smiting		
MISTRAL	Ramtils	NAGGERS	Gangers, Granges,
MISTUNE	Minuets, Minutes		Snagger
MISUSER	Surmise	NAGGING	Ganging
MITERED	Demerit, Dimeter,	NAILERY	Inlayer
	Merited, Retimed	NAILING	Alining
MITERER	Trireme	NAPPERS	Parsnep, Snapper
MITTENS	Smitten	NARCOSE	Carnose, Coarsen,
MOBBING	Bombing		Corneas, Sea-corn
MODELER	Remodel	NASTIER	Resiant, Restain,
MOILERS	Semilor		Retains, Retinas,
MOISTEN	Mintoes		Retsina, Stainer,
MOLDERS	Smolder		Stearin
MONACID	Monadic, Nomadic	NASTILY	Saintly
MONADIC	Monacid, Nomadic	NATURES	Saunter, Sea-turn
MONARCH	Nomarch	NEAREST	Earnest, Eastern
MONERAL	Almoner, Nemoral	NEARETH	Earneth, Earthen,
MONIALS	Malison, Osmanli,		Hearten, Teheran
	Somnial	NEARING	Earning, Engrain,
MONOCLE	Locomen		Grannie
MONSTER	Mentors, Montres	NECROSE	Encores
MONTRES	Mentors, Monster	NEEDING	Engined
MONTURE	Mounter, Remount	NEGATER	Grantee, Greaten,
MOONIES	Noisome		Reagent
MOORAGE	Roomage	NEGATUR	Ungrate
MOOR-HEN	Hormone	NEGLIGE	Gleeing
MOORING	Rooming	NEGRITO	Genitor, Trigone
MORAINE	Romaine	NEGROID	Eroding, Gironde,
MORDANT	Dormant		Groined, Ignored,
MORGUES	Grumose		Redoing
MORINGA	Roaming	NEIGHED	Heeding
MORONIC	Omicron	NEITHER	Therein

*NELIDES	Enisled, Ensiled,	NONSTOP	Pontons
	Linseed	NOOLOGY	Onology
NEMORAL	Almoner, Moneral	NORTHER	Horrent
NEPHRIC	Phrenic, Pincher	NOTICED	Condite, Ctenoid,
NERVATE	Veteran		Deontic
NERVINE	Innerve	NOTICES	Noetics, Section
NESTERS	Ernests, Resents,	NOTINGS	Stoning
	Streens, Strenes	NOUGHTS	Gunshot, Hognuts,
NESTING	Tensing		Shotgun
NESTLED	Dentels	NOVALIA	Valonia
NESTLER	Relents	NOWHERE	Erewhon, Whereon
NET-FISH	Fish-net	NUCLEAR	Lucarne, Unclear
NETTING	Tenting	NUDGING	Dunging
NETTLER	Lettern	NUPTIAL	Unplait
NEUTERS	Retunes, Tenures,	NUTATED	Attuned, Taunted
	Tureens, Unterse	NUTATES	Attunes, Tautens,
NEUTRAL	Renault		Tetanus, Unstate
NICKERS	Snicker	NUT-GALL	Gall-nut
NICTATE	Tetanic	NUT-WOOD	Woodnut
NIDGING	Dinging	NUZZLES	Snuzzle
NIFFLES	Sniffle		
NIGGARD	Grading		
NIGGERS	Gingers, Snigger	OBLIGER	Oilberg
NIGGERY	Gingery, Greying	OBSERVE	Obverse, Verbose
NIGGLED	Gelding, Gingled	OBTAINS	Bastion
NIGGLES	Gingles, Sniggle	OBTRUDE	Doubter, Redoubt
NIGRINE	Reining	OBVERSE	Observe, Verbose
NIGRITE	Igniter, Tiering,	OCARINA	Aaronic
	Tigrine	OCEANIC	Cocaine
NIPPERS	Snipper	OCELLUS	Locules
NITRATE	Intreat, Iterant,	OCELOTS	Coolest
	Tertian	OCHROID	Choroid
NITRIDE	Inditer	OCTANES	Costean
NITROSO	Torsion	OCTONAL	Coolant
NITTERS	Retints, Stinter,	OCTUPLE	Couplet
	Tinters	OCULARS	Carolus, Oscular
NIVEOUS	Envious	ODDNESS	Soddens
NOCKING	Conking	OERSTED	Teredos
NOCTUID	Conduit	OESTRUS	Ousters, Sourest,
NODATED	Donated		Souters, Trouses,
NODULES	Loudens, Unsoled		Trousse, Tussore
NOETICS	Notices, Section	OFFCAST	Cast-off
NOISIER	Ironies	OFFENDS	Send-off
NOISOME	Moonies	OFFERER	Reoffer
NO-KNOCK	Knock-on	OFF-SPIN	Spin-off
NOMADIC	Monacid, Monadic	OFF-STEP	Step-off
NOMARCH	Monarch	OFF-TAKE	Take-off
NON-CASH	Chanson	OGLINGS	Gosling
NON-PAID	Dipnoan	OILBERG	Obliger

OILINGS	Soiling	*OTRANTO	Arnotto, Rattoon
OIL-PALM	Palm-oil	OUSTERS	Oestrus, Sourest,
OLIVINE	Violine		Souters, Trouses,
OMELETS	Leemost		Trousse, Tussore
OMENTAL	Telamon	OUSTING	Outings, Outsing,
OMICRON	Moronic		Tousing
ONE-STEP	Pentose, Pontees,	OUTARDE	Outdare, Outread,
	Posteen, Poteens		Readout
ONOLOGY	Noology	OUT-BACK	Back-out
ONSHORE	Sorehon	OUTBLOW	Blow-out, Outbowl
ONSTEAD	Donates	OUTBOWL	Blow-out, Outblow
*ONTARIO	Oration	OUTBURN	Burnout
OOLITES	Ostiole	OUTDARE	Outarde, Outread,
OPERAND	Aproned, Padrone,		Readout
	Pandore	OUTDRAW	Drawout, Outward
OPERANT	Pronate, Protean	OUTFALL	Fall-out
OPETIDE	Epidote	OUTGRIN	Outring, Routing,
OPPOSER	Propose		Touring
OPPRESS	Porpess	OUTHIRE	Routhie
OPTICAL	Capitol, Coalpit,	OUTINGS	Ousting, Outsing,
	Pit-coal, Topical		Tousing
OPTIONS	Positon, Potions	OUTJEST	Outjets
OPUNTIA	Utopian	OUTJETS	Outjest
OPUSCLE	Close-up, Couples,	OUTLINE	Line-out
	Upclose	OUTLIVE	Live-out, Ovulite
ORACLES	Coalers, Recoals,	OUTLOOK	Lookout
	Solacer	OUTPASS	Passout
ORATION	Ontario	OUTPOST	Outtops, Puttoos,
ORBITED	Debitor, Deorbit		Stop-out
ORDAINS	Inroads, Sadiron	OUTPULL	Pull-out
ORDERER	Reorder	OUTRATE	Out-tear
ORDINAL	Lorinda	OUTREAD	Outarde, Outdare,
ORECTIC	Cerotic		Readout
ORGEATS	Storage, Tagsore	OUTRIDE	Ioduret
ORIGANS	Ignaros, Signora	OUTRING	Outgrin, Routing,
	Soaring		Touring
ORIGINS	Signior	OUTSELL	Sell-out
ORLEANS	Salerno	OUTSEND	Send-out
ORPINES	Sinoper	OUTSERT	Stouter, Touters
ORRICES	Cirrose, Corries,	OUTSIDE	Tedious
	Crosier	OUTSING	Ousting, Outings,
ORTHITE	Thorite		Tousing
OSCINES	Cession, Cosines	OUTSPIN	Spin-out
OSCULAR	Carolus, Oculars	OUT-TEAR	Outrate
*OSMANLI	Malison, Monials,	OUTTOPS	Outpost, Puttoos,
	Somnial		Stop-out
OSSETER	Stereos	OUTTURN	Turn-out
OSTIOLE	Oolites	OUTWALK	Walk-out
OSTRICH	Chorist	OUTWARD	Drawout, Outdraw

OUTWASH	Wash-out	
OUTWITH	Without	
OUTWORK	Work-out	
OUTWORN	Worn-out	
OVERALL	All-over	
OVER-ATE	Over-eat	
OVER-EAT	Over-ate	
OVERFLY	Fly-over	
OVERLAY	Layover	
OVERLIE	Relievo	
OVERRUN	Run-over	
OVERSET	Estover, Revotes,	
	Setover, Vetoers	
OVULITE	Live-out, Outlive	
PACABLE	Capable	
PACINGS	Spacing	
PACK-ICE	Icepack	
PACTION	Caption	
PADDLES	Spaddle	
PADRONE	Aproned, Operand,	
	Pandore	
PAD-TREE	Red-tape, Retaped,	
	Tapered	
PAGINGS	Gasping	
PAINTED	Depaint	
PAINTER	Pertain, Repaint	
PALETTE	Peltate	
PALINGS	Lapsing, Sapling,	
	Spaling	
PALMARY	Palmyra	
PALMATE	Lampate	
PALMERS	Lampers, Sampler	
PALMERY	Lamprey	
PALMIER	Impaler, Impearl,	
	Lempira	
PALMING	Lamping	
PALM-OIL	Oil-palm	
PALMYRA	Palmary	
PALPING	Lapping	
PALSHIP	Lappish	
PALSIED	Alipeds, Pleiads	
PALTERS	Persalt, Plaster,	
	Platers, Psalter,	
	Stapler	
PANDEAN	Pannade	
PANDORE	Aproned, Operand,	
	Padrone	

PANELER	Repanel	
*PANGAEA	Apanage	
PAN-HEAD	Headpan	
PANICLE	Capelin, Pelican	
PANNADE	Pandean	
PANNERS	Spanner	
PANTERS	Arpents, Entraps,	
	Parents, Pastern,	
	Persant, Trepans	
PANTLER	Planter, Replant	
PAPERER	Prepare, Repaper	
PAPULES	Appluse	
PARADES	Aspread, Saperda	
PARBOIL	Bipolar	
PARCELS	Carpels, Clasper,	
	Placers, Reclasp,	
	Scalper	
PARENTS	Arpents, Entraps,	
	Panters, Pastern,	
	Persant, Trepans	
PARESIS	Aspires, Praises,	
	Serapis, Spireas	
PARETIC	Picrate	
PARINGS	Parsing, Rasping,	
	Sparing	
PARISON	Soprani	
PARKERS	Reparks, Sparker	
PARLEYS	Parsley, Players,	
	Replays, Sparely	
PARODIC	Picador	
PAROLES	Reposal	
PAROTIC	Apricot, Patrico	
PARSEES	Asperse, Serapes	
PARSING	Parings, Rasping,	
	Sparing	
PARSLEY	Parleys, Players,	
	Replays, Sparely	
PARSNEP	Nappers, Snapper	
PARTANS	Spartan, Tarpans,	
	Trapans	
PARTIAL	Patrial	
PARTIES	Piaster, Piastre,	
	Pirates, Praties,	
	Traipse	
PARTING	Gin-trap, Prating	
PARTITE	Tearpit	
PARTLET	Platter, Prattle	
PARTONS	Patrons, Strap-on,	
	Tarpons	

PARTURE	Rapture
PARVISE	Paviers, Paviser
PASCUAL	Capsula, Scapula
PASSIVE	Pavises
PASSMAN	Sampans
PASSOUT	Outpass
PASTERN	Arpents, Entraps, Panters, Parents, Persant, Trepans
PASTIME	Impaste
PATCHER	Chapter, Repatch
PATINES	Sapient, Spinate
PATNESS	Aptness
PATRIAL	Partial
PATRICO	Apricot, Parotic
PATRONS	Partons, Strap-on, Tarpons
PATTERN	Reptant
PATTERS	Spatter, Tapster
PATTLES	Peltast, Spattle
PAVIERS	Parvise, Paviser
PAVISER	Parvise, Paviers
PAVISES	Passive
PAWLING	Lapwing
PAWNERS	Enwraps, Repawns, Spawner
PEACHER	Cheaper
PEALERS	Leapers, Pleaser, Preseal, Relapse, Repeals
PEALING	Leaping
PEANUTS	Unpaste
PEARLED	Pleader, Replead
PEASANT	Anapest
PECTINE	Pentice
PECTINS	Incepts, Inspect
PEDESIS	Despise
PEDICEL	Pedicle
PEDICLE	Pedicel
PEELERS	Sleeper
PEERESS	Presees
PELAMID	Impaled, Implead
PELICAN	Capelin, Panicle
PELMETS	Stempel, Stemple, Temples
PELORUS	Elopers, Leprous, Perlous, Sporule
PELOTAS	Apostle, Pot-ales
PELTAST	Pattles, Spattle
PELTATE	Palette

PELTERS	Petrels, Respelt, Spelter
PENCILS	Splenic
PENNATE	Pentane
PENNIES	Pinenes
PENSILE	Espinal, Sleep-in
PENSIVE	Vespine
PENTANE	Pennate
PENTICE	Pectine
PENTOSE	One-step, Pontees, Posteen, Poteens
PENULTS	Unspelt
PEONISM	Impones
PERACID	Preacid
PERBEND	Prebend
PERCALE	Replace
PERCASE	Escaper, Respace
PER-CENT	Precent
PERCEPT	Precept
PERCUSS	Spruces
PERFECT	Prefect
PERFORM	Preform
PERIDOT	Diopter, Dioptre, Proteid
PERIQUE	Re-equip, Repique
PERJINK	Prejink
PERLITE	Reptile
PERLOUS	Elopers, Leprous, Pelorus, Sporule
PERMITS	Imprest
PERSALT	Palters, Plaster, Platers, Psalter, Stapler
PERSANT	Arpents, Entraps, Panters, Parents, Pastern, Trepans
PERSEID	Preside
PERSEUS	Persues, Peruses
*PERSIAN	Rapines
PERSIST	Priests, Spriest, Sprites, Stirpes, Stripes
PERSUES	Perseus, Peruses
PERTAIN	Painter, Repaint
PERUSAL	Serpula
PERUSES	Perseus, Persues
PERVADE	Deprave, Repaved
PETEMAN	Tempean
PETERED	Depeter

PETRELS	Pelters, Respelt, Spelter	PISMIRE	Primsie
		PITCOAL	Capitol, Coal-pit, Optical, Topical
PETROUS	Posture, Pouters, Proteus, Septuor, Spouter, Troupes	PITTERS	Spitter, Tipster
		PLACERS	Carpels, Clasper, Parcels, Reclasp, Scalper
*PETULAS	Pulsate, Puteals, Spatule		
PEWTERS	Reswept	PLAGUER	Graupel
PHAETON	Phonate	PLAINER	Praline
PHASING	Hasping, Shaping	PLAITED	Taliped
PHILTER	Philtre	PLAITER	Replait
PHILTRE	Philter	PLANTER	Pantler, Replant
PHOCINE	Chopine	PLASHER	Spheral
PHOEBES	Ephebos	PLASMIC	Psalmic
PHONATE	Phaeton	PLASTER	Palters, Persalt, Platers, Psalter, Stapler
PHRASED	Sharped		
PHRENIC	Nephric, Pincher		
PHYTOID	Typhoid	PLATERS	Palters, Persalt, Plaster, Psalter, Stapler
PIASTER	Parties, Piastre, Pirates, Praties, Traipse		
		PLATTER	Partlet, Prattle
PIASTRE	Parties, Piaster, Pirates, Praties, Traipse	PLAYERS	Parleys, Parsley, Replays, Sparely
		PLAYFUL	Full-play
PICADOR	Parodic	PLEADER	Pearled, Replead
PICKETS	Skeptic	PLEASED	Elapsed
PICKLER	Prickle	PLEASER	Leapers, Pealers, Preseal, Relapse, Repeals
PICRATE	Paretic		
PICTURE	Cuprite		
PIECERS	Pierces, Precise, Recipes, Respice	PLEATER	Prelate, Replate
		PLEIADS	Alipeds, Palsied
PIERCER	Reprice	PLESSOR	Preloss, Splores
PIERCES	Piecers, Precise, Recipes, Respice	PLOPPED	Poppled
		PLOUTER	Poulter
PIGSKIN	Spiking	PLUMING	Lumping
PILINGS	Lisping, Spiling	POINTER	Protein, Pterion, Repoint, Tropine
PINCERS	Princes		
PINCHER	Nephric, Phrenic	POITREL	Politer
PINENES	Pennies	POLEMIC	Compile
PIN-HEAD	Head-pin	POLITER	Poitrel
PININGS	Sniping	POLOIST	Topsoil
PINKING	King-pin	PONDERS	Respond
PINNERS	Spinner	PONTEES	One-step, Pentose, Posteen, Poteens
PINNETS	Ten-pins		
PINOLES	Epsilon	PONTONS	Nonstop
PIRATES	Parties, Piaster, Piastre, Praties, Traipse	POOLING	Looping
		POOREST	Stooper
		POPPLED	Plopped
PIROGUE	Groupie	POPSTER	Stopper, Toppers

PORGIES	Serpigo	PRAISER	Aspirer, Rapiers, Repairs
PORPESS	Oppress		
PORRETS	Porters, Presort, Pretors, Reports, Sporter	PRAISES	Aspires, Paresis, Serapis, Spireas
		PRALINE	Plainer
PORTAGE	Potager	PRATIES	Parties, Piaster, Piastre, Pirates, Traipse
PORTEND	Drop-net, Protend		
PORTENT	Torpent		
PORTERS	Porrets, Presort, Pretors, Reports, Sporter	PRATING	Gin-trap, Parting
		PRATTLE	Partlet, Platter
		PRAWNER	Prewarn
PORTICO	Prootic	PRAYERS	Respray, Sprayer
PORTIFY	Torpify	PREACHY	Eparchy
POSITED	Deposit, Topside	PREACID	Peracid
POSITON	Options, Potions	PRE-ACTS	Carpets, Precast, Spectra
POSTAGE	Gestapo, Potages		
POST-BOY	Potboys	PRE-AGES	Presage
POSTEEN	One-step, Pentose, Pontees, Poteens	PREBEND	Perbend
		PRECAST	Carpets, Pre-acts, Spectra
POSTERN	Preston		
POSTING	Stoping	PRECENT	Per-cent
POSTMAN	Tampons, Topsman	PRECEPT	Percept
POSTURE	Petrous, Pouters, Proteus, Septuor, Spouter, Troupes	PRECISE	Piecers, Pierces, Recipes, Respice
		PRECITE	Receipt
POTAGER	Portage	PREDATE	Readept
POTAGES	Gestapo, Postage	PREDIAL	Lip-read
POT-ALES	Apostle, Pelotas	PREDIET	Pre-edit
POTASSA	Sapotas	PREDONE	Reponed
POTBOYS	Post-boy	PRE-EDIT	Prediet
POTEENS	One-step, Pentose, Pontees, Posteen	PREFECT	Perfect
		PREFORM	Perform
POTENTS	Ten-spot	PREJINK	Perjink
POTHERS	Strophe, Thorpes	PRELATE	Pleater, Replate
POTHOLE	Tophole	PRELIMS	Rimples, Simpler
POTIONS	Options, Positon	PRELOSS	Plessor, Splores
POTLINE	Topline	PREMATE	Tempera
POT-SHOT	Hotpots, Hotspot	PREMIER	Reprime
POTTERS	Protest, Spotter	PREMISE	Empires, Emprise, Spireme
POTWORK	Topwork		
POULTER	Plouter	PREMISS	Impress, Simpers
POUNDER	Unroped	PREPARE	Paperer, Repaper
POURING	Ingroup, Rouping	PRESAGE	Pre-ages
POUTERS	Petrous, Posture, Proteus, Septuor, Spouter, Troupes	PRESEAL	Leapers, Pealers, Pleaser, Relapse, Repeals
		PRESEES	Peeress
PRAETOR	Apertor, Prorate	PRESELL	Respell, Speller
PRAISED	Aspired, Despair, Diapers	PRESENT	Repents, Serpent

PRESHIP	Shipper	PROTEUS	Petrous, Posture,
PRESIDE	Perseid		Pouters, Septuor,
PRESORT	Porrets, Porters,		Spouter, Troupes
	Pretors, Reports,	PROTIST	Tropist
	Sporter	PROVIDE	Prevoid
PRESSED	Depress	PRUNERS	Spurner
PRESSER	Repress	PRYINGS	Springy
PRESS-UP	Suppers	PSALMIC	Plasmic
*PRESTON	Postern	PSALTER	Palters, Persalt,
PRESUME	Supreme		Plaster, Platers,
PRE-TEEN	Terpene		Stapler
PRETOLD	Droplet	PTERION	Pointer, Protein,
PRETORS	Porrets, Porters,		Repoint, Tropine
	Presort, Reports,	PTEROIS	Reposit, Riposte
	Sporter	PTYALIN	Inaptly
PREVOID	Provide	PULINGS	Pusling
PREWARN	Prawner	PULL-OUT	Outpull
PREWRAP	Wrapper	PULPITS	Split-up
PRICKLE	Pickler	PULSATE	Petulas, Puteals,
PRIESTS	Persist, Spriest,		Spatule
	Sprites, Stirpes,	PULSING	Pulings
	Stripes	PULSION	Upsilon
PRIEVED	Deprive	PUNKIES	Spunkie
PRIMAGE	Epigram	PUNSTER	Punters
PRIMSIE	Pismire	PUNTERS	Punster
PRINCES	Pincers	PURITAN	Up-train
PRINTER	Reprint	PURSUED	Usurped
PRISING	Spiring	PURSUER	Usurper
PRISTIS	Spirits, Tripsis	PUSHING	Gunship
PROCESS	Corpses	PUSHTOO	Shoot-up, Upshoot
PROCURE	Crouper	PUTEALS	Petulas, Pulsate,
PRO-EAST	Esparto, Seaport		Spatule
PRO-ETTE	Treetop	PUTTERS	Sputter
PROGENY	Pyrogen	PUTTOOS	Outpost, Outtops,
PROMISE	Imposer		Stop-out
PRONATE	Operant, Protean	PYROGEN	Progeny
PROOFER	Reproof		
PROOTIC	Portico		
PROPERS	Prosper	QUEERER	Requere
PROPOSE	Opposer	QUERIES	Esquire
PRORATE	Apertor, Praetor	QUESTER	Request
PROSPER	Propers	QUESTOR	Quoters, Roquets,
PROTEAN	Operant, Pronate		Torques
PROTEID	Diopter, Dioptre,	QUIETER	Requite
	Peridot	QUINATE	Antique
PROTEIN	Pointer, Pterion,	QUINNAT	Quintan
	Repoint, Tropine	QUINTAN	Quinnat
PROTEND	Drop-net, Portend	QUOTERS	Quester, Roquets,
PROTEST	Potters, Spotter		Torques

RABBETS	Barbets, Stabber	RASORES	Soarers
RABBLES	Barbels, Slabber	RASPING	Parings, Parsing,
RACEMED	Amerced, Creamed		Sparing
RACEMIC	Ceramic	RASURES	Assurer
RACINGS	Sacring, Scaring	RATABLE	Alberta, Latebra
RACKETS	Restack, Retacks,	RATBITE	Biretta
	Stacker, Tackers	RATCHED	Charted
RACKING	Carking, Craking	RATCHEL	Trachle, Relatch
RADDLES	Ladders, Saddler	RATCHET	Chatter
RADIATE	Tiaraed	RAT-HOLE	Loather
RADICEL	Decrial, Radicle	RATINGS	Gastrin, Gratins,
RADICLE	Decrial, Radicel		Staring
RAFFISH	Haffirs	RATITES	Artiste, Attires,
RAFTING	Farting, Ingraft		Striate, Tastier
RAGGLED	Draggle, Gargled	RATLINE	Entrail, Latrine,
RAGINGS	Gas-ring		Reliant, Retinal,
RAGTIME	Migrate		Trenail
RAG-WEED	Wagered	RATTEEN	Entreat, Ternate
RAILAGE	Lairage	RATTERS	Restart, Starter
RAILING	Lairing	RATTISH	Athirst, Tartish
RAILMAN	Laminar	RATTLES	Slatter, Starlet,
RAILMEN	Marline, Mineral,		Startle, Tatlers,
	Ramline		Telstar
RAIMENT	Minaret	RATTOON	Arnotto, Otranto
RAINING	Ingrain	RAVINED	Invader
RAISING	Airings, Arising,	RAVINES	Vansire
	Sairing	RAWHEAD	Warhead
RAKINGS	Sarking	RAWNESS	Answers
RALLIED	Dallier	RAYLESS	Slayers
RAMBLED	Marbled	REACTED	Catered, Cedrate,
RAMBLER	Marbler		Cerated, Created
RAMLINE	Marline, Mineral,	REACTOR	Creator
	Railmen	READAPT	Adapter
RAMPANT	Mantrap	READEPT	Predate
RAMTILS	Mistral	READERS	Redares, Redsear,
RANGERS	Garners		Rereads
RANGIER	Angrier, Earring,	READING	Deraign, Gradine,
	Grainer, Rearing		Grained
RANGING	Gnaring	READOPT	Adopter
RANKEST	Tankers	READORN	Adorner
RANKLED	Knarled	READ-OUT	Outarde, Outdare,
RAPIERS	Aspirer, Praiser,		Outread
	Repairs	REAGENT	Grantee, Greaten,
RAPINES	Persian		Negater
RAPPELS	Lappers, Slapper	REALIGN	Aligner, Engrail,
RAPTURE	Parture		Reginal
RAREBIT	Arbiter	REALINE	Aliener
RASHEST	Trashes	REALISE	Saliere
RASHING	Garnish, Sharing	REALISM	Mailers, Remails

REALIST	Alister, Retails, Saltier, Slatier, Tailers
REALITY	Irately
REALTER	Alterer, Relater
REALTOR	Relator
REAMASS	Amasser
REAMEND	Amender, Meander, Renamed
REANNEX	Annexer
REAPERS	Spearer
REARING	Angrier, Earring, Grainer, Rangier
REARMED	Dreamer
REAVING	Ginevra, Vinegar
REBATED	Berated, Betread, Debater
REBATOS	Boaster, Boaters, Sorbate
REBLEND	Blender
REBLOCK	Blocker
REBLOOM	Bloomer
REBOANT	Baronet
REBOARD	Arbored, Boarder, Broader
REBOLTS	Bolster, Bolters, Lobster
REBOUND	Bounder, Unbored, Unorbed, Unrobed
REBRAND	Brander
REBREED	Breeder
REBRUSH	Brusher
REBUILD	Builder
RECALKS	Calkers, Lackers, Slacker
RECALLS	Callers, Cellars, Scleral
RECASTS	Actress, Casters
RECEDED	Decreed
RECEDES	Decrees, Seceder
RECEIPT	Precite
RECEPTS	Respect, Scepter, Sceptre, Specter, Spectre
RECHART	Charter
RECHATE	Cheater, Hectare, Recheat, Reteach, Teacher
RECHEAT	Cheater, Hectare, Rechate, Reteach, Teacher
RECHECK	Checker
RECHOSE	Chorees, Coheres, Echoers
RECIPES	Piecers, Pierces, Precise, Respice
RECITAL	Article
RECLAIM	Almeric, Claimer, Miracle
RECLASP	Carpels, Clasper, Parcels, Placers, Scalper
RECLASS	Classer, Sarcels, Scalers
RECLEAN	Cleaner, Relance
RECLIMB	Climber
RECOALS	Coalers, Oracles, Solacer
RECOAST	Coaster, Coaters, Recoats
RECOATS	Coaster, Coaters, Recoast
RECOINS	Coiners, Cronies, Sericon
RECOLOR	Colorer
RECOMBS	Combers, Scomber
RECOOLS	Coolers, Creosol
RECOUNT	Cornute, Counter, Trounce
RECOVER	Coverer
RECRATE	Caterer, Retrace, Terrace
RECROSS	Crosser, Scorers
RECROWN	Crowner
RECTIFY	Certify, Cretify
RECUMBS	Cumbers, Scumber
RECURES	Rescuer, Securer
RECUSED	Rescued, Secured
REDARES	Readers, Red-sear, Rereads
REDATES	Dearest, Derates, Estrade
RED-BOOK	Brooked
RED-CAPS	Scarped
RED-CENT	Centred, Credent
RED-COAT	Cordate
RED-COCK	Crocked
REDDENS	Dresden

REDDEST	Tedders		REFACED	Defacer
REDDLES	Sledder		REFILED	Defiler, Fielder
REDEALT	Alerted, Altered,		REFINED	Definer
	Delater, Related,		REFINER	Reinfer
	Treadle		REFLOAT	Floater
REDECAY	Decayer		REFOCUS	Focuser
REDEEMS	Demerse, Emersed		REFOUND	Founder
RED-HATS	Hardest, Hardset,		REFRESH	Fresher
	Hatreds, Threads		REFUSAL	Earfuls, Ferules,
RED-HEAD	Adhered			Fur-seal
RED-HEAT	Earthed, Hearted		REFUSED	Defuser
RED-LEGS	Ledgers		REFUTAL	Faulter, Tearful
REDNESS	Resends, Senders		REGAINS	Angries, Erasing,
REDOING	Eroding, Gironde,			Earings, Gainers,
	Groined, Ignored,			Regians, Reginas,
	Negroid			Searing, Seringa
REDORSE	Reredos, Rose-red		REGALIA	Algeria
REDOUBT	Doubter, Obtrude		REGALLY	Allergy, Gallery,
REDOUND	Rounded, Underdo			Largely
REDRAFT	Drafter		REGIANS	Angries, Erasing,
REDRESS	Dresser			Earings, Gainers,
REDRIED	Deirdre, Derider,			Regains, Reginas,
	Ridered			Searing, Seringa
REDRILL	Driller		REGIMEN	Reeming
REDRIVE	Deriver		REGIMES	Emigres, Remiges
REDROOP	Drooper		REGINAL	Aligner, Engrail,
RED-SEAR	Readers, Redares,			Realign
	Rereads		REGINAS	Angries, Earsing,
RED-TAIL	Dilater, Trailed			Earings, Gainers,
RED-TAPE	Pad-tree, Retaped,			Regains, Regians,
	Tapered			Searing, Seringa
RED-TOPS	Deports, Sported		REGIONS	Eringos, Ignores,
REDUCES	Cerused, Seducer			Signore
REDWING	Wringed		REGLUED	Guelder
REEDING	Dreeing, Energid,		REGRAFT	Grafter
	Enridge, Reigned		REGRANT	Granter
REEFING	Feering, Freeing		REGRAPH	Grapher
REELING	Leering		REGRASP	Grasper, Sparger
REEMING	Regimen		REGRATE	Greater
RE-EMITS	Metiers, Retimes,		REGREET	Greeter
	Triseme		REGRIND	Grinder
RE-ENACT	Centare, Crenate		REGROUP	Grouper
RE-ENDOW	Endower		REGROWN	Wronger
RE-ENJOY	Enjoyer		REGULAE	Leaguer
RE-ENTER	Enterer, Terreen,		REHEADS	Adheres, Headers,
	Terrene			Hearsed, Sheared
RE-EQUIP	Perique, Repique		REHEARD	Adherer
RE-ERECT	Erecter		REHEARS	Hearers, Reshare,
REEVING	Veering			Shearer

REIGNED	Dreeing, Energid,	REMANET	Remeant
	Enridge, Reeding	REMATCH	Matcher
REINDEX	Indexer	REMBLAI	Embrail
REINFER	Refiner	REMEANT	Remanet
REINING	Nigrine	REMELTS	Melters, Smelter
REINTER	Rentier, Terrine	REMIGES	Emigrés, Regimes
REJOINT	Jointer	REMINTS	Minster, Minters
REJOLTS	Jolters, Jostler	REMIPED	Demirep, Epiderm,
REKNEAD	Kneader		Impeder
REKNITS	Kirsten, Stinker,	REMNANT	Rentman
	Tinkers	REMODEL	Modeler
REKNOCK	Knocker	REMOULD	Moulder
RELABEL	Labeler	REMOUNT	Monture, Mounter
RELACED	Cedrela, Cleared,	RENAMED	Amender, Meander,
	Declare		Reamend
RELANCE	Cleaner, Reclean	*RENAULT	Neutral
RELANDS	Darnels, Enlards,	RENDING	Grinned
	Landers, Slander	RENEGED	Greened
RELAPSE	Leapers, Pealers,	RENTALS	Antlers, Saltern,
	Pleaser, Preseal,		Sternal
	Repeals	RENTERS	Rerents, Sterner
RELATCH	Ratchel, Trachle	RENTIER	Reinter, Terrine
RELATED	Alerted, Altered,	RENTING	Ringent, Ring-net
	Delater, Redealt,	RENT-MAN	Remnant
	Treadle	REOFFER	Offerer
RELATER	Alterer, Realter	REORDER	Orderer
RELATOR	Realtor	REPAINT	Painter, Pertain
RELAYED	Delayer, Layered	REPAIRS	Aspirer, Praiser,
RELEARN	Learner		Rapiers
RELENDS	Lenders, Slender	REPANEL	Paneler
RELENTS	Nestler	REPAPER	Paperer, Prepare
RELEVEL	Leveler	REPARKS	Parkers, Sparker
RELEVER	Reveler	REPASTE	Repeats, Retapes,
RELIANT	Entrail, Latrine,		Sea-pert
	Ratline, Retinal,	REPATCH	Chapter, Patcher
	Trenail	REPAVED	Deprave, Pervade
RELIEVO	Overlie	REPAWNS	Enwraps, Pawners,
RELIGHT	Lighter		Spawner
RELIMIT	Leitrim, Limiter	REPEALS	Leapers, Pealers,
RELIVED	Deliver, Livered,		Pleaser, Preseal,
	Reviled		Relapse
RELIVES	Leviers, Reviles,	REPEATS	Repaste, Retapes,
	Servile, Veilers		Sea-pert
RELOVED	Lovered	REPENTS	Present, Serpent
RELOVES	Resolve	*REPHAIM	Ephraim
RELUCTS	Cluster, Culters,	REPINED	Ripened
	Custrel, Cutlers	REPINES	Erepsin
REMAILS	Mailers, Realism	REPIQUE	Perique, Re-equip
REMAINS	Marines, Seminar,	REPLACE	Percale
	Sirname		

REPLAIT	Plaiter		RESEAUS	Seasure, Ureases
REPLANT	Pantler, Planter		RE-SECTS	Cresset, Secrets
REPLATE	Pleater, Prelate		RESENDS	Redness, Senders
REPLAYS	Parleys, Parsley,		RESENTS	Ernests, Nesters,
	Players, Sparely			Streens, Strenes
REPLEAD	Pearled, Pleader		RESERVE	Reveres, Reverse,
REPLICA	Caliper			Severer
REPLUMS	Lumpers, Rumples,		RESHAKE	Harkees
	Slumper		RESHAPE	Rephase
REPOINT	Pointer, Protein,		RESHARE	Hearers, Reshears,
	Pterion, Tropine			Shearer
REPONED	Predone		RESHAVE	Heavers
REPORTS	Porrets, Porters,		RESHIFT	Shifter
	Presort, Pretors,		RESHINE	Inheres, Inherse
	Sporter		RESHOOK	Hookers
REPOSAL	Paroles		RESHOOT	Hooters, Shooter,
REPOSED	Deposer			Soother
REPOSIT	Pterois, Riposte		RESIANT	Nastier, Restain,
REPRESS	Presser			Retains, Retinas,
REPRICE	Piercer			Retsina, Stainer,
REPRIME	Premier			Stearin
REPRINT	Printer		RESIDED	Derides, Desired
REPRISE	Respire		RESIDER	Derries, Desirer,
REPROOF	Proofer			Serried
REPTANT	Pattern		RESIDUE	Ureides
REPTILE	Perlite		RESIGHT	Sighter
REPUTED	Erupted		RESIGNS	Ingress, Signers,
REQUERE	Queerer			Singers
REQUEST	Quester		RESOLVE	Reloves
REQUITE	Quieter		RESOUND	Enduros, Sounder,
RERATED	Retrade, Retread,			Undoers, Unrosed
	Treader		RESPACE	Escaper, Percase
RERATES	Retears, Serrate,		RESPEAK	Speaker
	Tearers		RESPECT	Recepts, Scepter,
REREADS	Readers, Redares,			Sceptre, Specter,
	Redsear			Spectre
REREDOS	Redorse, Rose-red		RE-SPELL	Presell, Speller
RERENTS	Renters, Sterner		RE-SPELT	Pelters, Petrels,
RESAILS	Airless, Sailers,			Spelter
	Serails, Serials		RESPICE	Piecers, Pierces,
RESALES	Earless, Leasers,			Precise, Recipes
	Reseals, Sealers		RESPIRE	Reprise
RESCIND	Cincers, Discern		RESPLIT	Spirtle
RESCUED	Recused, Secured		RESPOND	Ponders
RESCUER	Recures, Securer		RESPRAY	Prayers, Sprayer
RESEALS	Earless, Leasers,		RESTACK	Rackets, Retacks,
	Resales, Sealers			Stacker, Tackers
RESEATS	Easters, Seaters,		RESTAFF	Staffer
	Teasers, Tessera		RESTAIN	Nastier, Resiant,

	Retains, Retinas,	RETIMED	Demerit, Dimeter,
	Retsina, Stainer,		Merited, Mitered
	Stearin	RETIMES	Metiers, Re-emits,
RESTAMP	Stamper, Tampers		Triseme
RESTART	Ratters, Starter	RETINAL	Entrail, Latrine,
RESTATE	Estreat, Retaste,		Ratline, Reliant,
	Tearest		Trenail
RESTFUL	Fluster, Fluters	RETINAS	Nastier, Resiant,
RESTIFF	Stiffer		Restain, Retains,
RESTING	Stinger		Retsina, Stainer,
RESTIVE	Servite, Veriest		Stearin
RESTOCK	Rockets	RETINGE	Integer, Teering,
RESTUFF	Stuffer		Treeing,
RESURGE	Reurges	RETINTS	Nitters, Stinter,
RESWEAR	Rewears, Swearer,		Tinters
	Wearers	RETINUE	Reunite, Uterine
RESWEEP	Sweeper, Weepers	RETIRAL	Retrial, Trailer
RESWELL	Sweller	RETIRED	Retried
RESWEPT	Pewters	RETOAST	Rosetta, Rotates,
RETABLE	Bleater		Toaster
RETACKS	Rackets, Restack,	RETORTS	Rotters, Stertor
	Stacker, Tackers	RETOUCH	Toucher
RETAILS	Alister, Realist,	RETOURS	Rouster, Routers,
	Saltier, Saltire,		Tourers, Trouser
	Slatier, Tailers	RETRACE	Caterer, Recrate,
RETAINS	Nastier, Resiant,		Terrace
	Restain, Retinas,	RETRACK	Tracker
	Retsina, Stainer,	RETRADE	Rerated, Retread,
	Stearin		Treader
RETAPED	Pad-tree, Red-tape,	RETRAIN	Terrain, Trainer
	Tapered	RETRATE	Retreat, Treater
RETAPES	Repaste, Repeats,	RETREAD	Rerated, Retrade,
	Sea-pert		Treader
RETARDS	Darters, Starred,	RETREAT	Retrate, Treater
	Traders	RETRIAL	Retiral, Trailer
RETASTE	Estreat, Restate,	RETRIED	Retired
	Tearest	RETSINA	Nastier, Resiant,
RETEACH	Cheater, Hectare,		Restain, Retains,
	Rechate, Recheat		Retinas, Stainer,
	Teacher		Stearin
RETEARS	Rerates, Serrate,	RETTING	Gittern
	Tearers	RETUNED	Denture, Untreed
RETHANK	Thanker	RETUNES	Neuters, Tenures,
RETHINK	Thinker		Tureens, Unterse
RETICLE	Tiercel	RETWIST	Twister, Witster,
RETILED	Tile-red		Witters
RETILES	Leister, Sterile	REUNITE	Retinue, Uterine
RETILLS	Rillets, Stiller,	REURGES	Resurge
	Tillers, Trellis	REUTTER	Utterer

REVEALS	Laveers, Leavers, Several, Vealers	RIMPLES	Prelims, Simpler
REVELER	Relever	RINGENT	Renting, Ring-net
REVENUE	Unreeve	RINGING	Girning
REVERES	Reserve, Reverse, Severer	RINGLET	Tingler, Tringle
		RING-NET	Renting, Ringent
		RIOTERS	Roister
REVERSE	Reserve, Reveres, Severer	RIOTING	Ignitor
		RIPENED	Repined
REVERSI	Reviser	RIPOSTE	Pterois, Reposit
REVESTU	Vesture	RIPPLES	Lippers, Slipper
REVILED	Deliver, Livered, Relived	RIPPLET	Tippler, Tripple
		RIPTIDE	Tiderip
REVILES	Leviers, Relives, Servile, Veilers	RISKING	Girkins, Griskin
		RITUALS	Trisula
REVISED	Derives, Deviser, Diverse	RIVERET	Riveter
		RIVETED	Tivered
REVISER	Reversi	RIVETER	Riveret
REVISIT	Visiter	ROAD-BED	Boarded
REVOLVE	Evolver	ROADING	Adoring, Gordian
REVOTED	Devoter	ROADMAN	Mandora
REVOTES	Estover, Overset, Setover, Vetoers	ROAMING	Moringa
		ROASTED	Rosated, Torsade
REWAGER	Wagerer	ROCHETS	Hectors, Rotches, Tochers, Torches, Troches
REWAKEN	Wakener		
REWARMS	Swarmer, Warmers		
REWATER	Waterer	ROCK-DOE	Crooked
REWEARS	Reswear, Swearer, Wearers	ROCKETS	Restock
		ROCKING	Corking
REWEIGH	Weigher	ROGGLED	Doggrel
REWIDEN	Widener	ROGGLES	Loggers, Slogger
REWORDS	Sworder	ROGUING	Rouging
REWOUND	Wounder	ROISTER	Rioters
RHODIUM	Humidor	*ROLANDS	Rosland
RIBBING	Bribing	ROMAINE	Moraine
RIBLETS	Blister, Bristle	ROMANCE	Cameron, Cremona, Menorca
RICHEST	Estrich		
RICKETS	Sticker, Tickers	ROMANIC	Marconi, Minorca
RICKLES	Lickers, Sickler, Slicker	RONDEAU	Unoared
		RONDURE	Rounder, Unorder
RIDDELS	Riddles, Slidder	ROOMAGE	Moorage
RIDDLED	Diddler	ROOMING	Mooring
RIDDLES	Riddels, Slidder	ROOSTED	Stoored
RIDERED	Deirdre, Derider, Redried	ROOSTER	Rooters, Toreros
		ROOTERS	Rooster, Toreros
RIDGING	Girding, Griding	ROOTLET	Tootler
RIFFING	Griffin	ROQUETS	Questor, Quoters, Torques
RIGHT-UP	Upright		
RILLETS	Retills, Stiller, Tillers, Trellis	ROSATED	Roasted, Torsade
		ROSEATE	Tea-rose

ROSE-BUG	Brogues
ROSE-CUT	Scouter
ROSEOLA	Aerosol
ROSE-RED	Redorse, Reredos
ROSETTA	Retoast, Rotates, Toaster
ROSIEST	Sorites, Sorties, Stories
ROSINED	Indorse, Sordine
ROSLAND	Rolands
ROTATED	Troated
ROTATES	Retoast, Rosetta, Toaster
ROTCHES	Hectors, Rochets, Tochers, Torches, Troches
ROTTERS	Retorts, Stertor
ROUGHEN	Enrough
ROUGING	Roguing
ROULADE	Urodela
ROUNDED	Redound, Underdo
ROUNDEL	Lounder, Roundle
ROUNDER	Rondure, Unorder
ROUNDLE	Lounder, Roundel
ROUND-UP	Unproud
ROUPING	Ingroup, Pouring
ROUSING	Souring
ROUSTER	Retours, Routers, Tourers, Trouser
ROUTERS	Rouster, Retours, Tourers, Trouser
ROUTHIE	Out-hire
ROUTING	Outgrin, Outring, Touring
ROWDILY	Wordily
RUBBLES	Burbles, Lubbers, Slubber
RUBELLA	Rulable
RUBINES	Suberin
RUBYING	Burying
RUCKLES	Sculker, Suckler
RUFFIAN	Funfair
RUINATE	Taurine, Uranite, Urinate
RUINING	Inuring
RUINOUS	Urinous
RULABLE	Rubella
RUMBLED	Drumble
RUMBLES	Lumbers, Slumber, Umbrels

RUMPLES	Lumpers, Replums, Slumper
RUNCHED	Churned
RUNDALE	Arundel, Launder, Lurdane
RUNDLET	Trundle
RUN-OVER	Overrun
RUTHFUL	Hurtful
RUTTERS	Truster, Turrets
SABELLA	Lasable, Salable
SABRING	Barings
SACCADE	Cascade
SACKING	Casking
SACRING	Racings, Scaring
SADDLED	Daddles
SADDLER	Ladders, Raddles
SADIRON	Inroads, Ordains
SAFROLE	Loafers
SAGGERS	Aggress, Seggars
SAILERS	Airless, Resails, Serails, Serials
SAINTED	Detains, Instead, Satined, Stained
SAINTLY	Nastily
SAIRING	Airings, Arising, Raising
SALABLE	Lasable, Sabella
*SALERNO	Orleans
SALICET	Elastic, Latices
SALICIN	Sinical
SALIENT	Elastin, Entails, Slainte, Staniel, Tenails
SALIERE	Realise
SALLIED	Dallies
SALTERN	Antlers, Rentals, Sternal
SALTERS	Artless, Lasters, Slaters, Tarsels
SALTIER	Alister, Realist, Retails, Saltire, Slatier, Tailers
SALTING	Anglist, Lasting, Slating, Staling
SALTIRE	Alister, Realist, Retails, Saltier, Slatier, Tailers

SALVAGE	Lavages	
SALVING	Slaving	
SAMIELS	Aimless,	Melissa,
	Seismal	
SAMPANS	Passman	
SAMPLER	Lampers,	Palmers
SANGRIA	Sarangi	
SANHITA	Shaitan	
SANIOUS	Suasion	
SAPERDA	Aspread,	Parades
SAPIENT	Patines,	Spinate
SAPLING	Lapsing,	Palings,
	Spaling	
SAPOTAS	Potassa	
SARANGI	Sangria	
SARCELS	Classer,	Reclass,
	Scalers	
SARCINA	Arnicas,	Carinas
SARCINE	Arsenic,	Cerasin
SARDINE	Arnside	
SARGENT	Garnets,	Strange
SARKING	Rakings	
SATCHEL	Chalets,	Latches
SATEENS	Senates,	Sensate
SATIATE	Aetatis	
SATINED	Detains,	Instead,
	Sainted,	Stained
SATINET	Instate	
SATIRES	Tirasse	
SATIRIC	Iatrics	
SAUCING	Causing	
SAUMONT	Amounts	
SAUNTER	Natures,	Sea-turn
SAUSAGE	Assuage	
SAVINES	Vinasse	
SAVIOUR	Various	
SAWBUCK	Bucksaw	
SAWWHET	Wet-wash	
SCABIES	Ecbasis	
SCADDLE	Scalded	
SCALDED	Scaddle	
SCALDER	Cradles	
SCALENE	Cleanse,	Elances,
	Enlaces	
SCALERS	Classer,	Reclass,
	Sarcels	
SCALPED	Clasped	
SCALPER	Carpels,	Clasper,
	Parcels,	Placers,
	Reclasp	

SCAMBLE	Becalms	
SCAMPED	Decamps	
SCAMPER	Campers	
SCANNER	Canners	
SCANTED	Decants,	Descant
SCANTLE	Cantles,	Centals,
	Lancets	
SCAPULA	Capsula,	Pascual
SCARING	Racings,	Sacring
SCARLET	Cartels,	Clarets
SCARPED	Red-caps	
SCARRED	Carders	
SCENTED	Descent	
SCEPTER	Recepts,	Respect,
	Sceptre,	Specter,
	Spectre	
SCEPTRE	Recepts,	Respect,
	Scepter,	Specter,
	Spectre	
SCHEMER	Chermes	
S-CHISEL	Chisels	
SCHISMA	Chiasms	
SCHMEAR	Marches	
SCHOLAR	Chorals	
SCHOLIA	Lochias	
SCIATIC	Ascitic	
SCLERAL	Callers,	Cellars,
	Recalls	
SCOFFER	Coffers	
SCOLDED	Coddles	
SCOLLOP	Collops	
SCOMBER	Combers,	Recombs
SCOOPER	Coopers	
SCORERS	Crosser,	Recross
SCORNED	Corsned	
SCORNER	Corners	
SCOURED	Coursed	
SCOURER	Courser	
SCOURGE	Scrouge	
SCOURSE	Courses,	Croesus,
	Scouser,	Sources,
	Sucrose	
SCOUSER	Courses,	Croesus,
	Scourse,	Sources,
	Sucrose	
SCOUTED	Doucets	
SCOUTER	Rose-cut	
SCRAPER	Carpers	
SCREWED	Decrews	

SCRIEVE	Service	SECLUDE	Culdees
SCRINGE	Cringes	SECRETA	Cerates, Creates,
SCROUGE	Scourge		Ecartes
SCRYING	Cryings	SECRETS	Cresset, Re-sects
SCUDDLE	Cuddles	SECTION	Noetics, Notices
SCULKER	Ruckles, Suckler	SECULAR	Cesural
SCULLER	Cullers	SECURED	Recused, Rescued
SCULPIN	Insculp, Unclips	SECURER	Recures, Rescuer
SCUMBER	Cumbers, Recumbs	SEDILIA	Dailies
SCUMMER	Cummers	SEDUCED	Deduces
SCUNNER	Cunners	SEDUCER	Cerused, Reduces
SCUPPER	Cuppers	SEEINGS	Genesis
SCUTTER	Cutters	SEEKING	Skeeing
SCUTTLE	Cutlets, Cuttles	SEETHED	Sheeted
SEA-BIRD	Braised, Darbies	SEETHER	Sheeter, Therese
SEA-CARD	Arcades	SEGGARS	Aggress, Saggers
SEA-CORN	Carnose, Coarsen,	SEINING	Ingines
	Corneas, Narcose	SEISMAL	Aimless, Melissa,
SEA-FIRE	Arefies, Faeries,		Samiels
	Freesia	SELACHE	Chelsea
SEA-FOWL	Sea-wolf	SELENIC	License, Silence
SEA-GIRT	Agister, Aigrets,	SELFIST	Stifles
	Gaiters	SELL-OUT	Outsell
SEA-LEGS	Ageless	SEMILOR	Moilers
SEALERS	Earless, Leasers,	SEMINAL	Malines, Menials
	Resales, Reseals	SEMINAR	Marines, Remains,
SEALING	Leasing, Linages		Sirname
SEA-LUCE	Euclase	SEMIPED	Impedes
SEA-MILE	Mealies	SEMITIC	Miscite
SEAMING	Enigmas	SENATES	Sensate, Sateens
SEA-MONK	Sokeman	SENATOR	Atoners, Treason
SEA-PERT	Repaste, Repeats,	SENATUS	Austens, Unseats
	Retapes	SENDERS	Redness, Resends
SEAPORT	Esparto, Pro-east	SENDING	Endings
SEARING	Angries, Earings,	SEND-OFF	Offends
	Erasing, Gainers,	SEND-OUT	Outsend, Snouted
	Regains, Regians,	SEND-UPS	Suspend
	Reginas, Seringa	SENSATE	Sateens, Senates
SEA-RISK	Kaisers	SENSILE	Enisles, Ensiles,
SEASIDE	Disease		Silenes
SEASURE	Reseaus, Ureases	SENSING	Ensigns
SEATERS	Easters, Reseats,	SENSISM	Messins
	Teasers, Tessera	SENSUAL	Unseals
SEATING	Easting, Genista,	SEPTATE	Spattee
	Ingates, Ingesta,	SEPTICS	Cess-pit
	Signate, Teasing	SEPTUOR	Petrous, Posture,
SEA-TURN	Natures, Saunter		Pouters, Proteus,
SEA-WOLF	Sea-fowl		Spouter, Troupes
SECEDER	Decrees, Recedes	SERAPES	Asperse, Parsees

SERAPIS	Aspires,	Paresis,
	Praises,	Spireas
SERAILS	Airless,	Resails,
	Sailers,	Serials
SERENED	Sneered	
SERENER	Sneerer	
SERFDOM	Deforms	
SERIALS	Airless,	Resails,
	Sailers,	Serails
SERICON	Coiners,	Cronies,
	Recoins	
SERINGA	Angries,	Earings,
	Erasing,	Gainers,
	Regains,	Regians,
	Reginas,	Searing
SERINUS	Insures,	Sunrise
SERPENT	Present,	Repents
SERPIGO	Porgies	
SERPULA	Perusal	
SERRATE	Rerates,	Retears,
	Tearers	
SERRIED	Derries,	Desirer,
	Resider	
SERVAGE	Greaves	
SERVANT	Taverns,	Versant
SERVICE	Scrieve	
SERVILE	Leviers,	Relives,
	Reviles,	Veilers
SERVING	Versing	
SERVITE	Restive,	Veriest
SESELIS	Sessile	
SESOTHO	Soothes	
SESSILE	Seselis	
SESSION	Essoins	
SESTINA	Entasis,	Tisanes
SESTOLE	Toeless	
SET-BACK	Backset	
SETOVER	Estover,	Overset,
	Revotes,	Vetoers
SETTING	Testing	
SETTLER	Letters,	Sterlet,
	Trestle	
SETWALL	Swallet,	Wallets
SEVERAL	Laveers,	Leavers,
	Reveals,	Vealers
SEVERED	Deserve	
SEVERER	Reserve,	Reveres,
	Reverse	
SEXTAIN	Antisex	
SEXTERN	Ex-terns	

SHACKLE	Hackles	
SHADIER	Hardies	
SHADING	Dashing	
SHAITAN	Sanhita	
SHALLOW	Hallows	
SHAMBLE	Hambles	
SHAMERS	Mashers,	Smasher
SHAMING	Mashing	
SHAMMER	Hammers	
SHANGTI	Anights,	Hasting
SHANKER	Hankers,	Harkens
SHAPING	Hasping,	Phasing
SHARING	Garnish,	Rashing
SHARKER	Harkers	
SHARPED	Phrased	
SHARPER	Harpers	
SHATTER	Hatters,	Stareth,
	Threats	
SHAVING	Havings	
SHEARED	Adheres,	Headers,
	Hearsed,	Reheads
SHEARER	Hearers,	Rehears,
	Reshare	
SHEETED	Seethed	
SHEETER	Seether,	Therese
SHE-GOAT	He-goats,	Hostage
SHELLER	Hellers	
SHIFTER	Reshift	
SHINDIG	Dishing,	Hidings
SHINGLE	English	
SHIPPER	Preship	
SHOCKER	Chokers	
SHOOTER	Hooters,	Reshoot,
	Soother	
SHOOT-UP	Pushtoo,	Upshoot
SHOPPER	Hoppers	
SHORING	Horsing	
SHORTED	Dehorts	
SHORTEN	Hornets,	Threnos,
	Thrones	
SHORTIA	Thorias	
SHOTGUN	Gunshot,	Hognuts,
	Noughts	
SHOUTED	Southed	
SHOUTER	Souther	
SHRINED	Hinders	
SHRIVED	Dervish	
SHROUDY	Hydrous	
SHUNTER	Hunters	

SHYSTER	Thyrses	
SICKLED	Slicked	
SICKLER	Lickers,	Rickles,
	Slicker	
SIDEARM	Admires,	Misread
SIDEBAR	Abiders,	Air-beds
SIDECAR	Diceras	
SIDEMAN	Demains,	Maidens,
	Mandies,	Medians
SIDEWAY	Wayside	
SIDLING	Sliding	
SIFTING	Fisting	
SIGHTER	Resight	
SIGNATE	Easting,	Genista,
	Ingates,	Ingesta,
	Seating,	Teasing
SIGNERS	Ingress,	Resigns,
	Singers	
SIGNING	Singing	
SIGNIOR	Origins	
SIGNORA	Ignaros,	Origans,
	Soaring	
SIGNORE	Eringos,	Ignores,
	Regions	
SILENCE	License,	Selenic
SILENES	Enisles,	Ensiles,
	Sensile	
SILICAS	Liassic	
SILTING	Listing	
SIMARRE	Marries	
SIMILES	Missile	
SIMPERS	Impress,	Premiss
SIMPLED	Dimples	
SIMPLER	Prelims,	Rimples
SINCERE	Ceresin,	Cerines
SINEWED	Endwise	
SINGERS	Ingress,	Resigns,
	Signers	
SINGING	Signing	
SINGLED	Dingles	
SINGLER	Girnels,	Lingers,
	Slinger	
SINGLET	Glisten,	Lingets,
	Tingles	
SINGULT	Glutins,	Lusting,
	Lutings,	Sutling
SINICAL	Salicin	
SINNING	Innings	
SINOPER	Orpines	
SIPHONS	Sonship	

SIRNAME	Marines,	Remains,
	Seminar	
SISTRUM	Trismus,	Truisms
SITUATE	Usitate	
SKATING	Staking,	Takings,
	Tasking	
SKEEING	Seeking	
SKELTER	Kestrel	
SKEPTIC	Pickets	
SKID-PAN	Kidnaps	
SKIINGS	Kissing	
SKILLED	Deskill	
SKIMMER	Kimmers	
SKIPPER	Kippers	
SKIRRET	Skirter,	Striker
SKIRTER	Skirret,	Striker
SKITTLE	Kittles	
SKIVING	Vikings	
SLABBED	Dabbles	
SLABBER	Barbels,	Rabbles
SLACKER	Calkers,	Lackers,
	Recalks	
SLAINTE	Elastin,	Entails,
	Salient,	Staniel,
	Tenails	
SLAMKIN	Malkins	
SLANDER	Darnels,	Enlards,
	Landers,	Relands
SLANGED	Dangles	
SLANTED	Dentals,	Standel
SLAPPED	Dapples	
SLAPPER	Lappers,	Rappels
SLASHER	Lashers	
SLATERS	Artless,	Lasters,
	Salters,	Tarsels
SLATHER	Halters,	Harslet,
	Hastler,	Lathers,
	Thalers	
SLATIER	Alister,	Realist,
	Saltier,	Saltire,
	Tailers	
SLATING	Anglist,	Lasting,
	Salting,	Staling
SLATTER	Rattles,	Starlet,
	Startle,	Tatlers,
	Telstar	
SLAVING	Salving	
SLAYERS	Rayless	
SLAYING	Layings	

SLEDDER	Reddles	
SLEEKER	Keelers	
SLEEPER	Peelers	
SLEEP-IN	Espinel,	Pensile
SLEETED	Steeled	
SLENDER	Lenders,	Relends
SLEWING	Swingel,	Swingle
SLICKED	Sickled	
SLICKER	Lickers,	Rickles,
	Sickler	
SLIDDER	Riddels,	Riddles
SLIDING	Sidling	
SLINGER	Girnels,	Lingers,
	Singler	
SLIPPER	Lippers,	Ripples
SLITHER	Hitlers	
SLITTER	Litters,	Testril,
	Tilters,	Titlers
SLOBBER	Lobbers	
SLOCKEN	Enlocks	
SLOE-GIN	Eloigns,	Legions,
	Lignose,	Lingoes
SLOGGER	Loggers,	Roggles
SLOWING	Lowings	
SLUBBER	Burbles,	Lubbers,
	Rubbles	
SLUGGER	Gurgles,	Luggers
SLUICES	Celsius	
SLUMBER	Lumbers,	Rumbles,
	Umbrels	
SLUMISM	Muslims	
SLUMPER	Lumpers,	Replums,
	Rumples	
SMARTEN	Martens	
SMASHER	Mashers,	Shamers
SMATTER	Matters	
SMELTER	Melters,	Remelts
SMERLIN	Limners,	Merlins
SMILING	Lingism	
SMITING	Misting	
SMITTEN	Mittens	
SMOKIER	Irksome	
SMOLDER	Molders	
SMOTHER	Mothers,	Thermos
SMOUSER	Mousers	
SMYTRIE	Mistery	
SNAGGER	Gangers,	Granges,
	Naggers	
SNAPPED	Appends	

SNAPPER	Nappers,	Parsnep
SNEERED	Serened	
SNEERER	Serener	
SNICKED	Dickens	
SNICKER	Nickers	
SNIFFLE	Niffles	
SNIGGER	Gingers,	Niggers
SNIGGLE	Gingles,	Niggles
SNIPING	Pinings	
SNIPPER	Nippers	
SNIRTLE	Linters	
SNOFARI	Insofar	
SNOOPED	Spooned	
SNOOPER	Spooner	
SNORING	Sorning	
SNOUTED	Outsend,	Send-out
SNUZZLE	Nuzzles	
SOARERS	Rasores	
SOARING	Ignaros,	Origans,
	Signora	
SOBBING	Gibbons	
SOCAGER	Cargoes	
SOCKING	Gosnick	
SODDENS	Oddness	
SOILING	Oilings	
SOILURE	Lousier	
SOKEMAN	Sea-monk	
SOLACER	Coalers,	Oracles,
	Recoals	
SOLDIER	Solider	
SOLICIT	Colitis	
SOLIDER	Soldier	
SOLIPED	Despoil,	Dipoles,
	Diploes,	Spoiled
SOLUBLE	Lobules	
SOMATIC	Atomics	
SOMITIC	Mistico	
SOMNIAL	Malison,	Monials,
	Osmanli	
SONLESS	Lessons	
SONNITE	Intones,	Tension
SONSHIP	Siphons	
SOOTHES	Sesotho	
SOOTHER	Hooters,	Reshoot,
	Shooter	
SOPRANI	Parison	
SORBATE	Boaster,	Boaters,
	Rebatos	
SORDINE	Indorse,	Rosined

SORDINO	Indoors	
SOREHON	Onshore	
SORITES	Rosiest,	Sorties,
	Stories	
SORNING	Snoring	
SORTIES	Rosiest,	Sorites,
	Stories	
SORTING	Storing	
SOUCHET	Touches	
SOUNDER	Enduros,	Resound,
	Undoers,	Unrosed
SOUPCON	Coupons,	Uncoops
SOURCES	Croesus,	Courses,
	Scourse,	Scouser,
	Sucrose	
SOUREST	Oestrus,	Ousters,
	Souters,	Trouses,
	Trousse,	Tussore
SOURING	Rousing	
SOUTERS	Oestrus,	Ousters,
	Sourest,	Trouses,
	Trousse,	Tussore
SOUTHED	Shouted	
SOUTHER	Shouter	
SPACING	Pacings	
SPADDLE	Paddles	
SPALING	Lapsing,	Palings,
	Sapling	
SPANCEL	Enclasp	
SPANNER	Panners	
SPARELY	Parleys,	Parsley,
	Players,	Replays
SPARGED	Grasped	
SPARGER	Grasper,	Regrasp
SPARING	Parings,	Parsing,
	Rasping	
SPARKER	Parkers,	Reparks
SPARTAN	Partans,	Tarpans,
	Trapans	
SPATHED	Heptads	
SPATTEE	Septate	
SPATTER	Patters,	Tapster
SPATTLE	Pattles,	Peltast
SPATULE	Petulas,	Pulsate,
	Puteals	
SPAWNER	Enwraps,	Pawners,
	Repawns	
SPEAKER	Respeak	
SPEARER	Reapers	

SPECTRA	Carpets,	Pre-acts,
	Precast	
SPECTER	Recepts,	Respect,
	Scepter,	Sceptre,
	Spectre	
SPECTRE	Recepts,	Respect,
	Scepter,	Sceptre,
	Specter	
SPECULA	Capsule,	Lace-ups
SPELLER	Presell,	Respell
SPELTER	Pelters,	Petrels,
	Respelt	
SPHERAL	Plasher	
SPHERIC	Ceriphs,	Ciphers
SPICATE	Aseptic	
SPIKING	Pigskin	
SPILING	Lisping,	Pilings
SPINATE	Patines,	Sapient
SPINDLE	Splined	
SPINETS	Insteps,	Step-ins
SPINNER	Pinners	
SPIN-OFF	Off-spin	
SPIN-OUT	Outspin	
SPINULE	Line-ups,	Lupines,
	Unpiles,	Up-lines
SPIREAS	Aspires,	Paresis,
	Praises,	Serapis
SPIREME	Empires,	Emprise,
	Premise	
SPIRING	Prising	
SPIRITS	Pristis,	Tripsis
SPIRTED	Striped	
SPIRTLE	Resplit	
SPITTER	Pitters,	Tipster
SPLENIC	Pencils	
SPLINED	Spindle	
SPLIT-UP	Pulpits	
SPLORES	Plessor,	Pre-loss
SPOILED	Despoil,	Dipoles,
	Diploes,	Soliped
SPONDEE	Despones	
SPOONED	Snooped	
SPOONER	Snooper	
SPORTED	Deports,	Red-tops
SPORTER	Porrets,	Porters,
	Presort,	Pretors,
	Reports	
SPORULE	Elopers,	Leprous,
	Pelorus,	Perlous

SPOTTER	Potters, Protest
SPOUTER	Petrous, Posture,
	Pouters, Proteus,
	Septuor, Troupes
SPRAYER	Prayers, Respray
SPRIEST	Persist, Priests,
	Sprites, Stirpes,
	Stripes
SPRINGY	Pryings
SPRITES	Persist, Priests,
	Spriest, Stirpes,
	Stripes
SPRUCES	Percuss
SPUNKIE	Punkies
SPURIAE	Upraise
SPURNER	Pruners
SPUTTER	Putters
STABBER	Barbets, Rabbets
STABILE	Blastie
STABLED	Baldest, Blasted
STABLER	Alberts, Blaster,
	Labrets, Tablers
STACKER	Rackets, Restack,
	Retacks, Tackers
STAFFER	Restaff
STAGGER	Gargets, Taggers
STAGING	Gatings
STAIDER	Asterid, Astride,
	Disrate, Tirades
STAINED	Detains, Instead,
	Sainted, Satined
STAINER	Nastier, Resiant,
	Restain, Retains,
	Retinas, Retsina,
	Stearin
STAITHE	Atheist
STAKING	Skating, Takings,
	Tasking
STALING	Anglist, Lasting,
	Salting, Slating
STALKER	Talkers
STAMPER	Restamp, Tampers
STANDEE	East-end
STANDEL	Dentals, Slanted
STAND-UP	Upstand
STANIEL	Elastin, Entails,
	Salient, Slainte,
	Tenails
STAPLER	Palters, Persalt,

	Plaster, Platers,
	Psalter
STARDOM	Tsardom
STARETH	Hatters, Shatter,
	Threats
STARING	Gastrin, Gratins,
	Ratings
STARLET	Rattles, Slatter,
	Startle, Tatlers,
	Telstar
STARRED	Darters, Retards,
	Traders
STARTER	Ratters, Restart
STARTLE	Rattles, Slatter,
	Starlet, Tatlers,
	Telstar
STARVED	Adverts
STATING	Tasting
STAUNCH	Canthus
STAYING	Stygian
STEARIN	Nastier, Resiant,
	Restain, Retains,
	Retinas, Retsina,
	Stainer
STEELED	Sleeted
STEEPED	Deepest
STEEPEN	Ensteep
STEMLET	Mettles
STEMPEL	Pelmets, Stemple,
	Temples
STEMPLE	Pelmets, Stempel,
	Temples
STENCIL	Clients
STENTOR	Torsten
STEP-INS	Insteps, Spinets
STEP-OFF	Off-step
STEREOS	Osseter
STERILE	Leister, Retiles
STERLET	Letters, Settler,
	Trestle
STERNAL	Antlers, Rentals,
	Saltern
STERNED	Tenders
STERNER	Renters, Rerents
STERNUM	Munster
STEROID	Editors, Storied,
	Tie-rods, Triodes
STERTOR	Retorts, Rotters
STEVING	Vesting

STEWARD	Strawed	
STEWING	Twinges, Westing	
STEW-POT	Two-step	
STHENIC	Ethnics	
STICKER	Rickets, Tickers	
STICKLE	Tickles	
STIFFER	Restiff	
STIFLER	Filters, Lifters, Trifles	
STIFLES	Selfist	
STILLER	Retills, Rillets, Tillers, Trellis	
STIMIED	Misdiet	
STINGER	Resting	
STINKER	Kirsten, Reknits, Tinkers	
STINTED	Dentist, Distent	
STINTER	Nitters, Retints, Tinters	
STIPPLE	Tipples	
STIPULA	Tipulas	
STIRPES	Persist, Priests, Spriest, Sprites, Stripes	
STIVERS	Strives, Treviss, Verists	
STOCKED	Dockets	
STONILY	Tylosin	
STONING	Notings	
STOOPER	Poorest	
STOORED	Roosted	
STOOTER	Tooters	
STOPING	Posting	
STOP-OUT	Outpost, Outtops, Puttoos	
STOPPER	Popster, Toppers	
STOPPLE	Topples	
STORAGE	Orgeats, Tagsore	
STORIED	Editors, Steroid, Tie-rods, Triodes	
STORIES	Rosiest, Sorites, Sorties	
STORING	Sorting	
STORMER	Termors, Tremors	
STOTTER	Stretto, Totters	
STOUTER	Outsert, Touters	
STOVING	Votings	
STOWAGE	Towages	
STRAITS	Artists, Tsarist	

STRANGE	Garnets, Gerants, Sargent	
STRAP-ON	Partons, Patrons, Tarpons	
STRAWED	Steward	
STREAMY	Mastery, Mayster	
STREENS	Ernests, Nesters, Resents, Strenes	
STRENES	Ernests, Nesters, Resents, Streens	
STRETTA	Tatters	
STRETTO	Stotter, Totters	
STREWED	Wrested	
STREWER	Wrester	
STRIATE	Artiste, Attires, Ratites, Tastier	
STRIDES	Dissert	
STRIGES	Tigress	
STRIKER	Skirret, Skirter	
STRIPED	Spirted	
STRIPES	Persist, Priests, Spriest, Sprites, Stirpes	
STRIVED	Diverts	
STRIVEN	Inverts	
STRIVES	Stivers, Treviss, Verists	
STROPHE	Pothers, Thorpes	
STUDDIE	Studied	
STUDENT	Stunted	
STUDIED	Studdie	
STUDIER	Dustier	
STUFFER	Restuff	
STUMBLE	Tumbles	
STUMPER	Sumpter	
STUNNER	Unstern	
STUNTED	Student	
STURNUS	Untruss	
STYGIAN	Staying	
STYLITE	Testily	
STYRENE	Yestern	
SUASION	Sanious	
SUBERIN	Rubines	
SUB-KING	Busking	
SUBLIME	Bus-mile	
SUB-ORAL	Labours	
SUBSIGN	Bussing	
SUBTLER	Bluster, Brustle, Bustler, Butlers	

SUCCADE	Accused	
SUCKLER	Ruckles,	Sculker
SUCROSE	Courses,	Croesus,
	Scourse,	Scouser,
	Sources	
SUCTION	Unstoic	
SULLAGE	Ullages	
SULLIED	Illused	
SULLIES	Illuses	
SULTANE	Unslate	
SUMPTER	Stumper	
SUNBEAR	Unbares,	Unbears
SUNBEAT	Butanes	
SUNDARI	Durians	
SUNDERS	Undress	
SUNNITE	Tunnies	
SUNRISE	Insures,	Serinus
SUNROOF	Unroofs	
SUNROOM	Unmoors	
SUNSPOT	Unstops	
SUNTRAP	Unstrap	
SUNWARD	Undraws	
SUPPERS	Press-up	
SUPPING	Uppings	
SUPREME	Presume	
SURMISE	Misuser	
SURNAME	Manures	
SUSPEND	Send-ups	
SUSPIRE	Uprises	
SUSTAIN	Issuant	
SUTLING	Glutins,	Lusting,
	Lutings,	Singult
SWADDLE	Dawdles,	Waddles
SWAGING	Wagings	
SWALLET	Setwall,	Wallets
SWALLOW	Wallows	
SWARMER	Rewarms,	Warmers
SWASHER	Hawsers,	Washers
SWEARER	Reswear,	Rewears,
	Wearers	
SWEDISH	Swished	
SWEEPER	Resweep,	Weepers
SWELLER	Reswell	
SWELTER	Welters,	Wrestle
SWILLER	Willers	
SWINDLE	Windles	
SWINGEL	Slewing,	Swingle
SWINGER	Wingers	
SWINGLE	Slewing,	Swingel
SWISHED	Swedish	

SWISHER	Wishes	
SWITHER	Withers,	Writhes
SWORDER	Rewords	
TABARDS	Bastard	
*TABITHA	Habitat	
TABLEAU	Tabulae	
TABLERS	Alberts,	Blaster,
	Labrets,	Stabler
TABLIER	Librate,	Triable
	Trilabe	
TABORER	Arboret	
TABORET	Abettor	
TABULAE	Tableau	
TACITLY	Cattily	
TACKERS	Rackets,	Restack,
	Retacks,	Stacker
TACTILE	Lattice,	Talcite
TAGETES	Gestate	
TAGGERS	Gargets,	Stagger
TAGSORE	Orgeats,	Storage
TAILERS	Alister,	Realist,
	Saltier,	Saltire,
	Slatier	
TAILLES	Tallies	
TAKE-OFF	Off-take	
TAKINGS	Skating,	Staking,
	Tasking	
TALCITE	Lattice,	Tactile
TALCOSE	Alecost,	Lactose,
	Locates	
TALCOUS	Locusta	
TALIPED	Plaited	
TALIPES	Aplites	
TALKERS	Stalker	
TALLIER	Literal	
TALLIES	Tailles	
TALLY-HO	Loathly	
TAMALES	Malates,	Maltase
TAMINES	Emanist,	Inmates,
	Inmeats	
TAMPERS	Restamp,	Stamper
TAMPION	Maintop,	Timpano
TAMPONS	Postman,	Topsman
*TANCRED	Cantred,	Tranced
TANGENT	Gnat-net	
*TANGIER	Granite,	Ingrate,
	Tearing	

TANGLER	Trangle	TEARPIT	Partite
TANKERS	Rankest	TEASELS	Altesse, Tealess
TANRIDE	Anti-red, Detrain,	TEASERS	Easters, Reseats,
	Trade-in, Trained		Seaters, Tessera
TAPERED	Pad-tree, Red-tape,	TEASING	Easting, Genista,
	Retaped		Ingates, Ingesta,
TAPSTER	Patters, Spatter		Seating, Signate
TARPONS	Partons, Patrons,	TEDDERS	Reddest
	Strap-on	TEDIOUS	Outside
TARRIES	Tarsier	TEEMING	Meeting
TARSELS	Artless, Lasters,	TEERING	Integer, Retinge,
	Salters, Slaters		Treeing
TARSIER	Tarries	*TEHERAN	Earneth, Earthen,
TARTISH	Athirst, Rattish		Hearten, Neareth
TARTLET	Tattler	TELAMON	Omental
TASKING	Skating, Staking,	TELECAR	Treacle
	Takings	*TELSTAR	Rattles, Slatter,
TASTIER	Artiste, Attires,		Starlet, Startle,
	Ratites, Striate		Tatlers
TASTING	Stating	TEMPEAN	Peteman
TATLERS	Rattles, Slatter,	TEMPERA	Premate
	Starlet, Startle,	TEMPLAR	Trample
	Telstar	TEMPLES	Pelmets, Stempel,
TATTERS	Stretta		Stemple
TATTLER	Tartlet	TENABLE	Beltane
TAUNTED	Attuned, Nutated	TENAILS	Elastin, Entails,
TAURINE	Ruinate, Uranite,		Salient, Slainte,
	Urinate		Staniel
TAUTENS	Attunes, Nutates,	TENDERS	Sterned
	Tetanus, Unstate	TENDING	Denting
TAVERNS	Servant, Versant	TENDRIL	Trindle
TEA-BARS	Abaters, Abreast	TENIOID	Edition
TEACHER	Cheater, Hectare,	TENONER	Enteron
	Rechate, Recheat,	TEN-PINS	Pinnets
	Reteach	TENSING	Nesting
TEACHES	Escheat	TENSION	Intones, Sonnite
TEACUPS	Cuspate	TEN-SPOT	Potents
TEALESS	Altesse, Teasels	TENTING	Netting
TEAMING	Mintage	TENURES	Neuters, Retunes,
TEARERS	Rerates, Retears,		Tureens, Unterse
	Serrate	TERBIUM	Imbrute
TEAREST	Estreat, Restate,	TERCINE	Citrene, Enteric,
	Retaste		Enticer
TEARETH	Theater, Theatre,	TEREDOS	Oersted
	Thereat	TERMINI	Interim
TEARFUL	Faulter, Refutal	TERMITE	Emitter
TEARING	Granite, Ingrate,	TERMORS	Stormer, Tremors
	Tangier	TERNATE	Entreat, Ratteen
TEA-ROSE	Roseate	TERNION	Intoner

TERPENE	Pre-teen
TERRACE	Caterer, Recrate, Retrace
TERRAIN	Retrain, Trainer
TERREEN	Enterer, Re-enter, Terrene
TERRENE	Enterer, Re-enter, Terreen
TERRINE	Reinter, Rentier
TERSION	Triones
TERTIAN	Intreat, Iterant, Nitrate
TESSERA	Easters, Reseats, Seaters, Teasers
TESTILY	Stylite
TESTING	Setting
TESTRIL	Litters, Slitter, Tilters, Titlers
TETANIC	Nictate
TETANUS	Attunes, Nutates, Tautens, Unstate
THALERS	Halters, Harslet, Hastler, Lathers, Slather
THANKER	Rethank
THEATER	Teareth, Theatre, Thereat
THEATRE	Teareth, Theater, Thereat
THENARS	Anthers, Hanster
THEREAT	Teareth, Theater, Theatre
THEREIN	Neither
*THERESE	Seether, Sheeter
THERMOS	Mothers, Smother
THICKEN	Kitchen
THINKER	Rethink
THISTLE	Lettish
THORIAS	Shortia
THORITE	Orthite
THORPES	Pothers, Strophe
THREADS	Hardest, Hardset, Hatreds, Red-hats
THREADY	Hydrate
THREATS	Hatters, Shatter, Stareth
THRENOS	Hornets, Shorten, Thrones
THRONES	Hornets, Shorten, Threnos

THWAITE	Waiteth
THYRSES	Shyster
TIARAED	Radiate
TICKERS	Rickets, Sticker
TICKLER	Trickle
TICKLES	Stickle
TIDERIP	Riptide
TIDIEST	Dietist, Ditties
TIDYING	Dignity
TIERCEL	Reticle
TIE-RODS	Editors, Steroid, Storied, Triodes
TIERING	Igniter, Nigrite, Tigrine
TIGLINE	Lignite
TIGRESS	Striges
TIGRINE	Igniter, Nigrite, Tiering
TILE-RED	Retiled
TILLERS	Retills, Rillets, Stiller, Trellis
TILLING	Lilting
TILTERS	Litters, Slitter, Testril, Titlers
TILTING	Titling
TIMBALE	Limbate
TIMPANI	Impaint
TIMPANO	Maintop, Tampion
TINAMOU	Manitou
TINGLED	Glinted
TINGLER	Ringlet, Tringle
TINGLES	Glisten, Lingets, Singlet
TINIEST	Tinties
TINKERS	Kirsten, Reknits, Stinker
TINKLER	Trinkle
TINTERS	Nitters, Retints, Stinter
TINTIES	Tiniest
TIPPLER	Ripplet, Tripple
TIPPLES	Stipple
TIPSTER	Pitters, Spitter
TIPULAS	Stipula
TIRADES	Asterid, Astride, Disrate, Staider
TIRASSE	Satires
TISANES	Entasis, Sestina
TITHING	Hitting

TITLERS	Litters, Slitter,	TOUCHER	Retouch
	Testril, Tilters	TOUCHES	Souchet
TITLING	Tilting	TOURERS	Retours, Rouster,
TITRATE	Attrite		Routers, Trouser
TIVERED	Riveted	TOURING	Outgrin, Outring,
TOASTER	Retoast, Rosetta,		Routing
	Rotates	TOUSING	Ousting, Outsing,
TOCHERS	Hectors, Rochets,		Outings
	Rotches, Torches,	TOUTERS	Outsert, Stouter
	Troches	TOWAGES	Stowage
TOCSINS	Consist	TOWLINE	Two-line
TOELESS	Sestole	TRACHLE	Ratchel, Relatch
TOENAIL	Elation	TRACING	Carting, Crating
TOILETS	Litotes	TRACKER	Retrack
TO-NIGHT	Hotting	TRACTED	Detract
TONSILE	Entoils, Lionets	TRADE-IN	Anti-red, Detrain,
TOOLING	Looting		Tanride, Trained
TOOTERS	Stooter	TRADERS	Darters, Retards,
TOOTLER	Rootlet		Starred
TOPHOLE	Pothole	TRADING	Darting
TOPICAL	Capitol, Coalpit,	TRADUCE	Educrat
	Optical, Pit-coal	TRAGEDY	Gyrated
TOPLINE	Potline	TRAGICS	Catrigs, Gastric
TOPPERS	Popster, Stopper	TRAILED	Dilater, Red-tail
TOPPLES	Stopple	TRAILER	Retiral, Retrial
TOPSAIL	Apostil	TRAINED	Anti-red, Detrain,
TOPSIDE	Deposit, Posited		Tanride, Trade-in
TOPSMAN	Postman, Tampons	TRAINEE	Aintree
TOPSOIL	Poloist	TRAINER	Retrain, Terrain
TOPWORK	Potwork	TRAIPSE	Parties, Piaster,
TORCHES	Hectors, Rochets,		Piastre, Pirates,
	Rotches, Tochers,		Praties
	Troches	TRAMCAR	Carmart
TOREROS	Rooster, Rooters	TRAMPLE	Templar
TORNADO	Donator	TRANCED	Cantred, Tancred
TOROIDS	Disroot	TRANGLE	Tangler
TORPEDO	Trooped	TRANNEL	Lantern
TORPENT	Portent	TRANNIE	Entrain
TORPIDS	Disport, Tripods	TRANSOM	Matrons
TORPIFY	Portify	TRAPANS	Partans, Spartan,
TORQUES	Questor, Quoters,		Tarpans
	Roquets	TRASHES	Rashest
TORSADE	Roasted, Rosated	TREACLE	Telecar
TORSION	Nitroso	TREADER	Rerated, Retrade,
TORSTEN	Stentor		Retread
TORTILE	Triolet	TREADLE	Alerted, Altered,
TORYISH	History		Delater, Redealt,
TOTTERS	Stotter, Stretto		Related
TOUCANS	Conatus, Uncoats	TREASON	Atoners, Senator

TREATER	Retrate, Retreat	TROATED	Rotated
TREEING	Integer, Retinge,	TROCHES	Hectors, Rochets,
	Tearing		Rotches, Tochers,
TREETOP	Proette		Torches
TRELLIS	Retills, Rillets,	TROOPED	Torpedo
	Stiller, Tillers	TROPINE	Pointer, Protein,
TREMORS	Termors, Stormer		Pterion, Repoint
TRENAIL	Entrail, Latrine,	TROPISM	Imports
	Ratline, Reliant,	TROPIST	Protist
	Retinal	TROUBLE	Boulter
TREPANS	Arpents, Entraps,	TROUNCE	Cornute, Counter,
	Panters, Parents,		Recount
	Pastern, Persant	TROUPES	Petrous, Posture,
TRESSED	Deserts, Dessert		Pouters, Proteus,
TRESTLE	Letters, Settler,		Septuor, Spouter
	Sterlet	TROUSER	Retours, Rouster,
TREVISS	Stivers, Strives,		Routers, Tourers
	Verists	TROUSES	Oestrus, Ousters,
TRIABLE	Librate, Tablier,		Sourest, Souters,
	Trilabe		Trousse, Tussore
TRIACID	Triadic	TROUSSE	Oestrus, Ousters,
TRIADIC	Triacid		Sourest, Souters,
TRIBLET	Brittle		Trouses, Tussore
TRIBUNE	Turbine	TRUCIAL	Curtail
TRICKLE	Tickler	TRUFFLE	Fretful
TRIFLED	Flirted	TRUISMS	Sistrum, Trismus
TRIFLER	Flirter	TRUNDLE	Rundlet
TRIFLES	Filters, Lifters,	TRUSTER	Rutters, Turrets
	Stifler	TSABIAN	Abstain
TRIGONE	Genitor, Negrito	TSARDOM	Stardom
TRILABE	Librate, Tablier,	TSARINA	Antiars, Artisan
	Triable	TSARIST	Artists, Straits
TRINDLE	Tendril	TUMBLER	Tumbrel
TRINGLE	Ringlet, Tingler	TUMBLES	Stumble
TRINKET	Knitter	TUMBREL	Tumbler
TRINKLE	Tinkler	TUNABLE	Abluent
TRIODES	Editors, Steroid,	TUNG-OIL	Louting
	Storied, Tie-rods	TUNICLE	Untelic
TRIOLET	Tortile	TUNNIES	Sunnite
TRIONES	Tersion	TURBINE	Tribune
TRIPODS	Disport, Torpids	TURDINE	Intrude, Untired,
TRIPPLE	Ripplet, Tippler		Untried
TRIPSIS	Pristis, Spirits	TUREENS	Neuters, Retunes,
TRIREME	Miterer		Tenures, Unterse
TRISEME	Metiers, Re-emits,	TURN-OUT	Outturn
	Retimes	TURN-UPS	Upturns
TRISMUS	Sistrum, Truisms	TURRETS	Rutters, Truster
TRISULA	Rituals	TUSSORE	Oestrus, Ousters,
TRITELY	Littery		Sourest, Souters,
			Trouses, Trousse

TWEEDLE	Tweeled		UNEARTH	Haunter, Unheart,
TWEELED	Tweedle			Urethan
TWINGES	Stewing, Westing		UNFIRED	Unfried
TWISSEL	Witless		UNFRIED	Unfired
TWISTER	Retwist, Witster,		UNGIRTH	Unright
	Witters		UNGORED	Guerdon, Undergo
TWO-LINE	Towline		UNGRATE	Negatur
TWOSTEP	Stewpot		UNHEALS	Unleash, Unshale
TYLOSIN	Stonily		UNHEART	Haunter, Unearth,
TYPHOID	Phytoid			Urethan
TYPICAL	Claypit		UNIDEAL	Aliunde
TZARINA	Atrazin		UNLARGE	Granule, Unregal
			UNLEASH	Unheals, Unshale
			UNMANED	Mundane, Unnamed
UDALLER	Allured		UNMATED	Untamed
ULLAGES	Sullage		UNMINED	Minuend
UMBRELS	Lumbers, Rumbles,		UNMITER	Unmitre
	Slumber		UNMITRE	Unmiter
UNADEPT	Untaped		UNMOORS	Sunroom
UNARMED	Duramen, Manured,		UNNAILS	Unslain
	Maunder		UNNAMED	Mundane, Unmaned
UNAWNED	Unwaned		UNNOTED	Untoned
UNBARES	Sun-bear, Unbears		UNOARED	Rondeau
UNBEARS	Sun-bear, Unbares		UNORBED	Bounder, Rebound,
UNBELTS	Unblest			Unbored, Unrobed
UNBERTH	Burthen		UNORDER	Rondure, Rounder
UNBLEST	Unbelts		UNPACED	Uncaped
UNBONED	Bounden		UNPANEL	Unpenal
UNBORED	Bounder, Rebound,		UNPARED	Undrape, Unraped
	Unorbed, Unrobed		UNPASTE	Peanuts
UNCAPED	Unpaced		UNPENAL	Unpanel
UNCARED	Durance, Unraced		UNPILES	Line-ups, Lupines,
UNCASED	Cadenus			Spinule, Up-lines
UNCLEAR	Lucarne, Nuclear		UNPLACE	Clean-up
UNCLIPS	Insculp, Sculpin		UNPLAIT	Nuptial
UNCLOSE	Counsel		UNPROUD	Round-up
UNCOATS	Conatus, Toucans		UNRACED	Durance, Uncared
UNCOOPS	Coupons, Soupcon		UNRAPED	Undrape, Unpared
UNCRIED	Inducer		UNRATED	Durante, Untread
UNDATED	Daunted		UNRAYED	Unready
UNDEALT	Lunated		UNREADY	Unrayed
UNDERDO	Redound, Rounded		UNREEVE	Revenue
UNDERGO	Guerdon, Ungored		UNREGAL	Granule, Unlarge
UNDIGHT	Hindgut		UNRIGHT	Ungirth
UNDOERS	Enduros, Resound,		UNROBED	Bounder, Rebound,
	Sounder, Unrosed			Unbored, Unorbed
UNDRAPE	Unpared, Unraped		UNROBES	Unsober
UNDRAWS	Sunward		UNROOFS	Sunroof
UNDRESS	Sunders		UNROOST	Unroots

UNROOTS	Unroost	UP-LINES	Line-ups, Lupines,
UNROPED	Pounder		Spinule, Unpiles
UNROSED	Enduros, Resound,	UPPINGS	Supping
	Sounder, Undoers	UPRAISE	Spuriae
UNSEALS	Sensual	UPRIGHT	Right-up
UNSEATS	Austens, Senatus	UPRISES	Suspire
UNSHALE	Unheals, Unleash	UPSHOOT	Pushtoo, Shoot-up
UNSLAIN	Unnails	UPSILON	Pulsion
UNSLATE	Sultane	UPSPAKE	Upspeak
UNSOBER	Unrobes	UPSPEAK	Upspake
UNSOLED	Loudens, Nodules	UPSTAND	Stand-up
UNSPELT	Penults	UPSWARM	Warm-ups
UNSPILT	Unsplit	UPSWELL	Upwells
UNSPLIT	Unspilt	UP-TRAIN	Puritan
UNSTACK	Untacks	UPTURNS	Turn-ups
UNSTATE	Attunes, Nutates,	UPWELLS	Upswell
	Tautens, Tetanus	URANITE	Ruinate, Taurine,
UNSTERN	Stunner		Urinate
UNSTOIC	Suction	URANOUS	Anurous
UNSTOPS	Sunspot	UREASES	Reseaus, Seasure
UNSTRAP	Suntrap	UREIDES	Residue
UNSTUCK	Untucks	URETHAN	Haunter, Unearth,
UNSWEAR	Unwares		Unheart
UNTACKS	Unstack	URINALS	Insular, Ursinal
UNTAMED	Unmated	URINATE	Ruinate, Taurine,
UNTAPED	Unadept		Uranite
UNTELIC	Tunicle	URINOUS	Ruinous
UNTERSE	Neuters, Retunes,	URODELA	Roulade
	Tenures, Tureens	URSINAL	Insular, Urinals
UNTILED	Diluent	USITATE	Situate
UNTILES	Luniest, Utensil	USURPED	Pursued
UNTIRED	Intrude, Turdine,	USURPER	Pursuer
	Untried	UTENSIL	Luniest, Untiles
UNTONED	Unnoted	UTERINE	Reunite, Retinue
UNTREAD	Durante, Unrated	UTOPIAN	Opuntia
UNTREED	Denture, Retuned	UTTERER	Reutter
UNTRIED	Intrude, Turdine,		
	Untired		
UNTRUSS	Sturnus	VAGINAL	Gavilan
UNTUCKS	Unstuck	VALENCE	Enclave
UNWANED	Unawned	VALERIC	Caliver, Caviler,
UNWARES	Unswear		Clavier
UPBREAK	Break-up	VALIANT	Latvian
UPBUILD	Build-up	VALONIA	Novalia
UPBUILT	Built-up	VANSIRE	Ravines
UPBURST	Burst-up	VARICES	Viscera
UPCHEER	Cheer-up	VARIOUS	Saviour
UPCLOSE	Close-up, Couples,	VEALERS	Laveers, Leavers,
	Opuscle		Reveals

VEERING	Reeving
VEILERS	Leviers, Relives, Reviles, Servile
VELITES	Levites
VELOUTE	Evolute
VENDACE	Encaved
VERBOSE	Observe, Obverse
VERGLAS	Gravels
VERIEST	Restive, Servite
VERISTS	Stivers, Strives, Treviss
VERMIAN	Minerva
VERSANT	Servant, Taverns
VERSINE	Enviers, Inverse
VERSING	Serving
VESPINE	Pensive
VESTING	Steving
VESTURE	Revestu
VETERAN	Nervate
VETOERS	Estover, Overset, Revotes, Setover
VIALFUL	Fluvial
VIKINGS	Skiving
VINASSE	Savines
VINEGAR	Ginevra, Reaving
VIOLINE	Olivine
VISCERA	Varices
VISITER	Revisit
VISORED	Devisor
VITRAIN	Vitrina
VITRINA	Vitrain
VOLABLE	Lovable
VOMITED	Motived
VOTINGS	Stoving
WADDLED	Dawdled
WADDLER	Dawdler, Drawled
WADDLES	Dawdles, Swaddle
WAESOME	Awesome
WAGERED	Ragweed
WAGERER	Rewager
WAGINGS	Swaging
WAISTER	Waiters, Wastrie
WAITERS	Waister, Wastrie
WAITETH	Thwaite
WAKENER	Rewaken
WALK-OUT	Outwalk
WALLETS	Setwall, Swallet
WALLEYE	Eyewall
WALLOWS	Swallow
*WALTERS	Warstle, Wastrel
WANGLER	Wrangle
WARBLED	Brawled
WARBLER	Brawler
WARDING	Drawing
WARHEAD	Rawhead
WARMERS	Rewarms, Swarmer
WARM-UPS	Upswarm
WARSTLE	Walters, Wastrel
WASHERS	Hawsers, Swasher
WASH-OUT	Outwash
WASTREL	Walters, Warstle
WASTRIE	Waister, Waiters
WATERED	Dewater
WATERER	Rewater
WAYSIDE	Sideway
WEARERS	Reswear, Rewears, Swearer
WEATHER	Whereat, Wreathe
WEBSTER	Bestrew
WEDGING	Wind-egg
WEEPERS	Resweep, Sweeper
WEIGHER	Reweigh
WELTERS	Swelter, Wrestle
WELTING	Winglet
WESTING	Stewing, Twinges
WET-WASH	Sawwhet
WHEEDLE	Wheeled
WHEELED	Wheedle
WHEREAT	Weather, Wreathe
WHEREON	Erewhon, Nowhere
WHOEVER	However
WIDENER	Rewiden
WIGGLER	Wriggle
WILLERS	Swiller
WILTING	Witling
WIND-EGG	Wedging
WINDLES	Swindel
WINGERS	Swinger
WINGLET	Welting
WIRABLE	Brawlie
WISENTS	Witness
WISHERS	Swisher
WITHERS	Swither, Writhes
WITHOUT	Outwith
WITLESS	Twissel
WITLING	Wilting

WITNESS	Wisents		WRESTER	Strewer
WITSTER	Retwist, Twister, Witters		WRESTLE	Swelter, Welters
			WRIGGLE	Wiggler
*WITTERS	Retwist, Twister, Witster		WRINGED	Redwing
			WRITHES	Swither, Withers
WOLFING	Flowing, Fowling		WRONGER	Regrown
WOOD-BOX	Boxwood			
WOOD-GOD	Dogwood			
WOODNUT	Nutwood		XEROTIC	Excitor
WORDAGE	Dowager			
WORDILY	Rowdily			
WORKBOX	Boxwork		YARDAGE	Drayage
WORKDAY	Day-work		YARDING	Draying
WORK-OUT	Outwork		YARD-MAN	Drayman
WORN-OUT	Outworn		YEARNED	Deanery
WOUNDER	Rewound		YESTERN	Styrene
WRANGLE	Wangler			
WRAPPER	Prewrap			
WREATHE	Weather, Whereat		ZINCITE	Citizen
WRESTED	Strewed			

Eight letters

ABELMOSK	Smokable	ADAMSITE	Adamites,
ABETTALS	Statable,		Diastema
	Tastable	ADDUCERS	Crusaded
ABLUENTS	Unstable	ADENOIDS	Anodised
ABLUTION	Abutilon	ADHERENT	Neatherd
ABORTING	Borating,	ADHERERS	Redshare,
	Taboring		Reshared
ABRIDGED	Brigaded	ADHERING	Head-ring
ABSORBER	Reabsorb	ADHIBITS	Dishabit
ABUTILON	Ablution	ADJUSTER	Readjust
ACARIDAN	Arcadian	ADOPTERS	Asported,
ACCEPTER	Reaccept		Readopts
ACCOUTER	Accoutre	ADROITLY	Dilatory,
ACCOUTRE	Accouter		Idolatry
ACCRUALS	Caraculs,	ADSORBED	Roadbeds
	Saccular	ADULATOR	Laudator
ACCURATE	Carucate	AEROLOGY	Areology
ACETATES	Testacea	AESTIVAL	Salivate
ACETONES	Notecase	AFFECTER	Reaffect
ACHERSET	Cheaters,	AFFIRMER	Reaffirm
	Reachest,	AGENESIS	Assignee
	Recheats,	AGNOSTIC	Coasting,
	Teachers		Coatings,
ACLUTTER	Cultrate		Cotingas
ACONITES	Canoeist	AGONISED	Diagnose
ACOSMIST	Massicot	AILMENTS	Aliments,
ACREAGES	Gear-case		Saltmine,
ACROLEIN	Caroline		Smaltine
ACROSTIC	Socratic	AIRCREWS	Airscrew
ACTINIDE	Ctenidia,	AIRPOSTS	Prosaist,
	Diactine,		Protasis
	Indicate	AIRSCREW	Aircrews
ACTINOID	Diatonic	ALARMING	Marginal
ADAMITES	Adamsite,	ALARMIST	Alastrim
	Diastema	ALASTRIM	Alarmist

183

ALBURNUM	Laburnum		Germanic
*ALCESTIS	Elastics	AMORTISE	Atomiser
ALCHEMIC	Chemical	ANALCIME	Calamine
ALERTING	Altering,	ANARCHIC	Characin
	Integral,	ANCESTOR	Enactors
	Relating,	ANCIENTS	Instance
	Triangle	ANDIRONS	Iron-sand,
*ALGERIAN	Regalian		Sand-iron
ALGERIA'S	Gasalier	ANGERING	Enraging
	Regalias	ANGLINGS	Slanging
ALIENISM	Milesian	ANGRIEST	Astringe,
ALIENIST	Latinise,		Ganister,
	Litanies		Granites,
ALIGNERS	Engrails,		Ingrates,
	Realigns,		Reasting,
	Resignal,		Tangiers
	Sanglier,	ANIMATED	Diamante
	Signaler	ANIMATOR	Tamanoir
ALIMENTS	Ailments,	ANISETTE	Tetanise
	Saltmine,	ANODISED	Adenoids
	Smaltine	ANOINTER	Inornate,
*ALISTERS	Realists,		Reanoint
	Saltiers,	ANOTHER'S	Sheraton
	Saltires,	ANSWERER	Reanswer
	Slaister	ANT-BEARS	Ratsbane
ALKALIES	Alkalise	ANTEDATE	Edentata
ALKALISE	Alkalies	ANTHESIS	Shanties,
ALLIANCE	Canaille		Sheitans
ALLOTTED	Totalled	ANTICOUS	Auctions,
ALL-ROUND	Round-all		Cautions
ALMADIES	Maladies	ANTIDOTE	Tetanoid
ALTERANT	Alternat	*ANTIGONE	Negation
ALTERING	Alerting,	ANTILOPE	Antipole
	Integral,	ANTIMONY	Antinomy
	Relating,	ANTINOMY	Antimony
	Triangle	ANTIPOLE	Antilope
ALTERNAT	Alterant	ANTI-REDS	Detrains,
ALTITUDE	Latitude		Strained,
ALTRUISM	Muralist,		Trade-ins
	Ultraism	ANTISTES	Instates,
ALTRUIST	Titulars,		Satinets,
	Ultraist		Titaness
ALUNITES	Insulate	APHETISE	Hepatise
AMANITIN	Maintain	APHORISM	Morphias
AMASSING	Gas-mains,	APPARENT	Trappean
	Siamangs	APPEALER	Reappeal
AMENABLE	Nameable	APPEARER	Rapparee,
AMERCERS	Creamers,		Reappear
	Screamer	APRICOTS	Patricos,
AMERCING	Creaming,		Piscator

Word	Anagrams	Word	Anagrams
ARBORIST	Rib-roast		Sarsenet
ARBUSCLE	Curables	ASSERTER	Reassert,
ARCADIAN	Acaridan		Serrates
ARCHAISM	Charisma	ASSERTOR	Assorter,
AREOLOGY	Aerology		Oratress,
ARGENTIC	Catering,		Reassort,
	Creating,		Roasters
	Reacting	ASSIGNEE	Agenesis
ARIDNESS	Sardines	ASSIGNER	Reassign,
ARIETTAS	Aristate		Seringas
ARISTATE	Ariettas	ASSIGNOR	Signoras
*ARMENIAN	Marianne	ASSISTER	Reassist
ARRAIGNS	Srinagar	ASSORTED	Torsades
ARRESTED	Retrades,	ASSORTER	Assertor,
	Retreads,		Oratress,
	Serrated,		Reassort,
	Treaders		Roasters
ARRESTER	Rearrest	ASTERIDS	Disaster
ARROGANT	Tarragon		Disrates
ARSENICS	Cerasins,	*ASTERION	Senorita
	Raciness,	*ASTEROPE	Operates,
	Sarcines		Protease,
ARSENITE	Resinate,		Soap-tree
	Stearine,	ASTIGMIC	Sigmatic
	Teresian,	ASTRINGE	Angriest,
	Teresina,		Ganister,
	Trainees		Granites,
ARTESIAN	Erastian,		Ingrates,
	Resinata		Reasting,
ARTICLES	Recitals,		Tangiers
	Selictar	ASTURIAS	Austrias
ASCENDER	Reascend	ATELIERS	Earliest
ASCRIBED	Carbides	ATHEISMS	Mathesis
ASPERGES	Presages	ATOMISER	Amortise
ASPERSES	Passeres,	ATOMISMS	Somatism
	Repasses	ATOMISTS	Somatist
ASPHODEL	Pholades	ATRAZINE	Nazarite
ASPIRANT	Partisan	ATROCITY	Citatory
ASPIRATE	Parasite,	ATTACHER	Reattach
	Septaria	ATTACKER	Reattack
ASPIRING	Praising	ATTAINER	Reattain
ASPORTED	Adopters,	ATTESTER	Reattest
	Readopts	ATTESTOR	Testator
ASSAILER	Salaries	ATTRITED	Titrated
ASSAYING	Gainsays	ATTUNING	Taunting
ASSEMBLE	Beamless	AUCTIONS	Anticous,
ASSENTED	East-ends,		Cautions
	Standees	AURICLES	Escurial
ASSENTER	Earnests,	*AUSTRIAS	Asturias
	Reassent,	AVERTERS	Traverse

AWAKENER	Reawaken	BELLOWED	Bowelled
AWEATHER	Wheatear	*BENGALIS	Belgians,
			Signable,
			Singable
BAALITES	Labiates,	BERATING	Rebating
	Satiable	BEREAVED	Beavered
BABBLING	Blabbing	BERSEEMS	Bessemer
BABISHLY	Shabbily	BERTHING	Brighten
BACK-FIRE	Fireback	BESHADOW	Bowheads
BACK-HAUL	Haul-back	BESLAVER	Servable,
BACKWARD	Drawback		Versable
BAHADURS	Subahdar	BESORTED	Bestrode
BAIRNISH	Brainish	BESOTTED	Obtested
BALANCER	Barnacle	BESSEMER	Berseems
BALDNESS	Bandless	BESTIARY	Sybarite
BALE-FIRE	Fireable	BESTOWAL	Stowable
*BALINESE	Base-line,	BESTRODE	Besorted
	Sabeline	BETIDING	Debiting
BALK-LINE	Linkable	BETOKENS	Steenbok
BALLOTER	Reballot	BIG-SWOLN	Bowlings
BALMLIKE	Lamblike	BIOCIDAL	Diabolic
BALUSTER	Rustable	BIOCLEAN	Coinable
BANDLESS	Baldness	BIRD-CALL	Call-bird
BARITONE	Obtainer,	BIRD-SEED	Seed-bird
	Reobtain	BIRDSONG	Song-bird
BARNACLE	Balancer	BLABBING	Babbling
BARRACAN	Barranca	BLANKEST	Blankets
BARRANCA	Barracan	BLANKETS	Blankest
BASCINET	Cabinets	BLASTING	Stabling
BASE-LINE	Balinese,	BLEACHER	Rebleach
	Sabeline	BLEATERS	Restable,
BASINETS	Bassinet		Retables
BASSINET	Basinets	BLEATING	Belating,
BAUCHLES	Chasuble		Tangible
BEADINGS	Debasing	BLESSING	Glibness
BEAM-ENDS	Bedesman	BLOATERS	Sortable,
BEAMLESS	Assemble		Storable
BEANPOLE	Openable	BLOATING	Obligant
BEAVERED	Bereaved	BLOTLESS	Boltless
BED-CHAIR	Chair-bed	BLOTTING	Bottling
BEDESMAN	Beam-ends	BLOWFISH	Fishbowl
BEDMAKER	Embarked	BLUNGING	Bungling
BEETROOT	Boot-tree	BOASTING	Bostangi
BEGRUDGE	Buggered,	BOAT-HOOK	Book-oath
	Debugger	BODEMENT	Entombed
BELATING	Bleating,	BOLDNESS	Bondless
	Tangible	BOLTLESS	Blotless
*BELGIANS	Bengalis,	BONDAGES	Dogbanes,
	Signable		Dogsbane
	Singable		

BONDLESS	Boldness	CABALLER	Race-ball
BONE-FISH	Fishbone	CABINETS	Bascinet
BONELESS	Noblesse	CACKLING	Clacking
BOOKCASE	Casebook	CADASTER	Cadastre
BOOK-OATH	Boat-hook	CADASTRE	Cadaster
BOOTJACK	Jackboot	CALAMINE	Analcime
BOOTLACE	Lace-boot	CALAMINT	Claimant
BOOT-TREE	Beetroot	CALANDER	Calendar
BORATING	Aborting,	CALCINES	Scenical
	Taboring	CALENDAR	Calander
BORDURES	Suborder	CALENDER	Encradle
BOSTANGI	Boasting	CALENDRY	Dry-clean
BOTANIES	Botanise	CALIPEES	Especial
BOTANISE	Botanies	CALIPERS	Replicas,
BOTTLING	Blotting		Spiracle
BOUNDERS	Rebounds,	CALIVERS	Claviers,
	Suborned		Visceral
BOWELLED	Bellowed	CALL-BIRD	Bird-call
BOWHEADS	Beshadow	CALL-NOTE	Lancelot
BOWLINGS	Big-swoln	CALL-OVER	Cover-all,
BRAKEAGE	Breakage		Overcall
BRAINISH	Bairnish	CALORIES	Carioles,
BRAKE-MAN	Breakman		Escorial
BRANDIES	Brandise	CALOTTES	Salt-cote
BRANDISE	Brandies	CALOYERS	Coarsely
BRAWLING	Warbling	CALUMETS	Muscatel
BREAD-NUT	Turbaned	CAMBERED	Embraced
BREAKAGE	Brakeage	CAMBRELS	Clambers,
BREAKMAN	Brake-man		Scambler,
BREAKOUT	Outbreak		Scramble
BRIGADED	Abridged	CAMELINE	Melaenic
BRIGHTEN	Berthing	CAMERATE	Macerate,
BRISANCE	Carbines		Racemate
BRISTLED	Driblets	CANAILLE	Alliance
BROIDERS	Disrober	CANASTER	Caterans
BROKAGES	Grosbeak	CANCROID	Draconic
BUCKLERS	Sub-clerk	CANEPHOR	Chaperon
BUDGETER	Rebudget	CANISTER	Creatins
BUGGERED	Begrudge,	CANNINGS	Scanning
	Debugger	CANOEIST	Aconites
BUNGLING	Blunging	CANONESS	Sonances
BUNKERED	Debunker	CANONIST	Contains,
BURLETTA	Rebuttal		Sanction
BURNT-OUT	Outburnt	CANTEENS	Enascent
BUSH-BRED	Shrubbed	CANTERED	Crenated,
BUTCHERS	Schubert		Decanter,
BUTTERED	Rebutted		Nectared,
BUTTERIS	Tributes		Recanted
BUTTONER	Rebutton	CANTORIS	Cast-iron
BY-PASSER	Passer-by		

CAPERING	Preignac	CENTAURS	Etruscan,
CAPSULAR	Scapular		Recusant
CARACULS	Accruals,	CENTERED	Decenter,
	Saccular		Decentre
CARBIDES	Ascribed	CENTIARE	Creatine,
CARBINES	Brisance		Increate,
CARINATE	Craniate		Iterance
CARIOLES	Calories,	CENTIMOS	Centoism
	Escorial	CENTOISM	Centimos
CARMINES	Cremains	CENTROID	Doctrine
CARNEOUS	Nacreous	CERAMIST	Matrices
*CAROLINE	Acrolein	CERASINS	Arsenics,
CAROLLED	Collared		Raciness,
CARPINGS	Scarping,		Sarcines
	Scraping	CERASTES	Cateress
CARTOONS	Corantos,	CERATOSE	Creasote
	Ostracon	CEREMENT	Cementer,
CARUCATE	Accurate		Recement
CASEBOOK	Bookcase	CERVELAS	Cleavers
CASSETTE	Test-case	CESSIONS	Cosiness
CAST-IRON	Cantoris	CESTODES	Cosseted
CASTLING	Catlings	CHAINLET	Ethnical
CASTORES	Coarsest,	CHAINMAN	Chinaman
	Coasters,	CHAINMEN	Chinamen
	Recoasts	CHAIR-BED	Bed-chair
CASUALLY	Causally	CHALDRON	Chondrel
CATCHERS	Cratches	CHALKING	Hackling
CATEGORY	Grey-coat	CHANGING	Ganching
CATERANS	Canaster	CHANTERS	Snatcher,
CATERESS	Cerastes		Stancher
CATERING	Argentic,	CHAPERON	Canephor
	Creating,	CHAPITER	Phreatic
	Reacting	CHARACIN	Anarchic
CATHETER	Charette	CHARETTE	Catheter
CATLINGS	Castling	CHARISMA	Archaism
CAT'S-TAIL	Cattails,	CHARMING	Marching
	Statical	CHARPIES	Seraphic
CATTAILS	Cat's-tail,	CHARTERS	Recharts,
	Statical		Starcher
CAUSALLY	Casually	CHARTING	Ratching
CAUTIONS	Anticous,	CHASUBLE	Bauchles
	Auctions	*CHATWOOD	Woodchat
CAVATION	Octavian,	CHEATERS	Acherset,
	Vacation		Reachest,
CAVERNED	Cravened		Recheats,
CEMENTER	Cerement,		Teachers
	Recement	CHEATING	Teaching
CENSORED	Seconder,	CHEMICAL	Alchemic
	Seed-corn	CHEMISTS	Schemist

CHICK-PEA	Peachick	CLIMBOUT	Outclimb
CHILLERS	Schiller	CLOCKING	Cockling
CHINAMAN	Chainman	CLODDING	Coddling
CHINAMEN	Chainmen	CLOISTER	Costlier
CHINREST	Christen,	CLOSURES	Sclerous
	Citherns	CLOTHIER	Chlorite
CHITTERS	Restitch,	CLUTCHED	Declutch
	Stitcher	CLUTTERS	Scuttler
CHLORATE	Trochlea	COARSELY	Caloyers
CHLORITE	Clothier	COARSEST	Castores,
CHONDRAL	Chaldron		Coasters,
CHOPINES	Echinops		Recoasts
CHRISTEN	Chinrest,	CCASTERS	Castores,
	Citherns		Coarsest,
CHURNING	Runching		Recoasts
CILIATES	Silicate	COASTING	Agnostic,
CINEREAL	Reliance		Coatings,
CIPHERED	Decipher		Cotingas
CIPOLINS	Psilocin	COATINGS	Agnostic,
CISELEUR	Ciselure		Coasting,
CISELURE	Ciseleur		Cotingas
CISTVAEN	Vesicant	COAT-TAIL	Tailcoat
CITATORY	Atrocity	COAXIALS	Saxicola
CITHERNS	Chinrest,	COCKLING	Clocking
	Christen	CODDLERS	Scroddle
CITRATES	Cristate	CODDLING	Clodding
CLABBERS	Scrabble	CODLINGS	Lingcods,
CLACKING	Cackling		Scolding
CLAIMANT	Calamint	COEHORNS	Schooner
CLAMBERS	Cambrels,	COHERERS	Cosherer
	Scambler,	COIFFEUR	Coiffure
	Scramble	COIFFURE	Coiffeur
CLANGING	Glancing	COINABLE	Bioclean
CLATTERS	Scrattle	COINAGES	Cosinage
CLAVIERS	Calivers,	COITIONS	Isotonic
	Visceral	COLATION	Location
CLAY-MARL	Lacrymal	COLLAPSE	Escallop
CLAY-PIPE	Pipeclay	COLLARED	Carolled
CLEANERS	Cleanser,	COLONIES	Colonise
	Recleans,	COLONISE	Colonies
	Relances	COLOURED	Decolour
CLEANING	Elancing,	COLOURER	Recolour
	Enlacing	COMATOSE	Moot-case
CLEANSER	Cleaners,	COMEDIAN	Demoniac
	Recleans,	COMEDIST	Domestic
	Relances	COME-DOWN	Downcome
CLEAVERS	Cervelas	COMING-IN	Incoming
CLEMATIS	Climates	COMPARES	Compears,
CLERKESS	Reckless		Mesocarp
CLIMATES	Clematis		

COMPEARS	Compares,		Electros,
	Mesocarp		Selector
COMPILED	Complied	CORSETED	Escorted,
COMPILER	Complier		Recosted
COMPLIED	Compiled	CORSLETS	Costrels,
COMPLIER	Compiler		Croslets,
CONCETTI	Tectonic		Crosslet
CONDOLES	Consoled	COSHERER	Coherers
CONDUITS	Discount,	COSINAGE	Coinages
	Noctuids	COSINESS	Cessions
CONDYLES	Secondly	COSSETED	Cestodes
CONFLATE	Falconet	COST-FREE	Free-cost,
CONFRERE	Enforcer		Scot-free
CONGREET	Co-regent	COSTLIER	Cloister
CONGREVE	Converge	COSTRELS	Corslets,
CONIFERS	Fir-cones,		Croslets,
	Forensic,		Crosslet
	Forinsec	COSTUMED	Customed
CONSERVE	Converse	COSTUMER	Customer
CONSOLED	Condoles	CO-SURVEY	Courtesy
CONSOLES	Coolness	COTELINE	Election
CONSTRUE	Cornutes,	COTERIES	Esoteric
	Counters,	COTINGAS	Agnostic,
	Recounts,		Coasting,
	Trounces		Coatings
CONSULAR	Courlans	COUNTERS	Construe,
CONTAINS	Canonist,		Cornutes,
	Sanction		Recounts,
CONTOURS	Cornutos,		Trounces
	Croutons,	COUNTESS	Contuses
	Outscorn	COUPURES	Cupreous
CONTUSES	Countess	COURAGES	Scourage
CONVERGE	Congreve	COURANTE	Outrance
CONVERSE	Conserve	COURLANS	Consular
CONVEYER	Reconvey	COURSERS	Cursores,
COOLNESS	Consoles		Scourers
COPULATE	Outplace	COURSING	Scouring
CORANTOS	Cartoons,	COURTESY	Co-survey
	Ostracon	COURTIER	Outcrier
CORDAGES	God's-acre	COVER-ALL	Call-over,
CO-REGENT	Congreet		Overcall
CORNUTES	Construe,	COWLINGS	Scowling
	Counters,	*CRABTREE	Tree-crab
	Recounts,	CRANIATE	Carinate
	Trounces	CRAPPIES	Epicarps
CORNUTOS	Contours,	CRATCHES	Catchers
	Croutons,	CRAVENED	Caverned
	Outscorn	CRAWLERS	Scrawler
CORSELET	Electors,	CREAMERS	Amercers,
			Screamer

CREAMING	Amercing,
	Germanic
CREASOTE	Ceratose
CREATINE	Centiare,
	Increate,
	Iterance
CREATING	Argentic,
	Catering,
	Reacting
CREATINS	Canister
CREATION	Reaction
CREATIVE	Reactive
CREDITED	Directed
CREDITOR	Director
CREMAINS	Carmines
CREMOSIN	Incomers,
	Sermonic
CRENATED	Cantered,
	Decanter,
	Nectared,
	Recanted
CREPITUS	Cuprites,
	Pictures
	Piecrust
CRESCIVE	Crevices
*CRETHEIS	Heretics
CREVICES	Crescive
CRIBBLES	Scribble
CRIMEFUL	Merciful
CRISPATE	Picrates,
	Practise
CRISTATE	Citrates
CROSLETS	Corslets,
	Costrels,
	Crosslet
CROSSLET	Corslets,
	Costrels,
	Croslets
CROUTONS	Contours,
	Cornutos,
	Outscorn
CRUELEST	Lectures
CRUISERS	Scurries
CRUMPETS	Spectrum
CRUSADED	Adducers
CRUSTILY	Rusticly
CTENIDIA	Actinide,
	Diactine,
	Indicate

CULLINGS	Sculling
CULLIONS	Scullion
CULPRITS	Spit-curl
CULTRATE	Aclutter
CUMBERED	Recumbed
CUNIFORM	Nuciform,
	Unciform
CUPIDITY	Pudicity
CUPREOUS	Coupures
CUPRITES	Crepitus,
	Pictures,
	Piecrust
CURABLES	Arbuscle
CURELESS	Recluses
CURSORES	Coursers,
	Scourers
CURTAILS	Rustical
CURTNESS	Encrusts
CUSTOMED	Costumed
CUSTOMER	Costumer
CUTTABLE	Table-cut
CUTTINGS	Tungstic
CYSTINES	Encystis
DALESMAN	Leadsman
DALESMEN	Emendals,
	Leadsmen
DANGLERS	Glanders
DARNDEST	Stranded
DATE-LINE	Entailed,
	Lineated
DATE-PALM	Palmated
DATURINE	Indurate
DAWDLERS	Swaddler,
	Waddlers
DAWDLING	Waddling
DAWNLIKE	Wandlike
DAYLIGHT	Light-day
DEAD-LOCK	Deck-load
DEANSHIP	Headpins,
	Pinheads
DEBASING	Beadings
DEBITING	Betiding
DEBUGGER	Begrudge,
	Buggered
DEBUNKER	Bunkered
DECADENT	Decanted
DECANTED	Decadent

DECANTER	Cantered,	DEMESNES	Seedsmen
	Crenated,	DEMONIAC	Comedian
	Nectared,	DEMOTION	Motioned
	Recanted	DEMOUNTS	Unmodest
DECEIVER	Received	DEMURRED	Murdered
DECENTER	Centered,	DEMURRER	Murderer
	Decentre	DENARIUS	Unraised
DECENTRE	Centered,	DENOUNCE	Enounced
	Decenter	DENTINES	Desinent
DECIGRAM	Grimaced	DENTURES	Sederunt,
DECIMATE	Medicate		Underset,
DECIPHER	Ciphered		Unrested
DECK-LOAD	Dead-lock	DENUDERS	Sundered
DECLINER	Reclined	DEPARTED	Predated
DECLINES	Licensed,	DEPARTER	Reparted
	Silenced	DEPICTER	Decrepit
DECLUTCH	Clutched	DEPILATE	Pileated
DECOLOUR	Coloured	DEPLETES	Steepled
DECORATE	Recoated	DEPOSITS	Side-post,
DECREETS	Resected,		Topsides
	Secreted	DEPRAVED	Pervaded
DECREPIT	Depicter	DEPRIVES	Prevised
DEERFOOT	Refooted	DEPSIDES	Despised
DEER-LICK	Relicked	DEPUTIES	Deputise
DEER-PARK	Reparked	DEPUTISE	Deputies
DEFEATER	Redefeat	DERAILER	Re-railed
DEFERRER	Referred	DERATING	Gradient,
DEFILING	Fielding		Treading
DEFLOWER	Flowered,	DERATION	Ordinate,
	Reflowed		Rationed,
DEFORCES	Frescoed		Rodentia
DEFOREST	Forested,	DERELICT	Relicted
	Fostered	DERISION	Ironside,
DEFORMER	Reformed		Resinoid
DEGENDER	Gendered	DERMATIC	Time-card
DEGRADER	Regarded,	DESCHOOL	Schooled
	Regraded	DESELECT	Selected
DEIFYING	Edifying	DESERTER	Redesert
DELIGHTS	Slighted	DESERVER	Reserved,
DELIVERS	Desilver,		Reversed
	Silvered,	DESIGNER	Enridges,
	Slivered		Reedings,
DELUDING	Indulged,		Redesign,
	Ungilded		Resigned
DELUSION	Unsoiled	DESILVER	Delivers,
DEMANDED	Maddened		Silvered,
DEMENTIS	Sediment,		Slivered
	Tidesmen	DESINENT	Dentines
DEMERSAL	Emeralds	DESIRING	Residing,
			Ringside

DESPAIRS	Perissad		Proteids
DESPISED	Depsides	DIRECTED	Credited
DESPISER	Disperse,	DIRECTOR	Creditor
	Perseids,	DISASTER	Asterids,
	Presides		Disrates
DESPITES	Side-step	DISBURSE	Subsider
DESSERTS	Destress,	DISCOUNT	Conduits,
	Stressed		Noctuids
DESTRESS	Desserts,	DISCOVER	Divorces
	Stressed	DISCRASE	Sidecars
DETAILER	Retailed	DISCREET	Discrete
DETAINER	Retained	ISCRETE	Discreet
DETESTER	Retested	DISENDOW	Disowned
DETHRONE	Threnode	DISHABIT	Adhibits
DETRAINS	Anti-reds,	DISHEVEL	She-devil
	Strained,	DISINTER	Inditers,
	Trade-ins		Nitrides
DEVIATES	Sedative	DISORBED	Disrobed
DEWINESS	Wideness	DISOWNED	Disendow
DIABOLIC	Biocidal	DISPENSE	Piedness
DIACTINE	Actinide,	DISPERSE	Despiser,
	Ctenidia,		Perseids,
	Indicate		Presides
DIAGNOSE	Agnoised	DISPONER	Prisoned
DIAMANTE	Animated	DISPROVE	Prevoids,
DIAMETER	Remediat		Provides
DIARIANS	Sardinia	DISRATES	Asterids,
DIASTEMA	Adamites,		Disaster
	Adamsite	DISROBED	Disorbed
DIATONIC	Actinoid	DISROBER	Broiders
DIGESTER	Erdgeist,	DISSERTS	Distress
	Redigest	DISSERVE	Dissever,
DIGRAPHS	Sphragid		Divisers
DILATORY	Adroitly,	DISSEVER	Disserve,
	Idolatry		Divisers
DIOPTERS	Dioptres,	DISTRAIT	Triadist
	Dipteros,	DISTREAM	Misrated,
	Peridots,		Readmits
	Portside,	DISTRESS	Disserts
	Proteids	DIVERTER	Redivert,
DIOPTRES	Diopters,		Verditer
	Dipteros,	DIVISERS	Disserve,
	Peridots,		Dissever
	Portside,	DIVORCES	Discover
	Proteids	DOCTRINE	Centroid
DIPTERAL	Tripedal	DOGBANES	Bondages,
DIPTEROS	Diopters,		Dog'sbane
	Dioptres,	DOGHOUSE	Housedog
	Peridots,	DOG'SBANE	Bondages,
	Portside,		Dogbanes

DOG-WATCH	Watchdog		Sarsenet
DOLERITE	Loitered	EARTHIER	Heartier
DOMESTIC	Comedist	EARTHILY	Heartily
DOMIFIED	Modified	EARTHING	Hearting,
DOMINATE	Nematoid		Ingather
DOMINIES	Minidose	EASEMENT	Estamene
DONATION	Nodation	EAST-ENDS	Assented,
DOOR-POST	Door-stop		Standees
DOOR-STOP	Door-post	EASTINGS	Giantess,
DORMANCY	Mordancy		Seatings,
DOURINES	Sourdine		Teasings
DOURNESS	Resounds,	EASTLINS	Salients,
	Sounders		Staniels
DOVERING	Ringdove	ECHINOPS	Chopines
DOVETAIL	Violated	ECHOISMS	Mischose
DOWELLER	Rowelled,	ECLIPSED	Pedicels,
	Welldoer		Pedicles
DOWNCOME	Come-down	ECLIPSER	Resplice
DOWN-TAKE	Take-down	EDENTATA	Antedate
DOWN-TURN	Turndown	EDGINESS	Seedings
DOWNWARD	Drawdown	EDIFYING	Deifying
DOWNWASH	Washdown	EDITIONS	Sedition
DRACONIC	Cancroid	EDITRESS	Dress-tie
DRAG-NETS	Grandest	EEL-GRASS	Gearless
DRAINAGE	Gardenia	EEL-POUTS	Outsleep,
DRAWBACK	Backward		Sleep-out
DRAWBORE	Wardrobe	EEL-SPEAR	Prelease
DRAWDOWN	Downward	EFTSOONS	Festoons
DRAWINGS	Swarding,	EGG-SHELL	Shell-egg
	Wardings	EIDOLONS	Solenoid
DREAMING	Margined	*EINSTEIN	Nineties
DRESS-TIE	Editress	ELANCING	Cleaning,
DRIBLETS	Bristled		Enlacing
DROLLING	Lordling	ELAPSING	Pleasing
DROWSING	Wordings	ELAPSION	Opalines
DRUGGING	Grudging	ELASTICS	Alcestis
DRY-CLEAN	Calendry	ELATERIN	Entailer,
DRY-STEAM	Steam-dry		Treenail
DUPLEXES	Expulsed	ELATIONS	Insolate
DURAMENS	Maunders,	ELECTION	Coteline
	Surnamed	ELECTORS	Corselet,
DURANCES	Unsacred,		Electros,
	Unscared		Selector
DWINDLES	Swindled	ELECTROS	Corselet,
			Electors,
			Selector
EARLIEST	Ateliers	ELEGIACS	Legacies
EARLSHIP	Hare-lips	ELISIONS	Lionises,
EARNESTS	Assenter,		Oiliness
	Reassent,	EMBARKED	Bed-maker

EMBRACED	Cambered
EMENDALS	Dalesmen, Leadsmen
EMERALDS	Demersal
EMPANELS	Emplanes, Ensample
EMPERORS	Premorse
EMPHASIS	Misshape
EMPLANES	Empanels, Ensample
EMPLOYER	Re-employ
EMPRISES	Premises, Spiremes
ENACTORS	Ancestor
ENASCENT	Canteens
ENCASHED	Enchased
ENCASTRE	Reascent, Sarcenet
ENCHASED	Encashed
ENCOMIUM	Meconium
ENCRADLE	Calender
ENCRUSTS	Curtness
ENCYSTIS	Cystines
ENDITING	Indigent
ENERGIES	Energise
ENERGISE	Energies
ENERGIST	Integers, Reesting, Retinges, Steering
ENERVATE	Venerate
ENFORCER	Confrere
ENFOREST	Resoften, Softener
ENGIRDED	Enridged
ENGIRDLE	Lingered, Reedling
ENGLANTE	Entangle
ENGRAILS	Aligners, Realigns, Resignal, Sanglier, Signaler
ENGROOVE	Overgone
ENISLING	Ensiling
ENJOINER	Re-enjoin
ENKINDLE	Enlinked
ENLACING	Cleaning, Elancing
ENLINKED	Enkindle
ENLISTED	Lintseed,

	Listened
ENLISTEE	Selenite
ENLISTER	Leinster, Listener, Re-enlist, Relisten
ENORMOUS	Nemorous
ENOUNCED	Denounce
ENQUIRES	Squireen
ENRAGING	Angering
ENRIDGED	Engirded
ENRIDGES	Designer, Reedings, Redesign, Resigned
ENROBING	Ring-bone
ENSAMPLE	Empanels, Emplanes
ENSILAGE	Lineages
ENSILING	Enisling
ENSNARES	Nearness
ENSPIRIT	Pristine
ENTAILED	Date-line, Lineated
ENTAILER	Elaterin, Treenail
ENTANGLE	Englante
ENTASTIC	Nictates, Tetanics
ENTERERS	Re-enters, Resenter, Terreens, Terrenes
ENTICERS	Scienter, Secretin, Tercines
ENTIRELY	Lientery
ENTIRETY	Eternity, Trey-tine
ENTOMBED	Bodement
ENTOZOIC	Enzootic
ENTRAILS	Latrines, Ratlines, Trenails
ENTREATS	Ratteens, Seat-rent
ENTREPOT	Tent-rope
ENZOOTIC	Entozoic
EPICARPS	Crappies
EPISODAL	Opalised, Sepaloid

EPISTLER	Perlites,	ETHERISM	Erethism
	Repliest,	ETHICIST	Theistic
	Reptiles,	ETHNICAL	Chainlet
	Spirelet	ETHOLOGY	Theology
EPITAPHS	Happiest	*ETRUSCAN	Centaurs,
EPULOTIC	Poultice		Recusant
EQUATORS	Quaestor	EULOGIES	Eulogise
ERASURES	Reassure	EULOGISE	Eulogies
*ERASTIAN	Artesian,	EVERTORS	Restrove
	Resinata	EVILNESS	Liveness,
ERDGEIST	Digester,		Veinless,
	Redigest		Vileness
ERECTION	Neoteric,	EVOCATOR	Overcoat
	Renotice	EXCEPTED	Expected
ERECTORS	Secretor	EXCITORS	Exorcist
ERETHISM	Etherism	EXERTING	Genetrix
ERUPTING	Reputing	EXORCIST	Excitors
ESCALLOP	Collapse	EXPANDER	Re-expand
*ESCORIAL	Calories,	EXPECTED	Excepted
	Carioles	EXPLODER	Explored
ESCORTED	Corseted,	EXPLORED	Exploder
	Recosted	EXPORTER	Re-export
ESCURIAL	Auricles	EXPUGNED	Expunged
ESOTERIC	Coteries	EXPULSED	Duplexes
ESPALIER	Pearlies	EXPUNGED	Expugned
ESPECIAL	Calipees	EYEGLASS	Glass-eye
ESPOUSAL	Sepalous		
ESPOUSER	Repousse		
ESSORANT	Senators,	FAIRNESS	Sanserif
	Star-nose,	FALCONET	Conflate
	Treasons	FALLIBLE	Fillable
ESTAMENE	Easement	FAMELESS	Selfsame
ESTOVERS	Oversets	FARMABLE	Framable
ESTAMINE	Matinees,	FARROWED	Foreward
	Seminate	FASTENER	Fenestra,
*ESTRAGON	Rag-stone		Refasten
ESTRANGE	Grantees,	FATHEADS	Headfast
	Greatens,	FATTRELS	Flatters
	Negaters,	FELINITY	Finitely
	Reagents,	FENESTRA	Fastener,
	Segreant,		Refasten
	Sergeant,	FESTOONS	Eftsoons
	Sternage	FIDICULA	Fiducial
ESURIENT	Retinues,	FIDUCIAL	Fidicula
	Reunites	FIELDING	Defiling
ETAGERES	Steerage	FIGURATE	Fruitage
ETATISMS	Misstate	FILLABLE	Fallible
ETERNITY	Entirety,	FILTERER	Refilter
	Trey-tine	FINITELY	Felinity

FIR-CONES	Confiers,
	Forensic,
	Forinsec
FIREABLE	Bale-fire
FIREBACK	Back-fire
FIRE-POTS	Firestop
FIRESTOP	Fire-pots
FISH-BONE	Bone-fish
FISHBOWL	Blowfish
FISH-WORM	Worm-fish
FLATTERS	Fattrels
FLAUNTED	Unflated
FLIRTING	Trifling
FLOATERS	Forestal,
	Refloats
FLOUNDER	Unfolder
FLOURING	Fourling
FLOUTING	Outfling
FLOWERED	Deflower,
	Reflowed
FLOWERER	Reflower
FLUTINAS	Inflatus
FOREMAST	Formates
FOREMEAN	Forename
FORENAME	Foremean
FORENSIC	Conifers,
	Fir-cones,
	Forinsec
FOREPART	Raft-rope
FORESHEW	Whereofs
FORESTAL	Floaters,
	Refloats
FORESTED	Deforest,
	Fostered
FORESTER	Fosterer,
	Reforest
FOREWARD	Farrowed
FORINSEC	Conifers,
	Fir-cones,
	Forensic
FORMALIN	Informal
FORMATES	Foremast
FORMULAE	Fumarole
FOSTERED	Deforest,
	Forested
FOSTERER	Forester,
	Reforest
FOURLING	Flouring
FRAMABLE	Farmable

FREE-COST	Cost-free,
	Scot-free
FREEPOST	Post-free
FREE-REED	Refereed
FREE-SHOT	Shot-free
FRESCOED	Deforces
FROUNCED	Unforced
FRUITAGE	Figurate
FRUMENTY	Furmenty
FUMAROLE	Formulae
FUNDABLE	Unfabled
FURMENTY	Frumenty
GAINLESS	Glassine,
	Leasings,
	Sealings
GAINSAYS	Assaying
GALENIST	Gelatins,
	Genitals,
	Stealing
GALENITE	Gelatine,
	Legatine
GALILEES	Legalise
GAMESTER	Gas-meter
GANCHING	Changing
GANISTER	Angriest,
	Astringe,
	Granites,
	Ingrates,
	Reasting,
	Tangiers
GARDENER	Garnered
GARDENIA	Drainage
GARGLING	Raggling
GARNERED	Gardener
GAROTTER	Garrotte
GARRETED	Gartered
GARRISON	Roarings
GARROTTE	Garotter
GARTERED	Garreted
GASALIER	Algeria's,
	Regalias
GAS-MAINS	Amassing,
	Siamangs
GAS-METER	Gamester
GAS-RINGS	Grassing
GAS-WATER	Water-gas
GATE-VEIN	Negative

GATHERER	Regather	GLUTTING	Guttling
GEAR-CASE	Acreages	GNASHING	Hangings
GEARINGS	Greasing	GNATLING	Tangling
GEARLESS	Eel-grass	GNOMONIC	Oncoming
GELATINE	Galenite,	GOATLING	Gloating
	Legatine	GOAT'S-RUE	Outrages
GELATINS	Galenist,	GOBELINS	Ignobles
	Genitals,	GOD'S-ACRE	Cordages
	Stealing	GOINGS-ON	Ongoings
GELATION	Legation	GOSLINGS	Glossing
GELDINGS	Sledging,	GRADIENT	Derating,
	Sniggled		Treading
GENDERED	Degender	GRAECISM	Grimaces
GENERATE	Green-tea,	GRAIN-TIN	Training
	Renegate,	GRANDEST	Drag-nets
	Teenager	GRANITES	Angriest,
GENETRIX	Exerting		Astringe,
GENITALS	Galenist,		Ganister,
	Gelatins,		Ingrates,
	Stealing		Reasting,
GENTILES	Sleeting,		Tangiers
	Steeling	GRANTEES	Estrange,
GEORGIAN	Georgina		Greatens,
*GEORGINA	Georgian		Negaters,
GERANIOL	Regional		Reagents,
GERMANIC	Amercing,		Segreant,
	Creaming		Sergeant,
GERMINAL	Maligner,		Sternage
	Malinger	GRANTERS	Regrants,
GIANTESS	Eastings,		Stranger
	Seatings,	GRANULES	Laser-gun
	Teasings	GRASPING	Sparging
GINGLING	Niggling	GRASSING	Gas-rings
GIN-SLING	Singling,	GRASS-OIL	Girasols
	Slinging	GRAUPELS	Plaguers,
GIRASOLE	Seraglio		Spergula
GIRASOLS	Grass-oil	GREASING	Gearings
GLAD-RAGS	Laggards	GREATENS	Estrange,
GLANCING	Clanging		Grantees,
GLANDERS	Danglers		Negaters,
GLASS-EYE	Eye-glass		Reagents,
GLASSINE	Gainless,		Segreant,
	Leasings,		Sergeant,
	Sealings		Sternage
GLENOIDS	Sidelong	GREENISH	Sheering
GLIBNESS	Blessing	GREEN-TEA	Generate,
GLINTING	Tingling		Renegate,
GLOATING	Goatling		Teenager
GLOSSING	Goslings		

GREMIALS	Regalism	HEADLONG	Long-head
GREY-COAT	Category	HEADPINS	Deanship,
GRIMACED	Decigram		Pinheads
GRIMACES	Graecism	HEAD-RING	Adhering
GROINING	Ignoring	HEADSKIN	Skinhead
GROPINGS	Proggins	HEALINGS	Leashing,
GROSBEAK	Brokages		Shealing
GROUNDED	Underdog,	HEARINGS	Hearsing,
	Under-god		Shearing
GRUDGING	Drugging	HEARKENS	Reshaken
GRUNTERS	Restrung	HEARSING	Hearings,
GUANINES	Sanguine		Shearing
GUTTLING	Glutting	HEARTENS	Hastener
		HEARTIER	Earthier
		HEARTILY	Earthily
HACKLING	Chalking	HEARTING	Earthing,
HADDOCKS	Shaddock		Ingather
HALCYONS	Synochal	HEATABLE	Hateable
HALF-NOTE	Half-tone	HEAVINGS	Sheaving
HALF-TONE	Half-note	HEIRLESS	Hireless,
HALLOOED	Holloaed		Relishes
HALTERED	Lathered	HEMATICS	Misteach
HALTERES	Leathers	HEPATICS	Pastiche,
HAMMERER	Rehammer		Scaphite
HANDLESS	Handsels	HEPATISE	Aphetise
HANDMILL	Millhand	HERETICS	Cretheis
HANDOUTS	Thousand	HERONSEW	Nowheres,
HANDOVER	Overhand		Whereons
HANDSELS	Handless	HETAIRAI	Hetairia
HANGINGS	Gnashing	HETAIRIA	Hetairai
HANG-OVER	Overhang	HILL-BORN	Hornbill
HANKERED	Harkened	HILLSIDE	Side-hill
HAPLOIDS	Shipload	HINDERED	Rehidden
HAPPIEST	Epitaphs	HIPPINGS	Shipping
HARA-KIRI	Hari-kari	HIRELESS	Heirless,
HARDENER	Reharden		Relishes
HARELIPS	Earlship	HITTABLE	Tithable
HARI-KARI	Hara-kiri	HOGMANAY	Mahogany
HARKENED	Hankered	HOLLOAED	Hallooed
HARPINGS	Phrasing,	HOOTINGS	Soothing,
	Sharping		Shooting
HARP-SEAL	Pearl-ash	HOPLITES	Isopleth
HASTENER	Heartens	HOPPINGS	Shopping
HATBANDS	Sandbath	HORNBILL	Hill-born
HATCHETS	Thatches	HORSEMAN	Shoreman
HATEABLE	Heatable	HORSEMEN	Shoremen
HAUL-BACK	Back-haul	HOSELESS	Shoeless
HEADFAST	Fatheads	HOSPODOR	Shop-door
HEADINGS	Sheading	HOUSEDOG	Doghouse

HOUSETOP	Pot-house		Creatine,
HOWEVERS	Whosever		Iterance
HUMORIST	Thoriums	INDENTED	Intended
HUNG-OVER	Overhung	INDENTER	Intender,
HUNTINGS	Shunting		Interned,
HUNTRESS	Shunters		Retinned
HUNTSMAN	Manhunts	INDICATE	Actinide,
HURTLESS	Hustlers,		Ctenidia,
	Ruthless		Diactine
HUSTINGS	Unsights	INDICTER	Indirect,
HUSTLERS	Hurtless,		Reindict
	Ruthless	INDIGENT	Enditing
HUSTLING	Sunlight	INDIRECT	Indicter,
HYPNOTIC	Pythonic,		Reindict
	Typhonic	INDITERS	Disinter,
			Nitrides
		INDULGED	Deluding,
ICE-WATER	Water-ice		Ungilded
IDEATION	Taenioid	INDURATE	Daturine
IDLENESS	Linseeds	INFECTER	Reinfect
IDOLATRY	Adroitly,	INFESTER	Reinfest
	Dilatory	INFLATUS	Flutinas
IDOLISMS	Solidism	INFORMAL	Formalin
IDOLISTS	Solidist	INFORMER	Reinform,
IGNOBLES	Gobelins		Reniform
IGNORING	Groining	INFRINGE	Refining
ILMENITE	Menilite	INGATHER	Earthing,
IMBRUTES	Resubmit,		Hearting
	Terbiums	INGRATES	Angriest,
IMITANCY	Intimacy,		Astringe,
	Minacity		Ganister,
IMITANTS	Titanism		Granites,
IMITATOR	Timariot		Reasting,
IMMERSED	Simmered		Tangiers
IMPEDING	Impinged	INGROWTH	Throwing,
IMPINGED	Impeding		Worthing
IMPLEADS	Misplead	INKLINGS	Linkings,
IMPLORES	Pelorism,		Slinking
	Sperm-oil	INKWOODS	Woodskin
IMPORTER	Reimport	INNOVATE	Venation
IMPRINTS	Misprint	INORNATE	Anointer,
INACTION	Nicotian		Reanoint
INCENSES	Niceness	INSECURE	Sinecure
INCEPTOR	Pretonic	INSERTED	Resident
INCISURE	Sciurine	INSERTER	Reinsert,
INCLUDES	Unsliced		Reinters,
INCOMERS	Cremosin,		Rentiers,
	Sermonic		Terrines
INCOMING	Coming-in	INSISTED	Tidiness
INCREATE	Centiare,	INSISTER	Reinsist

INSOLATE	Elations		Theorise
INSTANCE	Ancients	ISOTONIC	Coitions
INSTATES	Antistes,	ITERANCE	Centiare,
	Satinets,		Creatine,
	Titaness		Increate
INSTREAM	Minarets,	ITERATES	Treaties
	Raiments		Treatise
INSULATE	Alunites		
INSUREDS	Sundries		
INTAGLIO	Ligation	JACKBOOT	Bootjack
INTEGERS	Energist,		
	Reesting,		
	Retinges,	KEYNOTES	Keystone
	Steering	KEYSTONE	Keynotes
INTEGRAL	Alerting,	KILLINGS	Skilling
	Altering,		
	Relating,		
	Triangle	LABIATES	Baalites,
INTENDED	Indented		Satiable
INTENDER	Indenter,	LABRADOR	Larboard
	Interned,	LABURNUM	Alburnum
	Retinned	LACE-BOOT	Bootlace
INTEREST	Interset,	LACROSSE	Solacers
	Sternite,	LACRYMAL	Clay-marl
	Trestine	LACTEOUS	Osculate
INTERIMS	Minister	LADRONES	Solander
INTERNED	Indenter,	LAGGARDS	Glad-rags
	Intender,	LAKELETS	Skeletal
	Retinned	LAMBKINS	Lambskin
INTERSET	Interest,	LAMBLIKE	Balmlike
	Sternite,	LAMBSKIN	Lambkins
	Trestine	LAMELLAS	Small-ale
INTIMACY	Imitancy,	LAMENESS	Maneless,
	Minacity		Nameless,
INTREATS	Nitrates,		Salesmen
	Straiten,	LAMINOSE	Semolina
	Tertians	*LANCELOT	Call-note
INTROITS	Tritonis	LAND-ARMY	Maryland
INVADERS	Sandiver	LAPIDATE	Talpidae
INVENTER	Reinvent	LAPSTONE	Polentas
INVENTOR	Noverint	LARBOARD	Labrador
IRELAND'S	Islander	LASER-GUN	Granules
IRON-SAND	Andirons,	LASHINGS	Slashing
	Sand-iron	LATERITE	Literate
IRONSIDE	Derision,	LATHERED	Haltered
	Resinoid	LATINISE	Alienist,
*ISABELLA	Sailable		Litanies
ISLANDER	Ireland's	LATITUDE	Altitude
ISOPLETH	Hoplites	LATRINES	Entrails,
ISOPRENE	Pioneers		Ratlines,
ISOTHERE	Theories,		Trenails

LAUDATOR	Adulator	LINEATED	Date-line,
LAUNCHER	Relaunch		Entailed
LAYERING	Relaying,	LINESIDE	Side-line
	Yearling	LINESMAN	Melanins
LEADSMAN	Dalesman	LINGCODS	Codlings,
LEADSMEN	Dalesmen,		Scolding
	Emendals	LINGERED	Engirdle,
*LEANDERS	Sand-reel		Reedling
LEASABLE	Saleable	LINKABLE	Balk-line
LEASHING	Healings,	LINKINGS	Inklings,
	Shealing		Slinking
LEASINGS	Gainless,	LINSEEDS	Idleness
	Glassine,	LINTSEED	Enlisted,
	Sealings		Listened
LEATHERS	Halteres	LIONISES	Elisions,
LEAVINGS	Sleaving,		Oiliness
	Svengali	LISTENED	Enlisted,
LECTURES	Cruelest		Lintseed
LEGACIES	Elegiacs	LISTENER	Enlister,
LEGALISE	Galilees		Leinster,
LEGALIST	Stillage,		Re-enlist,
	Tillages		Relisten
LEGATINE	Galenite,	LITANIES	Alienist,
	Gelatine		Latinise
LEGATION	Gelation	LITERATE	Laterite
*LEINSTER	Enlister,	LIVENESS	Evilness,
	Listener		Veinless,
	Re-enlist		Vileness
	Relisten	LOBATELY	Oblately
LEISTERS	Riteless,	LOBATION	Oblation
	Tireless	LOCATION	Colation
LEPIDOTE	Petioled	LOGGINGS	Slogging
LESSENED	Needless	LOG-SLATE	Tollages
LETTERER	Reletter	LOITERED	Dolerite
LEVANTER	Relevant	LONG-HEAD	Headlong
LEVERETS	Verselet	LONG-SLIP	Pollings
LEVIRATE	Relative	LOOKER-ON	Onlooker
LIBRETTO	Tribolet	LORDLING	Drolling
LICENSED	Declines,	LOW-DOWNS	Slow-down
	Silenced	LUNATICS	Sultanic
LICENSER	Reclines,	LUNETTES	Unsettle
	Silencer	LUSTRATE	Tutelars
LICKINGS	Slicking	LUSTRING	Rustling
LIENTERY	Entirely		
LIGATION	Intaglio		
LIGHT-DAY	Daylight	MACARONI	Marocain
LIME-PITS	Slime-pit	*MACASSAR	Marascas,
LIMITARY	Military		Mascaras
LIMITATE	Militate	MACERATE	Camerate,
LINEAGES	Ensilage		Racemate

MADDENED	Demanded	MATINEES	Seminate
MAESTOSO	Osteomas	MATRICES	Ceramist
MAGISTER	Migrates,	MATTRESS	Smartest,
	Ragtimes		Smatters
MAHOGANY	Hogmanay	MAUNDERS	Duramens,
MAIDENLY	Medianly		Surnamed
MAINTAIN	Amanitin	MEAGERLY	Meagrely
MALADIES	Almadies	MEAGRELY	Meagerly
MALETOTE	Matelote	MEASURES	Reassume
MALIGNER	Germinal,	MEATLESS	Mateless,
	Malinger		Tameless
MALINGER	Germinal,	MECONIUM	Encomium
	Maligner	MEDALIST	Misdealt
MALTSTER	Martlets	MEDIANLY	Maidenly
MANDORAS	Roadsman	MEDICATE	Decimate
MANELESS	Lameness,	MELAENIC	Cameline
	Nameless,	MELANICS	Meniscal,
	Salesmen		Mescalin
MANHUNTS	Huntsman	MELANINS	Linesman
MANNERED	Remanned	MELODIAS	Soda-lime
MAN-POWER	Powerman	MELODIES	Melodise
MANROPES	Proseman	MELODISE	Melodies
MANTISSA	Satanism,	MEMORIES	Memorise
	Staminas	MEMORISE	Memories
MARASCAS	Macassar,	MENILITE	Ilmenite
	Mascaras	MENISCAL	Melanics,
MARBLING	Rambling		Mescalin
MARCHING	Charming	MENTALLY	Tallymen
MARGINAL	Alarming	MERCIFUL	Crimeful
MARGINED	Dreaming	MERRIEST	Miterers,
*MARIANNE	Armenian		Triremes
MARKETER	Remarket	MESCALIN	Melanics,
MAROCAIN	Macaroni		Meniscal
MARTLETS	Maltster	MESOCARP	Compares,
*MARYLAND	Land-army		Compears
MASCARAS	Macassar,	MESOTRON	Monteros
	Marascas	MESSIDOR	Misdoers
MASSETER	Seamster,	MIGRANTS	Smarting
	Steamers	MIGRATES	Magister,
MASSICOT	Acosmist		Ragtimes
MASTERED	Remasted,	MILDNESS	Mindless
	Streamed	MILESIAN	Alienism
MASTERER	Remaster,	MILITARY	Limitary
	Streamer	MILITATE	Limitate
MASTICOT	Stomatic	MILL-HAND	Handmill
MATELESS	Meatless,	MINACITY	Imitancy,
	Tameless		Intimacy
MATELOTE	Maletote	MINARETS	Instream,
MATESHIP	Shipmate		Raiments
MATHESIS	Atheisms		

MINDLESS	Mildness	MOTORAIL	Motorial
MINIDOSE	Dominies	MOTORIAL	Motorail
MINISTER	Interims	MOULDERS	Remoulds,
MINUTELY	Untimely		Smoulder
MISCHOSE	Echoisms	MOUNTERS	Montures,
MISDEALT	Medalist		Remounts
MISDOERS	Messidor	MUNERARY	Numerary
MISPLEAD	Impleads	MURALIST	Altruism,
MISPRINT	Imprints		Ultraism
MISPRISE	Pismires	MURDERED	Demurred
MISRATED	Distream,	MURDERER	Demurrer
	Readmits	MURMURER	Remurmur
MISREADS	Sidearms	MUSCATEL	Calumets
MISSHAPE	Emphasis	MUTENESS	Tenesmus
MISSPELL	Psellism	MUTILATE	Ultimate
MISSTATE	Etatisms	MUTINOUS	Untimous
MISTEACH	Hematics		
MISTICOS	Stoicism		
MISTIMES	Semitism	NACREOUS	Carneous
MISTRIAL	Trialism	NAMEABLE	Amenable
MISUNION	Unionism	NAMELESS	Lameness,
MITERERS	Merriest,		Maneless,
	Triremes		Salesmen
MOCKINGS	Smocking	NARGHILE	Nargileh
MODIFIED	Domified	NARGILEH	Narghile
MONADISM	Nomadism	NASALISE	Sea-snail
MONARCHS	Nomarchs,	NATANTES	Stannate,
	Romansch		Tannates
MONARCHY	Nomarchy	NATIVELY	Venality
MONETISE	Semitone	NATIVISM	Vitamins
MONISTIC	Nomistic	NATIVIST	Visitant
MONOGENY	Nomogeny	NAVIGATE	Vaginate
MONOGRAM	Nomogram	*NAZARITE	Atrazine
MONOLOGY	Nomology	NEARNESS	Ensnares
MONOTYPE	Moon-type	NEATHERD	Adherent
MONTEROS	Mesotron	NECTARED	Cantered,
MONTURES	Mounters,		Crenated,
	Remounts		Decanter,
MOON-TYPE	Monotype		Recanted
MOOT-CASE	Comatose	NEEDLESS	Lessened
MOOTINGS	Stooming	NEGATERS	Estrange,
MORAINES	Romanise		Grantees,
MORDANCY	Dormancy		Greatens,
MORINGAS	Organism,		Reagents,
	Roamings,		Segreant,
	Sinogram		Sergeant,
MORPHIAS	Aphorism		Sternage
MOTIONED	Demotion	NEGATION	Antigone
MOTIONER	Remotion	NEGATIVE	Gate-vein

NEMATOID	Dominate	NUPTIALS	Unplaits
NEMOROUS	Enormous	NURLINGS	Nursling
NEOPLASM	Pleonasm	NURSLING	Nurlings
NEOTERIC	Erection,	NUTTINGS	Stunting
	Renotice		
NEPHRITE	Trephine		
NEPOTISM	Pimentos	OBLATELY	Lobately
NEPOTIST	Point-set	OBLATION	Lobation
NEUROSIS	Resinous	OBLIGANT	Bloating
NICENESS	Incenses	OBTAINER	Baritone,
NICKINGS	Snicking		Reobtain
NICOTIAN	Inaction	OBTESTED	Besotted
NICTATES	Entastic,	OBTURATE	Tabouret
	Tetanics	OCHEROUS	Ochreous
NIGGLING	Gingling	OCHREOUS	Ocherous
NIGHTCAP	Patching	*OCTAVIAN	Cavation,
NINETIES	Einstein		Vacation
NIPPINGS	Snipping	OERSTEDS	Retossed
NITRATES	Intreats,	OFFENDER	Reoffend
	Straiten,	OFF-SHOOT	Shoot-off
	Tertians	OILINESS	Elisions,
NITRIDES	Disinter,		Lionises
	Inditers	ONCOMING	Gnomonic
NOBLESSE	Boneless	ONGOINGS	Goings-on
NOCARDIA	Orcadian	ONLOOKER	Looker-on
NOCTUIDS	Conduits,	OPALINES	Elapsion
	Discount	OPALISED	Episodal,
NODATION	Donation		Sepaloid
NOMADISM	Monadism	OPENABLE	Bean-pole
NOMARCHS	Monarchs,	OPERATES	Asterope,
	Romansch		Protease,
NOMARCHY	Monarchy		Soap-tree
NOMISTIC	Monistic	OPSONINS	Sponsion
NOMOGENY	Monogeny	OPTOLOGY	Topology
NOMOGRAM	Monogram	OPTOTYPE	Topotype
NOMOLOGY	Monology	ORATRESS	Assertor,
NORTHING	Throning		Assorter,
NOSELESS	Soleness		Reassort,
NOTARIAL	Rational		Roasters
NOTECASE	Acetones	ORCADIAN	Nocardia
NOTELESS	Toneless	ORDAINER	Reordain
NOVELIST	Violents	ORDINATE	Deration,
NOVERINT	Inventor		Rationed,
NOWHERES	Heronsew,		Rodentia
	Whereons	ORGANISM	Moringas,
NUCIFORM	Cuniform,		Roamings,
	Unciform		Sinogram
NUMBERER	Renumber	ORGANIST	Roasting
NUMERARY	Munerary	ORIENTAL	Relation,
			Tirolean

ORNATELY	Tyrolean	OUTWATCH	Watch-out
ORNITHIC	Trichion	OUTWEARS	Outswear
OSCITANT	Tactions	OUTWEIGH	Weigh-out
OSCULATE	Lacteous	OUTWELLS	Outswell
OSTEOMAS	Maestoso	OUTWINGS	Outswing
OSTRACON	Cartoons,	OUTWORTH	Outthrow,
	Corantos		Throw-out
OUTBREAK	Breakout	OVERACTS	Overcast
OUTBURNT	Burnt-out	OVERBLOW	Overbowl
OUTCHARM	Outmarch	OVERBOWL	Overblow
OUTCLIMB	Climbout	OVERBUSY	Overbuys
OUTCRIER	Courtier	OVERBUYS	Overbusy
OUTCURES	Outcurse	OVERCALL	Call-over,
OUTCURSE	Outcures		Cover-all
OUTDEVIL	Outlived	OVERCAST	Overacts
OUTFLING	Flouting	OVERCOAT	Evocator
OUTKILLS	Outskill	OVERDARE	Overdear,
OUTLIVED	Outdevil		Overread
OUTMARCH	Outcharm	OVERDEAL	Overlade
OUTMATES	Outsteam	OVERDEAR ·	Overdare,
OUTPLACE	Copulate		Overread
OUTPORTS	Outsport	OVERDOER	Overrode
OUTRAGES	Goat's-rue	OVERDOES	Overdose
OUTRANCE	Courante	OVERDOSE	Overdoes
OUTRATES	Outstare,	OVEREATS	Oversate
	Out-tears	OVERGONE	Engroove
OUTREIGN	Routeing	OVERHAND	Hand-over
OUTRIDES	Outsider	OVERHANG	Hangover
OUTSCORN	Contours,	OVERHUNG	Hung-over
	Cornutos,	OVERKEEN	Overknee
	Croutons	OVERKING	Revoking
OUTSIDER	Outrides	OVERKNEE	Overkeen
OUTSKILL	Outkills	OVERLADE	Overdeal
OUTSLEEP	Eel-pouts	OVERLAPS	Pro-slave
	Sleep-out	OVERLIVE	Overveil
OUTSLIDE	Solitude,	OVERMANS	Oversman
	Toluides	OVERNEAT	Renovate
OUTSPORT	Outports	OVERPASS	Passover
OUTSTAND	Stand-out	OVERPOST	Overtops,
OUTSTARE	Outrates,		Stop-over
	Out-tears	OVER-READ	Overdare,
OUTSTEAM	Outmates		Overdear
OUTSWEAR	Outwears	OVERRODE	Overdoer
OUTSWELL	Outwells	OVERSATE	Overeats
OUTSWING	Outwings	OVERSEEN	Veronese
OUT-TEARS	Outrates,	OVERSETS	Estovers
	Outstare	OVERSLIP	Slipover
OUTTHROW	Outworth,	OVERSMAN	Overmans
	Throw-out	OVERTAKE	Take-over

OVERTOPS	Overpost,	PATRIOTS	Protista
	Stop-over	PATTENED	Patented
OVERTURE	Trouvere	PATTERNS	Transept
OVERTURN	Turnover	PEACHICK	Chickpea
OVERVEIL	Overlive	PEARL-ASH	Harp-seal
OXAZINES	Saxonise	PEARLIES	Espalier
OYSTERED	Storeyed	PEARTREE	Repartee,
			Repeater
		PECTINAL	Planetic
*PAIGNTON	Poignant	PEDERAST	Predates,
PAINLESS	Spaniels		Repasted
PAINTERS	Pertains,	PEDICELS	Eclipsed,
	Pinaster,		Pedicles
	Repaints	PEDICLES	Eclipsed,
PALENESS	Paneless		Pedicels
PALMATED	Date-palm	PEELINGS	Sleeping
PALMATES	Plateasm	PEERLESS	Sleepers
PALMISTS	Psalmist	PELORIAS	Polarise
PALSYING	Splaying	PELORISM	Implores,
PANELESS	Paleness		Sperm-oil
PARABLES	Sparable	PELTINGS	Pestling
PARADISE	Sparidae	PENALISE	Sepaline
PARASITE	Aspirate,	PENDULAR	Uplander
	Septaria	PEOPLING	Popeling
PARENTAL	Paternal,	PERDENDO	Pondered
	Prenatal	PERIDOTS	Diopters,
PARIETAL	Pteralia		Dioptres,
*PARMESAN	Spearman		Dipteros,
PARODIST	Parotids		Portside,
PAROTIDS	Parodist		Proteids
PARSLEYS	Sparsely	PERIPLUS	Supplier
PARTIALS	Triapsal	PERISSAD	Despairs
PARTISAN	Aspirant	PERLITES	Epistler,
PARTLETS	Platters,		Repliest,
	Prattles,		Reptiles,
	Splatter		Spirelet
PASSER-BY	By-passer	PERSEIDS	Despiser,
PASSERES	Asperses,		Disperse,
	Repasses		Presides
PASSOVER	Overpass	PERSONAS	Responsa
PASTICHE	Hepatics,	PERTAINS	Painters,
	Scaphite		Pinaster,
PASTRIES	Piastres,		Repaints
	Traipses	PERTNESS	Presents,
PATCHING	Nightcap		Serpents
PATENTED	Pattened	PERUSERS	Pressure
PATERNAL	Parental,	PERVADED	Depraved
	Prenatal	PERVERSE	Preserve
PATRICOS	Apricots,	PERVIOUS	Previous,
	Piscator		Viperous

PESTLING	Peltings	PLAISTER	Pilaster,
PETALINE	Tape-line		Plaiters,
PETIOLED	Lepidote		Replaits
PETROSAL	Pole-star,	PLAITERS	Pilaster,
	Prolates		Plaister,
PETUNIAS	Supinate		Replaits
PHAETONS	Stanhope	PLANETIC	Pectinal
PHOLADES	Asphodel	PLANTAIN	Plainant
PHRASING	Harpings,	PLANTPOT	Pot-plant
	Sharping	PLASHERS	Splasher
PHREATIC	Chapiter	PLASTERY	Psaltery
PIASABAS	Piassaba	PLATEASM	Palmates
PIASSABA	Piasabas	PLATINGS	Stapling
PIASTRES	Pastries,	PLATTERS	Partlets,
	Traipses		Prattles,
PICADORS	Sporadic		Splatter
PICRATES	Crispate,	PLEADERS	Relapsed,
	Practise		Repleads
PICTURES	Crepitus,	PLEASANT	Sea-plant
	Cuprites,	PLEASING	Elapsing
	Piecrust	PLEONASM	Neoplasm
PIECRUST	Crepitus,	PLOPPING	Poppling
	Cuprites,	*PLOTINUS	Unspoilt
	Pictures	PODISMUS	Spodiums
PIEDNESS	Dispense	POIGNANT	Paignton
PIKELETS	Spikelet	POINT-SET	Nepotist
PILASTER	Plaister,	POLARISE	Pelorias
	Plaiters,	POLENTAS	Lapstone
	Replaits	POLE-STAR	Petrosal,
PILEATED	Depilate		Prolates
PIMENTOS	Nepotism	POLISHER	Repolish
PINASTER	Painters,	POLLINGS	Long-slip
	Pertains,	PONDERED	Perdendo
	Repaints	PONDERER	Reponder
PINHEADS	Deanship,	PONTOONS	Spontoon
	Headpins	POPELING	Peopling
PINNINGS	Spinning	POPPLING	Plopping
PINTAILS	Tail-spin	PORINESS	Pression,
PIONEERS	Isoprene		Ropiness
PIPE-CLAY	Clay-pipe	PORTFIRE	Profiter
PISCATOR	Apricots,	PORTHOLE	Potholer
	Patricos	PORTINGS	Sporting
PISMIRES	Misprise	PORTIONS	Positron,
PISTOLED	Postiled		Sorption
PISTOLES	Spilotes	PORTSIDE	Diopters,
PLACINGS	Scalping		Dioptres,
PLAGUERS	Graupels,		Dipteros,
	Spergula		Peridots,
PLAINANT	Plantain		Proteids

POSHTEEN	Potheens	PRELEASE	Eel-spear
POSITION	Sopition	PRELUDES	Repulsed
POSITRON	Portions,	PREMATES	Presteam,
	Sorption		Temperas
POSTABLE	Potables	PREMIERS	Reprimes,
POST-FREE	Freepost		Simperer
POSTICHE	Potiches	PREMISES	Emprises,
POSTILED	Pistoled		Spiremes
POSTINGS	Signpost,	PREMORSE	Emperors
	Stopings	PRENATAL	Parental,
POSTLESS	Spotless,		Paternal
	Stopless	PRESAGES	Asperges
POSTLIKE	Spotlike	PRESENTS	Pertness,
POST-NOTE	Potstone,		Serpents
	Topstone	PRESERVE	Perverse
POSTURAL	Pulsator	PRESIDES	Despiser,
POSTURER	Sprouter,		Disperse,
	Troupers		Perseids
POTABLES	Postable	PRESOUND	Pounders
POTHEENS	Poshteen	PRESSING	Springes
POTHOLER	Porthole	PRESSION	Poriness,
POT-HOUSE	Housetop		Ropiness
POTICHES	Postiche	PRESS-UPS	Suppress
POT-PLANT	Plantpot	PRESSURE	Perusers
POT-ROAST	Taproots	PRESTEAM	Premates,
POTSTONE	Post-note,		Temperas
	Topstone	PRETONIC	Inceptor
POTTERED	Repotted	*PRETORIA	Priorate
POTTINGS	Spotting	PREVIOUS	Pervious,
POULTICE	Epulotic		Viperous
POUNDERS	Presound	PREVISED	Deprives
POWERMAN	Manpower	PREVOIDS	Disprove,
PRACTISE	Crispate,		Provides
	Picrates	PRIESTED	Respited
PRAETORS	Prorates,	PRIESTLY	Spritely
	Raptores	PRIMROSE	Promiser
PRAISING	Aspiring	PRINTERS	Reprints,
PRATTLES	Partlets,		Sprinter
	Platters,	PRIORATE	Pretoria
	Splatter	PRISONED	Disponer
PRAYINGS	Spraying	PRISTINE	Enspirit
PREBOAST	Probates	PROBATES	Pre-boast
PRECIOUS	Rice-soup	PROCURED	Producer
PREDATED	Departed	PRODUCER	Procured
PREDATES	Pederast,	PROFITER	Portfire
	Repasted	PROGGINS	Gropings
PREDATOR	Tear-drop	PROLAPSE	Sapropel
PRE-ENTER	Repenter	PROLATES	Petrosal,
PREIGNAC	Capering		Pole-star

PROMISEE	Reimpose	RACE-BALL	Caballer
PROMISER	Primrose	RACEMATE	Camerate,
PRORATES	Praetors,		Macerate
	Raptores	RACINESS	Arsenics,
PROSAIST	Airposts,		Cerasins,
	Protasis		Sarcines
PROSEMAN	Manropes	RAFT-ROPE	Forepart
PROSLAVE	Overlaps	RAGGLING	Gargling
PROSTYLE	Protyles	RAG-STONE	Estragon
PROTASIS	Airposts,	RAGTIMES	Magister,
	Prosaist		Migrates
PROTEASE	Asterope,	RAIMENTS	Instream,
	Operates,		Minarets
	Soap-tree	RAINTREE	Retainer
PROTEIDS	Diopters,	RAMBLING	Marbling
	Dioptres,	RANCHERO	Reanchor
	Dipteros,	RAPPAREE	Appearer,
	Peridots,		Reappear
	Portside	RAPTORES	Praetors,
PROTISTA	Patriots		Prorates
PROTYLES	Prostyle	RARERIPE	Repairer
PROVIDES	Disprove,	RATCHING	Charting
	Prevoids	RATEABLE	Tearable
PRUNINGS	Spurning	RATIONAL	Notarial
PSALMIST	Palmists	RATIONED	Deration,
PSALTERY	Plastery		Ordinate,
PSELLISM	Misspell		Rodentia
PSILOCIN	Cipolins	RATLINES	Alternis,
PTERALIA	Parietal		Entrails,
PUDICITY	Cupidity		Latrines,
PULPITER	Repulpit		Trenails
PULP-WOOD	Wood-pulp	RATLINGS	Starling,
PULSATOR	Postural		Trasling
PUNISHER	Repunish	RATSBANE	Ant-bears
PURPOSES	Supposer	RATTEENS	Entreats,
PURRINGS	Spurring		Seat-rent
PURSLANE	Supernal	RATTLERS	Startler
PURSUING	Usurping	REABSORB	Absorber
PYTHONIC	Hypnotic,	REACCEPT	Accepter
	Typhonic	REACHERS	Research,
			Searcher
		REACHEST	Acherset
QUAESTOR	Equators		Cheaters,
QUARTETS	Squatter		Recheats,
QUICKEST	Quickset		Teachers
QUICKSET	Quickest	REACTING	Argentic,
			Catering,
			Creating
		REACTION	Creation

REACTIVE	Creative
READJUST	Adjuster
READMITS	Distream,
	Misrated
READOPTS	Adopters,
	Asported
REAFFECT	Affecter
REAFFIRM	Affirmer
REAGENTS	Estrange,
	Grantees,
	Negaters,
	Segreant,
	Sergeant,
	Sternage
REALIGNS	Aligners,
	Engrails,
	Resignal
	Sanglier,
	Signaler
REALISED	Resailed
REALISTS	Alisters,
	Saltiers,
	Saltires,
	Slaister
REANCHOR	Ranchero
REANOINT	Anointer,
	Inornate
REANSWER	Answerer
REAPPEAL	Appealer
REAPPEAR	Appearer,
	Rapparee
REARGUED	Redargue
REARMING	Remargin
REARREST	Arrester
REASCEND	Ascender
REASCENT	Encastre,
	Sarcenet
REASSENT	Assenter,
	Earnests,
	Sarsenet
REASSERT	Asserter,
	Serrates
REASSIGN	Assigner,
	Seringas
REASSIST	Assister
REASSORT	Assertor,
	Assorter,
	Oratress,
	Roasters

REASSUME	Measures
REASSURE	Erasures
REASTING	Angriest,
	Astringe,
	Ganister,
	Granites,
	Ingrates,
	Tangiers
REATTACH	Attacher
REATTACK	Attacker
REATTAIN	Attainer
REATTEST	Attester
REAWAKEN	Awakener
REBALLOT	Balloter
REBATING	Berating
REBLEACH	Bleacher
REBOUNDS	Bounders,
	Suborned
REBUDGET	Budgeter
REBUTTAL	Burletta
REBUTTED	Buttered
REBUTTON	Buttoner
RECANTED	Cantered,
	Crenated,
	Decanter,
	Nectared
RECANTER	Recreant
RECEIVED	Deceiver
RECEMENT	Cementer,
	Cerement
RECESSED	Seceders
RECHARTS	Charters,
	Starcher
RECHEATS	Acherset,
	Cheaters,
	Reachest,
	Teachers
RECITALS	Articles,
	Selictar
RECKLESS	Clerkess
RECLEANS	Cleaners,
	Cleanser,
	Relances
RECLINED	Decliner
RECLINES	Licenser,
	Silencer
RECLUSES	Cureless
RECOASTS	Castores,
	Coarsest,
	Coasters

RECOATED	Decorate		Terreens,
RECOLOUR	Colourer		Terrenes
RECONVEY	Conveyer	REESTING	Energist,
RECORDER	Re-record		Integers,
RECOSTED	Corseted,		Retinges,
	Escorted		Steering
RECOUNTS	Cornutes,	RE-EXPAND	Expander
	Construe,	RE-EXPORT	Exporter
	Counters,	REFASTEN	Fastener,
	Trounces		Fenestra
RECOURSE	Resource	REFEREED	Free-reed
RECREANT	Recanter	REFERRED	Deferrer
RECUMBED	Cumbered	REFILTER	Filterer
RECUSANT	Centaurs,	REFINING	Infringe
	Etruscan	REFLOATS	Floaters,
RECUSING	Rescuing,		Forestal
	Securing	REFLOWED	Deflower,
REDARGUE	Reargued		Flowered
REDEFEAT	Defeater	REFLOWER	Flowerer
REDELESS	Reedless	REFOOTED	Deerfoot
REDEMISE	Remedies	REFOREST	Forester,
REDENTED	Tendered		Fosterer
REDESERT	Deserter	REFORMED	Deformer
REDESIGN	Designer,	REFUNDED	Underfed
	Enridges,	REGALIAN	Algerian
	Reedings,	REGALIAS	Algeria's,
	Resigned		Gasalier
REDIGEST	Digester,	REGALISM	Gremials
	Erdgeist	REGARDED	Degrader,
REDIVERT	Diverter,		Regraded
	Verditer	REGATHER	Gatherer
REDOLENT	Rondelet	REGELATE	Relegate
REDSHARE	Adherers,	REGIONAL	Geraniol
	Reshared	REGRADED	Degrader,
REEDINGS	Designer,		Regarded
	Enridges,	REGRANTS	Granters,
	Redesign,		Stranger
	Resigned	REHAMMER	Hammerer
REEDLESS	Redeless	REHARDEN	Hardener
REEDLING	Engirdle,	REHIDDEN	Hindered
	Lingered	REIMPORT	Importer
REED-STOP	Reposted	REIMPOSE	Promisee
RE-EMPLOY	Employer	REINDICT	Indicter,
RE-ENJOIN	Enjoiner		Indirect
RE-ENLIST	Enlister,	REINFECT	Infecter
	Leinster,	REINFEST	Infester
	Listener,	REINFORM	Informer,
	Re-enlist		Reniform
RE-ENTERS	Enteres,	REINSERT	Inserter,
	Resenter,		

		REMEDIES	Redemise
	Reinters,	REMITTER	Trimeter
	Rentiers,	REMOTION	Motioner
	Terrines	REMOULDS	Moulders,
REINSIST	Insister		Smoulder
REINTERS	Inserter,	REMOUNTS	Montures,
	Reinsert,		Mounters
	Rentiers,	REMURMUR	Murmurer
	Terrines	RENEGATE	Generate,
REINVENT	Inventer		Green-tea,
REINVEST	Servient		Teenager
REISSUED	Residues	RENIFORM	Informer,
RELANCES	Cleaners,		Reinform
	Cleanser,	RENOTICE	Erection,
	Recleans		Neoteric
RELAPSED	Pleaders,	RENOVATE	Overneat
	Repleads	RENTIERS	Inserter,
RELATING	Alerting,		Reinsert,
	Altering,		Reinters,
	Integral,		Terrines
	Triangle	RENUMBER	Numberer
RELATION	Oriental,	REOBTAIN	Baritone,
	Tirolean		Obtainer
RELATIVE	Levirate	REOFFEND	Offender
RELAUNCH	Launcher	RE-OILING	Religion
RELAYING	Layering,	REORDAIN	Ordainer
	Yearling	REPAINTS	Painters,
RELEASED	Resealed		Pertains,
RELEGATE	Regelate		Pinaster
RELETTER	Letterer	REPAIRER	Rareripe
RELEVANT	Levanter	REPARKED	Deer-park
RELIANCE	Cinereal	REPARTED	Departer
RELICKED	Deer-lick	REPARTEE	Pear-tree,
RELICTED	Derelict		Repeater
RELIGION	Re-oiling	REPASSES	Asperses,
RELISHES	Heirless,		Passeres
	Hireless	REPASTED	Pederast,
RELISTEN	Enlister,		Predates
	Leinster,	REPEATER	Pear-tree,
	Listener,		Repartee
	Re-enlist	REPENTED	Repetend
RELIVING	Reviling	REPENTER	Pre-enter
RÉMANNED	Mannered	REPERTOR	Reporter
REMARGIN	Rearming	REPETEND	Repented
REMARKET	Marketer	REPINING	Ripening
REMASTED	Mastered,	REPLAITS	Pilaster,
	Streamed		Plaister,
REMASTER	Masterer,		Plaiters
	Streamer	REPLEADS	Pleaders,
REMEDIAT	Diameter		Relapsed

REPLICAS	Calipers,	RESIDENT	Inserted
	Spiracle	RESIDING	Desiring,
REPLIEST	Epistler,		Ringside
	Perlites,	RESIDUES	Reissued
	Reptiles,	RESIGNAL	Aligners,
	Spirelet		Engrails,
REPOLISH	Polisher		Realigns,
REPONDER	Ponderer		Sanglier,
REPORTER	Repertor		Signaler
REPOSTED	Reed-stop	RESIGNED	Designer,
REPOTTED	Pottered		Enridges,
REPOUSSE	Espouser		Redesign,
REPRIMES	Premiers,		Reedings
	Simperer	RESILVER	Revilers,
REPRINTS	Printers,		Silverer,
	Sprinter		Sliverer
REPRISAL	Sarplier	RESINATA	Artesian,
REPTILES	Epistler,		Erastian
	Perlites,	RESINATE	Arsenite,
	Repliest,		Stearine,
	Spirelet		Teresian,
REPULPIT	Pulpiter		Teresina,
REPULSED	Preludes		Trainees
REPUNISH	Punisher	RESINOID	Derision,
REPUTING	Erupting		Ironside
RE-RAILED	Derailer	RESINOUS	Neurosis
RE-RECORD	Recorder	RESISTED	Sistered
REREWARD	Rewarder	RESISTOR	Roisters,
RESAILED	Realised		Sorriest
RESCREEN	Screener	RESITING	Strigine
RESCUING	Recusing,	RESKETCH	Sketcher
	Securing	RESMOOTH	Smoother
RESEALED	Released	RESOFTEN	Enforest,
RESEARCH	Reachers,		Softener
	Searcher	RESOLDER	Solderer
RESEASON	Seasoner	RESORTED	Restored,
RESECTED	Decreets,		Rostered
	Secreted	RESORTER	Restorer,
RESENTER	Enterers,		Retrorse
	Re-enters,	RESOUNDS	Dourness,
	Terreens,		Sounders
	Terrenes	RESOURCE	Recourse
RESERVED	Deserver,	RESPIRED	Serriped
	Reversed	RESPITED	Priested
RESERVER	Reverser	RESPLICE	Eclipser
RESHAKEN	Hearkens	RESPONSA	Personas
RESHARED	Adherers,	RESPREAD	Spreader
	Redshare	RESPRING	Springer
RESICKEN	Sickener	RESTABLE	Bleaters,
			Retables

Headword	Anagrams
RESTATED	Retasted
REST-HOME	Theorems
RESTITCH	Chitters, Stitcher
RESTLESS	Tressels
RESTORED	Resorted, Rostered
RESTORER	Resorter, Retrorse
RESTRAIN	Strainer, Terrains, Trainers, Transire
RESTRICT	Stricter
RESTRING	Ringster, Stringer
RESTRIVE	Reverist, Riverets, Riveters
RESTROVE	Evertors
RESTRUNG	Grunters
RESUBMIT	Imbrutes, Terbiums
RESUMMON	Summoner
RETABLES	Bleaters, Restable
RETAILED	Detailer
RETAINED	Detainer
RETAINER	Raintree
RETASTED	Restated
RETEMPER	Temperer
RETESTED	Detester
RETHATCH	Thatcher
RETHREAD	Threader
RETHRESH	Thresher
RETICLES	Sclerite, Tiercels
RETIMING	Ring-time
RETINGES	Energist, Integers, Reesting, Steering
RETINNED	Indenter, Intender, Interned
RETINUES	Esurient, Reunites
RETOSSED	Oersteds
RETRADES	Arrested, Retreads, Serrated, Treaders
RETREADS	Arrested, Retrades, Serrated, Treaders
RETRENCH	Trencher
RETRORSE	Resorter, Restorer
RETUNDED	Rudented
REUNITES	Esurient, Retinues
REVENANT	Venerant
REVERIST	Restrive, Riverets, Riveters
REVERSAL	Slaverer
REVERSED	Deserver, Reserved
REVERSER	Reserver
REVERSIS	Revisers
REVILERS	Resilver, Silverer, Sliverer
REVILING	Reliving
REVISERS	Reversis
REVOKING	Overking
REVOLUTE	Truelove
REWARDER	Rereward
REWEAKEN	Weakener
RIB-ROAST	Arborist
RICE-SOUP	Precious
RING-BONE	Enrobing
RING-DOVE	Dovering
RINGLESS	Slingers
RINGLETS	Sterling, Tinglers, Tringles
RING-LOCK	Rock-ling
RING-SIDE	Desiring, Residing
RINGSTER	Restring, Stringer
RING-TAIL	Trailing
RING-TIME	Retiming
RING-TOSS	Sortings
RIPENING	Repining
RIPPLETS	Stippler,

	Tipplers,	ROWELLED	Doweller,
	Tripples		Welldoer
RIPTIDES	Spirited	ROYALIST	Solitary
RITELESS	Leisters,	RUDENTED	Retunded
	Tireless	RUNCHING	Churning
RIVALING	Virginal	RUSTABLE	Baluster
RIVERETS	Restrive,	RUSTICAL	Curtails
	Reverist,	RUSTICLY	Crustily
	Riveters	RUSTLING	Lustring
RIVETERS	Restrive,	RUTHLESS	Hurtless
	Reverist,		Hustlers
	Riverets		
RIVETING	Tivering		
ROADBEDS	Adsorbed	SABELINE	Balinese,
ROADSIDE	Side-road		Base-line
ROADSMAN	Mandoras	SACCULAR	Accruals,
ROAMINGS	Moringas,		Caraculs
	Organism,	SAILABLE	Isabella
	Sinogram	SAINTING	Staining
ROARINGS	Garrison	SALARIES	Assailer
ROASTERS	Assertor,	SALEABLE	Leasable
	Assorter,	SALESMEN	Lameness,
	Oratress,		Maneless,
	Reassort		Nameless
ROASTING	Organist	SALIENTS	Eastlins,
ROCK-LING	Ring-lock		Staniels
ROCK-WOOD	Woodrock	SALIVANT	Valiants
RODENTIA	Deration,	SALIVATE	Aestival
	Ordinate,	SALLYING	Signally
	Rationed	SALT-COTE	Calottes
ROISTERS	Resistor,	SALTIERS	Alisters,
	Sorriest		Realists,
ROMANISE	Moraines		Saltires,
ROMANSCH	Monarchs,		Slaister
	Nomarchs	SALTIEST	Slatiest
RONDELET	Redolent	SALTIRES	Alisters,
RONDURES	Rounders,		Realists,
	Unorders		Saltiers,
ROOSTING	Stooring		Slaister
ROPINESS	Poriness,	SALTMINE	Ailments,
	Pression		Aliments,
ROSTERED	Resorted,		Smaltine
	Restored	SAMPHIRE	Seraphim
ROTATING	Troating	SANCTION	Canonist,
ROUND-ALL	All-round		Contains
ROUNDERS	Rondures,	SAND-BATH	Hatbands
	Unorders	SAND-IRON	Andirons,
ROUSTERS	Trousers		Ironsand
ROUTEING	Outreign	SANDIVER	Invaders

SAND-REEL	Leanders	SCHOOLED	Deschool
SANGLIER	Aligners,	SCHOONER	Coehorns
	Engrails,	*SCHUBERT	Butchers
	Realigns,	SCIENTER	Enticers,
	Resignal,		Secretin,
	Signaler		Tercines
SANGUINE	Guanines	SCIOLIST	Solicits
SANSERIF	Fairness	SCIURINE	Incisure
SAPROPEL	Prolapse	SCLERITE	Reticles,
SARCENET	Encastre,		Tiercels
	Reascent	SCLEROUS	Closures
SARCINES	Arsenics,	SCOLDING	Codlings,
	Cerasins,		Lingcods
	Raciness	SCOT-FREE	Cost-free,
SARCITIS	Triassic		Free-cost
SARDINES	Aridness	SCOURAGE	Courages
*SARDINIA	Diarians	SCOURERS	Coursers,
SARPLIER	Reprisal		Cursores
SARSENET	Assenter,	SCOURGED	Scrouged
	Earnests,	SCOURGER	Scrouger
	Reassent	SCOURING	Coursing
SATANISM	Mantissa,	SCOUTHER	Touchers
	Staminas	SCOWLING	Cowlings
SATELESS	Seatless	SCRABBLE	Clabbers
SATIABLE	Baalites,	SCRAMBLE	Cambrels,
	Labiates		Clambers,
SATINETS	Antistes,		Scambler
	Instates,	SCRAPING	Carpings,
	Titaness		Scarping
SAXICOLA	Coaxials	SCRATTLE	Clatters
SAXONIZE	Oxazines	SCRAWLER	Crawlers
SCALENUS	Unscales	SCREAMER	Amercers,
SCALPING	Placings		Creamers
SCAMBLER	Cambrels,	SCREENED	Secerned
	Clambers,	SCREENER	Rescreen
	Scramble	SCRIBBLE	Cribbles
SCANNING	Cannings	SCRODDLE	Coddlers
SCAPHITE	Hepatics,	SCROUGED	Scourged
	Pastiche	SCROUGER	Scourger
SCAPULAR	Capsular	SCULLING	Cullings
SCARIOUS	Urocissa	SCULLION	Cullions
SCARPING	Carpings,	SCURRIES	Cruisers
	Scraping	SCUTTLER	Clutters
SCELERAT	Telecars,	SEA-HORSE	Sea-shore
	Treacles	SEA-LEMON	Sea-melon
SCENICAL	Calcines	SEALINGS	Gainless,
SCEPTRAL	Spectral		Glassine,
SCHEMIST	Chemists		Leasings
SCHILLER	Chillers	SEA-MELON	Sea-lemon

SEAMSTER	Masseter,		Sergeant,
	Steamers		Sternage
SEA-PLANE	Spelaean	SEIZABLE	Sizeable
SEA-PLANT	Pleasant	SELECTED	Deselect
SEARCHER	Reachers,	SELECTOR	Corselet,
	Research		Electors,
SEARWOOD	Wood-sear		Electros
SEA-SHORE	Sea-horse	SELENITE	Enlistee
SEA-SNAIL	Nasalise	SELFSAME	Fameless
SEASONER	Reseason	SELICTAR	Articles,
SEATINGS	Eastings,		Recitals
	Giantess,	SEMINATE	Matinees
	Teasings	SEMITISM	Mistimes
SEATLESS	Sateless	SEMITONE	Monetise
SEAT-RENT	Entreats,	SEMOLINA	Laminose
	Ratteens	SENATORS	Essorant,
SECEDERS	Recessed		Star-nose,
SECERNED	Screened		Treasons
SECONDER	Censored,	SENORITA	Asterion
	Seed-corn	SEPALINE	Penalise
SECONDLY	Condyles	SEPALOID	Episodal,
SECRETED	Decreets,		Opalised
	Resected	SEPALOUS	Espousal
SECRETES	Sesterce	SEPTARIA	Aspirate,
SECRETIN	Enticers,		Parasite
	Scienter,	SERAGLIO	Girasole
	Tercines	SERAPHIC	Charpies
SECRETOR	Erectors	SERAPHIM	Samphire
SECURING	Rescuing,	SERAPIAS	Spiraeas
	Recusing	SERGEANT	Estrange,
SEDATIVE	Deviates		Grantees,
SEDERUNT	Dentures,		Greatens,
	Underset,		Negaters,
	Unrested		Reagents,
SEDIMENT	Dementis,		Segreant,
	Tidesmen		Sternage
SEDITION	Editions,	SERINGAS	Assigner,
	Tenioids		Reassign
SEED-BIRD	Bird-seed	SERMONIC	Cremosin,
SEED-CORN	Censored,		Incomers
	Seconder	SERPENTS	Pertness,
SEEDINGS	Edginess		Presents
SEEDSMEN	Demesnes	SERRATED	Arrested,
SEETHING	Sheeting		Retrades,
SEGREANT	Estrange,		Retreads,
	Grantees,		Treaders
	Greatens,	SERRATES	Asserter,
	Negaters,		Reassert
	Reagents,	SERRIPED	Respired

SERVABLE	Beslaver,	SIDE-LINE	Lineside
	Versable	SIDELONG	Glenoids
SERVIENT	Reinvest	SIDE-NOTE	Side-tone
SESTERCE	Secretes	SIDE-POST	Deposits,
SESTOLET	Teleosts		Topsides
SEVERING	Veerings	SIDE-ROAD	Roadside
SHABBILY	Babishly	SIDE-STEP	Despites
SHADDOCK	Haddocks	SIDE-TONE	Side-note
SHANTIES	Anthesis,	SIDEWAYS	Waysides
	Sheitans	SIGMATIC	Astigmic
SHARPING	Harpings,	SIGNABLE	Belgians,
	Phrasing		Bengalis,
SHEADING	Headings		Singable
SHEALING	Healings,	SIGNALER	Aligners,
	Leashing		Engrails,
SHEARING	Hearings,		Realigns,
	Hearsing		Resignal,
SHEAVING	Heavings		Sanglier
SHE-DEVIL	Dishevel	SIGNALLY	Sallying
SHEERING	Greenish	SIGNORAS	Assignor
SHEETING	Seething	SIGNPOST	Postings,
SHEITANS	Anthesis,		Stopings
	Shanties	SILENCED	Declines,
SHELL-EGG	Eggshell		Licensed
*SHERATON	Another's	SILENCER	Licenser,
SHIPLOAD	Haploids		Reclines
SHIPMATE	Mateship	SILICATE	Ciliates
SHIPPING	Hippings	SILVERED	Delivers,
SHOELESS	Hoseless		Desilver,
SHOOTING	Hootings,		Slivered
	Soothing	SILVERER	Resilver,
SHOOT-OFF	Offshoot		Revilers,
SHOP-DOOR	Hospodor		Sliverer
SHOPPING	Hoppings	SIMMERED	Immersed
SHOPWORK	Workshop	SIMPERER	Premiers,
SHOREMAN	Horseman		Reprimes
SHOREMEN	Horsemen	SIMULARS	Surmisal
SHOT-FREE	Free-shot	SINECURE	Insecure
SHOTTING	Tonights	SINGABLE	Belgians,
SHOUTING	Southing		Bengalis,
SHRUBBED	Bush-bred		Signable
SHUNTERS	Huntress	SINGLING	Gin-sling,
SHUNTING	Huntings		Slinging
SIAMANGS	Amassing,	SINOGRAM	Moringas,
	Gas-mains		Organism,
SICKENER	Resicken		Roamings
SIDEARMS	Misreads	SISTERED	Resisted
SIDECARS	Discrase	SIZEABLE	Seizable
SIDE-HILL	Hillside	SKELETAL	Lakelets

SKETCHER	Resketch	SMARTING	Migrants
SKILLING	Killings	SMATTERS	Mattress,
SKINHEAD	Headskin		Smartest
SKIRTING	Striking	SMELTERS	Termless
SLAISTER	Alisters,	SMOCKING	Mockings
	Realists,	SMOKABLE	Abelmosk
	Saltiers,	SMOOTHER	Resmooth
	Saltires	SMOULDER	Moulders,
SLANGING	Anglings		Remoulds
SLASHING	Lashings	SNATCHED	Stanched
SLATIEST	Saltiest	SNATCHER	Chanters,
SLATTERN	Trentals		Stancher
SLAVERER	Reversal	SNICKING	Nickings
SLEAVING	Leavings,	SNIGGLED	Geldings,
	Svengali		Sledging
SLEDGING	Geldings,	SNIPPING	Nippings
	Sniggled	SNOOPIER	Spoonier
SLEEPERS	Peerless	SNOOPING	Spooning
SLEEPING	Peelings	SNOWLESS	Slowness
SLEEP-OUT	Eel-pouts	SOAP-TREE	Asterope,
	Outsleep		Operates,
SLEETING	Gentiles,		Protease
	Steeling	SOCRATIC	Acrostic
SLEWINGS	Swingles,	SODA-LIME	Melodias
	Wingless	SOFTENER	Enforest,
SLICKETS	Stickles		Resoften
SLICKING	Lickings	SOLACERS	Lacrosse
SLIGHTED	Delights	SOLANDER	Ladrones
SLIME-PIT	Lime-pits	SOLDERER	Resolder
SLINGERS	Ringless	SOLECIST	Solstice
SLINGING	Gin-sling,	SOLENESS	Noseless
	Singling	SOLENOID	Eidolons
SLINKING	Inklings,	SOLICITS	Sciolist
	Linkings	SOLIDISM	Idolisms
SLIPOVER	Overslip	SOLIDIST	Idolists
SLIVERED	Delivers,	SOLITARY	Royalist
	Desilver,	SOLITUDE	Outslide,
	Silvered		Toluides
SLIVERER	Resilver,	SOLSTICE	Solecist
	Revilers,	SOMATISM	Atomisms
	Silverer	SOMATIST	Atomists
SLOGGING	Loggings	SOMBERLY	Sombrely
SLOW-DOWN	Low-downs	SOMBRELY	Somberly
SLOWNESS	Snowless	SONANCES	Canoness
SMALL-ALE	Lamellas	SONG-BIRD	Bird-song
SMALTINE	Ailments,	SOOTHING	Hootings,
	Aliments,		Shooting
	Saltmine	SOPITION	Position
SMARTEST	Mattress,	SORPTION	Portions,
	Smatters		Positron

SORRIEST	Resistor,	SPLAYING	Palsying
	Roisters	SPLENDID	Spindled
SORTABLE	Bloaters,	SPLENIUS	Spinules
	Storable	SPLITTER	Triplets
SORTINGS	Ring-toss	SPODIUMS	Podismus
SORTMENT	Torments	SPONSION	Opsonins
SOUNDERS	Dourness,	SPONTOON	Pontoons
	Resounds	SPOONIER	Snoopier
SOUNDING	Undoings	SPOONING	Snooping
SOURDINE	Dourines	SPORADIC	Picadors
SOUTHING	Shouting	SPORTING	Portings
SPANIELS	Painless	SPOTLESS	Postless,
SPARABLE	Parables		Stopless
SPARGING	Grasping	SPOTLIKE	Postlike
SPARIDAE	Paradise	SPOTTING	Pottings
SPARLING	Springal	SPRAINTS	Spirants
SPARSELY	Parsleys	SPRAYING	Prayings
SPEARMAN	Parmesan	SPREADER	Respread
SPECTRAL	Sceptral	SPRINGAL	Sparling
SPECTRUM	Crumpets	SPRINGER	Respring
SPELAEAN	Sea-plane	SPRINGES	Pressing
SPERGULA	Graupels,	SPRINTER	Printers,
	Plaguers		Reprints
SPERM-OIL	Implores,	SPRITELY	Priestly
	Pelorism	SPROUTER	Posturer,
SPHRAGID	Digraphs		Troupers
SPIKELET	Pikelets	SPURNING	Prunings
SPILOTES	Pistoles	SPURRING	Purrings
SPINDLED	Splendid	SQUATTER	Quartets
SPINNING	Pinnings	SQUIREEN	Enquires
SPINSTRY	Trypsins	*SRINAGAR	Arraigns
SPINULES	Splenius	STABLING	Blasting
SPIRACLE	Calipers,	STACCATO	Toccatas
	Replicas	STAINING	Sainting
SPIRAEAS	Serapias	STAKE-OUT	Take-outs
SPIRANTS	Spraints	STALLAGE	Tallages
SPIRELET	Epistler,	STAMINAL	Talisman
	Perlites,	STAMINAS	Mantissa,
	Repliest,		Satanism
	Reptiles	STAMPEDE	Step-dame
SPIREMES	Emprises,	STAMPING	Tampings
	Premises	STANCHED	Snatched
SPIRITED	Riptides	STANCHER	Chanters,
SPIRTING	Striping		Snatcher
SPIT-CURL	Culprits	STANDEES	Assented,
SPLASHER	Plashers		East-ends
SPLATTER	Partlets,	STANDOUT	Oustand
	Platters,	STANHOPE	Phaetons
	Prattles	STANIELS	Eastlins,
			Salients

*STANMORE	Storeman	STERNITE	Interest,
STANNATE	Natantes,		Interset,
	Tannates		Trestine
STAPLING	Platings	STIBBLER	Tribbles
STARCHER	Charters,	STICKETH	Thickest,
	Recharts		Thickets,
STARLING	Ratlings,		Thickset
	Trasling	STICKING	Tickings
STAR-NOSE	Essorant,	STICKLER	Strickle,
	Senators,		Ticklers,
	Treasons		Trickles
STARTLER	Rattlers	STICKLES	Slickest
STATABLE	Abbetals,	STILLAGE	Legalist,
	Tastable		Tillages
STATICAL	Cat's-tail,	STILLING	Tillings
	Cattails	STILTING	Tiltings,
STEALERS	Tearless,		Titlings
	Tesseral	STING-RAY	Straying
STEALING	Galenist,	STINTING	Tintings
	Gelatins,	STIPPLER	Ripplets,
	Genitals		Tipplers,
STEAM-DRY	Dry-steam		Tripples
STEAMERS	Masseter,	STITCHER	Chitters,
	Seamster		Restitch
STEARINE	Arsenite,	STOATING	Toasting
	Resinate,	STOICISM	Misticos
	Teresian,	STOMATIC	Masticot
	Teresina,	STOOLING	Toolings
	Trainees	STOOMING	Mootings
STEELING	Gentiles,	STOORING	Roosting
	Sleeting	STOPINGS	Postings,
STEENBOK	Betokens		Signpost
STEEPLED	Depletes	STOPLESS	Postless,
STEERAGE	Etageres		Spotless
STEERING	Energist,	STOP-OVER	Overpost,
	Integers,		Overtops
	Reesting,	STOPPING	Toppings
	Retinges	STORABLE	Bloaters,
STEP-DAME	Stampede		Sortable
STERLING	Ringlets,	STOREMAN	Stanmore
	Tinglers,	STOREYED	Oystered
	Tringles	STOWABLE	Bestowal
STERNAGE	Estrange,	STRAINED	Anti-reds,
	Grantees,		Detrains,
	Greatens,		Trade-ins
	Negaters,	STRAINER	Restrain,
	Reagents		Terrains,
	Segreant,		Trainers,
	Sergeant		Transire

STRAITEN	Intreats,	SUB-TOPIC	Sub-optic
	Nitrates,	SUBVERSE	Subserve
	Tertians	SUITINGS	Tissuing
STRAMMEL	Trammels	SULTANIC	Lunatics
STRANDED	Darndest	SUMMONER	Resummon
STRANGER	Granters,	SUN-BLIND	Unblinds
	Regrants	SUNDERED	Denuders
STRANGLE	Tanglers,	SUNDRIES	Insureds
	Trangles	SUNLIGHT	Hustling
STRAPPER	Trappers	SUPERNAL	Purslane
STRAYING	Sting-ray	SUPINATE	Petunias
STREAMED	Mastered,	SUPPLIER	Periplus
	Remasted	SUPPOSER	Purposes
STREAMER	Masterer,	SUPPRESS	Press-ups
	Remaster	SURMISAL	Simulars
STRESSED	Desserts,	SURNAMED	Duramens,
	Destress		Maunders
STREWING	Wresting	*SVENGALI	Leavings,
STRICKLE	Stickler,		Sleaving
	Ticklers,	SWADDLER	Dawdlers,
	Trickles		Waddlers
STRICTER	Restrict	SWAGGING	Waggings
STRIDDLE	Tiddlers	SWARDING	Drawings,
STRIDENT	Tridents		Wardings
STRIGINE	Resiting	SWASHING	Washings
STRIKING	Skirting	SWEARING	Wearings
STRINGER	Restring,	SWEEPING	Weepings
	Ringster	SWIGGING	Wiggings
STRINKLE	Tinklers,	SWINDGED	Weddings
	Trinkles	SWINDLED	Dwindles
STRIPING	Spirting	SWINDLES	Wildness,
STRIPPER	Trippers		Windless
STROLLER	Trollers	SWINGLES	Slewings,
STRUMPET	Trumpets		Wingless
STUBBING	Tubbings	SWINKING	Winkings
STUMBLER	Tumblers,	SYBARITE	Bestiary
	Tumbrels	SYNOCHAL	Halycons
STUNTING	Nuttings		
SUBAHDAR	Bahadurs	TABLEAUS	Sub-alate
SUB-ALATE	Tableaus	TABLE-CUT	Cuttable
SUB-CLERK	Bucklers	TABORING	Aborting,
SUBLIMES	Sub-smile		Borating
SUB-OPTIC	Sub-topic	TABOURET	Obturate
SUBORDER	Bordures	TACTIONS	Oscitant
SUBORNED	Bounders,	TAENIOID	Ideation
	Rebounds	TAIL-COAT	Coat-tail
SUBSERVE	Subverse	TAIL-SPIN	Pintails
SUBSIDER	Disburse	TAKE-DOWN	Down-take
SUB-SMILE	Sublimes	TAKE-OUTS	Stake-out

TAKE-OVER	Overtake	TELECARS	Scelerat,
TALISMAN	Staminal		Treacles
TALLAGES	Stallage	TELEOSTS	Sestolet
TALLYMEN	Mentally	TELESTIC	Testicle
TALPIDAE	Lapidate	TEMPERAS	Premates,
TAMANOIR	Animator		Presteam
TAMELESS	Mateless,	TEMPERER	Retemper
	Meatless	TENDERED	Redented
TAMPINGS	Stamping	TENESMUS	Muteness
TANGIBLE	Belating,	TENORIST	Tritones
	Bleating	TENT-ROPE	Entrepot
*TANGIERS	Angriest,	TERBIUMS	Imbrutes,
	Astringe,		Resubmit
	Ganister,	TERCINES	Enticers,
	Granites,		Scienter,
	Ingrates,		Secretin
	Reasting	*TERESIAN	Arsenite,
TANGLERS	Strangle,		Resinate,
	Trangles		Stearine,
TANGLING	Gnatling		Teresina,
TANNATES	Natantes,		Trainees
	Stannate	*TERESINA	Arsenite,
TANTRISM	Transmit		Resinate,
TAPE-LINE	Petaline		Stearine,
TAPROOTS	Pot-roast		Teresian,
TAPWATER	Water-tap		Trainees
TARRAGON	Arrogant	TERMINAL	Tram-line
TAR-WATER	Water-rat	TERMINUS	Unmiters,
TASTABLE	Abbetals,		Unmitres
	Statable	TERMLESS	Smelters
TAUNTING	Attuning	TERRAINS	Restrain,
TAUTNESS	Unstates		Strainer,
TEACHERS	Acherset,		Trainers,
	Cheaters,		Transire
	Reachest,	TERREENS	Enterers,
	Recheats		Re-enters,
TEACHING	Cheating		Resenter,
TEAMWORK	Workmate		Terrenes
TEARABLE	Rateable	TERRENES	Enterers,
TEAR-DROP	Predator		Re-enters,
TEARLESS	Stealers,		Resenter,
	Tesseral		Terreens
TEASINGS	Eastings,	TERRINES	Inserter,
	Giantess,		Reinsert,
	Seatings		Reinters,
TECTONIC	Concetti		Rentiers
TEENAGER	Generate,	TERTIANS	Intreats,
	Green-tea,		Nitrates,
	Renegate		Straiten

TESSERAL	Stealers,	TIDINESS	Insisted
	Tearless	TIERCELS	Reticles,
TESTACEA	Acetates		Sclerite
TESTATOR	Attestor	TILLAGES	Legalist,
TEST-CASE	Cassette		Stillage
TESTICLE	Telestic	TILLINGS	Stilling
TETANICS	Entastic,	TILTINGS	Stilting,
	Nictates		Titlings
TETANISE	Anisette	TIMARIOT	Imitator
TETANOID	Antidote	TIME-CARD	Dermatic
THATCHER	Rethatch	TINGLERS	Ringlets,
THATCHES	Hatchets		Sterling,
THEISTIC	Ethicist		Tringles
THEOLOGY	Ethology	TINGLING	Glinting
THEOREMS	Rest-home	TINKLERS	Strinkle,
THEORIES	Isothere,		Trinkles
	Theorise	TINSTONE	Tontines
THEORISE	Isothere,	TINTINGS	Stinting
	Theories	TIPPLERS	Ripplets,
THEORIST	Thorites		Stippler,
THICKEST	Sticketh,		Tripples
	Thickets,	TIRELESS	Leisters,
	Thickset		Riteless
THICKETS	Sticketh,	TIROLEAN	Oriental,
	Thickest,		Relation
	Thickset	TISSUING	Suitings
THICKSET	Sticketh,	TITANESS	Antistes,
	Thickest,		Instates,
	Thickets		Satinets
THORACIC	Trochaic	TITANISM	Imitants
THORITES	Theorist	TITHABLE	Hittable
THORIUMS	Humorist	TITLINGS	Stilting,
THOUSAND	Handouts		Tiltings
THREADER	Rethread	TITRATED	Attrited
THRENODE	Dethrone	TITRATES	Tri-state
THRESHER	Rethresh	TITULARS	Altruist,
THRONING	Northing		Ultraist
THROWING	Ingrowth,	TIVERING	Riveting
	Worthing	TOASTING	Stoating
THROW-OUT	Outthrow,	TOCCATAS	Staccato
	Outworth	TOLLAGES	Log-slate
THYROIDS	Thyrsoid	TOLUIDES	Outslide,
THYRSOID	Thyroids		Solitude
TICKINGS	Sticking	TONELESS	Noteless
TICKLERS	Stickler,	TONIGHTS	Shotting
	Strickle,	TONSURED	Unsorted,
	Trickles		Unstored
TIDDLERS	Striddle	TONTINES	Tinstone
TIDESMEN	Dementis,	TOOLINGS	Stooling
	Sediment		

TOPOLOGY	Optology		Serrated
TOPOTYPE	Optotype	TREADING	Derating,
TOPPINGS	Stopping		Gradient
TOPSIDES	Deposits,	TREASONS	Essorant,
	Side-post		Senators,
TOPSTONE	Post-note,		Star-nose
	Potstone	TREATIES	Iterates,
TORMENTS	Sortment		Treatise
TORSADES	Assorted	TREATISE	Iterates,
TOTALLED	Allotted		Treaties
TOUCHERS	Scouther	TREE-CRAB	Crabtree
TOUSLING	Tung-oils	TREENAIL	Elaterin,
TOWNLESS	Wontless		Entailer
TRADE-INS	Anti-reds,	TRENAILS	Entrails,
	Detrains,		Latrines,
	Strained		Ratlines
TRAILING	Ringtail	TRENCHER	Retrench
TRAINEES	Arsenite,	TRENTALS	Slattern
	Resinate,	TREPHINE	Nephrite
	Stearine,	TRESSELS	Restless
	Teresian,	TRESTINE	Interest,
	Teresina		Interset,
TRAINERS	Restrain,		Sternite
	Strainer,	TREY-TINE	Entirety,
	Terrains,		Eternity
	Transire	TRIADIST	Distrait
TRAINING	Grain-tin	TRIALISM	Mistrial
TRAIPSES	Pastries,	TRIANGLE	Alerting,
	Piastres		Altering,
TRAM-LINE	Terminal		Integral,
TRAMMELS	Strammel		Relating
TRANGLES	Strangle,	TRIAPSAL	Partials
	Tanglers	TRIASSIC	Sarcitis
TRANSEPT	Patterns	TRIBBLES	Stibbler
TRANSIRE	Restrain,	TRIBOLET	Libretto
	Strainer,	TRIBUNAL	Turbinal
	Terrains,	TRIBUTES	Butteris
	Trainers	TRICHION	Ornithic
TRANSMIT	Tantrism	TRICKLES	Stickler,
TRAPPEAN	Apparent		Strickle,
TRAPPERS	Strapper		Ticklers
TRASLING	Ratlings,	TRIDENTS	Strident
	Starling	TRIFLING	Flirting
TRAVERSE	Averters	TRIMETER	Remitter
TREACLES	Scelerat,	TRINGLES	Ringlets,
	Telecars		Sterling,
TREADERS	Arrested,		Tinglers
	Retrades,	TRINKLES	Strinkle
	Retreads,		Tinklers

TRIPEDAL	Dipteral	ULTRAIST	Altruist,
TRIPLETS	Splitter		Titulars
TRIPPERS	Stripper	UMBELLAR	Umbrella
TRIPPLES	Ripplets,	UMBRELLA	Umbellar
	Stippler,	UNBELIED	Unedible
	Tipplers	UNBLINDS	Sun-blind
TRIREMES	Merriest,	UNBOILED	Unilobed
	Miterers	UNBOMBED	Unmobbed
TRI-STATE	Titrates	UNBRIBED	Unribbed
TRITONES	Tenorist	UNBURDEN	Unburned
*TRITONIS	Introits	UNBURNED	Unburden
TROATING	Rotating	UNCARTED	Uncrated,
TROCHAIC	Thoracic		Underact,
TROCHLEA	Chlorate		Untraced
TROLLERS	Stroller	UNCASKED	Unsacked
TROUNCES	Cornutes,	UNCAUSED	Unsauced
	Construe,	UNCIFORM	Cuniform,
	Counters,		Nuciform
	Recounts	UNCORKED	Unrocked
TROUPERS	Posturer,	UNCRATED	Uncarted,
	Sprouter		Underact,
TROUSERS	Rousters		Untraced
TROUTING	Tutoring	UNDASHED	Unshaded
TROUVERE	Overture	UNDENTED	Untended
TRUELOVE	Revolute	UNDERACT	Uncarted,
TRUMPETS	Strumpet		Uncrated,
TRYPSINS	Spinstry		Untraced
TUBBINGS	Stubbing	UNDERAGE	Ungeared
TUMBLERS	Stumbler,	UNDERAID	Unraided
	Tumbrels	UNDERARM	Unmarred
TUMBRELS	Stumbler,	UNDER-DOG	Grounded,
	Tumblers		Under-god
TUNG-OILS	Tousling	UNDERFED	Refunded
TUNGSTIC	Cuttings	UNDER-GOD	Grounded,
TURBANED	Bread-nut		Under-dog
TURBINAL	Tribunal	UNDERPAY	Unprayed
TURNDOWN	Down-turn	UNDERSEA	Unseared
TURNINGS	Unstring	UNDERSET	Dentures,
TURNOVER	Overturn		Sederunt,
TUTELARS	Lustrate		Unrested
TUTORING	Trouting	UNDOINGS	Sounding
TWISTING	Wittings	UNDRAPES	Unparsed,
TYPHONIC	Hypnotic,		Unrasped,
	Pythonic		Unspared,
TYROLEAN	Ornately		Unspread
		UNEDIBLE	Unbelied
		UNFABLED	Fundable
ULTIMATE	Mutilate	UNFARMED	Unframed
ULTRAISM	Altruism,	UNFISTED	Unsifted
	Muralist		

UNFLATED	Flaunted	UNRENTED	Untender
UNFOLDER	Flounder	UNREPAID	Unpaired
UNFORCED	Frounced	UNRESTED	Dentures,
UNFRAMED	Unfarmed		Sederunt,
UNGAINLY	Unlaying		Underset
UNGEARED	Underage	UNRIBBED	Unbribed
UNGILDED	Deluding,	UNRIDGED	Ungirded
	Indulged	UNROCKED	Uncorked
UNGIRDED	Unridged	UNROUTED	Untoured
UNHASPED	Unphased,	UNRUINED	Uninured
	Unshaped	UNSACKED	Uncasked
UNHORSED	Unshored	UNSACRED	Durances,
UNILOBED	Unboiled		Unscared
UNINURED	Unruined	UNSALTED	Unslated,
UNIONISM	Misunion		Unstaled
UNKILNED	Unlinked	UNSASHED	Unshades
UNLAYING	Ungainly	UNSAUCED	Uncaused
UNLEASED	Unsealed	UNSCALES	Scalenus
UNLINKED	Unkilned	UNSCARED	Durances,
UNLOOPED	Unpooled		Unsacred
UNLUMPED	Unplumed	UNSEALED	Unleased
UNMARRED	Underarm	UNSEARED	Undersea
UNMASHED	Unshamed	UNSEATED	Unsedate,
UNMITERS	Terminus,		Unteased
	Unmitres	UNSEDATE	Unseated,
UNMITRES	Terminus,		Unteased
	Unmiters	UNSERVED	Unversed
UNMOBBED	Unbombed	UNSETTLE	Lunettes
UNMODEST	Demounts	UNSHADED	Undashed
UNNETTED	Untented	UNSHADES	Unsashed
UNORDERS	Rondures,	UNSHAMED	Unmashed
	Rounders	UNSHAPED	Unhasped,
UNPAIRED	Unrepaid		Unphased
UNPARSED	Undrapes,	UNSHORED	Unhorsed
	Unrasped,	UNSIFTED	Unfisted
	Unspared,	UNSIGHTS	Hustings
	Unspread	UNSIGNED	Unsinged
UNPHASED	Unhasped,	UNSINGED	Unsigned
	Unshaped	UNSLATED	Unsalted,
UNPLAITS	Nuptials		Unstaled
UNPLUMED	Unlumped	UNSLICED	Includes
UNPOOLED	Unlooped	UNSOILED	Delusion
UNPRAYED	Underpay	UNSOMBER	Unsombre
UNRAIDED	Underaid	UNSOMBRE	Unsomber
UNRAISED	Denarius	UNSORTED	Tonsured,
UNRASPED	Undrapes,		Unstored
	Unparsed,	UNSPARED	Undrapes,
	Unspared,		Unparsed,
	Unspread		Unrasped,
			Unspread

UNSPOILT	Plotinus	*VERONESE	Overseen
UNSPREAD	Undrapes,	VERSABLE	Beslaver,
	Unparsed,		Servable
	Unrasped,	VERSELET	Leverets
	Unspared	VESICANT	Cistvaen
UNSTABLE	Abluents	VILENESS	Evilness,
UNSTALED	Unsalted,		Liveness,
	Unslated		Veinless
UNSTATED	Untasted	VIOLATED	Dovetail
UNSTATES	Tautness	VIOLENTS	Novelist
UNSTORED	Tonsured,	VIPEROUS	Pervious,
	Unsorted		Previous
UNSTRING	Turnings	VIRGINAL	Rivaling
UNTASTED	Unstated	VIRTUOSE	Vitreous
UNTEASED	Unseated,	VISCERAL	Calivers,
	Unsedate		Claviers
UNTENDED	Undented	VISITANT	Nativist
UNTENDER	Unrented	VITAMINS	Nativism
UNTENTED	Unnetted	VITREOUS	Virtuose
UNTHRUST	Untruths	VOCALIST	Voltaics
UNTILTED	Untitled	VOLTAICS	Vocalist
UNTIMELY	Minutely		
UNTIMOUS	Mutinous		
UNTITLED	Untilted	WADDLERS	Dawdlers,
UNTOURED	Unrouted		Swaddler
UNTRACED	Uncarted,	WADDLING	Dawdling
	Uncrated,	WAGGINGS	Swagging
	Underact	WAISTERS	Waitress
UNTRUTHS	Unthrust	WAITRESS	Waisters
UNVERSED	Unserved	WANDLIKE	Dawnlike
UPLANDER	Pendular	WARBLING	Brawling
UROCISSA	Scarious	WARDINGS	Drawings,
USURPING	Pursuing		Swarding
		WARDROBE	Drawbore
		WASHDOWN	Downwash
VACATION	Cavation,	WASHINGS	Swashing
	Octavian	WATCHDOG	Dog-watch
VAGINATE	Navigate	WATCH-OUT	Outwatch
VALIANTS	Salivant	WATER-DOG	Water-god
VEERINGS	Severing	WATER-GAS	Gas-water
VEINLESS	Evilness,	WATER-GOD	Water-dog
	Liveness,	WATER-HEN	Wreathen
	Vileness	WATER-ICE	Ice-water
VENALITY	Natively	WATER-RAT	Tar-water
VENATION	Innovate	WATER-TAP	Tap-water
VENERANT	Revenant	WAYSIDES	Sideways
VENERATE	Enervate	WEAKENER	Reweaken
VERDITER	Diverter,	WEARINGS	Swearing
	Redivert	WEDDINGS	Swindged

WEEPINGS	Sweeping	WOOD-SEAR	Searwood
WEIGH-OUT	Outweigh	WOOD-SEER	Wood-sere
WELLDOER	Doweller,	WOOD-SERE	Wood-seer
	Rowelled	WOODSKIN	Inkwoods
WENCHERS	Wrenches	WOOD-WORM	Wormwood
WHEATEAR	Aweather	WORDINGS	Drowsing
WHEREOFS	Foreshew	WORKMATE	Teamwork
WHEREONS	Heronsew,	WORKSHOP	Shopwork
	Nowheres	WORM-FISH	Fish-worm
WHOSEVER	Howevers	WORMWOOD	Woodworm
WIDENESS	Dewiness	*WORTHING	Ingrowth,
WIGGINGS	Swigging		Throwing
WILDNESS	Swindles,	WREATHEN	Water-hen
	Windless	WRENCHES	Wenchers
WINDLESS	Swindles,	WRESTING	Strewing
	Wildness		
WINGLESS	Slewings,		
	Swingles	XANTHEIN	Xanthine
WINKINGS	Swinking	XANTHINE	Xanthein
WITTINGS	Twisting		
WONTLESS	Townless		
WOODCHAT	Chatwood	YEARLING	Layering,
WOOD-PULP	Pulp-wood		Relaying
WOODROCK	Rock-wood		

Nine letters

ABANDONER	Reabandon	ALTERNATS	Alterants,
ABHORRENT	Earth-born		Translate
ABORIGINE	Baignoire	AMPLENESS	Ensamples
ABOUT-TURN	Turnabout	ANACRUSES	Assurance
ACALEPHAN	Acephalan	ANALGESIC	Angelicas
ACCIDENTS	Desiccant	ANALOGIES	Analogise
ACCLAIMER	Reacclaim	ANALOGISE	Analogies
ACCOUTERS	Accoutres,	ANALOGIST	Nostalgia
	Coruscate	ANATOMIES	Anatomise
ACCOUTRES	Accouters,	ANATOMISE	Anatomies
	Coruscate	ANCESTRAL	Lancaster
ACEPHALAN	Acalephan	ANDESITIC	Indicates
ACETAMIDE	Emaciated	*ANDROCLES	Colanders
ACIERATED	Eradicate	ANGELICAL	Englacial,
ACROTISMS	Castroism,		Galenical
	Ostracism	ANGELICAS	Analgesic
ADDRESSER	Readdress	ANGERLESS	Largeness
ADMINICLE	Medicinal	ANGLESITE	Galenites,
ADMONITOR	Dominator		Gelatines
ADSORBATE	Tea-boards	*ANGOSTURA	Argonauts
ADULATION	Laudation	ANICONISM	Insomniac
ADULATORY	Laudatory	ANICONIST	Inactions,
AEROLOGIC	Areologic		Nicotians,
AEROMETER	Areometer		Onanistic
AFFRONTER	Reaffront	ANTELOPES	Pleonaste
ALCHEMIES	Alchemise	ANTENATAL	Atlantean
ALCHEMISE	Alchemies	ANTIDOTES	Stationed
ALIENATOR	Rationale	ANTIGENIC	Gentianic
ALIGNMENT	Lamenting	ANTIMONIC	Antinomic
ALINEMENT	Lineament	ANTINOMIC	Antimonic
ALLOTTING	Totalling	ANTIPHONY	Typhonian
ALMANDITE	Laminated	ANTI-TRADE	Attainder
ALSATIANS	Assailant	APERIENTS	Postareen
ALTERANTS	Alternats,	APHERESIS	Pharisees
	Translate	APHETIZED	Hepatized

231

APOLOGIES	Apologise	BACKWARDS	Drawbacks
APOLOGISE	Apologies	BACTERIAL	Calibrate
APPLAUDER	Reapplaud	BACULITES	Bisulcate
APPOINTER	Reappoint	BAIGNOIRE	Aborigine
APSIDIOLE	Episodial	BALE-FIRES	Bas-relief
ARCHERESS	Searchers	BANDEROLE	Bandoleer
AREOLOGIC	Aerologic	BANDOLEER	Banderole
AREOMETER	Aerometer	BARGAINED	Gabardine
*ARGENTINA	Tanagrine	BASANITES	Sebastian
ARGENTINE	Tangerine	BAS-RELIEF	Bale-fires
ARGENTITE	Integrate	BASSETING	Beastings
ARGONAUTS	Angostura	BEARDLESS	Breadless
*ARMSTRONG	Strongarm	BEASTINGS	Basseting
ARSENICAL	Carnalise	BECHARMED	Chambered
ASCENSION	Canonises	BESAINTED	Bestained
ASCERTAIN	Cartesian,	BESTAINED	Besainted
	Sectarian	BIANGULAR	Bulgarian
ASCITICAL	Sciatical	BIGENTIAL	Ignitable
ASHLERING	Narghiles,	BILL-BOARD	Broadbill
	Nargilehs,	BIRGANDER	Debarring
	Shearling	BISULCATE	Baculites
ASSAILANT	Alsatians	BOARD-FOOT	Foot-board
ASSERTION	Senoritas	BOARDINGS	Signboard
ASSESSING	Gassiness	BOATHOUSE	Houseboat
ASSISTANT	Satanists	BRAINCASE	Carabines
ASSURANCE	Anacruses	BRAKELESS	Breakless
ASTHENICS	Caithness	BRASSERIE	Brassiere
ASTRINGED	Gradients	BRASSIERE	Brasserie
ASTROPHEL	Plethoras	BREAD-CORN	Corn-bread
ASYNDETIC	Syndicate	BREADLESS	Beardless
ATLANTEAN	Antenatal	BREAKLESS	Brakeless
ATTAINDER	Anti-trade	BREAST-PIN	Step-bairn
ATTEMPTER	Reattempt	BRIEFLESS	Fiberless,
ATTENTIVE	Tentative		Fibreless
ATTRACTER	Reattract	BROADBILL	Bill-board
ATTRITING	Titrating	BROAD-HEAD	Headboard
ATTRITION	Titration	BROADSIDE	Sideboard
AUCTIONED	Cautioned,	BROADTAIL	Tail-board
	Education,	BRUSHLESS	Shrubless
	Noctuidae	BRUSHLIKE	Shrublike
AUTHORESS	Share-outs	*BULGARIAN	Biangular
AVERTIBLE	Veritable	BURNED-OUT	Out-burned
		BURN-SIDES	Sideburns
		BUTTERING	Rebutting
BACK-CHECK	Check-back	BUTTER-NUT	Nut-butter
BACKCLOTH	Clothback	BYSTANDER	Stander-by
BACKSHORE	Horseback		
BACK-SWEPT	Swept-back		
BACK-SWING	Swing-back		

*CAITHNESS	Asthenics	CERTOSINA	Creations,
CALENDERS	Encradles,		Narcotise,
	Esclandre		Reactions
CALENTURE	Crenulate	CERULEINS	Licensure
CALIBRATE	Bacterial	CERUSITES	Cerussite
CALIPHATE	Hepatical	CERUSSITE	Cerusites
CALLOSITY	Stoically	CESSATION	Canoeists
CAMERATED	Demarcate,	CHAMBERED	Becharmed
	Macerated	CHANNELER	Rechannel
CANEPHORE	Chaperone	CHAPERONE	Canephore
CANE-SUGAR	Sugar-cane	CHAPTERED	Repatched
CANOEISTS	Cessation	CHARACINS	Saccharin
CANONISES	Ascension	CHARRETTE	Chatterer
CANTERING	Recanting	CHARTERED	Three-card
CANTINESS	Incessant,	CHARTERER	Recharter
	Instances	CHATTERER	Charrette
CAPSULARY	Scapulary	CHARTISMS	Christmas
CAPSULATE	Scapulate	CHEATABLE	Teachable
CARABINES	Braincase	CHECK-BACK	Back-check
CARCINOMA	Macaronic	CHERALITE	Etherical,
CARNALISE	Arsenical		Heretical
*CAROLINES	Censorial	CHEST-NOTE	Chest-tone
CAROLLING	Collaring	CHEST-TONE	Chest-note
CARTESIAN	Ascertain,	CHORISTER	Rhetorics
	Sectarian	CHRISTIAN	Christina,
CART-HORSE	Orchestra		Trichinas
CARUCATES	Crustacea	*CHRISTINA	Christian,
CASTALIAN	Satanical		Trichinas
*CASTROISM	Acrotisms,	CHRISTMAS	Chartisms
	Ostracism	CHROMATES	Stomacher
CATALOGUE	Coagulate	CISTERNAL	Clarinets,
CATECHISM	Schematic		Larcenist
CAT-SILVER	Verticals	CLARINETS	Cisternal,
CAUTIONED	Auctioned,		Larcenist
	Education,	CLAUSTRAL	Lacustral
	Noctuidae	CLAYMORES	Lacrymose
CAUTIONER	Cointreau,	CLEANSERS	Clearness
	Recaution	CLEARNESS	Cleansers
CEILINGED	Diligence	CLIENTAGE	Genetical
CELANDINE	Decennial	CLOTHBACK	Backcloth
CENSORIAL	Carolines	COAGULATE	Catalogue
CENTIARES	Creatines,	COASTLINE	Sectional
	Iterances,	COETERNAL	Tolerance
	Nectarise	COGNATION	Contagion
CENTURION	Continuer	COGNITION	Incognito
CERTIFIED	Cretified,	COINTREAU	Cautioner,
	Rectified		Recaution
CERTIFIER	Rectifier	COLANDERS	Androcles
CERTITUDE	Rectitude	COLLARING	Carolling

COLLINEAR	Coralline
COLLUSIVE	Colluvies
COLLUVIES	Collusive
COMFORTER	Recomfort
COMMENDER	Recommend
COMPLAINT	Compliant
COMPLEXED	Decomplex
COMPLIANT	Complaint
CONCEDERS	Crescendo
CONCENTER	Concentre,
	Connecter,
	Reconnect
CONCENTRE	Concenter,
	Connecter,
	Reconnect
CONDEMNER	Recondemn
CONFIRMER	Reconfirm
CONFORMER	Reconform
CONGERIES	Recognise
CONGESTED	Decongest
CONNECTER	Concenter,
	Concentre,
	Reconnect
CONNOTATE	Notonecta
CONSENTER	Cretonnes,
	Reconsent
CONSERVED	Conversed
CONSERVER	Converser
CONSIGNER	Necrosing,
	Reconsign
CONSPIRES	In-process
CONSTRAIN	Transonic
CONSULTER	Reconsult
CONTAGION	Cognation
CONTAINER	Crenation,
	Rocinante
CONTENDER	Recontend
CONTESTER	Recontest
CONTINUAL	Inoculant
CONTINUED	Unnoticed
CONTINUER	Centurion
CONVERSED	Conserved
CONVERSER	Conserver
CONVERTER	Reconvert
CO-PARTNER	Procreant
COPEMATES	Copesmate
COPESMATE	Copemates
CORALLINE	Collinear
CORAL-TREE	Correlate
*CORISANDE	Dinocerus
CORK-BORER	Rock-borer
CORKINESS	Rockiness
CORN-BREAD	Bread-corn
*CORNELIUS	Inclosure
CORRELATE	Coral-tree
CORSETING	Escorting,
	Recosting
CORUSCATE	Accouters,
	Accoutres
COTELINES	Elections,
	Selection
COTILLION	Octillion
COTTON-GIN	Cottoning
COTTONING	Cotton-gin
COUNTERED	Recounted
COURANTES	Courtesan,
	Nectarous,
	Outrances
COURBARIL	Orbicular
COURTESAN	Courantes,
	Nectarous,
	Outrances
COVERABLE	Revocable
CREAMINGS	Germanics,
	Screaming
CREATABLE	Traceable
CREATINES	Centiares,
	Iterances,
	Nectarise
CREATIONS	Certosina,
	Narcotise,
	Reactions
CREDITING	Directing
CREDITRIX	Directrix
CREMATION	Manticore
CRENATION	Container,
	Rocinante
CRENULATE	Calenture
CRESCENDO	Conceders
CRETIFIED	Certified,
	Rectified
CRETINOID	Direction
CRETINOUS	Neurotics
CRETONNES	Consenter,
	Reconsent
CRIMELESS	Merciless
CRISPATED	Practised
CRUSTACEA	Carucates

CTENIDIAL	Identical	DEMURRING	Murdering
CTESIPHON	Phonetics	DENOTATED	Detonated
CUMBERING	Recumbing	DENOUNCER	Renounced
CURTATION	Ructation	DENTALISE	Date-lines
		DEPARTING	Predating
		DEPASTURE	Depurates
DAMNATORY	Mandatory	DEPLENISH	Plenished
DATE-LINES	Dentalise	DEPLUMING	Implunged
DATE-SUGAR	Graduates	DEPRAVING	Pervading
DAUNDERED	Undreaded	DEPURATES	Depasture
DEBARRING	Birgander	DEREPRESS	Repressed
DECADENTS	Descanted	DESCANTED	Decadents
DECALITER	Decalitre	DESCANTER	Decanters
DECALITRE	Decaliter	DESCENDER	Redescend
DECAMETER	Decametre	DESECRATE	Decastere
DECAMETRE	Decameter	DESERTION	Detersion
DECANTERS	Descanter	DESICCANT	Accidents
DECASTERE	Desecrate	DESPAIRER	Draperies,
DECELERON	Redolence		Repraised
DECEMVIRI	Vermicide	DESTINATE	Tetanised
DECENNIAL	Celandine	DESULPHUR	Sulphured
DECILITER	Decilitre	DETERSION	Desertion
DECILITRE	Deciliter	DETONATED	Denotated
DECIMALLY	Medically	DEVELOPER	Redevelop
DECIMATED	Medicated	DEVITRIFY	Fervidity
DECIMATOR	Medicator	DIAMETRIC	Matricide
DECIMETER	Decimetre	DIGNIFIES	Signified
DECIMETRE	Decimeter	DILIGENCE	Ceilinged
DECLAIMER	Reclaimed	DILUVIONS	Divulsion
DECOLLATE	Ocellated	DINOCERUS	Corisande
DECOMPLEX	Complexed	DIRECTING	Crediting
DECONGEST	Congested	DIRECTION	Cretinoid
DEER-MOUSE	Mouse-deer	DIRECTRIX	Creditrix
DEFERMENT	Fermented	DIREPTION	Perdition
DEFLORATE	Floreated,	DIRTINESS	Disinters
	Refloated	DISCERNED	Rescinded
DEGARNISH	Garnished	DISCERNER	Rescinder
DEISTICAL	Silicated	DISCUSSER	Rediscuss
DELAPSION	Palinodes	DISENDOWS	Dowdiness
DELATIONS	Insolated	DISHONEST	Hedonists
DELIGHTER	Relighted	DISINTERS	Dirtiness
DELIVERER	Redeliver	DISPLAYER	Redisplay
DEMANDING	Maddening	DISSEISOR	Siderosis
DEMARCATE	Camerated,	DISSENTER	Residents,
	Macerated		Tiredness
DEMEANOUR	Enamoured	DISSOLUTE	Outslides,
DEMERSION	Domineers,		Solitudes
	Modernise	DISTILLER	Redistill
DEMI-LANCE	Endemical	DISTRAINS	Sinistrad

DIVULSION	Diluvions	ENCRADLES	Calenders,
DOMINATES	Staminode		Esclandre
DOMINATOR	Admonitor	ENCRATISM	Miscreant
DOMINEERS	Demersion,	ENDEARING	Engrained,
	Modernise		Grenadine
DOOMWATCH	Matchwood	ENDEMICAL	Demi-lance
DOVEHOUSE	House-dove	ENERGICAL	Generical
DOWDINESS	Disendows	ENERVATED	Venerated
DOWELLING	Well-doing	ENERVATOR	Venerator
DOWNRIGHT	Right-down	ENGLACIAL	Angelical,
DRAGOONED	Gadrooned		Galenical
DRAPERIES	Despairer,	ENGRAINED	Endearing,
	Repraised		Grenadine
DRAWBACKS	Backwards	ENGROSSER	Re-engross
		ENLISTING	Listening
		ENSAMPLES	Ampleness
EAGERNESS	Sea-greens	ENSTATITE	Intestate,
EARTH-BORN	Abhorrent		Satinette
EARTHIEST	Heartiest	ENSTEEPED	Steepened
EARTHLING	Haltering,	ENTERTAIN	Terentian
	Heartling,	ENTRANCES	Renascent
	Lathering	ENTROPIUM	Importune
EARTHWORM	Heartworm	EPICENTER	Epicentre
EASTER-EGG	Segregate	EPICENTRE	Epicenter
ECONOMIES	Economise	EPIDERMAL	Impleader
ECONOMISE	Economies	EPISODIAL	Apsidiole
ECSTASIES	Ecstasise	ERADICATE	Acierated
ECSTASISE	Ecstasies	ERASTIANS	Star-anise
EDUCATION	Auctioned,	ERECTIONS	Necrotise,
	Cautioned,		Resection,
	Noctuidae		Secretion
EDUCTIONS	Seduction	ERISTICAL	Realistic
EGLANTINE	Inelegant	EROTICISM	Isometric,
EIDOGRAPH	Ideograph		Meroistic
ELECTIONS	Cotelines,	ERUPTIONS	Pertusion
	Selection	ESCLANDRE	Calenders,
ELECTIVES	Selective		Encradles
EMACIATED	Acetamide	ESCORTING	Corseting,
EMANATING	Man-eating,		Recosting
	Manganite	ESPERANTO	Personate
EMERSIONS	Sermonise	ESTRANGES	Greatness,
EMIGRANTS	Germanist,		Sergeants
	Mastering,	ETHERICAL	Cheralite,
	Remasting,		Heretical
	Streaming	ETHOLOGIC	Theologic
ENAMELIST	Melanites	EXCEPTANT	Expectant
ENAMOURED	Demeanour	EXCEPTING	Expecting
ENCASHING	Enchasing	EXHIBITER	Re-exhibit
ENCHASING	Encashing	EXPECTANT	Exceptant
ENCLASPED	Spanceled	EXPECTING	Excepting

EXPLAINER	Re-explain
EXPRESSER	Re-express
FACTIONAL	Falcation
FACTORIES	Factorise
FACTORISE	Factories
FALCATION	Factional
FANTASIES	Fantasise
FANTASISE	Fantasies
FASHIONER	Refashion
FERMENTED	Deferment
FERVIDITY	Devitrify
FIBERFILL	Fibrefill
FIBERLESS	Briefless,
	Fibreless
FIBREFILL	Fiberfill
FIBRELESS	Briefless,
	Fiberless
FIREIRONS	Inferiors
FIRSTLING	Flirtings,
	Triflings
FLIRTINGS	Firstling,
	Triflings
FLOREATED	Deflorate,
	Refloated
FLOWERING	Reflowing
FOOT-BOARD	Board-foot
FORCE-LAND	Land-force
FORE-HORSE	Foreshore
FOREMEANS	Forenames,
	Freemason
FORENAMES	Foremeans,
	Freemason
FOREPEAKS	Forespake,
	Forespeak
FORESHORE	Fore-horse
FORESPAKE	Forepeaks,
	Forespeak
FORESPEAK	Forepeaks,
	Forespake
FORESTAGE	Fosterage
FORESTING	Fostering
FORFEITER	Reforfeit
FORWARDER	Reforward
FORWARDLY	Frowardly
FOSTERAGE	Forestage
FOSTERING	Foresting
FOUNDLING	Unfolding

FREEMASON	Foremeans,
	Forenames
FRESHENER	Refreshen
FRIENDING	Infringed
FRINGILLA	Ill-faring
FROWARDLY	Forwardly
FURBISHER	Refurbish
FURNISHER	Refurnish
GABARDINE	Bargained
GADROONED	Dragooned
GALENICAL	Angelical,
	Englacial
GALENITES	Anglesite,
	Gelatines
GANTRISIN	Straining,
	Trainings
GARNISHED	Degarnish
GARNISHER	Regarnish,
	Resharing
GARRETING	Gartering
GARTERING	Garreting
GASSINESS	Assessing
GATHERING	Nightgear
GEE-STRING	Greetings
GELATINES	Anglesite,
	Galenites
GELIDNESS	Seedlings
GEMINATES	Magnesite,
	Magnetise
GENERATED	Renegated
GENERICAL	Energical
GENETICAL	Clientage
GENITIVAL	Vigilante
GENITIVES	Ingestive
GENTIANIC	Antigenic
GERMANICS	Creamings,
	Screaming
GERMANIST	Emigrants,
	Mastering,
	Remasting,
	Streaming
GIRANDOLE	Negroidal,
	Reloading
GNOMONICS	Oncomings
GOVERNORS	Grosvenor
GRADATION	Indagator
GRADIENTS	Astringed
GRADUATES	Date-sugar

GRANDIOSE	Organised	HETEROSIS	Isotheres,
GRANULITE	Traguline		Theorises
GRAVELESS	Verglases	HIBERNATE	Inbreathe
GREATNESS	Estranges,	HISPANIST	Saintship
	Sergeants	HOLLOAING	Hallooing
GREETINGS	Gee-string	HORSEBACK	Backshore
GREGARIAN	Gregarina	HORSEBANE	Horsebean
GREGARINA	Gregarian	HORSEBEAN	Horsebane
GRENADINE	Endearing,	HORSE-BOAT	Shoreboat
	Engrained	HORSEFACE	Shoreface
GROOMSMAN	Monograms,	HORSE-HOES	Horseshoe
	Nomograms	HORSELESS	Shoreless
*GROSVENOR	Governors	HORSEMEAT	Heartsome
GYRATIONS	Signatory	HORSESHOE	Horse-hoes
		HORSEWEED	Shoreweed
HALF-GROWN	Half-wrong	HOUSE-BOAT	Boathouse
HALF-WRONG	Half-grown	HOUSE-DOVE	Dovehouse
HALLOOING	Holloaing	HOUSE-TOPS	Posthouse,
HALTERING	Earthling,		Pothouses
	Heartling,	HOUSEWORK	Workhouse
	Lathering	HOWSOEVER	Whosoever
HANKERING	Harkening	HURTFULLY	Ruthfully
HARKENING	Hankering		
HARMONIES	Harmonise	IDENTICAL	Ctenidial
HARMONISE	Harmonies	IDEOGRAPH	Eidograph
HARNESSER	Reharness	IGNITABLE	Bigential
HARVESTER	Reharvest	ILL-FARING	Fringilla
HEAD-BOARD	Broad-head	IMMERSING	Simmering
HEADLAMPS	Lampshade	IMPARTIAL	Primatial
HEADNOTES	Headstone	IMPLANTER	Reimplant
HEADSTONE	Headnotes	IMPLEADER	Epidermal
HEADWATER	Waterhead	IMPLUNGED	Depluming
HEART-FREE	Hereafter	IMPORTERS	Misreport,
HEARTIEST	Earthiest		Reimports
HEARTLING	Earthling,	IMPORTUNE	Entropium
	Haltering,	IMPRESSER	Reimpress,
	Lathering		Simperers
HEARTSOME	Horsemeat	IMPRINTER	Reimprint
HEARTWORM	Earthworm	IMPUGNERS	Presuming
HEDONISTS	Dishonest	INACTIONS	Aniconist,
HELLFIRES	Shellfire		Nicotians,
HELL-HOLES	Shell-hole		Onanistic
HEPATICAL	Caliphate	INBREATHE	Hibernate
HEPATIZED	Aphetized	INCEPTORS	Inspector,
HEREAFTER	Heart-free		Pre-tonics
HERETICAL	Cheralite,	INCESSANT	Cantiness,
	Etherical		Instances
HESPERIAN	Inspheare,	INCLOSURE	Cornelius
	Seraphine	INCOGNITO	Cognition

INCONDITE	Nicotined	INTESTATE	Enstatite,
INCREASES	Scenarise		Satinette
INDAGATOR	Gradation	INTIMATES	Mini-state
INDENTING	Intending	INTRICATE	Triactine
INDICATES	Andesitic	INTRODUCE	Reduction
INELASTIC	Sciential	INUNDATES	Unsainted,
INELEGANT	Eglantine		Unstained
INFARCTED	Infracted	IRRADIANT	Triandria
INFERIORS	Fireirons	ISOMETRIC	Eroticism,
INFERRING	Infringer		Meroistic
INFRACTED	Infarcted	ISOSCELES	Solecises
INFRINGED	Friending	ISOTHERES	Heterosis,
INFRINGER	Inferring		Theorises
INGESTIVE	Genitives	ISSUANCES	Sauciness
INHABITER	Reinhabit	ITERANCES	Centiares,
INOCULANT	Continual		Creatines,
IN-PROCESS	Conspires		Nectarise
INSOLATED	Delations	ITINERANT	Nitratine
INSOMNIAC	Aniconism		
INSPECTOR	Inceptors,		
	Pre-tonics	JESSERANT	Serjeants
INSPHEARE	Hesperian,		
	Seraphine		
INSTALLER	Reinstall	KILOLITER	Kilolitre
INSTANCES	Cantiness,	KILOLITRE	Kiloliter
	Incessant	KILOMETER	Kilometre
INSTANTER	Transient	KILOMETRE	Kilometer
INSURABLE	Sublinear	KITCHENED	Thickened
INSURGENT	Unresting	KITCHENER	Rethicken,
INTEGRANT	Nattering		Thickener
INTEGRATE	Argentite		
INTENDING	Indenting		
INTER-ARTS	Restraint	LACERTINE	Interlace,
INTERESTS	Intersets,		Reclinate
	Resistent,	LACQUERER	Relacquer
	Sternites,	LACRYMOSE	Claymores
	Triteness	LACUSTRAL	Claustral
INTERLACE	Lacertine,	LAMENTING	Alignment
	Reclinate	LAMINATED	Almandite
INTERLOPE	Repletion,	LAMPSHADE	Headlamps
	Terpineol	*LANCASTER	Ancestral
INTERMITS	Terminist	LAND-FORCE	Force-land
INTERPAGE	Pignerate,	LAPIDATES	Stapedial
	Repeating	LARCENIST	Cisternal,
INTERPLAY	Party-line		Clarinets
INTERSETS	Interests,	LARGENESS	Angerless
	Resistent,	LARGITION	Tailoring
	Sternites,	LATESCENT	Tentacles
	Triteness	LATHERING	Earthling,

	Haltering,	MARONITES	Matronise
	Heartling	MARSHALER	Remarshal
LAUDATION	Adulation	MARTIALLY	Maritally
LAUDATORY	Adulatory	MARTINETS	Stream-tin,
LAUGHTERS	Slaughter		Tarentism
LAUNDERER	Relaunder	MASTERING	Emigrants,
LAVATIONS	Salvation		Germanist,
LEASE-LEND	Lend-lease		Remasting,
LEND-LEASE	Lease-lend		Streaming
LETTERING	Reletting	MATCHWOOD	Doomwatch
LEVANTINE	Valentine	MATERIALS	Mare's-tail
LICENSING	Silencing	MATRICIDE	Diametric
LICENSURE	Ceruleins	MATRONISE	Maronites
LIGHTINGS	Slighting	MAUNDERED	Undreamed
LIGHTNESS	Nightless	MEANDRIAN	Meandrina
LIMESTONE	Milestone	MEANDRINA	Meandrian
LINEAMENT	Alinement	MEANS-TEST	Statesmen
LIONESSES	Noiseless	MECHANICS	Mischance
LISTENING	Enlisting	MECHANISE	Manichees
LISTERISE	Sterilise	MEDICALLY	Decimally
LONGUETTE	Tonguelet	MEDICATED	Decimated
LORICATES	Sclerotia,	MEDICATOR	Decimator
	Sectorial	MEDICINAL	Adminicle
LUCRATIVE	Revictual	MELANITES	Enamelist
LUMBERERS	Slumberer	MELANOSIS	Semolinas
LUMP-SUGAR	Sugar-plum	MENTALISM	Simmental
		MENTIONER	Remention
		MERCILESS	Crimeless
MACARONIC	Carcinoma	MEROISTIC	Eroticism,
MACERATED	Camerated,		Isometric
	Demarcate	METRONOME	Monometer,
MADDENING	Demanding		Monotreme
MAGNESITE	Geminates,	MILESTONE	Limestone
	Magnetise	MINI-STATE	Intimates
MAGNETISE	Geminates,	*MINNESOTA	Nominates
	Magnesite	MINORITES	Misorient
MANDATORY	Damnatory	MISAUNTER	Ruminates
MAN-EATING	Emanating,	MISCHANCE	Mechanics
	Manganite	MISCREANT	Encratism
MANGANITE	Emanating,	MISCREDIT	Misdirect
	Man-eating	MISDEALER	Misleader
MANICHEES	Mechanise	MISDIRECT	Miscredit
MANICURES	Muscarine	MISLEADER	Misdealer
MANOEUVER	Manoeuvre	MISORIENT	Minorites
MANOEUVRE	Manoeuver	MISREFORM	Reformism
MANTICORE	Cremation	MISREPORT	Importers,
MARE'S-NEST	Steersman		Reimports
MARE'S-TAIL	Materials	MISSIONER	Remission
MARITALLY	Martially	MOBILISES	Omissible

MODERNISE	Demersion,
	Domineers
MONERGISM	Sommering
MONGOLISE	Neulogism
MONOCRACY	Nomocracy
MONOGRAMS	Groomsman,
	Nomograms
MONOGRAPH	Nomograph,
	Phonogram
MONOMETER	Metronome,
	Monotreme
MONOTONES	Moonstone
MONOTREME	Metronome,
	Monometer
MOONSTONE	Monotones
MORPHINES	Premonish
MOUSE-DEER	Deer-mouse
MOUSETRAP	Route-maps
MURDERING	Demurring
MUSCARINE	Manicures
MUTILATES	Stimulate,
	Ultimates
NARCOTISE	Certosina,
	Creations,
	Reactions
NARCOTISM	Romancist,
	Romantics
NARCOTIST	Tractions
NARGHILES	Ashlering,
	Nargilehs,
	Shearling
NARGILEHS	Ashlering,
	Narghiles,
	Shearling
NATTERING	Integrant
NAVIGATED	Vaginated
NECROSING	Consigner,
	Reconsign
NECROTISE	Erections,
	Resection,
	Secretion
NECTARISE	Centiares,
	Creatines,
	Iterances
NECTAROUS	Courantes,
	Courtesan,
	Outrances

NEGROIDAL	Girandole,
	Reloading
NEO-GOTHIC	Theogonic
NEOLOGIES	Neologise
NEOLOGISE	Neologies
NEOLOGISM	Mongolise
NEOTERISM	Timoneers
NEPHOLOGY	Phenology
NEPHRITIC	Phrenitic
NEPHRITIS	Phrenitis
NEPHROSIS	Phronesis
NERVATION	Vernation
NESTORIAN	Rosinante
NEUROTICS	Cretinous
NICCOLOUS	Occlusion
NICOTIANS	Aniconist,
	Inactions,
	Onanistic
NICOTINED	Incondite
NIGHTGEAR	Gathering
NIGHTLESS	Lightness
NIGHTWEAR	Wreathing
NITRATINE	Itinerant
NOCTUIDAE	Auctioned,
	Cautioned,
	Education
NOISELESS	Lionesses
NOMINATES	Minnesota
NOMOCRACY	Monocracy
NOMOGRAMS	Groomsman,
	Monograms
NOMOGRAPH	Monograph,
	Phonogram
NORMALISE	Orleanism
NORTHWEST	Westnorth
NOSTALGIA	Analogist
NOTONECTA	Connotate
NOURISHER	Renourish
NUT-BUTTER	Butter-nut
OBVERSELY	Verbosely
OCCLUSION	Niccolous
OCELLATED	Decollate
OCTILLION	Cotillion
OCULARIST	Suctorial
ODOMETERS	Osteoderm
OMISSIBLE	Mobilises
ONANISTIC	Aniconist,

	Inactions,	OVERTHROW	Throw-over
	Nicotians	OVERTRADE	Overrated,
ONCOMINGS	Gnomonics		Overtread
OPERATING	Pignorate	OVERTREAD	Overrated,
OPERETTAS	Poetaster		Overtrade
OPPRESSOR	Proposers	OVERWEARS	Overswear
OPTICALLY	Topically	OVERWREST	Overstrew
OPTICIANS	Panoistic	OWNERSHIP	Shipowner
OPTOMETER	Potometer		
OPTOMETRY	Potometry	PAILLASSE	Palliasse
ORBICULAR	Courbaril	*PALESTINE	Tapelines
ORCADIANS	Sarcodina	PALINODES	Delapsion
ORCHESTRA	Cart-horse	PALLIASSE	Paillasse
ORDERLESS	Resolders,	PALM-SUGAR	Sugar-palm
	Solderers	PALTERERS	Plasterer,
ORGANISED	Grandiose		Replaster
ORIENTALS	Orleanist,	PANOISTIC	Opticians
	Relations,	PAROTITIS	Topiarist
	Tiroleans	PARTERRES	Pre-arrest
ORLEANISM	Normalise	PARTY-LINE	Interplay
ORLEANIST	Orientals,	PASSENGER	Sap-greens
	Relations,	PASSIONAL	Sponsalia
	Tiroleans	PATRIARCH	Phratriac
OSTEODERM	Odometers	PATRONESS	Transpose
OSTRACISM	Acrotisms,	PATTERNER	Repattern
	Castroism	PECULATES	Speculate
OUT-BURNED	Burned-out	PELAGIANS	Pelasgian
OUTMASTER	Outstream	PELASGIAN	Pelagians
OUTRANCES	Courantes,	PENDULATE	Unpleated
	Courtesan,	PENETRANT	Repentant
	Nectarous	PERCALINE	Periclean
OUTSLIDES	Dissolute,	PERCOLATE	Prelocate
	Solitudes	PERDITION	Direption
OUTSPRING	Sprouting	PERFORMED	Preformed
OUTSPRINT	Print-outs	PERFORMER	Prereform,
OUTSTREAM	Outmaster		Reperform
OUTSTRIKE	Strike-out	PERICLEAN	Percaline
OUTSTRIPS	Posturist	PERICOPES	Periscope
OVERBRAKE	Overbreak	PERISCOPE	Pericopes
OVERBREAK	Overbrake	PERISTOME	Temporise
OVERDATES	Oversated	PERMITTER	Pretermit
OVERRATED	Overtrade,	PERSONATE	Esperanto
	Overtread	PERTAINED	Repainted
OVERRATES	Overstare	PERTUSION	Eruptions
OVERSATED	Overdates	PERVADING	Depraving
OVERSPILL	Spill-over	PHARISEES	Apheresis
OVERSTARE	Overrates	PHASELESS	Shapeless
OVERSTREW	Overwrest	PHENOLOGY	Nephology
OVERSWEAR	Overwears	PHONETICS	Ctesiphon

PHONOGRAM	Monograph,	PRE-ENTERS	Presenter,
	Nomograph		Repenters,
PHOTOGRAM	Tomograph		Represent
PHRATRIAC	Patriarch	PRE-EXCEPT	Pre-expect
PHRENITIC	Nephritic	PRE-EXPECT	Pre-except
PHRENITIS	Nephritis	PREFORMED	Performed
PHRONESIS	Nephrosis	PRE-LEASED	Pre-sealed
PIECEWORK	Work-piece	PRELOCATE	Percolate
PIERRETTE	Preterite	PRELUSIVE	Pulverise,
PIGNERATE	Interpage,		Repulsive
	Repeating	PRELUSORY	Repulsory
PIGNORATE	Operating	PREMONISH	Morphines
PISTAREEN	Aperients	PRENOTION	Pontonier
PISTOLING	Postiling	PRENTICES	Prescient,
PISTOLLED	Postilled		Reinspect
PLASTERER	Palterers,	PREREFORM	Performer,
	Replaster		Reperform
PLATINOUS	Pulsation	PRE-RESORT	Reporters
PLENISHED	Deplenish	PRESCIENT	Prentices,
PLENISHES	Spleenish		Reinspect
PLEONASTE	Antelopes	PRE-SEALED	Pre-leased
PLETHORAS	Astrophel	PRESEARCH	Preachers
POETASTER	Operettas	PRESENTED	Pretensed,
POLYTHENE	Telephony		Repetends,
PONTONIER	Prenotion		Serpented
PORTERAGE	Reportage	PRESENTER	Pre-enters,
PORTIONER	Reportion		Repenters,
POSTHOUSE	House-tops,		Represent
	Pothouses	PRESIGNED	Predesign
POSTILING	Pistoling	PRESTRAIN	Terrapins,
POSTILLED	Pistolled		Transpire
POSTURIST	Outstrips	PRESUMING	Impugners
POTHOUSES	House-tops,	PRETENSED	Presented,
	Posthouse		Repetends,
POTOMETER	Optometer		Serpented
POTOMETRY	Optometry	PRETERITE	Pierrette
POTTERING	Pottinger,	PRETERMIT	Permitter
	Repotting	PRE-TONICS	Inceptors,
POTTINGER	Pottering,		Inspector
	Repotting	PRIMATIAL	Impartial
PRACTISED	Crispated	PRINTINGS	Sprinting
PREACHERS	Presearch	PRINT-OUTS	Outsprint
PRE-ARREST	Parterres	PROCEDURE	Reproduce
PRECEDENT	Precented	PROCEEDER	Reproceed
PRECENTED	Precedent	PROCREANT	Copartner
PRECREDIT	Predirect	PROPOSERS	Oppressor
PREDATING	Departing	PROTESTER	Reprotest
PREDESIGN	Presigned	PROTISTIC	Tropistic
PREDIRECT	Precredit	*PTERELAUS	Pulse-rate

PUBLISHER	Republish	RECONSENT	Consenter,
PULSATION	Platinous		Cretonnes
PULSE-RATE	Pterelaus	RECONSIGN	Consigner,
PULVERISE	Prelusive,		Necrosing
	Repulsive	RECONSULT	Consulter
PUNCTILIO	Unpolitic	RECONTEND	Contender
		RECONTEST	Contester
		RECONVERT	Converter
QUAKERESS	Squeakers	RECOSTING	Corseting,
QUICKENER	Requicken		Escorting
		RECOUNTED	Countered
		RECTIFIED	Certified,
RACIALIST	Satirical		Cretified
RAININESS	Sirenians	RECTIFIER	Certifier
RAINTREES	Retainers,	RECTITUDE	Certitude
	Ternaries	RECUMBING	Cumbering
RASPINGLY	Sparingly	REDELIVER	Deliverer
RATIONALE	Alienator	REDESCEND	Descender
REABANDON	Abandoner	REDEVELOP	Developer
REACCLAIM	Acclaimer	REDISCUSS	Discusser
REACTIONS	Certosina,	REDISPLAY	Displayer
	Creations,	REDISTILL	Distiller
	Narcotise	REDOLENCE	Deceleron
READDRESS	Addresser	REDRAWING	Rewarding
REAFFRONT	Affronter	REDUCTION	Introduce
REALISTIC	Eristical	RE-ENGROSS	Engrosser
REAPPLAUD	Applauder	RE-EXHIBIT	Exhibiter
REAPPOINT	Appointer	RE-EXPLAIN	Explainer
REATTEMPT	Attempter	RE-EXPRESS	Expresser
REATTRACT	Attracter	RE-FASHION	Fashioner
REBUTTING	Buttering	REFLOATED	Deflorate,
RECANTING	Cantering		Floreated
RECAUTION	Cautioner,	REFLOWING	Flowering
	Cointreau	REFORFEIT	Forfeiter
RECHANNEL	Channeler	REFORMISM	Misreform
RECHARTER	Charterer	REFORWARD	Forwarder
RECLAIMED	Declaimer	REFRESHEN	Freshener
RECLINATE	Interlace,	REFURBISH	Furbisher
	Lacertine	REFURNISH	Furnisher
RECOGNISE	Congeries	REGARNISH	Garnisher,
RECOMFORT	Comforter		Resharing
RECOMMEND	Commender	REGAUGING	Ring-gauge
RECONCEAL	Concealer	REGELATED	Relegated
RECONDEMN	Condemner	REHARNESS	Harnesser
RECONDITE	Renoticed	REHARVEST	Harvester
RECONFIRM	Confirmer	REIMPLANT	Implanter
RECONFORM	Conformer	REIMPORTS	Importers,
RECONNECT	Concenter,		Misreport
	Concentre,	REIMPRESS	Impresser,
	Connecter		Simperers

REIMPRINT	Imprinter	REPORTAGE	Porterage
REINHABIT	Inhabiter	REPORTERS	Pre-resort
REINSPECT	Prentices,	REPORTION	Portioner
	Prescient	REPOTTING	Pottering,
REINSTALL	Installer		Pottinger
RELACQUER	Lacquerer	REPRAISED	Despairer,
RELATIONS	Orientals,		Draperies
	Orleanist,	REPRESENT	Pre-enters,
	Tiroleans		Presenter,
RELATIVES	Versatile		Repenters
RELAUNDER	Launderer	REPRESSED	Derepress
RELEGATED	Regelated	REPROCEED	Proceeder
RELETTING	Lettering	REPRODUCE	Procedure
RELIANCES	Scare-line	REPROTEST	Protester
RELIGHTED	Delighter	REPUBLISH	Publisher
RELOADING	Girandole,	REPULSIVE	Prelusive,
	Negroidal		Pulverise
REMARSHAL	Marshaler	REPULSORY	Prelusory
REMASTING	Emigrants,	REQUICKEN	Quickener
	Germanist,	RESCINDED	Discerned
	Mastering,	RESCINDER	Discerner
	Streaming	RESCUABLE	Securable
REMENTION	Mentioner	RESECTION	Erections,
REMISSION	Missioner		Necrotise,
REMITTERS	Trimester,		Secretion
	Trimeters	RESERVING	Reversing
RENASCENT	Entrances	RESHARING	Garnisher,
RENEGATED	Generated		Regarnish
RENOTICED	Recondite	RESHARPEN	Sharpener
RENOUNCED	Denouncer	RESHORTEN	Shortener
RENOURISH	Nourisher	RESIDENTS	Dissenter,
RENVERSED	Reverends		Tiredness
REPAINTED	Pertained	RESISTANT	Straitens
REPATCHED	Chaptered	RESISTENT	Interests,
REPATTERN	Patterner		Intersets,
REPEATING	Interpage,		Sternites,
	Pignerate		Triteness
REPENTANT	Penetrant	RESISTING	Sistering
REPENTERS	Pre-enters,	RESLANDER	Slanderer
	Presenter,	RESOLDERS	Orderless
	Represent		Solderers
REPERFORM	Performer,	RESORTING	Restoring
	Prereform	RESPIRATE	Sparterie
REPETENDS	Presented,	RESTATION	Stationer
	Pretensed,	RESTORING	Resorting
	Serpented	RESTRAINT	Inter-arts
REPLASTER	Palterers,	RESUSPEND	Suspender
	Plasterer	RESWALLOW	Swallower,
REPLETION	Interlope,		Wallowers
	Terpineol		

RESWEETEN	Sweetener	SALTPETRE	Saltpeter,
RETAINERS	Raintress,		Steel-trap
	Ternaries	SALVATION	Lavations
RETHICKEN	Kitchener,	SAP-GREENS	Passenger
	Thickener	SARCODINA	Orcadians
RETIGHTEN	Tightener	SATANICAL	Castalian
REVARNISH	Varnisher	SATANISTS	Assistant
REVERENDS	Renversed	SATINETTE	Enstatite,
REVERSING	Reserving		Intestate
REVICTUAL	Lucrative	SATIRICAL	Racialist
REVISABLE	Verbalise	SATURNIAN	Turanians
REVOCABLE	Coverable	SAUCINESS	Issuances
REWARDING	Redrawing	SAVOURILY	Variously
REWARRANT	Warranter	SCAPULARY	Capsulary
RHETORICS	Chorister	SCAPULATE	Capsulate
RHETORISE	Theoriser	SCARE-LINE	Reliances
RICE-WATER	Water-rice	SCATTERER	Street-car
RIGHT-DOWN	Downright	SCENARISE	Increases
RING-GAUGE	Regauging	SCHEMATIC	Catechism
RINGSTAND	Stranding	SCIATICAL	Ascitical
*ROCINANTE	Container,	SCIENTIAL	Inelastic
	Crenation	SCLEROSIS	Scoreless
ROCK-BORER	Cork-borer	SCLEROTIA	Loricates,
ROCKINESS	Corkiness		Sectorial
ROISTERER	Terrorise	SCORELESS	Sclerosis
ROMANCIST	Narcotism,	SCREAMING	Creamings,
	Romantics		Germanics
ROMANISER	Rosmarine	SCREENING	Secerning
ROMANTICS	Narcotism,	SEAGREENS	Eagerness
	Romancist	SEARCHERS	Archeress
ROSINANTE	Nestorian	*SEBASTIAN	Basanites
ROSMARINE	Romaniser	SECERNENT	Sentencer
ROUTE-MAPS	Mousetrap	SECERNING	Screening
ROWDINESS	Windroses,	SECRETION	Erections,
	Wordiness		Necrotise,
RUCTATION	Curtation		Resection
RUINATION	Urination	SECTARIAN	Ascertain,
RUMINATES	Misaunter		Cartesian
RUNCINATE	Uncertain	SECTIONAL	Coastline
RUSTICATE	Urticates	SECTORIAL	Loricates,
RUTHFULLY	Hurtfully		Sclerotia
		SECURABLE	Rescuable
		SEDERUNTS	Undersets,
SACCHARIN	Characins		Untressed
SAINTSHIP	Hispanist	SEDUCTION	Eductions
SALTATION	Stational	SEEDLINGS	Gelidness
SALTINESS	Slatiness,	SEGREGATE	Easter-egg
	Stainless	SELECTION	Cotelines,
SALTPETER	Saltpetre,		Elections
	Steel-trap		

SELECTIVE	Electives	SINISTRAD	Distrains
SEMOLINAS	Melanosis	SIRENIANS	Raininess
SENESCENT	Sentences	SISTERING	Resisting
SENORITAS	Assertion	SLANDERER	Reslander
SENTENCER	Secernent	SLATINESS	Saltiness,
SENTENCES	Senescent		Stainless
SEPULCHER	Sepulchre	SLAUGHTER	Laughters
SEPULCHRE	Sepulcher	SLIGHTING	Lightings
SERAPHINE	Hesperian,	SLIVERING	Silvering
	Inspheare	SLUMBERER	Lumberers
SERGEANTS	Estranges,	SNATCHING	Stanching
	Greatness	SNOOPIEST	Spconiest
SERJEANTS	Jesserant	SOLDERERS	Orderless,
SERMONISE	Emersions		Resolders
SERPENTED	Presented,	SOLECISES	Isosceles
	Pretensed,	SOLITUDES	Dissolute,
	Repetends		Outslides
SERRATURE	Treasurer	*SOMMERING	Monergism
SESTERTIA	Treatises	SORTMENTS	Sternmost
SHAPELESS	Phaseless	SPANCELED	Enclasped
SHARE-OUTS	Authoress	SPARINGLY	Raspingly
SHARPENER	Resharpen	SPARTERIE	Respirate
SHEARLING	Ashlering,	SPECULATE	Peculates
	Narghiles,	SPILL-OVER	Overspill
	Nargilehs	SPLEENISH	Plenishes
SHELLFIRE	Hellfires	SPLIT-RING	Stripling
SHELL-HOLE	Hell-holes	SPOLIATOR	Troopials
SHIPMATES	Steamship	SPONSALIA	Passional
SHIPOWNER	Ownership	SPOONIEST	Snoopiest
SHOREBOAT	Horse-boat	SPOTTABLE	Tabletops
SHOREFACE	Horseface	SPRINTING	Printings
SHORELESS	Horseless	SPROUTING	Outspring
SHOREWEED	Horseweed	SQUEAKERS	Quakeress
SHORTENER	Reshorten	STABILISE	Sibilates
SHRUBLESS	Brushless	STAINLESS	Saltiness,
SHRUBLIKE	Brushlike		Slatiness
SIBILATES	Stabilise	STAMINODE	Dominates
SIDEBOARD	Broadside	STANCHING	Snatching
SIDEBURNS	Burnsides	STANDER-BY	Bystander
SIDEROSIS	Disseisor	STAPEDIAL	Lapidates
SIGNATORY	Gyrations	STAR-ANISE	Erastians
SIGNBOARD	Boardings	STATEABLE	Tasteable
SIGNIFIED	Dignifies	STATELESS	Tasteless
SILENCING	Licensing	STATEMENT	Testament
SILICATED	Deistical	STATESMEN	Means-test
SILVERING	Slivering	STATIONAL	Saltation
SIMMENTAL	Mentalism	STATIONED	Antidotes
SIMMERING	Immersing	STATIONER	Restation
SIMPERERS	Impresser,	STEAMSHIP	Shipmates
	Reimpress		

STEEL-TRAP	Saltpeter,	SUSPENDER	Resuspend
	Saltpetre	SUSPIRING	Uprisings
STEEPENED	Ensteeped	SWALLOWER	Reswallow,
STEERSMAN	Mare's-nest		Wallowers
STEP-BAIRN	Breast-pin	SWEETENER	Resweeten
STERILISE	Listerise	SWEPT-BACK	Back-swept
STERNITES	Interests,	SWING-BACK	Back-swing
	Intersets,	SWING-TREE	Westering
	Resistent,	SWORDPLAY	Wordplays
	Triteness	SYNDICATE	Asyndetic
STERNMOST	Sortments		
STIMULATE	Mutilates,		
	Ultimates	TABLETOPS	Spottable
STOICALLY	Callosity	TABLE-WORK	Work-table
STOMACHER	Chromates	TAILBOARD	Broadtail
STRAINING	Gantrisin,	TAILORING	Largition
	Trainings	TANAGRINE	Argentina
STRAITENS	Resistant	TANGERINE	Argentine
STRANDING	Ringstand	TAPELINES	Palestine
STRAPPING	Trappings	TARENTISM	Martinets,
STREAMING	Emigrants,		Stream-tin
	Germanist,	TARPAULIN	Unpartial
	Mastering,	TASTEABLE	Stateable
	Remasting	TASTELESS	Stateless
STREAM-TIN	Martinets,	TEA-BOARDS	Adsorbate
	Tarentism	TEACHABLE	Cheatable
STREET-CAR	Scatterer	TELEPHONY	Polythene
STRIKE-OUT	Outstrike	TEMPORISE	Peristome
STRIPLING	Split-ring	TENTACLES	Latescent
STRONGARM	Armstrong	TENTATIVE	Attentive
SUABILITY	Usability	TERENTIAN	Entertain
SUB-DEALER	Sub-leader	TERMINIST	Intermits
SUB-LEADER	Sub-dealer	TERNARIES	Raintrees,
SUBLINEAR	Insurable		Retainers
SUBSIDIES	Subsidise	TERPINEOL	Interlope,
SUBSIDISE	Subsidies		Repletion
SUCTIONAL	Sulcation,	TERRAPINS	Prestrain,
	Unstoical		Transpire
SUCTORIAL	Ocularist	TERRORISE	Roisterer
SUGAR-CANE	Cane-sugar	TESTAMENT	Statement
SUGAR-PALM	Palm-sugar	TETANISED	Destinate
SUGAR-PLUM	Lump-sugar	THEOGONIC	Neo-gothic
SULCATION	Suctional,	THEOLOGIC	Ethologic
	Unstoical	THEORISER	Rhetorise
SULPHURED	Desulphur	THEORISES	Heterosis,
SUMMARIES	Summarise		Isotheres
SUMMARISE	Summaries	THICKENED	Kitchened
SUNBONNET	Unbonnets	THICKENER	Kitchener,
SUNDERING	Undersign		Rethicken
SUNFLOWER	Unflowers	THREE-CARD	Chartered

THROW-OVER	Overthrow	TROOPIALS	Spoliator
TIGHTENER	Retighten	TROPISTIC	Protistic
TIMONEERS	Neoterism	TURANIANS	Saturnian
TIREDNESS	Dissenter,	TURBINATE	Tribunate
	Residents	TURNABOUT	About-turn
TIROLEANS	Orientals,	TYPHONIAN	Antiphony
	Orleanist,		
	Relations		
TITRATING	Attriting	ULTIMATES	Mutilates,
TITRATION	Attrition		Stimulate
TOILET-SET	Toilettes	UNALTERED	Unrelated
TOILETTES	Toilet-set	UNATTUNED	Untaunted
TOLERANCE	Coeternal	UNBEARDED	Unbreaded
TOMOGRAPH	Photogram	UNBLASTED	Unstabled
TONGUELET	Longuette	UNBLOTTED	Unbottled
TONSORIAL	Torsional	UNBONNETS	Sunbonnet
TOPIARIST	Parotitis	UNBOTTLED	Unblotted
TOPICALLY	Optically	UNBREADED	Unbearded
TORSIONAL	Tonsorial	UNCATERED	Uncreated
TOTALLING	Allotting	UNCERTAIN	Runcinate
TRACEABLE	Creatable	UNCHALKED	Unhackled
TRACTIONS	Narcotist	UNCLAIMED	Undecimal,
TRAGULINE	Granulite		Unmedical
TRAININGS	Gantrisin,	UNCREATED	Uncatered
	Straining	UNDECIMAL	Unclaimed,
TRANSIENT	Instanter		Unmedical
TRANSLATE	Alterants,	UNDEFILED	Unfielded
	Alternats	UNDELIGHT	Unlighted
TRANSONIC	Constrain	UNDERACTS	Undercast
TRANSPIRE	Prestrain,	UNDERCAST	Underacts
	Terrapins	UNDERFLOW	Wonderful
TRANSPOSE	Patroness	UNDERNOTE	Undertone
TRAPPINGS	Strapping	UNDERSETS	Sederunts,
TREASURER	Serrature		Untressed
TREATISES	Sestertia	UNDERSIDE	Undesired
TRIACTINE	Intricate	UNDERSIGN	Sundering
TRIANDRIA	Irradiant	UNDERTIME	Unmerited
TRIBUNATE	Turbinate	UNDERTONE	Undernote
TRICHINAS	Christian,	UNDESERVE	Unsevered
	Christina	UNDESIRED	Underside
TRIFLINGS	Firstling,	UNDREADED	Daundered
	Flirtings	UNDREAMED	Maundered
TRIMESTER	Remitters,	UNELAPSED	Unpleased
	Trimeters	UNERODING	Ungroined,
TRIMETERS	Remitters,		Unignored
	Trimester	UNERUPTED	Unreputed
TRITENESS	Interests,	UNFEEDING	Unfeigned
	Intersets,	UNFEELING	Unfleeing
	Resistent,	UNFEIGNED	Unfeeding
	Sternites		

UNFIELDED	Undefiled	VAGINATED	Navigated
UNFLEEING	Unfeeling	VALENTINE	Levantine
UNFLOWERS	Sunflower	VARIOUSLY	Savourily
UNFOLDING	Foundling	VARNISHER	Revarnish
UNGROINED	Uneroding,	VASTITUDE	Vedutista
	Unignored	VEDUTISTA	Vastitude
UNHACKLED	Unchalked	VENERATED	Enervated
UNHEARSED	Unsheared	VENERATOR	Enervator
UNIGNORED	Uneroding,	VERBALISE	Revisable
	Ungroined	VERBOSELY	Obversely
UNLIGHTED	Undelight	VERGLASES	Graveless
UNMEDICAL	Unclaimed,	VERIFIERS	Versifier
	Undecimal	VERITABLE	Avertible
UNMERITED	Undertime	VERMICIDE	Decemviri
UNNOTICED	Continued	VERNATION	Nervation
UNPARTIAL	Tarpaulin	VERSATILE	Relatives
UNPHRASED	Unsharped	VERSIFIER	Verifiers
UNPLEASED	Unelapsed	VERTICALS	Cat-silver
UNPLEATED	Pendulate	VIGILANTE	Genitival
UNPOLITIC	Punctilio		
UNRASPING	Unsparing		
UNRELATED	Unaltered	WAGNERIST	Waterings
UNREPINED	Unripened	WALLOWERS	Reswallow,
UNREPUTED	Unerupted		Swallower
UNRESCUED	Unsecured	WARRANTER	Rewarrant
UNRESTING	Insurgent	WATERFLEA	Waterleaf
UNRIPENED	Unrepined	WATERFLOW	Waterfowl
UNSAINTED	Inundates,	WATERFOWL	Waterflow
	Unstained	WATERHEAD	Head-water
UNSECURED	Unrescued	WATERINGS	Wagnerist
UNSEVERED	Undeserve	WATERLEAF	Waterflea
UNSHARPED	Unphrased	WATER-RICE	Rice-water
UNSHEARED	Unhearsed	WELLDOING	Dowelling
UNSPARING	Unrasping	WELL-NOTED	Well-toned
UNSTABLED	Unblasted	WELL-TONED	Well-noted
UNSTAINED	Inundates,	WESTERING	Swing-tree
	Unsainted	WESTNORTH	Northwest
UNSTOICAL	Suctional,	WHOSOEVER	Howsoever
	Sulcation	WINDROSES	Rowdiness,
UNSTREWED	Unwrested		Wordiness
UNTAUNTED	Unattuned	WONDERFUL	Underflow
UNTRESSED	Sederunts,	WORDINESS	Rowdiness,
	Undersets		Windroses
UNWRESTED	Unstrewed	WORDPLAYS	Swordplay
UPRISINGS	Suspiring	WORKHOUSE	Housework
URINATION	Ruination	WORK-PIECE	Piecework
URTICATES	Rusticate	WORK-TABLE	Table-work
USABILITY	Suability	WREATHING	Nightwear

Ten letters

ABSORPTION	Probations	AREOLOGIST	Aerologist
ACCRETIONS	Cestracion	ARGENTEOUS	Entourages
ACHERONTIC	Anchoretic	ASCRIPTION	Crispation
ACHROMATIN	Machinator	ASPIRINGLY	Praisingly
ACIDIMETER	Mediatrice	ASTRINGENT	Integrants
ADAMANTINE	Amantadine,	ASTRODROME	Moderators
	Diamantane	AUCTIONARY	Cautionary
ADMONITION	Domination	AUCTIONING	Cautioning
ADULTERIES	Adulterise	AUSTRALIAN	Saturnalia
ADULTERISE	Adulteries		
AEROLOGIST	Areologist		
ALARMINGLY	Marginally	BANDEROLES	Bandoleers,
ALIENATION	Alineation		Endorsable
ALIENATORS	Rationales,	BANDOLEERS	Banderoles,
	Senatorial		Endorsable
ALINEATION	Alienation	BASKETWORK	Workbasket
ALIGNMENTS	Signalment	BAS-RELIEFS	Bass-relief
ALLEGORIES	Allegorise	BASS-RELIEF	Bas-reliefs
ALLEGORISE	Allegories	BOLSTERING	Lobstering
ALLEGORIST	Legislator	BREAKWATER	Waterbreak
ALMOND-TREE	Entodermal	BREAST-DEEP	Predebates
ALPHAMETIC	Emphatical	BRIDLE-HAND	Hildebrand
ALTRUISTIC	Ultraistic	BRIGHTENER	Rebrighten
AMANTADINE	Adamantine,	BRIGHTEYES	Eyebrights
	Diamantane	BRINGING-UP	Upbringing
ANCHORETIC	Acherontic	BROADTREAD	Treadboard
ANEMOGRAPH	Phanerogam	BURGLARIES	Burglarise
ANTAGONIST	Stagnation	BURGLARISE	Burglaries
ANTIMONIAL	Lamination		
ANTISEPSIS	Inspissate		
ANTISEPTIC	Psittacine	CAMERATING	Macerating
ANTI-SOVIET	Novitiates	CAMERATION	Maceration,
APHETIZING	Hepatizing		Racemation
APPROACHER	Reapproach	CAMPAIGNER	Recampaign

CANE-CHAIRS	Saccharine	CO-ORDINATE	Carotenoid,
CAPSULATED	Scapulated		Decoration
CAROTENOID	Co-ordinate,	CO-RELATION	Iconolater,
	Decoration		Relocation
CATALOGUED	Coagulated	COSMODROME	Commodores
CATECHESIS	Catechises	COUNTERING	Recounting
CATECHISES	Catechesis	COVENANTER	Contravene
CATEGORIES	Categorise	CREATININE	Incinerate
CATEGORISE	Categories	CREATIONAL	Laceration,
CAUTIONARY	Auctionary		Reactional
CAUTIONING	Auctioning	CREATIVELY	Reactively
CENTERINGS	Nigrescent	CREATIVITY	Reactivity
CENTESIMAL	Lemniscate	CREDENTIAL	Interlaced
CENTILITER	Centilitre	CREDITABLE	Directable
CENTILITRE	Centiliter	CRENATIONS	Containers,
CENTIMETER	Centimetre		Resanction,
CENTIMETRE	Centimeter		Sanctioner
CENTRALISE	Interlaces,	CRESCENTED	Decrescent
	Linecaster	CRESCENTIC	Eccentrics
CENTROIDAL	Declinator	CRETIFYING	Certifying,
CERTIFYING	Cretifying,		Rectifying
	Rectifying	CRETINISED	Indiscreet,
CESTRACION	Accretions		Indiscrete,
CHIMNEYPOT	Chimneytop		Iridescent
CHIMNEYTOP	Chimneypot	CRISPATION	Ascription
CHRISTENER	Rechristen	CRUSTINESS	Rusticness
CHRYSOLITE	Chrysotile		
CHRYSOTILE	Chrysolite		
CISPONTINE	Inceptions,	DEALERSHIP	Leadership
	Inspection	DECIMATING	Medicating
COAGULATED	Catalogued	DECIMATION	Medication
COMMODORES	Cosmodrome	DECLENSION	Indolences
COMPOUNDED	Decompound	DECLINATOR	Centroidal
COMPOUNDER	Recompound	DECOMPOUND	Compounded
COMPRESSED	Decompress	DECOMPRESS	Compressed
CONCREATES	Consecrate	DECORATION	Carotenoid,
CONFRONTER	Reconfront		Co-ordinate
CONSECRATE	Concreates	DECRESCENT	Crescented
CONSERVANT	Conversant	DENOMINATE	Emendation
CONSERVING	Conversing	DENOTATION	Detonation
CONSTRAINS	Trans-sonic	DENSIMETER	Determines
CONTAINERS	Crenations,	DENTITIONS	Distention
	Resanction,	DENUNCIATE	Enunciated
	Sanctioner	DEPOSITION	Positioned
CONTENTING	Contingent	DEPRESSING	Predesigns
CONTINGENT	Contenting	DERACINATE	Ecardinate
CONTRAVENE	Covenanter	DEROGATION	Gerodontia
CONVERSANT	Conservant	DESCRIPTOR	Predictors
CONVERSING	Conserving	DETERMINES	Densimeter

DETONATION	Denotation	ENTOURAGES	Argenteous
DIAMANTANE	Adamantine,	ENTREATIVE	Inveterate
	Amantadine	ENTROPIUMS	Importunes,
DICTATIONS	Donatistic		Resumption
DICTIONARY	Indicatory	ENUNCIATED	Denunciate
DIRECTABLE	Creditable	ESCHAROTIC	Octarchies
DIRECTIONS	Discretion	ETHOLOGIST	Theologist
DIRECTIVES	Discretive	EXCEPTABLE	Expectable
DIRUPTIONS	Disruption	EXCITATION	Intoxicate
DISCERNING	Rescinding	EXPECTABLE	Exceptable
DISCOUNTER	Introduces,	EXPLOITERS	Sexploiter
	Reductions	EXTIRPATES	Sexpartite
DISCOVERER	Rediscover	EYEBRIGHTS	Brighteyes
DISCREETLY	Discretely		
DISCREPANT	Predicants		
DISCRETELY	Discreetly	FIBERBOARD	Fibreboard
DISCRETION	Directions	FIBERGLASS	Fibreglass
DISCRETIVE	Directives	FIBREBOARD	Fiberboard
DISPATCHER	Redispatch	FIBREGLASS	Fiberglass
DISRUPTION	Diruptions	FILTRATION	Flirtation
DISTENTION	Dentitions	FINGERLESS	Fringeless
DOMINATION	Admonition	FITTING-OUT	Outfitting
*DONATISTIC	Dictations	FLIRTATION	Filtration
DRAGOONING	Gadrooning	FLIRTINGLY	Triflingly
		FLOODWATER	Waterflood
		FORECASTER	Reforecast
EARTHINESS	Heartiness	FORTEPIANO	Pianoforte
EARTHQUAKE	Heartquake	FRINGELESS	Fingerless
EAR-WITNESS	Wateriness		
EASTERLING	Generalist		
ECARDINATE	Deracinate	GADROONING	Dragooning
ECCENTRICS	Crescentic	GENERALIST	Easterling
EDITORIALS	Idolatries,	GENERATING	Renegating
	Idolatrise	GENERATION	Renegation
EGOCENTRIC	Geocentric	GEOCENTRIC	Egocentric
EMACULATES	Emasculate	GERODONTIA	Derogation
EMASCULATE	Emaculates	GINGERSNAP	Engrasping
EMENDATION	Denominate	GLOOMINESS	Neologisms
EMPHATICAL	Alphametic	GRANULITES	Resaluting
ENCLASPING	Spanceling	GRAPHOLOGY	Logography
ENCOPRESIS	Precession	GRAPHONOMY	Monography,
ENDEARMENT	Man-entered		Nomography
ENDORSABLE	Banderoles,	GROUNDLESS	Groundsels
	Bandoleers	GROUNDSELS	Groundless
ENERVATING	Venerating		
ENERVATION	Veneration		
ENERVATIVE	Venerative	HARMONICAS	Maraschino
ENGRASPING	Gingersnap	HEADMASTER	Headstream
ENTODERMAL	Almond-tree	HEADSPRING	Springhead

HEADSTREAM	Headmaster	INSOUCIANT	Incautions
HEARTINESS	Earthiness	INSPECTION	Cispontine,
HEARTQUAKE	Earthquake		Inceptions
HECTOLITER	Hectolitre	INSPISSATE	Antisepsis
HECTOLITRE	Hectoliter	INSTRUMENT	Nutriments
HECTOMETER	Hectometre	INTEGRANTS	Astringent
HECTOMETRE	Hectometer	INTERLACED	Credential
HEPATIZING	Aphetizing	INTERLACES	Centralise,
HIBERNATED	Inbreathed		Linecaster
*HILDEBRAND	Bridle-hand	INTERVENED	Reinvented
HOMOLOGIES	Homologise	INTOXICATE	Excitation
HOMOLOGISE	Homologies	INTRENCHER	Reintrench
HOWSOMEVER	Whomsoever	INTRODUCES	Discounter,
HURTLESSLY	Ruthlessly		Reductions
		INVETERATE	Entreative
		IRIDECTOMY	Mediocrity
ICONOLATER	Co-relation,	IRIDESCENT	Cretinised,
	Relocation		Indiscreet,
IDOLATRIES	Editorials,		Indiscrete
	Idolatrise	IRONSMITHS	Mini-shorts
IDOLATRISE	Editorials,		
	Idolatries		
IMPENITENT	Pentimenti	JEOPARDIES	Jeopardise
IMPERFECTS	Perfectism	JEOPARDISE	Jeopardies
IMPORTUNES	Entropiums,		
	Resumption		
IMPRECATES	Spermaceti	KITCHENING	Thickening
IMPRESSION	Permission		
IMPRESSIVE	Permissive		
IMPRISONER	Reimprison	LACE-PILLOW	Pillow-lace
INBREATHED	Hibernated	LACERATION	Creational,
INCAUTIONS	Insouciant		Reactional
INCEPTIONS	Cispontine,	LACUSTRINE	Nuclearist
	Inspection	LAMINATION	Antimonial
INCINERATE	Creatinine	LAZINESSES	Sleaziness
INDICATORY	Dictionary	LEADERSHIP	Dealership
INDISCREET	Cretinised,	LEAD-PENCIL	Pencil-lead
	Indiscrete,	LEBENSRAUM	Mensurable
	Iridescent	LEGISLATOR	Allegorist
INDISCRETE	Cretinised,	LEMNISCATE	Centesimal
	Indiscreet,	LENTAMENTE	Tenemental
	Iridescent	LETHARGIES	Lethargise
INDOLENCES	Declension	LETHARGISE	Lethargies
INFARCTION	Infraction	LEVITATION	Tonalitive,
INFRACTION	Infarction		Velitation
INOCULATES	Inosculate	LIMITATION	Militation
INOSCULATE	Inoculates	LINECASTER	Centralise,
INSINUATOR	Ruinations,		Interlaces
	Urinations	LOBSTERING	Bolstering

LOGOGRAPHY	Graphology
LOUVER-DOOR	Louvre-door
LOUVRE-DOOR	Louver-door
LUSTRELESS	Resultless
MACERATING	Camerating
MACERATION	Cameration, Racemation
MACHINATOR	Achromatin
MAIN-STREET	Terminates
MAN-ENTERED	Endearment
MANIFESTER	Remanifest
MANNERISMS	Mismanners
MARASCHINO	Harmonicas
MARCIONIST	Morticians, Romanistic
MARGARINES	Misarrange
MARGINALLY	Alarmingly
MASTERLESS	Streamless
MASTERSHIP	Shipmaster
MAUNDERING	Undreaming
MEAGERNESS	Meagreness
MEAGRENESS	Meagerness
MEDIATRICE	Acidimeter
MEDICATING	Decimating
MEDICATION	Decimation
MEDIOCRITY	Iridectomy
MENSURABLE	Lebensraum
METRONOMIC	Monometric
MICA-SCHIST	Schismatic
MILITARIES	Militarise
MILITARISE	Militaries
MILITATION	Limitation
MILLILITER	Millilitre
MILLILITRE	Milliliter
MILLIMETER	Millimetre
MILLIMETRE	Millimeter
MINI-SHORTS	Ironsmiths
MISARRANGE	Margarines
MISDEALING	Misleading
MISLEADING	Misdealing
MISMANNERS	Mannerisms
MODERATORS	Astrodrome
MONARCHIES	Monarchise
MONARCHISE	Monarchies
MONOGRAPHY	Graphonomy, Nomography
MONOLOGIST	Nomologist, Ontologism

MONOMETRIC	Metronomic
MONOPOLIES	Monopolise
MONOPOLISE	Monopolies
MONOTHETIC	Nomothetic
MORTICIANS	Marcionist, Romanistic
MUTILATORS	Stimulator
NARCOTISED	Redactions
NECTARINES	Transience
NECTARLIKE	Trancelike
NEOLOGISMS	Gloominess
NEOPLASTIC	Pleonastic
NEPHROLOGY	Phrenology
NIGRESCENT	Centerings
NOMOGRAPHY	Graphonomy, Monography
NOMOLOGIST	Monologist, Ontologism
NOMOTHETIC	Monthetic
NOTARIALLY	Rationally
NOTELESSLY	Tonelessly
NOVITIATES	Anti-Soviet
NUCLEARIST	Lacustrine
NUTRIMENTS	Instrument
OCTARCHIES	Escharotic
OLIVACEOUS	Violaceous
ONTOLOGISM	Monologist, Nomologist
OPTOLOGIST	Topologist
ORCHESTRAL	Trochlears
ORNAMENTER	Reornament
OUTFITTING	Fitting-out
OUTLANDERS	Outslander
OUTSLANDER	Outlanders
OVERDRAPES	Overspread, Spread-over
OVERDRAWER	Overreward
OVERLIGHTS	Overslight
OVERMASTER	Overstream
OVERREWARD	Overdrawer
OVERSLIGHT	Overlights
OVERSPREAD	Overdrapes, Spread-over
OVERSTRAIN	Overtrains
OVERSTREAM	Overmaster

OVERSTRIKE	Strikeover	PHRENOLOGY	Nephrology
OVERTRAINS	Overstrain	PHYTOGENIC	Pythogenic,
			Typhogenic
		PIANOFORTE	Fortepiano
PARADISAIC	Paradisiac	PICTORIALS	Poristical,
PARADISIAC	Paradisaic		Saprolitic
PARENTALLY	Paternally,	PILFERAGES	Persiflage
	Prenatally	PILLOW-BEER	Pillow-bere
PARTIALISM	Patrialism	PILLOW-BERE	Pillow-beer
PARTIALITY	Patriality	PILLOW-LACE	Lace-pillow
PARTIALIZE	Patrialize	PISTOLLING	Postilling
PATERNALLY	Parentally,	PLAGIARIES	Plagiarise
	Prenatally	PLAGIARISE	Plagiaries
PATRIALISM	Partialism	PLEONASTIC	Neoplastic
PATRIALITY	Partiality	PORISTICAL	Pictorials,
PATRIALIZE	Partialize		Saprolitic
PATRONISER	Periastron	POSITIONAL	Spoliation
PATRONYMIC	Pyromantic	POSITIONED	Deposition
PECULATION	Unpoetical	POSTILLING	Pistolling
PECULATORS	Speculator	PRAETORIAN	Reparation
PEDERASTIC	Predicates	PRAISINGLY	Aspiringly
PENCIL-LEAD	Lead-pencil	PREADMIRER	Premarried
PENETRANCE	Repentance	PRE-ALTERED	Pre-related
PENSIONERS	Presension	PRECEDENTS	Predescent
PENTIMENTI	Impenitent	PRECEPTION	Perception
PERCEPTION	Preception	PRECEPTIVE	Perceptive
PERCEPTIVE	Preceptive	PRECESSION	Encopresis
PERCOLATED	Pre-located	PRECLAIMED	Pre-medical
PERCURRENT	Precurrent	PRECURRENT	Percurrent
PERCURSORY	Precursory	PRECURSORY	Percursory
PERCUSSION	Supersonic	PREDEBATES	Breast-deep
PERFECTISM	Imperfects	PREDESCENT	Precedents
PERFORMING	Preforming	PREDESIGNS	Depressing
PERIASTRON	Patroniser	PREDICANTS	Discrepant
PERICENTER	Pericentre	PREDICATES	Pederastic
PERICENTRE	Pericenter	PREDICTORS	Descriptor
PERISPERMS	Pre-impress	PREFORMING	Performing
PERMISSION	Impression	PRE-IMPRESS	Perisperms
PERMISSIVE	Impressive	PRE-LEASING	Pre-sealing
PERSIFLAGE	Pilferages	PRELOCATED	Percolated
PERSISTENT	Prettiness	PREMARRIED	Preadmirer
PERTAINING	Repainting	PRE-MEDICAL	Preclaimed
PERVERSION	Pre-version	PRENATALLY	Parentally,
PERVIOUSLY	Previously,		Paternally
	Viperously	PRE-RELATED	Pre-altered
PESTICIDAL	Septicidal	PRE-SEALING	Pre-leasing
PETITIONER	Repetition	PRESENSION	Pensioners
PETROLEUMS	Pulsometer	PRESENTING	Serpenting
PHANEROGAM	Anemograph	PRESENTIVE	Vespertine
*PHILIPPIAN	Philippina	PRESHARING	Rangership,
*PHILIPPINA	Philippian		Spring-hare

PRE-SYSTOLE	Proselytes	REFORECAST	Forecaster
PRETTINESS	Persistent	REGELATING	Relegating
PREVERSION	Perversion	REGELATION	Relegation
PREVIOUSLY	Perviously,	REGISTERER	Reregister
	Viperously	REGULATION	Urogenital
PRIESTLESS	Stripeless	REHEARINGS	Rehearsing
PROBATIONS	Absorption	REHEARSING	Rehearings
PROCLAIMER	Reproclaim	REIMPRISON	Imprisoner
PROSELYTES	Pre-systole	REINTRENCH	Intrencher
PSALMODIES	Psalmodise	REINVENTED	Intervened
PSALMODISE	Psalmodies	RELEASABLE	Resealable
PSITTACINE	Antisepsis	RELEGATING	Regelating
PULSOMETER	Petroleums	RELEGATION	Regelation
PURSUINGLY	Usurpingly	RELEVATION	Revelation
PYROMANTIC	Patronymic	RELOCATION	Co-relation,
PYTHOGENIC	Phytogenic,		Iconolater
	Typhogenic	REMANIFEST	Manifester
		REMUNERATE	Renumerate
		RENEGATING	Generating
QUESTIONER	Requestion	RENEGATION	Generation
		RENUMERATE	Remunerate
		REORNAMENT	Ornamenter
RACEMATION	Cameration,	REPAINTING	Pertaining
	Maceration	REPARATION	Praetorian
RANGERSHIP	Presharing	REPENTANCE	Penetrance
	Spring-hare	REPETITION	Petitioner
RATIONALES	Alienators,	REPROCLAIM	Proclaimer
	Senatorial	REQUESTION	Questioner
RATIONALLY	Notarially	REREGISTER	Registerer
REACTIONAL	Creational,	RESALUTING	Granulites
	Laceration	RESANCTION	Containers,
REACTIVELY	Creatively		Crenations,
REACTIVITY	Creativity	·	Sanctioner
REAPPROACH	Approacher	RESCINDING	Discerning
REBRIGHTEN	Brightener	RESEALABLE	Releasable
RECAMPAIGN	Campaigner	RESERVEDLY	Reversedly
RECENTNESS	Secernents,	RESHOULDER	Shoulderer
	Sentencers	RESISTLESS	Sisterless
RECHRISTEN	Christener	RESQUANDER	Squanderer
RECOMPOUND	Compounder	RESTOCKING	Stockinger
RECONFRONT	Confronter	RESULTLESS	Lustreless
RECOUNTING	Countering	RESUMPTION	Entropiums,
RECTIFYING	Certifying,		Importunes
	Cretifying	RESUPPRESS	Suppresser
REDACTIONS	Narcotised	RETHREATEN	Threatener
REDISCOVER	Discoverer	RETRACTION	Triaconter
REDISPATCH	Dispatcher	REVELATION	Relevation
REDUCTIONS	Discounter,	REVERSEDLY	Reservedly
	Introduces	RHAPSODIES	Rhapsodise

RHAPSODISE	Rhapsodies	SLIVERLIKE	Silverlike
RHEINBERRY	Rhineberry	SOMBERNESS	Sombreness
RHINEBERRY	Rheinberry	SOMBRENESS	Sombement
ROMANISTIC	Marcionist,	SPANCELING	Enclasping
	Morticians	SPECULATOR	Peculators
ROTULIFORM	Toruliform	SPERMACETI	Imprecates
RUINATIONS	Insinuator	SPIROMETER	Temporiser
	Urinations	SPOLIATION	Positional
RUSTICNESS	Crustiness	SPREAD-OVER	Overdrapes,
RUTHLESSLY	Hurtlessly		Overspread
		SPRING-HARE	Presharing,
			Rangership
SACCHARINE	Cane-chairs	SPRINGHEAD	Headspring
SANCTIONER	Containers,	SQUANDERER	Resquander
	Crenations,	STAGNATION	Antagonist
	Resanction	STEELINESS	Sleetiness
SANDERLING	Slandering	STIMULATOR	Mutilators
SAPROLITIC	Pictorials,	STOCKINGER	Restocking
	Poristical	STRAIGHTEN	Shattering
SASH-WINDOW	Window-sash	STREAMIEST	Tasimeters
SATURNALIA	Australian	STREAMLESS	Masterless
SCAPULATED	Capsulated	STRIKEOVER	Overstrike
SCHISMATIC	Mica-schist	STRIPELESS	Priestless
SCRUTINIES	Scrutinise,	SUPERSONIC	Percussion
	Sinecurist	SUPPRESSER	Resuppress
SCRUTINISE	Scrutinies,	SYMPATHIES	Sympathise
	Sinecurist	SYMPATHISE	Sympathies
SECERNENTS	Recentness,	SYMPHONIES	Symphonise
	Sentencers	SYMPHONISE	Symphonies
SENATORIAL	Alienators,		
	Rationales		
SENTENCERS	Recentness,	TABLEWATER	Watertable
	Secernents	TASIMETERS	Streamiest
SEPTICIDAL	Pesticidal	TEMPORISER	Spirometer
SERPENTING	Presenting	TENEMENTAL	Lentamente
SEXPARTITE	Extirpates	TERMINATES	Main-street
SEXPLOITER	Exploiters	TESTICULAR	Trisulcate
SHATTERING	Straighten	THEOLOGIES	Theologise
SHIPMASTER	Mastership	THEOLOGISE	Theologies
SHOPWINDOW	Window-shop	THEOLOGIST	Ethologist
SHOULDERER	Reshoulder	THICKENING	Kitchening
SIGNALMENT	Alignments	THREATENER	Rethreaten
SILVERLIKE	Sliverlike	TONALITIVE	Levitation,
SINECURIST	Scrutinies,		Velitation
	Scrutinise	TONELESSLY	Notelessly
SISTERLESS	Resistless	TOPOLOGIST	Optologist
SLANDERING	Sanderling	TORULIFORM	Rotuliform
SLEAZINESS	Lazinesses	TRANCELIKE	Nectarlike
SLEETINESS	Steeliness	TRANSIENCE	Nectarines

TRANS-SONIC	Constrains	UNRESERVED	Undeserver,
TREADBOARD	Broad-tread		Unreversed
TRIACONTER	Retraction	UNREVERSED	Undeserver,
TRICHINOUS	Unhistoric		Unreserved
TRIFLINGLY	Flirtlingly	UNSILENCED	Unlicensed
TRISULCATE	Testicular	UNSOMBERLY	Unsombrely
TROCHLEARS	Orchestral	UNSOMBRELY	Unsomberly
TWELVE-NOTE	Twelve-tone	UPBRINGING	Bringing-up
TWELVE-TONE	Twelve-note	URINATIONS	Insinuator,
TYPHOGENIC	Phytogenic,		Ruinations
	Pythogenic	UROGENITAL	Regulation
		USURPINGLY	Pursuingly
ULTRAISTIC	Altruistic		
UNBUTTERED	Unrebutted	VELITATION	Levitation,
UNCAROLLED	Uncollared		Tonalitive
UNCOLLARED	Uncarolled	VENERATING	Enervating
UNCORSETED	Unescorted	VENERATION	Enervation
UNCREDITED	Undirected	VENERATIVE	Enervative
UNDEIFYING	Unedifying	VESPERTINE	Presentive
UNDELUDING	Unindulged	VICEGERENT	Viceregent
UNDEMANDED	Unmaddened	VICEREGENT	Vicegerent
UNDERBRUSH	Undershrub	VIOLACEOUS	Olivaceous
UNDERDRAWS	Undersward	VIPEROUSLY	Perviously,
UNDERNOTED	Undertoned		Previously
UNDERSHRUB	Underbrush	VISITATION	Vitiations
UNDERSIGNS	Undressing	VITIATIONS	Visitation
UNDERSWARD	Underdraws		
UNDERTONED	Undernoted		
UNDESERVER	Unreserved,	WARRANTIES	Warrantise
	Unreversed	WARRANTISE	Warranties
UNDIRECTED	Uncredited	WATER-BREAK	Breakwater
UNDREAMING	Maundering	WATERFLOOD	Floodwater
UNDRESSING	Undersigns	WATERINESS	Ear-witness
UNEDIFYING	Undeifying	WATER-LEMON	Water-melon
UNESCORTED	Uncorseted	WATER-MELON	Water-lemon
UNFORESTED	Unfostered	WATERTABLE	Tablewater
UNFOSTERED	Unforested	WELL-LEASED	Well-sealed
UNHALTERED	Unlathered	WELL-SEALED	Well-leased
UNHISTORIC	Trichinous	WHOMSOEVER	Howsomever
UNINDULGED	Undeluding	WILDFLOWER	Wildfowler
UNLATHERED	Unhaltered	WILDFOWLER	Wildflower
UNLICENSED	Unsilenced	WINDOW-SASH	Sash-window
UNMADDENED	Undemanded	WINDOW-SHOP	Shop-window
UNPOETICAL	Peculation	WORK-BASKET	Basketwork
UNREBUTTED	Unbuttered		

Eleven letters

ACTIVATIONS	Vacationist	CENTRALISES	Treacliness
ADULTERINES	Neutralised	CERTIFIABLE	Rectifiable
AEROLOGICAL	Areological	COAGULATING	Cataloguing
ALTITUDINAL	Latitudinal	COLONIALIST	Oscillation
ANACREONTIC	Conceration	COMEDIETTAS	Domesticate
ANEMOGRAPHY	Phanerogamy	CONDITIONER	Recondition
ANGELICALLY	Englacially	CONSERVABLE	Conversable
ANTHOLOGIES	Anthologise	CONSERVANCY	Conversancy
ANTHOLOGISE	Anthologies	CONSIDERATE	Desecration
ANTIMONIALS	Laminations,	CONSTRUCTER	Reconstruct
	Nationalism	CONSUMERIST	Misconstrue
ANTIPYRETIC	Pertinacity	CONVERSABLE	Conversable
APPORTIONER	Reapportion	CONVERSANCY	Conservancy
APPREHENDER	Reapprehend	COPULATIONS	Unapostolic
AREOLOGICAL	Aerological	CREATIONARY	Reactionary
ARTILLERIST	Triliterals	CREATIONISM	Miscreation,
ASTRONOMIES	Astronomise		Reactionism,
ASTRONOMISE	Astronomies		Romanticise
ATTENTIVELY	Tentatively	CREATIONIST	Reactionist,
			Recitations
		CREDENTIALS	Centralised
BROADCASTER	Rebroadcast	CRYPTOMERIA	Imprecatory
CALLIGRAPHY	Graphically	DEGRADATION	Gradationed
CANCERATION	Anacreontic	DEIFICATION	Edification
CAPERNOITED	Deprecation	DEPRECATION	Capernoited
CAPILLARITY	Piratically	DESCRIPTION	Predictions
CAPTAINSHIP	Ship-captain	DESECRATION	Considerate
CATALOGUING	Coagulating	DETERMINANT	Detrainment
CATAPULTIER	Particulate	DETRAINMENT	Determinant
CATECHISMAL	Schematical	DISCERNABLE	Rescindable
CAVILLATION	Vacillation	DISCERNMENT	Rescindment
CENTRALISED	Credentials	DOMESTICATE	Comediettas

EDIFICATION	Deification	IMPRESSIBLE	Permissible
ELECTORSHIP	Helicopters	IMPRESSIBLY	Permissibly
ELIMINATORS	Misrelation,	INBREATHING	Hibernating
	Orientalism,	INCORPORATE	Procreation
	Relationism	INFESTATION	Festination
EMBELLISHER	Re-embellish	INFRACOSTAL	Fractionals
ENGLACIALLY	Angelically	INTERPRETER	Reinterpret
ENGRAILMENT	Realignment	INTERRUPTER	Reinterrupt
ENLIGHTENER	Re-enlighten	INTERSPERSE	Enterprises
ENTAILMENTS	Sentimental	INTERVIEWER	Reinterview
ENTERPRISES	Intersperse		
ENUMERATION	Mountaineer		
ESTABLISHER	Re-establish	LAMINATIONS	Antimonials,
ETHOLOGICAL	Theological		Nationalism
		LATITUDINAL	Altitudinal
		LEVITATIONS	Neovitalist
FESTINATION	Infestation	LIGHTHOUSES	House-lights
FORWARDNESS	Frowardness	LOGOGRAPHIC	Graphologic
FRACTIONALS	Infracostal		
FROWARDNESS	Forwardness		
		MEMORIALIST	Immortalise
		MENSURATION	Numerations
GENEALOGIES	Genealogise	MISCONSTRUE	Consumerist
GENEALOGISE	Genealogies	MISCREATION	Creationism,
GENERATIONS	Nitrogenase		Reactionism,
GRADATIONED	Degradation		Romanticise
GRAMOPHONIC	Monographic,	MISCREDITED	Misdirected
	Nomographic,	MISDIRECTED	Miscredited
	Phonogramic	MISRELATION	Eliminators,
GRAPHICALLY	Calligraphy		Orientalism,
GRAPHOLOGIC	Logographic		Relationism
GRAPHOTYPIC	Typographic	MONOGENESIS	Nomogenesis
		MONOGRAPHER	Nomographer
		MONOGRAPHIC	Gramophonic,
HELICOPTERS	Electorship		Nomographic,
HIBERNATING	Inbreathing		Phonogramic
HISTRIONICS	Trichinosis	MONOLOGICAL	Nomological
HOMOGENESIS	Homogenises	MOUNTAINEER	Enumeration
HOMOGENISES	Homogenesis	MUTILATIONS	Stimulation
HORSERIDING	Riding-horse	MYTHOLOGIES	Mythologise
HOUSE-LIGHTS	Lighthouses	MYTHOLOGISE	Mythologies
HURTFULNESS	Ruthfulness		
		NATIONALISM	Antimonials,
IMMORTALISE	Memorialist		Laminations
IMPERSONALS	Personalism	NECESSARIAN	Renaissance
IMPERSONATE	Permeations	NEOTERISING	Nitrogenise
IMPORTUNATE	Permutation	NEOTROPICAL	Percolation
IMPRECATORY	Cryptomeria	NEOVITALIST	Levitations

NEPHOLOGIST	Phenologist	PHENOLOGIST	Nephologist
NEPHROSTOME	Nephrotomes	PHONOGRAMIC	Gramophonic,
NEPHROTOMES	Nephrostome		Monographic,
NEUTRALISED	Adulterines		Nomographic
NIGHTINGALE	Tile-hanging	PHOTO-RESIST	Orthoepists
NITROGENASE	Generations	PIRATICALLY	Capillarity
NITROGENISE	Neoterising	PLANIMETERS	Sempiternal
NOMOGENESIS	Monogenesis	POTOMETRIST	Optometrist
NOMOGRAPHER	Monographer	PRECIPITATE	Peripatetic
NOMOGRAPHIC	Gramophonic,	PRECREDITOR	Predirector
	Monographic,	PREDICTIONS	Description
	Phonogramic	PREDIRECTOR	Precreditor
NOMOLOGICAL	Monological	PRE-LOCATING	Percolating
NON-CREATIVE	Non-reactive	PRERATIONAL	Proletarian
NON-PARENTAL	Non-paternal	PROBATIONER	Reprobation
NON-PATERNAL	Non-parental	PROCREATION	Incorporate
NON-REACTIVE	Non-creative	PROLETARIAN	Prerational
NUMERATIONS	Mensuration	PROLETARIES	Proletarise
		PROLETARISE	Proletaries
		PROTECTRESS	Retrospects
OPTOMETRIST	Potometrist	PROVISIONER	Reprovision
ORIENTALISM	Eliminators,	PTEROGRAPHY	Petrography,
	Misrelation,		Typographer
	Relationism		
ORIENTALIST	Relationist		
ORTHOEPISTS	Photo-resist	QUARTER-NOTE	Quarter-tone
OSCILLATION	Colonialist	QUARTER-TONE	Quarter-note
PARLIAMENTS	Paternalism	RATIONALISE	Realisation
PARTICULATE	Catapultier	REACTIONARY	Creationary
PATERNALISM	Parliaments	REACTIONISM	Creationism,
PATERNOSTER	Penetrators		Miscreation,
PECULATIONS	Speculation		Romanticise
PENETRATORS	Paternoster	REACTIONIST	Creationist,
PERCOLATING	Pre-locating		Recitations
PERCOLATION	Neotropical	REALIGNMENT	Engrailment
PERIPATETIC	Precipitate	REALISATION	Rationalise
PERISTALTIC	Triplicates	REAPPORTION	Apportioner
PERMEATIONS	Impersonate	REAPPREHEND	Apprehender
PERMISSIBLE	Impressible	REBROADCAST	Broadcaster
PERMISSIBLY	Impressibly	RECITATIONS	Creationist,
PERMUTATION	Importunate		Reactionist
PERSONALISM	Impersonals	RECONDITION	Conditioner
PERTINACITY	Antipyretic	RECONNOITER	Reconnoitre
PESTIFEROUS	Septiferous	RECONNOITRE	Reconnoiter
PETROGRAPHY	Pterography,	RECONSTRUCT	Constructer
	Typographer	RECTIFIABLE	Certifiable
PHANEROGAMY	Anemography	RE-EMBELLISH	Embellisher

RE-ENLIGHTEN	Enlightener	TABERNACLES	Scarlet-bean
RE-ESTABLISH	Establisher	TAUTOLOGIES	Tautologise
REINTERPRET	Interpreter	TAUTOLOGISE	Tautologies
REINTERRUPT	Interrupter	TELEGRAPHER	Retelegraph
REINTERVIEW	Interviewer	TENTATIVELY	Attentively
RELATIONISM	Eliminators,	TETRASPORIC	Triceratops
	Misrelation,	THEATERGOER	Theatregoer
	Orientalism	THEATREGOER	Theatergoer
RELATIONIST	Orientalist	THEOLOGICAL	Ethological
REMUNERATED	Renumerated	THEOSOPHIES	Theosophise
RENAISSANCE	Necessarian	THEOSOPHISE	Theosophies
RENUMERATED	Remunerated	TILE-HANGING	Nightingale
REPAINTINGS	Signpainter	TREACLINESS	Centralises
REPROBATION	Probationer	TRICERATOPS	Tetrasporic
REPROVISION	Provisioner	TRICHINOSIS	Histrionics
RESCINDABLE	Discernable	TRILITERALS	Artillerist
RESCINDMENT	Discernment	TRIPLICATES	Peristaltic
RESIDENTERS	Retiredness	TRIVIALNESS	Silvestrian
RESPECTLESS	Sceptreless	TYPOGRAPHER	Petrography,
RESPIRATION	Retinispora		Pterography
RETELEGRAPH	Telegrapher	TYPOGRAPHIC	Graphotypic
RETINISPORA	Respiration		
RETIREDNESS	Residenters		
RETROSPECTS	Protectress	UNAPOSTOLIC	Copulations
REUPHOLSTER	Upholsterer	UNAUCTIONED	Uncautioned
RIDING-HORSE	Horseriding	UNCAUTIONED	Unauctioned
ROMANTICISE	Creationism,	UNCERTIFIED	Unrectified
	Miscreation,	UNDERLEASED	Undersealed
	Reactionism	UNDERSEALED	Underleased
RUSTICATION	Urtications	UNRECTIFIED	Uncertified
RUTHFULNESS	Hurtfulness	UNRESPECTED	Unsceptered
		UNSCEPTERED	Unrespected
		UPHOLSTERER	Reupholster
SANCTUARIES	Sanctuarise	URTICATIONS	Rustication
SANCTUARISE	Sanctuaries		
SAVOURINESS	Variousness		
SCARLET-BEAN	Tabernacles	VACATIONIST	Activations
SCEPTRELESS	Respectless	VACILLATION	Cavillation
SCHEMATICAL	Catechismal	VARIOUSNESS	Savouriness
SEMPITERNAL	Planimeters	VICE-GERENCY	Vice-regency
SENTIMENTAL	Entailments	VICE-REGENCY	Vice-gerency
SEPTIFEROUS	Pestiferous		
SHIP-CAPTAIN	Captainship		
SIGNPAINTER	Repaintings	WATERSPRING	Springwater
SILVESTRIAN	Trivialness	WEATHERINGS	Weather-sign
SPECULATION	Peculations	WEATHER-SIGN	Weatherings
SPRINGWATER	Waterspring		
STIMULATION	Mutilations		

Twelve letters

ACHERONTICAL   Anchoretical   DISCONSOLATE   Consolidates
ACROSTICALLY   Socratically   DISCREETNESS   Discreteness
ALTITUDINOUS   Latitudinous   DISCRETENESS   Discreetness
AMPHITHEATER   Amphitheatre   DISHARMONIES   Disharmonise
AMPHITHEATRE   Amphitheater   DISHARMONISE   Disharmonies
ANCHORETICAL   Acherontical
ANEMOGRAPHIC   Phanerogamic
ANTI-CREATION   Anti-reaction   ENERGETICIST   Energetistic
ANTI-CREATIVE   Anti-reactive   ENERGETISTIC   Energeticist
ANTI-REACTION   Anti-creation   ENTOMOLOGIES   Entomologise
ANTI-REACTIVE   Anti-creative   ENTOMOLOGISE   Entomologies
ARISTOTELIAN   Retaliations   EXPERIMENTER   Re-experiment

CARTESIANISM   Sectarianism   GRAPHOPHONIC   Phonographic
COLLIMATIONS   Collision-mat
COLLISION-MAT   Collimations
COMMISSIONER   Recommission   HURTLESSNESS   Ruthlessness
CONSERVATION   Conversation
CONSOLIDATES   Disconsolate
CONVERSATION   Conservation   IMPRESSIVELY   Permissively
CORPOREALIST   Prosectorial   INDISCREETLY   Indiscretely,
COUNTERCHARM   Countermarch   Iridescently
COUNTERMARCH   Countercharm   INDISCRETELY   Indiscreetly,
COUNTERPALED   Counterplead   Iridescently
COUNTERPLEAD   Counterpaled   INOCULATIONS   Inosculation
CREATIVENESS   Reactiveness   INOSCULATION   Inoculations
CREDITORSHIP   Directorship   IRIDECTOMIES   Iridectomise
CREMATIONIST   Metrications   IRIDECTOMISE   Iridectomies
                                  IRIDESCENTLY   Indiscreetly,
                                                  Indiscretely

DELICATENESS   Delicatessen
DELICATESSEN   Delicateness
DIRECTORSHIP   Creditorship

LATITUDINOUS	Altitudinous
LOUVER-WINDOW	Louvre-window
LOUVRE-WINDOW	Louver-window
MANSLAUGHTER	Slaughterman
METRICATIONS	Cremationist
METRONOMICAL	Monometrical
MISCREDITING	Misdirecting
MISDIRECTING	Miscrediting
MONOMETRICAL	Metronomical
NEBULISATION	Sublineation
NEPHOLOGICAL	Phenological
NEPHROLOGIST	Phrenologist
NON-CERTIFIED	Non-rectified
NON-RECTIFIED	Non-certified
NOTELESSNESS	Tonelessness
OBSCURANTIST	Subtractions
PARADISAICAL	Paradisiacal
PARADISIACAL	Paradisaical
PENETRATIONS	Presentation
PERCEPTIVELY	Preceptively
PERMISSIVELY	Impressively
PERVIOUSNESS	Previousness
PETROGRAPHER	Pterographer
PETROGRAPHIC	Pterographic
PHANEROGAMIC	Anemographic
PHENOLOGICAL	Nephological
PHILOSOPHIES	Philosophise
PHILOSOPHISE	Philosophies
PHONOGRAPHIC	Graphophonic
PHOTOGRAPHER	Rephotograph
PHRENOLOGIST	Nephrologist
PHYTOGENESIS	Pythogenisis
POST-ARTERIAL	Proletariats
PRECEPTIVELY	Perceptively
PRE-CREDITING	Pre-directing
PRE-DIRECTING	Pre-crediting
PRESENTATION	Penetrations
PREVIOUSNESS	Perviousness
PROBATIONERS	Reabsorption,
	Reprobations
PROLETARIATS	Post-arterial
PROPORTIONER	Reproportion

PROSECTORIAL	Corporealist
PTEROGRAPHER	Petrographer
PTEROGRAPHIC	Petrographic
PYTHOGENESIS	Phytogenesis
RATEABLENESS	Tearableness
REABSORPTION	Probationers,
	Reprobations
REACTIVENESS	Creativeness
RECOMMISSION	Commissioner
REDINTEGRATE	Reintegrated
RE-EXPERIMENT	Experimenter
REINTEGRATED	Redintegrate
REMUNERATING	Renumerating
RENUMERATING	Remunerating
REPHOTOGRAPH	Photograp/her
REPROBATIONS	Probationers,
	Reabsorption
REPROPORTION	Proportioner
RESTRAIGHTEN	Straightener
RETALIATIONS	Aristotelian
RETRANSPLANT	Transplanter
RUTHLESSNESS	Hurtlessness
SECTARIANISM	Cartesianism
SLAUGHTERMAN	Manslaughterl
SOCRATICALLY	Acrostically
STRAIGHTENER	Restraighten
SUBLINEATION	Nebulisation
SUBTRACTIONS	Obscurantist
TEARABLENESS	Rateableness
TONELESSNESS	Notelessness
TRANSPLANTER	Retransplant
UNDERLEASING	Undersealing
UNDERSEALING	Underleasing
UNSOMBERNESS	Unsombreness
UNSOMBRENESS	Unsomberness
WELL-CORSETED	Well-escorted
WELL-CREDITED	Well-directed
WELL-DIRECTED	Well-credited
WELL-ESCORTED	Well-corseted

Thirteen letters

```
ATTENTIVENESS      Tentativeness

BALANCE-SHEETS     Teachableness

CERTIFICATION      Cretification, Rectification
CRETIFICATION      Certification, Rectification

DESERTISATION      Disorientates
DISORIENTATES      Desertisation

ETHOLOGICALLY      Theologically
EXPLOITATIONS      Sexploitation

GRAMOPHONICAL      Monographical, Phonogramical
GRAPHOLOGICAL      Logographical

IMPRESSIONIST      Permissionist

LOGOGRAPHICAL      Graphological

MONOGRAPHICAL      Gramophonical, Phonogramical

PERMISSIONIST      Impressionist
PHONOGRAMICAL      Gramophonical, Monographical
```

RECTIFICATION	Certification, Cretification
RUMEL-GUMPTION	Rumle-gumption
RUMLE-GUMPTION	Rumel-gumption
SEXPLOITATION	Exploitations
SOUNDBOARDING	Soundingboard
SOUNDINGBOARD	Soundboarding
STATELESSNESS	Tastelessness
TASTELESSNESS	Statelessness
TEACHABLENESS	Balance-sheets
TENTATIVENESS	Attentiveness
THEOLOGICALLY	Ethologically
UNCERTIFIABLE	Unrectifiable
UNCONSERVABLE	Unconversable
UNCONVERSABLE	Unconservable
UNRECTIFIABLE	Uncertifiable
VERIFICATIONS	Versification
VERSIFICATION	Verifications